2—

THOMAS BERRY

THOMAS BERRY

A Biography

MARY EVELYN TUCKER,
JOHN GRIM,
AND ANDREW ANGYAL

Columbia University Press

New York

Columbia University Press
Publishers Since 1893
New York   Chichester, West Sussex
cup.columbia.edu
Library of Congress Cataloging-in-Publication Data
{to come}

Columbia University Press books are printed on permanent
and durable acid-free paper.

Printed in the United States of America
Add cover/jacket credit information

To future generations who will take up the Great Work

Contents

Acknowledgments

This biography has been many years in the making, as Thomas Berry's life embraced so many people and ideas over nine decades. We are pleased that it is being published by Columbia to celebrate the ten-year anniversary of his passing on June 1, 2009.

We are especially grateful to Brian Thomas Swimme for his unflagging support and encouragement over so many years. We thank him for reading the manuscript and providing insightful feedback. Others who generously read the whole manuscript and gave valuable suggestions include: Judith Emery, Donald St. John, Stephen Dunn, Ann Marie Dalton, Ann Berry Somers, Susan Ernst, Nathan Empsall, Lauren Griffith, Sam Mickey, Jennifer Angyal; as well as those who read individual chapters or sections: Brian Brown, John Borelli, Liz Hosken, Fiona Wilton, Jules Cashford, Ursula King, John Haught, Kathleen Duffy, Brett de Bary, Anne Roberts, and Carlton Tucker.

We are indebted to Berry Family members who gave interviews or advice: Margaret Berry, Ann Berry Somers, Teresa Kelleher, Mary Elizabeth (Merse) Berry, Frank Berry, Thomas Gabriel Berry, Ben Berry, and Thomas Berry, Jr.

Others who were helpful in their interviews were: Ted and Fanny de Bary, Ewert Cousins, Daniel Sheridan, Gail Worcelo, Mike Bell, Tom McKenna, Bob Molyneaux, Beatrice Bruteau, James Somerville, Joseph Shoffity, Andrew Schlosser, and Eileen Doyle.

Assistance also came from the Passionist community including: Stephen Dunn, Conrad Federspeil, Rob Carbonneau, Thomas Brendan Keevey, Joseph Mitchell, Quentin Amehein, Ronan Calchan, Damian Carroll, Victor Donovan, and Simon Wood.

Those who were consulted or have shared aspects of the influence of Thomas on their life and work include: Robert McDermott, Jim Conlon, Franklin Vilas, Fritz and Vivienne Hull, Heather Eaton, Ann Marie Dalton, Drew Dellinger, Steve Snider, Paul Winter, Chris Loughlin, Lauren deBoer, John Surrette, Mary Southard, Toni Nash, Carl Anthony, Paloma Pavel, Carolyn Toben, Peggy Whalen-Levitt, Herman Greene, Nelson Stover, Jim Schenk, Dennis O'Hara, Christina Vanin, Suzanne Golas, Elizabeth Ferrero, Sam and Paula Guarnaccia, and Cami Davis. Some of this work and other projects that are inspired by Berry can be seen at www.thomasberry.org. Please feel free to contact us to add more, as this is intended to be part of the living legacy of Thomas Berry. We thank Elizabeth McAnally for her careful curating of this website on Berry's life and thought over many years.

We are grateful, too, for the support and friendship of many women and men who appreciate the depths of Berry's contributions. We thank especially the Sisters of Earth and the nuns in the United States, Canada, England, Ireland, and Australia who have helped birth Thomas's vision into our world.

For assistance with photographs we extend appreciation to: Ann Berry Somers, Rob Carbonneau and the Passionist Archives, Stephen Dunn, Lou Niznik and Jane Blewett, Judith Emery, Gretchen McHugh and J. Murray McHugh, Marnie Mueller, Brian Thomas Swimme, Miriam MacGillis, Brian Brown, Amarylis Cortijo, Paul de Bary, Merce Prats, Craig Kochel, Paul Winter, Kusumita Pedersen, Peggy Whalen-Levitt, Teresa Berger, Charles Adams, Michael Greenlar, Alan Delozier, and Larry Petrovick.

At Columbia University Press we thank our publisher, Wendy Lochner, and associate editor, Lowell Frye, for their patience and assistance in bringing this work to fruition, and for eliciting responses from readers, John Cobb and Christopher Key Chapple. Susan Zorn did an excellent job editing the manuscript, and Marisa Lastres and Ben Kolstad shepherded it carefully through production on a tight schedule.

William C. Clark at the Kennedy School at Harvard was a key collaborator in bringing Berry's papers to Harvard where they were placed in the Environmental Sciences and Public Policy Archives. Margaret Berry assembled and sent the papers to Harvard. George E. Clark, the curator of these archives, was unfailingly helpful in our research in the archives. Martin S. Kaplan was instrumental in the establishment of the Berry Archives and the Thomas Berry Foundation. His assistance for over twenty years has been incomparable.

John Grim and Mary Evelyn Tucker are indebted for support for many years of work on this book from the Germeshausen Foundation, Charles Engelhard Foundation, Margaret Mead Bateson Trust, Marianne and Jim Welch, Reverend Albert P. Neilson, Paul Minus, and Frances Beinecke. Andrew Angyal acknowledges support for his research from Elon University and the Institute for Research on Unlimited Love.

Special acknowledgement goes to Tara C. Trapani for her expert assistance in attending to the endless details of preparing the manuscript for publication. Our gratitude knows no bounds, as this biography was enhanced not only by her efficiency and care, but also by her spirit of dedication to Thomas Berry's vision for so many years. This means more than we can fully express, except to say that she and her husband, Paul Trapani, are cherished companions on this journey.

0.1 Thomas Berry.

Lou Niznik, courtesy of Jane Blewett

Introduction

Thomas Berry and the Arc of History

The account of how I became increasingly aware of the cosmological and biological dimensions of existence is the story of my life. My quest for understanding this larger context of things conditioned all the decisions I made about my life. I saw life within its larger context, eventually within the context of the universe itself. I was immersed in the mystery of things, in the mysterious powers expressed in natural phenomena. The various living beings I experienced as integral with my own existence.

Thomas Berry, *Goldenrod: Reflections on the Twentieth Century*

In the autumn of 1994, Thomas Berry turned eighty. Still in good health, he was planning to move from New York City back to his birthplace in Greensboro, North Carolina. As Mary Evelyn Tucker and John Grim were helping him pack up and distribute his library, they would pause at the end of the day and share a meal and a glass of wine together. While the sun set over the ancient rock cliffs of the Palisades across the Hudson River, they sensed the transition of a life lived in the depths of time—biological and geological. As they began to reflect together on the best approach to his biography, Thomas would invariably say: "Tell my story in the context of the times."

That refrain was a guiding mantra in preparing his biography within the arc of history. It was a formidable task, as Thomas Berry's long life (1914–2009) spanned the major events of the twentieth century, from the First World War at the time of his birth to significant climatic and ecological disruption around the planet in his later years. Moreover, his intellectual breadth and spiritual depth defy adequate description. He was widely read in world history and religions and spent his early years within the contemplative rhythms of monastic life.

He lived immersed in the narratives of time that were continually expanding—from human history, to Earth history, to universe history. He sought a way to be grounded in the great vessel of life, the cosmos itself. He evoked this grounding with the power of story. He could tell stories that would capture a room and would leave the audience clamoring for more. His storytelling was based on a profound attention to the past, a passion for history, and a comprehensive compassion for the present with its multifaceted challenges. These sensibilities rested in the "mysterious powers expressed in natural phenomena": the bird songs and migrations, the living forests and ancient mountains, and the roaring force of oceans and rivers. All these powers were connected to star birth, out of which the elements of life emerged.

He spoke from a place of erudition mingled with an engaging poetic rhetoric. His presence was one of laughter and luminosity; his words penetrated the soul and enlivened the mind. Indeed, his lucid language broke out of scholarly constraints to bring rays of hope into the eyes of young and old alike. There are few people who have grappled for so long and so steadfastly with bringing a healing vision for the Earth community.[2]

What motivated him in this task? Thomas lived through some of the most remarkable and rapid changes in recorded history—from electrical energy to solar energy, from community phone lines to personal cell phones and computers, from horse-and-buggy travel to placing a man on the moon. He sought throughout his life to make sense of these changes. His constant question was: "What is progress, and what is its real cost?" He intuited at a very early age that something was being lost—not just in the agrarian life of the South, where he was raised, but also in the depths of the integral functioning of the planet itself with the race to industrialize and modernize. Toxic chemicals seeped into soils and streams while greenhouse gases in the atmosphere caused massive climate change. He would spend his life trying to respond to the loss of ecosystem health and biodiversity with an encompassing and enlivening vision. He began where the environmentalist John Muir ended. Indeed, Thomas came into the world in 1914, the same year Muir died. They shared a love of wilderness and consternation at its destruction due to unregulated logging, overgrazing by pastoralists, and relentless extractive industries.

Thomas was born into a recently expanded Union and a newly initiated world war. Two years earlier, in 1912, Arizona and New Mexico joined the Union, thus completing the forty-eight states of the United States mainland. The westward expansion of the prior hundred years was over, and joyful celebrations were held. However, as Thomas understood later, this "Union" came at the expense of Native Americans, who were subsumed into a new republic that had long suppressed their traditional cultures and lifeways. Similarly, while slavery was legally outlawed, full participation of African Americans in educational or economic opportunities was still unrealized. An economy and politics of inclusion were struggling to emerge across the country and throughout his lifetime. He lamented that this aspiration toward broader inclusion was still not realized at the time of his death.

Ethnic, political, and economic tensions were not restricted to the United States but were a worldwide phenomenon of the twentieth century. In July 1914, just four months before Thomas was born, World War I broke out in Europe with the unpredictable assassination of Archduke Ferdinand by a Serbian nationalist. By the end of the war, four great empires had collapsed: German, Russian, Austro-Hungarian, and Ottoman. The Russian Revolution had taken place in 1917. A new world order was coming into being with the armistice in 1919 and the formation of the League of Nations in 1920. Its goal was to promote peace and disarmament through negotiations and arbitration. But President Woodrow Wilson could not persuade the United States to join due to the strength of the isolationist lobby. Moreover, because the League had no military power, various international conflicts could not be resolved. Thus, the League faltered, and the peace did not last. It would take the Depression of the 1930s and another world war for the United Nations to be founded in 1945 and the European Union to emerge in the postwar period. These international and regional institutions also faced upheavals caused by ethnic differences and political conflicts. A continuing challenge was the growing ideology of nationalism, which led to tensions on the international scene as well as within nation states. Indeed, European historian Carlton J. H. Hayes, who was an important influence on Berry, titled his last book, *Nationalism: A Religion*.[3]

All of this was part of the world in which Thomas Berry was born and grew up, and to which he eventually responded. He was searching for a way beyond such divisions, toward a story that could draw the human community together into a whole that was larger than the nation-state. He created the term *Earth community* to indicate our shared sense of belonging to something greater—humans and nature in continuity. Against all odds, and in the midst of endless conflicts, he persisted in his quest to understand how such an enlivening narrative could emerge from the upheavals of modern history and rapid technological change. He experienced these upheavals in China with the Maoist revolution and in Germany with the Cold War. He had to leave China in 1948 as Mao's troops moved into Peking. He lived for three years in the 1950s with American troops in a Germany divided between a communist East and democratic West. And in the 1960s he witnessed demonstrations on American campuses against the Vietnam War and for civil rights. He, like President Dwight Eisenhower, grew wary of the power of the "military-industrial complex."[4]

The post–World War II economic boom brought growth and prosperity to various parts of the world, but at immense cost to the environment and to social equity. As the human community exploded from 2 billion, when he was born, to 7 billion three years after he died, these environmental and social problems became exacerbated. Thus, it would require two United Nations conferences (in Stockholm in 1972 and Rio in 1992) to call the nations of the world to address the escalating tensions of economic development and environmental protection.

In the decade between these conferences, the World Charter for Nature was written and endorsed in 1982 by all members of the United Nations except the United States. Thomas held this Charter in high esteem for its eloquent recognition of nature as the basis of all life. The leaders of the Rio Earth Summit expanded on this idea by calling for an Earth Charter in 1992. This initiated many years of careful drafting by an international committee led by Steven Rockefeller, a professor of religion at Middlebury College. The Earth Charter was completed at the end of the twentieth century, a decade before Thomas died. The document is a comprehensive vision of the interconnections of cosmology, ecology, justice, and peace. It has been called a Declaration of Interdependence for a shared planetary future. The preamble includes Thomas's view that "[h]umanity is part of a vast evolving universe. Earth, our home, is alive with a unique community of life."[5]

Thomas spent his life navigating between the forces of nationalism and internationalism and between the tensions of ecological conservation and economic growth. All the while, he was working on a new inclusive framework for humans and nature, eventually articulating a comprehensive ecological sense of the Earth community. From this perspective, humans are seen not simply as political or economic entities, but as biocultural beings amidst the vast diversity of life systems and species. This viewpoint, he felt, changes everything. Thus, Thomas Berry expanded his life quest to articulate an engaging evolutionary narrative that would respond to the overwhelming ecological and social crises facing the human community.

Thomas's journey has shaped the structure of this biography: the first eight chapters focus on the chronological unfolding of his life, and the final four chapters elaborate his thought. He began his life in Greensboro, North Carolina, entered the monastery, did graduate studies in history, went to China, then to Germany, and returned to the United States to begin teaching. He built a History of Religions program at Fordham and a place for broader reflection at the Riverdale Center for Religious Research along the Hudson River. Even in his retirement back to Greensboro he inspired programs in education, law, religion, and agriculture.

From his beginnings as a cultural and intellectual historian, Berry became a historian of the Earth. While some described him as a theologian, as he taught in a theology department at Fordham, Berry preferred to describe himself as a "geologian." The movement from human history to Earth history was a necessary progression for Berry. He witnessed in his own lifetime the emergence of a multicultural planetary civilization as cultures came in contact around the globe, often for the first time. But he wanted to place this emergence in the larger arc of Earth history and the evolution of the universe. He saw humans as arising out of the journey of the universe, unfolding over billions of years of dynamic evolution. He recognized the power of an evolutionary story to engage humans in the great questions: where have we come from, how do we belong, why are we here?

This is what led to his signature essay "The New Story" in 1978. A new universe story, he felt, could help humans become mutually enhancing participants in the life community.[6] He worked for over a decade to write *The Universe Story* with Brian Thomas Swimme. This was the grounding for the transformations that he saw were needed for a new period in human history, one he called the Ecozoic era.

Inspired by creative thinkers in ecological forms of economics, politics, education, law, and religion, Berry believed that such a period was not only possible but already emerging. This is the promise of Berry's perspective. It is one that adds fresh energy to what he called the "Great Work," namely, what each person and community can contribute to a flourishing future. As he would say, "This work is for the future generations of all species." It is in this context of a great story inspiring great work that he saw the arc of history unfolding.

THOMAS BERRY

CHAPTER 1

An Independent Youth

The story that I tell of the city where I was born is, I think, a typical story of the twentieth century in America, the story of a lovely small town with tree-shaded streets and neighborhoods, of people who knew each other and delighted in the more simple things of life, a city with a strong sense of tradition, where in the early decades of this century people still told stories of the late reconstruction period after the Civil War. It is a city that, because of its location on the railroad between Washington and New Orleans, had possibilities of expansion in the commercial world. A city that I knew at the beginning of World War I, that passed through the Depression years of the 1930s, that experienced World War II, that became a small city and then a growing city, a commercial city.

Thomas Berry, *Goldenrod: Reflections on the Twentieth Century*

Thomas Berry's hometown of Greensboro is located in the gently rolling Piedmont area of North Carolina between the coastal plain and the Blue Ridge Mountains of the Appalachian range. Thomas would later describe this Greensboro region with a deep appreciation for the diversity of its life forms and the beauty of the seasons:

It is not too far from the mountains around the Asheville region where there was one of the greatest number of plant and botanical species anywhere in the northern hemisphere, varieties fostered by such a favorable climate, ... long spring and fall seasons, with mild winters and summers that can be hot, but not unendurable.

As soon as the heat became intolerable, it would often be relieved by the lightning storms that would break over the region in the afternoon of a blazing day. Some of the most glorious moments of my childhood were spent on a side porch of the house on Colonial Avenue listening to the evening symphony of the bull-frogs, the cicada, the katydids.

In springtime, the dogwood trees brought a sense of refinement to the region in mid April and May. In autumn there was the brilliance of the various trees, the maples and oaks and poplar and sweet gum and sycamore, and willow growths along the creek beds. The sweet-smelling honeysuckle experienced at nightfall, when the mist gathers over the lowlands and everything is quiet except for the rising and falling away of the crickets and tree frogs.

The bird variety was wonderful. The wood thrush and the bluebirds in springtime, the warblers coming through with all their colorful array, the red-winged blackbirds down by the wetlands along the old pond, the mourning doves in the evening and the whip-poor-will throughout the night—an almost endless number of species. There were the creeks where the sun-perch were found and the lakes with their bullheads and other bottom dwellers as well as the small-mouth and large-mouth bass.[1]

Thomas would see this small southern town of 12,000 become a burgeoning city of nearly 300,000 people in his lifetime. Its rapid growth paralleled the extensive changes he would observe around the globe.

A NEW BEGINNING

It was in the spring of 1913 that a young, handsome couple disembarked at the striking Romanesque railroad depot in Greensboro. William Nathan Berry had come east from Owensboro, Kentucky, with his wife, Bess,[2] and their two small children. He was to take on a new job as a dispatcher for the Southern Railroad Company. "I had two dollars and two children," William recalled. "I was carrying the bags. Jack, almost two, was tugging at his mother's skirts; Mary Elizabeth was carried in her arms."[3] After a brief stay at the Hotel Clegg, which was located across from the train station, the family settled into a modest house on Edgeworth Street, just below the large, historic Greenhill Cemetery.

Thomas was born on November 9, a year after his parents arrived in Greensboro, and was christened on November 22, 1914 as William Nathan Jr. He came to be called "Brother" by his family, in the southern tradition of deferring to an older male sibling. In 1935, in religious life, he took the name Thomas after the medieval theologian Thomas Aquinas. He used this name for the rest of his life.

The family grew rapidly to thirteen children—eight boys and five girls: John Vize (Jack, 1911–1990), Mary Elizabeth (Merse, 1913–2004), William Nathan Jr. (Brother/Fr. Thomas, 1914–2009), Francis Xavier (Frank, 1916–2006), James (Jim, 1917–1997), Margaret (1918–living), Katherine (1920–1983), Joseph Louis (Joe, 1921–1996), Ann Louise (Sr. Zoe Marie, 1922–1958), Teresa Marie (1924–1999), Benedict Regis (Ben, 1926–2017), Thomas Gabriel (Tom, 1929–2009), and Stephan Badin (Steve, 1933–2011). "As more babies came," William observed, "the older children looked after the younger while their mother and I worked."[4] By 1920 they had to move to a larger house. Seven years later they settled in the home they built on Colonial Avenue in the Kirkwood neighborhood of northern Greensboro.[5] They moved in just a few months before Charles Lindbergh completed his historic flight across the Atlantic in May 1927.

It had become clear to William and Bess that his railroad salary was no longer sufficient to feed their growing family. Looking for alternatives, they considered the residential coal business. After observing the increase in Southern Railroad's coal car deliveries in the years following World War I, William recognized the potential for an energetic and motivated businessman in this burgeoning

1.1 Berry family, circa 1931.
Courtesy of Ann Berry Somers for the Berry family

industry. More and more families were installing coal-burning furnaces in their homes instead of relying on wood for winter comfort, and the demand for dependable coal delivery was steadily increasing.

In 1924, William resigned his job with Southern Railroad and went into business full-time for himself. He formed the Berry Coal Company and displayed its motto—"Always Dependable"—on the sides of his Model T. Ford. That same year he purchased the first truck of what would become a fleet of thirteen by 1933. The Berry Coal Company prospered, first under William's leadership, and later under the direction of sons Jack and Joe. It eventually became Berico Fuels, Inc., one of North Carolina's largest fuel distributors, which still exists today.

THOMAS'S EARLY YEARS: INDEPENDENCE AND DREAMING OF THE WILD

Berry family life was warm, stable, and affectionate. Moreover, by 1920 standards, William and Bess were quite progressive. "We always asked our children to 'please' do things," William later recalled. Both parents encouraged their children to speak up and think for themselves—an approach that clearly went against the "children should be seen and not heard" attitude of the time. William and Bess were dedicated to their family and were judicious in making each child feel valued. One time Thomas was talking with a young friend who claimed that his own parents played favorites with their children and loved some more than others. Wondering about this custom, Thomas asked his mother whether she loved "some of us better than others." Unhesitatingly, Bess replied, "It's not that I love one better than another, but I always feel closest to the child who needs me the most."[6] Thomas later declared that his sense of integrity came from his father and his sense of wonder from his mother.

By all accounts, Thomas was a kind and caring older brother and the peacemaker in his family. Still, Thomas later recalled that as a child he presented his parents with challenges:

> My mother told me once that I was so difficult as a child, that by the age of four, my mother and father had a conference one day about me, and my father said, "We have been nice and sweet and kind to this boy. We have

rewarded him. We have spanked him. We have punished him. Just nothing's going to work. I guess he will just have to raise himself."[7]

And so, he did, acknowledging, "I was fortunate. From the beginning my parents let me get on with my own thinking" (*Goldenrod*, 30). This kind of independence was evident in the story Thomas recalls from his youth:

> One of the most memorable events was when I was nine years old, and my father took me to the downtown section to an old building on West Market Street just west of Greene Street where the *Daily Record* was published in a rickety old loft. There he showed me how to buy papers for three cents. Then we went to the crossroads of the city where he showed me how to sell the papers for a nickel. We started with ten papers. He went back to his job as timekeeper at the railway station. I stood on the corner and sold my papers to the business people coming out of their offices in the middle and later afternoon. It was for me a liberating experience. I was being put on my own. I had a need for independence. Evidently my father saw this.
>
> Some days later he took me to Vanstory clothing store and set up an account for me, telling the clerk that I would buy and pay for my clothes. It was a typical small town way of leading a young boy to a capacity for survival on his own. This was one of the most basic principles of my father in raising his children. He would always see that his children were assisted when they needed assistance. But he knew that the greatest thing he could do for his children would be to let us shape our own lives and also to support ourselves as early and as completely as we could. I remember especially my feeling of elation when we walked out of the clothing store. I was in command of my destiny.
>
> (*Goldenrod*, 104–5)

This singular drive and self-determination were evident throughout his life.

So was his intense love of reading. As a young person, Thomas devoured the *Tom Swift* books, Zane Grey's writing, and the Pony Rider Series of boys' adventure stories. Along with his brothers, he enjoyed the camaraderie of a local Boy Scout troop, where he learned to appreciate outdoor life, woodcraft, fishing, hunting, camping, and Native American lore. The idea of wilderness especially attracted him, and he pored over *Boy's Life* advertisements to order catalogues of outdoor equipment. This was his escape, dreaming of being part of a larger world:

> My own attractions to the wild and my aversion to the ordering processes of the civilizational order were evident at a rather early period. At the ages of nine and ten, when I was reading Boy's Life and other adventure publications, I would read the advertising sections where I could learn of the equipment a person would need for living in a wilderness setting. By the time I was 10, I had a five-inch stack of catalogues that I had sent for to learn about going to the north woods. This was my escape world. In a sense, my wonderworld. Of course I never got there. I never had the money to buy the equipment or to find transportation to this region. My family context, my life situation did not permit it. To go to the wilderness was never an available option.
>
> (*Goldenrod*, 29)

He was instinctively drawn to the dramatic geography of the Northwest region of the United States. While he never lived there, years later when he met Brian Thomas Swimme, who was from that region, he would say with a smile that the Pacific Northwest had finally come to him. His longing for adventure in remote locales persisted through his attraction to travel and study, first in China, then Germany, and later in Japan and the Philippines.

By his teens, Thomas was a tall, lanky athletic youth, built much like his father and sharing his features. Thomas and his friends played hockey on the streets, raced scooters, and took up sandlot baseball. Bicycling around Greensboro was a favorite pastime, and Thomas estimated that he sometimes rode over two hundred miles a week, which included his daily paper route.[8] He was a lover of animals early on and was devoted to the family dog, Prince. Thomas once carried the injured dog home in his arms after a milk delivery truck struck him. With equal care, Thomas raised an abandoned baby red-winged blackbird until it fledged.[9]

He recalled when the family got their first radio and, later, going to the movies to see Charlie Chaplin and Buster Keaton, as well as Douglas Fairbanks, Mary Pickford, and Greta Garbo. As a teenager, Thomas had friends and even dated, but he remained critical of the triviality and anti-intellectualism of the southern social milieu. He was, in fact, a born rebel and an independent thinker who had the self-confidence to question things. Perhaps this was because he grew up as something of an outsider himself.

Religious Formation: A Catholic Family in the South

Growing up Catholic in the South in the 1920s was not easy. Greensboro was overwhelmingly Protestant, and Catholic customs and beliefs were not well understood or appreciated. There was often a sense of being tolerated as outsiders, rather than being fully accepted by the community. Through personal appeal and honest business practices, William allayed much local prejudice, but for many years some people refused to do business with a Catholic. During the 1928 campaign of Al Smith, the first Catholic to run for president of the United States, Greensboro suffered considerable anti-Catholic sentiment often fueled by the Ku Klux Klan and a revival of old prejudices. Some of this prejudice was in the tradition of "papistry," which arose originally in England with the Anglican Church and which suggested that Catholic loyalty would be primarily to the pope.

In a time when fewer Catholics lived in North Carolina than anywhere else in the country, the Berrys were nonetheless conscientious observers of their religion. Their parish, St. Benedict's, was at the time the only Catholic parish in Greensboro.[10] However, the Berrys practiced their religion with a sense of celebration. Sunday Mass was generally followed by a big breakfast for family and friends at the Berry home. This social dimension of church life was true for all the churches in the area and created a strong basis for the social life of the community. As Thomas noted, throughout Greensboro "there were church affairs constantly, church dinners or outdoor celebrations. In summers there were the encampments, the bible learning sessions" (*Goldenrod*, 11).

In his later years Thomas observed:

Undoubtedly, the thing of greatest value to me, the thread of continuity in my deeper life commitments, has been the religious training that I received quite early and the family religious observances as a Roman Catholic in a region so completely Protestant that Catholics constituted only about one-half of 1 percent of the population. This provided a profound awareness of identity, a purely religious identity that had no ethnic sensitivity that I am aware of.[11]

(*Goldenrod*, 65-66)

Thomas's religious training at home, and later at school, shaped him for a lifelong spiritual journey marked by inclusion and compassion.

One person who exemplified such compassion was Katharine Drexel (1858-1955), a wealthy Catholic woman from Philadelphia who worked tirelessly to assist African Americans and Native Americans, giving funds and championing their rights. In the late 1890s, she made a donation of $1,500 to St. Benedict's parish in Greensboro to build a church with the stipulation that pews would be reserved for African Americans and that integration would be part of the church policy. Sixty years before the sit-in at the Woolworth lunch counter, just down the road, a glimmer of integration in the segregated South was felt at the city's first Catholic parish.

Both parents were strongly committed to their children's education and sought out Catholic schools. When, in 1926, the Sisters of Charity opened a parochial grammar school, the Berry children were promptly enrolled. Thomas completed seventh and eighth grades there, graduating with the first class in 1928. Moreover, despite the expense, the children were sent away to Catholic boarding schools for secondary school. The girls attended St. Joseph's College High School in Emmitsburg, Maryland, which was founded in 1809 by Elizabeth Seton. This was the first free parochial school for girls in the United States. The Berry boys were sent to nearby Mount St. Mary's Preparatory School and College, which was founded in 1808.[12]

Each child was also encouraged to pursue as much higher education as he or she wished. All the Berry children earned college degrees, and between them there were also two doctoral degrees, three master's degrees, and one medical doctorate. In addition, reflecting the strong family ethos to be of service, four of the thirteen Berry children entered Catholic religious orders. Two joined the Daughters of Charity—Mary Elizabeth and Margaret—while Ann joined the Maryknoll Sisters. Thomas eventually entered the Passionist Congregation.

Awareness of Inequities: Social Justice of Father and Son

The Church in the early twentieth century was encouraging social justice for workers, based on the encyclical *Rerum Novarum* of Pope Leo XIII.[13] This letter to the faithful created the foundations for modern Catholic social teachings on such topics as the limits of both capitalism and communism as just economic systems, the rights and responsibilities of workers and employers, and the duty to care for the poor.

No doubt, William was influenced by such teachings and tried to put them into practice. He was noted for his generosity to the poor, often providing them with free coal and asking them to pay only what they could. Once, during the Depression years, when a local portrait artist fell behind in his payments, William accepted his proposal to provide art lessons for son Frank as payment.

Troubled by racial injustice, William made an effort to hire African Americans and pay them a decent wage. He provided dental benefits for them, knew the names of their spouses and children, and attended family funerals at local African American churches. By standards of the time and place, the Berrys were progressive in their racial attitudes. Their children were not allowed to use racial epithets, and they inherited their father's sense of social justice.

Thomas was keenly aware of the inequities of life for African Americans, especially in housing and jobs. He later wrote of the injustices in his hometown:

> Greensboro was an attractive city in its residential houses, its job opportunities, its sense of community. This might be said, except for the Black population which, in these earlier decades of the twentieth century, lived in rather miserable conditions in shacks outside the residential area of the white community. This "Negro" section of the city extended to the east of the main business district out Market Street and to the south of the city out Ash Street. Until after World War II, these streets were lined with shacks built originally for a few hundred dollars by White owners who made substantial amounts of money from rents. These rents, while quite low, looked at from the present, were in reality quite high for the situation. In my early years at least, the houses had running water and electricity, yet not all the streets were paved. Many had only back-house toilets.
>
> (*Goldenrod*, 12)

He reflected, too, on the difficulty of employment for African Americans:

> Because they were not included in the mill organization, the only work
> left for the blacks in the South was tenant farming and subservient types
> of labor in the more burdensome occupations of hauling and digging and
> trash-disposal; service work of a type not far different from what they were
> doing as slaves prior to liberation. There were more jobs available for black
> women in the white-dominated society as cooks and housekeepers and
> caregivers for the children, the elderly, and the incapacitated.
>
> (*Goldenrod*, 33-34)

Thomas's sense of justice and compassion was already developing at an early age. He acknowledges being influenced as a boy by Catholic social teachings regarding concern for the poor: "Saints Benedict and Leo and Vincent de Paul, the creator of the modern Catholic tradition of concern for the poor, were present in my mind from this early period" (*Goldenrod*, 43).

Indeed, young Thomas was an "easy touch" for workers needing an advance on their next paycheck. Money simply didn't interest him. Once, sent by his father to the bank with a company deposit, Thomas left the deposits on the back seat of the car while it was being serviced. Later, rebuked by his father for his carelessness, Thomas replied, "It's just money." Though annoyed by this lack of business sense, William was known to be secretly proud of his son's detachment.

The Berry children often worked in the family business after school hours or in the summer. They all, including Thomas, had great respect for their father and his work ethos. But, while understanding his father's drive to succeed in business, Thomas did not share it, and in the end he sought another path. A life-changing experience contributed to this decision.

In the summer of 1928, after his eighth-grade graduation, Thomas and his cousin Kitty took the train to visit her father in Stone, Kentucky, where he worked as a mining engineer at the Ford Motor Company. Thomas recalls witnessing dismal conditions in the coal mine and in the company town, where miners were paid in a currency that was only redeemable at the company store. One of the first indications of Thomas's discontent with the modern industrial order grew out of his awareness of the miners' plight. It is ironic that the son of a family that prospered by selling coal mined in the Appalachian Mountains would later turn so strongly against the commercial-industrial order that brought economic prosperity to his home state. Yet, early in life Thomas was beginning to see the human and environmental cost of this prosperity:

> From the time I was nine years old I worked with my father in the small commercial concern that he ran at the time. I saw something of the conditions under which commercial transactions were carried out. I knew the stench and smoke of railway engines and the fumes of automobile engines, the grime and exhaustion of workingmen coming home from machine work. I knew the type of lives that people were living, the unrelieved hours of work, the limited time available for children and play and home living, the severity of a commercial world where money was the basic value and where kindness was often seen more in its economic value than as authentic feeling.
>
> (*Goldenrod*, 24)

The Newly Industrializing South: A Changing Bioregion

The South went through its own industrial revolution in the decades after the Civil War. Born only fifty years after the war, Thomas grew up in a South that had residues of that conflict still alive in its historical memory: "The year of my birth was the end of that fifty-year period between the Civil War and World War I. It was the beginning of a new phase of life not only for the South, but for the entire nation" (*Goldenrod*, 30–31). He reflected on the cultural milieu of the post–Civil War South:

> A new type of feeling about life, in all its aspects, came into being in this postwar period. In the prewar period, the South had begun to define itself as a distinctive cultural region over against the other sections of the country. The South had developed, after 1800, a life mystique strongly influenced by the romantic tradition that had originated in Europe at the end of the eighteenth century, and which dominated much of English thought and

literature throughout the earlier part of the nineteenth century. It was this sense of a more gracious way of life that gave to the South its disdain for the Northern states with their emphasis on industry, trade, and commerce as the basic values, values inculcated by earlier training in the "useful arts and sciences."

(*Goldenrod*, 38)

However, North Carolina, the "Old North State," was searching for a new identity, having lost a war it never really wanted to fight and rejecting a plantation identity that never really fit its agricultural history. The traditional agrarian economy of the South could not compete successfully with northern industrial enterprise. Though rich in natural resources, especially coal and timber, the South, as yet, offered little regional manufacturing. It was seeking ways to industrialize. The North Carolina Piedmont region did, in fact, find its modern identity in textile mills and furniture industries. By the end of the nineteenth century it had adopted its own southern form of belief in progress through industrial development.

The region was transitioning from an agrarian folk culture to that of an industrial working class. With the lure of cash or scrip wages, textile mills gradually supplanted subsistence farming. People focused on new jobs and cultivated habits of industry. In mill villages, later incorporated into cities such as Greensboro, entire families worked sixty or more hours a week and were paid in scrip redeemable only in company stores. Cone Mills and Lorillard Tobacco came to dominate Greensboro's economy. Rural village culture of nineteenth-century North Carolina gave way to the new industrial culture dependent on low wages and easily available labor. This was often at the expense of African American communities, where opportunities were restricted and Jim Crow laws enforced segregation. Consequently, many African Americans moved north to cities like New York, Chicago, and Detroit, where jobs could be found.

A rising class of merchants and manufacturers who were risk-taking entrepreneurs soon dominated the economy. Southern businessmen, such as Moses Cone—the "Denim King"—and his brother Caesar, made a name for themselves by being some of the first textile manufacturers in the nation to offer finished clothing for sale, instead of merely fabric. New technology, too, was changing the world in which Thomas was growing up. Movie theaters opened and commercial radio spread. Telephones were now available, and electricity had recently been introduced, thanks to James B. Duke's power plants. Streetcars ran in downtown Greensboro, and in the 1920s the age of the automobile was launched. Thomas recalled when cars began to have roll-up windows. He lamented this change, as he couldn't breathe in the fresh air and feel the wind on his face as easily. With the automobile came asphalt roads and highway construction. Known for some time as "the good roads state," North Carolina now linked not just farms but also growing industrial markets. Greensboro had come to redefine itself as "the Gate City," a regional transportation and manufacturing center.

The new technologies and paved roads were equated with progress and the promise of a modernized North Carolina. Yet, in the general culture, there was little awareness of the hidden costs of this industrializing in terms of both humans and nature. African Americans were still not integrated into the workforce or housing or schools, and voting rights were restricted.[14] Piedmont rivers were polluted with dyes dumped by textile mills and by untreated municipal sewage. Across North Carolina, widespread clear-cutting of timber and soil erosion from poor farming practices prevailed.[15]

The Growing Tensions: Commerce Versus Nature

Thomas later reflected on the implications of these trends for Greensboro: "It was increasingly clear that society's entire cultural commitment was to an ever-increasing exploitation of the natural world by expanding the city limits, paving the roads, polluting the rivers, cutting the finest available trees, exalting the human to the exclusion of nature in literary studies" (*Goldenrod*, 23). What he longed for, and gave expression to in his later years, was that, given the right conditions, the South might have created a rich culture congruent with its geography, climate, soils, vegetation, wildlife, and indigenous peoples. But, devastated by the Civil War and Reconstruction, the southern states felt they needed to catch up with the North. The southern myth of a gracious and genteel culture gave way to the myth of progress in a society still rife with the racial tensions of segregation. Moreover, this southern myth rarely acknowledged the slave culture on which it was based. Thomas described the ambiguities:

> The orientation of the South was toward a more leisurely culture, at one time a more gracious and yet socially, in its oppression of the blacks, a more violent culture than existed in the north. It was a culture filled with contradictions that the South never succeeded in overcoming. It might even be said that the South has, from its beginning, lived in a dreamworld of self-idealization. That this had its charm is evident in the fascination for this period that still remains for the white population of the country, not simply for Southerners.
>
> (*Goldenrod*, 38)

As he grew up, Thomas sensed this loss of a more leisurely, reflective life: "Development was taking over an increasing amount of farmland. I thought then that there must be a better way of interacting with the natural world. But for people generally there was seldom a question of anything other than survival in the business world" (*Goldenrod*, 24). As Thomas observes: "The absence of any mystique of the land in the general culture of society was the central difficulty I encountered in my effort to attain some integral mode of being for myself" (*Goldenrod*, 20). He would spend decades of his life trying to uncover the roots of this absence, all the while seeking to remedy this loss.

CHILDHOOD MEMORIES: SOLACE IN NATURE

The experiences of seeing the destruction of nature contrasted with Thomas's strong sensibilities toward the natural world that were cultivated during his early years in Greensboro. He was a brooding youth and spent hours on his own, roaming in nature and trying to understand what was missing in others' experiences. He cherished this independence and relished the time for thinking. But he was puzzled about what he saw lacking in his parents' generation:

> Already in childhood, in the mid-1920's, I knew that there were difficulties in the way humans were relating to the natural world. There were sensitivities that the adult generation did not have. There were voices they could not hear.

My awareness of this brought about an extensive isolation early in my life. Yet it was perhaps not so much isolation as independence, for at this time children had a range of freedom from immediate supervision that could hardly be granted children in the more troubled world of the present.

(Goldenrod, 20)

From a very young age, Thomas was keenly aware of the power of nature and found solace there:

In the late summer of 1920, when I was six years old, the family moved to a house on Douglas Street at the southeast corner of Macon, in the southeast part of the city. I remember vividly the Sweet Gum tree in the small back yard. The yard itself was mostly bare, but beyond the house, across Macon Street, a small stream ran through a meadow on down to South Buffalo creek. Willow trees grew alongside the stream, while along the road there were white oaks. Often, I sat by the stream and simply watched the flow of the water, especially in those places where it flowed over rocks to make a tiny waterfall. This was not wilderness. Yet, it was away from houses and away from people. A mysterious place, I found here something beyond what I experienced elsewhere. It was a healing place. It affected my thinking throughout the years to come.

(Goldenrod, 19)

When they moved again seven years later, Thomas discovered a wide range of places for his wanderings and thus spent hours immersing himself in nature:

Later, after we moved across town, I found more extensive range for my roaming through the woodlands north of the city where I could camp out on occasion on the shores of a nearby lake. Meadows and creeks and woodlands, mockingbirds and red-winged blackbirds, and the sound of crickets in the fields were always nearby in summer; while in the winter there was the stillness of the land, only the sound of the wind flowing through the pines. There was an infinite distance between these realities and the realities that impinged on my awakening consciousness from the human world. . . . I needed a way of life integral with these modes of life expression. Among my most vivid memories are those of the bluebirds coming through in the last week of February or the early days of March and resting on a nearby fence-rail before continuing their journey.

(*Goldenrod*, 19)

A Defining Moment: The Meadow Across the Creek

In spring 1926, eleven-year-old Thomas had a transformative experience of nature, one that would influence his basic life orientation. He recounts that experience in his essay, "The Meadow Across the Creek."[16] On an early May afternoon, he had bicycled to Kirkwood, a new suburb in northern Greensboro, near Irving Park. There, on Colonial Avenue, his family was having land cleared and construction had begun on a new home. Men with mules and a drag pan had dug out the basement, the foundation had been laid, and the framing was ready to begin.

Beyond this site, situated on a slight ridge overlooking South Buffalo Creek, lay a wet meadow of wildflowers. Standing with his bicycle, Thomas gazed beyond the house at the spring meadow "covered with white lilies rising above

1.2 Field of lilies.
Larry Petrovick

the thick grass."[17] He was transfixed by the wonder and beauty of the scene—not merely the flowers, but the entire field: the crickets, the distant woods, and the clouds in the clear blue sky. This experience deepened his profound sensitivity to nature, a disposition that became increasingly normative for him over his lifetime. Indeed, even at such a young age he felt intuitively that "whatever preserves and enhances this meadow in the natural cycles of its transformation is good; whatever opposes this meadow or negates it is not good."[18] The integrity of the meadow became apparent to him, with its variety of interdependent life forms. It was a complex, beautiful, and vibrant ecosystem that needed to be preserved.

Navigating Creativity: Between the Wild and the Domestic

These reflections of Thomas on his early experiences in nature were elaborated over the years in the mystique he developed regarding the dynamic forces of nature. His was not simply a romantic view of the natural world, nor was it one that prized domestication. The power of his imagination allowed him to join his personal experiences in nature as a youth with the expansive wildness that is also part of nature's power and attraction. Indeed, one might say that nature was "numinous" for him—simultaneously alluring and fearful. How to navigate these responses was one of his challenges—both personally and with his students.

It was many years later that Thomas wrote an article on the "Apollonian and Dionysian" tensions in human societies and individuals. There, he highlighted the interplay of the rational and emotional sides of humans as a counterpart to the creative and destructive dynamics of nature. He observed that we have arisen from these processes and needed to learn to integrate them. The interaction of the domestic and the wild were the tensions he identified. The creativity he sought was in wildness:

> I wished to escape from this reengineered world into what can only be identified as the wild. Wildness might be considered as the rootedness of the authentic spontaneities of any being. It is that wellspring of creativity whence comes the instinctive activities of the living world that enable all living beings to obtain their food, to find shelter, to perform their mating rituals.

This is the same inner tendency that evokes the insight of the poet, the skill of the artist, and the power of the shaman.

(Goldenrod, 25)

His own creative path was poetic and shamanic, entering into nature's vital forces to bring back a healing vision. It is noteworthy that he could manage this creative attraction to the wild amidst the contemplative and restrained demands of the monastic life that he later chose. The chaotic and unifying tensions of the larger world around him were mirrored in the destructive and creative choices a person makes as a human life unfolds.

In all of this, Thomas was sustained during his life by an abiding attention to nature that was, for him, ineffable and yet felt, intimate and vast, enduring and yet ever changing.

This presence to the natural world has been the saving dimension of my life. Although I could not name it at the time, I was aware of some absorbing mystery present throughout the natural world. This I experienced at all times but more profoundly while lying on my back in a meadow or along a nearby lake and watching the clouds as they would take on such playful shapes in the sky. This was no experience of the Rocky Mountain peaks or of Mount Rainier, or even the experience of Mount Mitchell in the Southern Appalachians. It was no experience of the Sonora desert of the Southwest. Nor the coasts of Maine. Yet, it was my childhood wilderness.

(Goldenrod, 53)

Out of this childhood experience of the mysterious power in nature arose a New Story and a Great Work that he felt would guide humans through this next century of upheaval and uncertainty. The power of these youthful experiences remained with Thomas throughout his life. Indeed, it became a bass note for a journey that took him from North Carolina to Maryland and on to New York and Washington, D.C., then to China and Germany, back to New York, and at last home to Greensboro. It was a journey of ninety-four years lived across a century of massive disruptions and widespread suffering.

CHAPTER 2

The Call to Contemplation

For myself, I needed a sense of the Great Work of the historical moment. My life quest has been to identify this. Just what this Great Work is, or the precise pattern of its achievement, has never been entirely clear. For me, identifying this work and finding my own role in achieving it has been itself the journey.

I found this in the monastery world. For me, this was the appropriate context for the type of thinking that I needed to do. I needed time, I needed solitude, I needed to live in a religious context as I sought out the comprehensive wisdom of the human heritage. This would require a lifetime.

Thomas Berry, *Goldenrod: Reflections on the Twentieth Century*

LEAVING HOME: STUDY AT MOUNT ST. MARY'S

In September 1928, when he was not yet fourteen, Thomas's parents sent him to study at Mount St. Mary's Preparatory School, a Catholic boys school with an enrollment of about a hundred students. It was located on the outskirts of Emmitsburg, Maryland, in the foothills of the Blue Ridge Mountains, just south of Gettysburg. There he spent his high school years, except the holidays. As he reflected on this moment, he wrote, "Leaving home at this time gave me an increased sense of independence that I had developed from earlier years" (*Goldenrod*, 67). He would not return to Greensboro to live permanently until he was eighty years old. His life journey apart from his family was launched in Maryland on a rolling campus at the foot of an imposing mountain. These years

2.1 Mount St. Mary's Prep School in Emmitsburg, Maryland.
Photo courtesy of Mount St. Mary's

were surrounded by the calamity of the Depression, increasing his sense that the world of business and finance was inadequate for his own path. He knew he had to find another direction.

THE DEPRESSION YEARS

Within a year of Thomas's coming to Mount St. Mary's, the Depression had begun. In October of his sophomore year, the stock market crashed, and the United States was plunged into a chaotic period of uncertainty and anguish brought on by the financial turmoil. Many people lost their jobs, homes, or businesses, as well as their life savings. Effective plans for recovery were not on the horizon; nothing of this magnitude had ever happened before. The entire world was drawn into the downward spiral.

President Herbert Hoover, despite his economic expertise and strong support from the business community, seemed unable to stem the collapse. Inept decisions led to further decline of the economic system. Maintaining the gold standard and resisting government spending proved inadequate to reduce the scale of the problems. The decline continued throughout Thomas's high school years. It was not until he graduated, and Franklin Delano Roosevelt came into office in 1932, that the United States began to dig its way out.

The New Deal that Roosevelt developed held great promise for many who were out of work. The Civilian Conservation Corps and other public work projects put people back into the labor force. This kind of government spending was a driving engine of the New Deal, and the economy began to sputter back to life. Reform of the financial system was initiated with programs to insure deposits, such as the Federal Deposit Insurance Corporation (FDIC), and regulation of capital markets through the Securities and Exchange Commission (SEC). Recovery would take years, and another dip occurred in the market in 1938. Many conjectured that it was the Second World War that finally reignited the economy, with factories producing munitions and supplies for the Allied troops.

All through this period, Thomas was hungry for learning, trying to find his way forward in a world that was unraveling and a new one that was being born. His vocation emerged from this chrysalis of knowledge, unfolding amid the economic uncertainties of his youth. As the United States groped its way through times of immense human tragedy, he was immersing himself in western European history and the Greek classics. These early studies, steeped in narratives of time and tradition, nourished him in his teenage years and yet propelled him toward new areas of reading and reflection.

THE BEGINNINGS OF AN INTELLECTUAL LIFE

The complex of buildings on the Mount St. Mary's campus included not only the high school but also the Seminary, which is the second oldest Catholic seminary in the United States. Still active today, it is known as "the cradle of American bishops" for its education of many church leaders. There was also the college where Thomas spent his freshman year. Unique in American Catholic education, Mount St. Mary's College was not associated with any order or diocese and was governed by its own administration and board of trustees. Founded in 1808, it is the oldest private, independent Catholic college in the United States.[1]

Marked by imposing granite buildings, the campus is laid out on descending terraces against the lower slopes of St. Mary's Mountain. On the hills above the campus was the Grotto of Our Lady of Lourdes.[2] This grotto was beloved to Elizabeth Seton, the founder of the Sisters of Charity, who lived in a log cabin near the grotto in 1809 before moving to the nearby town of Emmitsburg. A large rock in the grotto is dedicated to her, as she often preached there on Sundays to the children of the local parish. The exquisite beauty of the grotto, as Thomas knew it, was thanks to the French priest Simon Brute (Seton's spiritual adviser), who believed the sacred could be found in all of nature.[3] At the peak of the mountain is an old Indian lookout that had served as a Union outpost during the Civil War.

During Thomas's years there (1928–1933), the Mount was governed by the formidable Monsignor Bernard Bradley, president of both the prep school and the college from 1911 until his death in 1936. Bradley himself attended the college and seminary and, after ordination, returned to teach logic and liturgy. He was revered by students and faculty for his dedication to the Mount as well as for his inspiring character. Bradley was recognized in his time as one of the foremost Catholic educators in the United States. It was he who helped shape Thomas's course of studies.

Under Bradley's guidance, the school offered scientific and classical curricula with a competent faculty composed of both lay and religious persons. Thomas enrolled in the classical curriculum, which included courses in English, Latin, French, history, and religion, as well as mathematics and physical science. Student life at the prep school included intellectual and social activities: a debating club, weekly movies, visiting lecturers, and dances with girls from nearby St. Joseph's College High School, which his sisters attended. Thomas enjoyed team sports and played on the varsity football and basketball teams. He also spent time hiking in the Catoctin Mountains, east of the Blue Ridge.

On weekends, students would often leave the secluded campus to hitchhike or walk a mile into Emmitsburg to eat at the Green Parrot Tea Shop (a favorite Emmitsburg spot, located on the green) or go to movies in nearby Gettysburg. A strict curfew prevailed at the school, and during his senior year Thomas lost the privilege of delivering the valedictory address for being out after hours. His independent streak continued from his youthful Greensboro years.

Thomas's grades, however, were excellent, and throughout his four years at the school, he won the highest academic awards in his class. Still, he did not find the classes particularly challenging:

> I learned very little in high school, although I was consistently among those with the higher grades. I had chosen the liberal-arts program rather than the science program as the pattern of my thinking. Perhaps the best thing that I learned was the rudiments of the Latin language, still a requirement for those entering into humanistic studies.
>
> (*Goldenrod*, 66)

On June 5, 1931, at the height of the Depression, Thomas graduated from the prep school, first in a senior class of eighteen. In his commencement address, Vincentian priest William McClimont spoke of the Catholic missions in China. No doubt something was sparked in Thomas that resulted in his lifelong interest in China and his travel there in 1948. But he writes that "at the end of high school I was still wondering just what direction to take" (*Goldenrod*, 66).

Not yet ready to apply elsewhere for college or to pursue a religious vocation, Thomas entered Mount St. Mary's College for his freshman year with 244 other young men. Of the eight majors offered, he enrolled in the classics program. In addition to classes in Greek and Latin, he read Greek authors such as the epic writer Homer and the lyric poet Pindar, the philosophers Plato and Aristotle, and the Roman poets Virgil and Horace. He also absorbed such Western texts as *Beowulf*, *The Song of Roland*, *El Cid*, the Arthurian legends, and the *Divine Comedy*.[4] Despite good grades, he did not find the coursework engaging and decided after his first year to leave college.

The Mount St. Mary's experience was invaluable in getting Thomas away from home during his teenage years and increasing his sense of independence. There, he received a broad liberal arts education and began discerning his calling toward the priesthood. With the Great Depression still engulfing the country and with his aversion to the growing industrialization of the South, he sought a place of reflection. The monastery was to be a refuge from the world and yet a place where he found his way back into the world with a healing vision.

PATH OF DISCERNMENT: ENTERING THE MONASTERY

During the summer of 1933, after completing his freshman year of college, Thomas returned to Greensboro. He was still uncertain about his future but was increasingly drawn to the contemplative life for time to think and meditate. His choice of the Passionist Congregation was perhaps fortunate, since it was not a strictly monastic order but engaged in giving parish talks and retreats. The order combined prayer and preaching, a rigorous monastic rule and broader church outreach, and an intense devotion to the Passion of Christ and a commitment to alleviate suffering.

Thomas's deep compassion for human suffering led him to try to comprehend its meaning. He was inspired by the Christian notion of redemptive or vicarious suffering on behalf of others. The Passionists made this their highest aspiration, namely, that through such compassion one could relieve the ordeals and anguish of others. This empathy for the pathos of life, and sympathy for human tragedy, marked Thomas throughout his life. Indeed, it is one of the reasons he eventually sought a "new story" to guide the human venture.

The Passionists are officially named the Congregation of the Passion (C.P.). The founder was an Italian mystic called Paul Francis Danei (1694-1775), later known as St. Paul of the Cross. Grounded in the works of medieval mystics Meister Eckhart and John Tauler, Paul spent a season in contemplation and then went out to preach to the people, focusing on divine participation in human suffering.[5] This model marked the order he founded. In its combination of contemplation and action, monastic prayer and apostolic work, the Passionist Congregation was somewhat unusual. For most of the twentieth century, its priests and brothers resided in monasteries, living a common life of prayer and contemplation in between their preaching.[6]

Thomas had become aware of the Passionist Congregation in the 1920s through their presence in North Carolina. The state was still considered mission territory, as this was an overwhelmingly Protestant region at the time. The Passionists sometimes visited his family's parish, St. Benedict's Church in Greensboro, as guest preachers. On one such occasion, at age thirteen, Thomas heard Father Egbert Albert, a noted Passionist priest, lead an engaging parish retreat. With an eloquent style and vivid images, Father Egbert mesmerized listeners. Several years later, another Passionist who lived in Greensboro, Father Patrick Darrah, advised Thomas about applying for entrance into the Passionist Congregation.

Thomas was not familiar with other religious orders, as they were not present in North Carolina, except the Benedictines, who had a monastic community outside of Charlotte. However, he realized he didn't want to be primarily a contemplative monk, as these Benedictines were. He wanted some engagement with the world, other than being a parish priest. He also wanted to move outside of North Carolina, and the Benedictines in those days took a vow of commitment to remain at a particular monastery.

On September 5, 1933, Thomas wrote Provincial Father Justin Carey asking to be accepted into the Passionist community: "It has taken me several years to remove all the doubts that have arisen, but always the call to the priesthood has persisted until now it is calling with a force, which can no longer be denied."[7] Father Carey advised him instead to apply to become a diocesan or secular priest, rather than enter a demanding religious community like the Passionists. But Thomas wrote again:

> It has taken me three years to make a decision as to whether I should become a secular priest or whether I should join an Order. My knowledge of the life of both is not complete in every detail, but it is sufficient for me to decide as to where my vocation lies. I have chosen the Passionists because of the special devotion to the Passion of Christ, because of the missionary work, which the Order does, and because of the strictness of the Order.[8]

Thomas's determination to pursue religious life with the Passionists was clear. He was especially attracted to the Passionists because of the possibility of going to their missions in China. Father Carey soon relented, and, in late September of 1933, Thomas was accepted into the community. Accordingly, that fall he was sent to begin his studies toward priesthood at Holy Cross Preparatory Seminary in Dunkirk, New York. This was located on Lake Erie, some forty miles west of Buffalo.

Thus, Thomas's life journey brought him out of Greensboro and into an unknown future. He left behind family and the familiar customs of a small southern community. He realized he had to branch out from Greensboro: "Just how I came to leave my close association with all this to venture into the monastery and its enclosure is more than I can say. I knew that I needed to leave my

2.2 Holy Cross Passionist Preparatory Seminary, Dunkirk, New York.
Photo courtesy of the Passionist Historical Archives

hometown." Indeed, he observes that in Greensboro "there was no context for anything other than a commercial career or that of law or medicine within the newly developing technological world. There was the career of teaching, but that too was questionable as regards just how to get the training and even what to teach." He knew he was not "suited to or attracted to any kind of ministerial career." But he writes of his deeper sense of calling: "I envisaged myself as a religious personality" (*Goldenrod*, 49).

MONASTIC RELIGIOUS FORMATION

Just under nineteen years of age in 1933, Thomas was leaving the secular world of early twentieth-century America for the highly structured world of traditional monastic life. Having spent the summer mulling over his decision and hoping to avoid anything that might dissuade him, Thomas did not inform his family of his choice until the day before his departure for the seminary. There he began a period of rigorous religious formation to determine his suitability for a life of prayer, study, and preaching.[9]

It was a choice with immense consequences. In the pre-Vatican II period before 1962, Catholic monastic training was quite demanding. Sacrifice was at the heart of this life path. Except for a monthly letter to parents and a short visit home between first year postulancy and the second yearlong novitiate, most contact with the outer world would be severed. All letters, including those from home, would be opened and read. In an age before television, other modes of communication like the radio, telephone, and newspapers were restricted. This severity of monastic life would change significantly in the 1960s with Vatican Council II and the liberalizing spirit of Pope John XXIII, who wished to open the doors of the Church to contemporary life and thought.

In a letter home on December 18, 1933, Thomas reflected on how much he was looking forward to the Christmas holiday because of the rigor of his first semester at Dunkirk:

> Everything here seems to be hanging in suspense awaiting the holiday, which will begin Wednesday. We are working on the decorations now. By Thursday the study hall will be transformed into a brilliantly decorated recreation room. We will take out all the desks, put up two or three chandeliers bedecked with the usual red and green, and then after putting streamers all over the walls and a Christmas tree in each corner, we will put up a few wreaths here and there; haul in the radio; put up an aerial and declare that the holidays have begun. The most rigid part of the discipline—arising at five thirty and classes will be dispensed for a week or so.
>
> I will welcome the holiday with a deep sigh of relief, for I am beginning to get dizzy every time I try to interpret some of this Greek, which a certain Demosthenes handed down for the ensuing generations.[10]

DAILY MONASTIC LIFE

Holy Cross Preparatory seminary was on an expansive seventy-five-acre campus in rural Chautauqua County, on the shores of Lake Erie. Its natural setting offered groves of pine and spruce and magnificent clouds and snow in the wintertime. The seminary studies were aimed for completion of high school and two required years of college. Thomas finished his second year of college here. When he entered, about one hundred young men were enrolled there; twenty-eight of these were in his class.[11]

Dunkirk's isolated location fostered an intense atmosphere of academic study and prayerful contemplation, but there were also diversions. Sports programs afforded relief, including basketball in a new gymnasium and, in winter, hockey on frozen Lake Erie. Occasionally, movies were brought in, and a drama club staged plays, especially Lenten passion plays. Once, during Thomas's time there, seminarians performed T. S. Eliot's *Murder in the Cathedral* with a stage set featuring cellophane stained-glass windows. One of the priests, Father Francis Kuba, directed an excellent choir.

Seminarians were encouraged to correspond with foreign missionaries and to think about volunteering for an overseas assignment. Thomas corresponded with Father James Lambert, who had been sent to China in 1933 and served there until 1941. Passionate about his missionary work, Lambert returned in 1945, but the Communist takeover in 1949 forced the evacuation of all American missionaries. Lambert passed away in 1951.[12] His death, no doubt, affected Thomas deeply.[13]

The yearlong postulancy in Dunkirk was followed by a novitiate year in the monastery of Our Lady of Sorrows in West Springfield, Massachusetts. There Thomas undertook spiritual formation in preparation for his first profession of vows. Included in this year were lectures on the nature and practice of prayer; meditations on the passion of Christ taken from the *Ignatian Exercises*; and spiritual readings such as Reginald Garrigou-Lagrange's *Christian Perfection and Contemplation*.[14] This was a time of close consultation with a spiritual director to assess a candidate's suitability for the arduous life ahead.

On August 15, 1935, at the end of his novitiate year in West Springfield, Thomas's parents were present for his first profession of vows ceremony, in which he chose his religious name, Thomas, after Thomas Aquinas.[15] Because of the strict rules of monastic life, they were only permitted to visit with him for an hour after the ceremony, even though they had made the long trip north from Greensboro. They witnessed Thomas profess the three vows of religious life, namely, commitment to poverty, chastity, and obedience, along with a fourth vow of the Passionists, to promote devotion to the Passion of Christ. Later in his life, Thomas would expand his fourth vow to include dedication to the Passion of Earth.[16] His sense of vocation and commitment was continually broadening.

2.3 Our Lady of Sorrows Monastery in West Springfield, Massachusetts.
Photo courtesy of the Passionist Historical Archives

2.4 Thomas Berry with his parents in 1935 for first profession of vows.
Courtesy of Ann Berry Somers for the Berry family

LIFE AS A PROFESSED PASSIONIST STUDENT

After his year in West Springfield, Thomas completed seven years of study before his ordination to the priesthood in 1942. Student life from novitiate to ordination was a participation in the monastic life of the priests and brothers with permanent vows. Monastery life and meals were simple and austere, with meatless Wednesdays, Fridays, and Saturdays, in addition to Advent and Lent fasting before Christmas and Easter. Sign language was used for passing of food or utensils, and wooden spoons and forks sufficed for meals. During meals, seminarians took turns reading from spiritual works. Monastic life was hierarchical, with monks respecting rank and seniority, as reflected in the seating arrangements in the refectory.

Inspired by the vow of poverty, the monks made their own sleeping pallets filled with straw and crafted their own leather belts and sandals, along with their habits, rosaries, and black felt caps. They even fashioned their Passionist insignias and ironed on the white acetate letters.[17] Barbering and haircutting were among their other skills. However, the Passionist brothers, not the monks, did the manual work of gardening, cooking, and laundry.[18] Summer assignments included a three-week vacation on Lake Erie or at the Passionist summer retreat on Shelter Island, New York. Despite the proximity to Long Island Sound and beautiful natural surroundings, Thomas dreaded this "vacation" assignment, as seminarians were required to work on landscaping the property. Manipulating the environment added to the drudgery of the work.

During his studies for the priesthood, which included three years of philosophy and four of theology, the Congregation moved the seminarians each year among its various monasteries. After spending 1935–1936 in Pittsburgh, Thomas's class alternated between Immaculate Conception Monastery, Jamaica, in Queens, New York, and St. Michael's Monastery in Union City, New Jersey, along the Hudson River.[19] Besides philosophy and theology, his classes during this period included scripture, canon law, mysticism, history, sociology, psychology, rhetoric, and music. His lifelong appreciation for music was fostered during these years, as he served as class organist, becoming sufficiently proficient to play the works of Palestrina.

Once a week, seminarians were allowed out in pairs to experience the local environs with very modest spending money. For instance, at St. Michael's they were given fifty cents' spending money and a nickel for the ferry fare from Hoboken to Manhattan's Twenty-Third Street terminal. Thomas could then enjoy New York's cultural life, visiting museums or attending concerts, operas, or lectures. Perhaps harkening back to his childhood love of solitude and independence, Thomas and his companions would usually go their separate ways, agreeing to meet later. He would visit such places as the American Museum of Natural History, the construction site of the Cathedral of St. John the Divine, and the old Metropolitan Opera House. There, he could get a ticket high up in the sixth tier of the balcony to hear Wagner's operas, such as *Die Walkure* from *The Ring of the Nibelung* cycle.

Thomas would often head downtown for dinner at Ratner's Restaurant on Second Avenue and, afterwards, to Union Square to hear radical social and

2.5 St. Michael's Monastery, Union City, New Jersey.
Photo courtesy of the Passionist Historical Archives

political speakers. Sometimes he would continue down to the Catholic Worker House on Mott Street for roundtable discussions with Peter Maurin regarding his call for social change. Father Gerard Rooney at St. Michael's in Union City had introduced his class to Dorothy Day and Peter Maurin of the Catholic Worker Movement. The progressive tradition of the Catholic Worker newspaper and Dorothy Day's commitment to pacifism and social justice strongly appealed to Thomas. He would meet with her on occasion and exchange views on current affairs.

Thomas was a southerner in a class of mostly northerners, and he was remembered by fellow seminarians as a bit of a rebel. He acknowledged he could be withdrawn, noncommunicative, and critical of rules. While adjusting reasonably well to strict monastic life, at times he bent regulations for his own purposes. His remarkable stamina and strong constitution enabled him, for example, to get by with little sleep. He would read from three to six in the morning after early morning prayers. He taped the cracks around the door and transom of his monastic cell to mask the light from his gooseneck lamp. He also draped himself in the heavy black cloth used to make caps for the seminarians.

Thomas's hunger for learning began to be satisfied as he read his way through various Passionist libraries during his studies toward ordination. Largely restricted to Catholic theological works, the library holdings nevertheless offered full collections of the Church Fathers and medieval theologians. Thomas was thus able to raise probing questions in class about seminary assignments. In many respects these years of self-education were vital to Thomas's formation, especially his earliest encounters with scriptures from non-Christian religions. Of this time he later wrote:

> For almost ten years I began my study each day at three o'clock in the morning, after celebrating the night liturgy by choral chanting of the psalms and meditation on the great mysteries of the universe. This night study was followed by a day of further study, broken only by periods of work and prayer. I read extensively, in translated versions, in Greek philosophy, Biblical studies, the Fathers of the Church, Upanishadic literature and the classical writings of the Chinese for over ten years before I began my advanced studies in history at the Catholic University in Washington.[20]

STUDY OF ARISTOTLE AND AQUINAS

During this period, Thomas was able to acquire even further knowledge of the classical world that he had begun to study at St. Mary's prep school. "Of special importance for me during my years of personal study was the reading of Aristotle and the commentaries of St. Thomas on Aristotle's physics, metaphysics, biology, ethics, and politics, as well as his *Prior Analytics* and *Posterior Analytics*."[21] He immersed himself in Aristotle, but also in Thomas Aquinas. He read and reread Aquinas's *Summa Theologica*. He always had a copy of this book close at hand, even in his final years at his retirement community in Greensboro.

Through Aquinas and other medieval scholastic theologians (first Islamic and then Christian), the legacy of Aristotle had endured in the West. Thomas appreciated the range and diversity of Aristotle's thought and was profoundly drawn to the commentaries on it. Most Catholic seminaries and universities in this period were dominated by Thomistic thought.

Thomas's feel for Aristotelian empiricism, rather than Platonic idealism, helped to shape his thinking regarding the dynamic processes of evolution. Nonetheless, Thomas also read Plato and the Neo-Platonist Dionysius, and he later encouraged his students to do the same. Other medieval theologians whom he read and valued were Duns Scotus and Bonaventure. He also drank deeply of the medieval mystics, such as Teresa of Avila, John of the Cross, Meister Eckhart, and Hildegard of Bingen. He was profoundly influenced by Dante's *Divine Comedy*, to which he returned throughout his life.

Thomas was drawn to understand and contemplate the world, not simply escape from it in transcendental prayer or meditation. He maintained this focus throughout his life, against the usual tendency of monastics to withdraw from the world and be absorbed in contemplating a transcendent divine force. For Thomas, that divine force was also evident within the world and was present in matter itself. He found this reality in Aristotle, whose work *On the Soul* (*De Anima*) has been translated as "Life Force." This perspective of the subjectivity of matter, from Aristotle and later from Pierre Teilhard de Chardin (1881–1955), had a significant influence on Thomas. Matter was not dead, but alive with divine immanence. As Pierre Teilhard de Chardin wrote, "By means of all created things, without exception, the divine assails us, penetrates us, and molds us. We imagined it as distant and inaccessible, when in fact we live steeped in its burning layers."[22]

All of Thomas's intense reading of Teilhard de Chardin was done in the context of finding an effective way into the next phase of human history beyond the clash of nations and fall of empires seen in World War I.

> In these years, I was also fascinated with the writings of St. Augustine, especially *The City of God*, a work that, together with the Bible and the ritual books of the Church and the Neoplatonic writings of Dionysius, enabled the peoples of Europe to survive the Dark Ages and to build the medieval civilization out of which emerged what we now consider as Western civilization.[23]

Thomas continually reread *The City of God*. He would often speak in vivid terms of the degeneration of the Roman Empire and the struggle of the two cities—the "city of God" and the "city of man"—that so preoccupied Augustine. He saw the early twentieth century as a similar period of upheaval amidst the contestations of war and economic disruption.

MONASTIC LIFE: CONTEMPLATION AND STUDY

Thomas knew that to find his voice he needed time to read and, as he often said, a place to brood. He felt that this is what a monastic life would offer him. He later wrote: "A decisive moment of my life was when I entered the monastery, as the context in which I would be able to reflect on the deeper issues that were presenting themselves to my mind."[24] He was drawn to contemplation within the depths of silence:

> I left college and entered a monastery, not with the idea of ministerial functioning, but for its sense of the sacred that somehow survived amid all the inadequacies of the establishment. It provided the opportunity I needed for the study and thought that I would need later on in life as I began to articulate a vision of the future that would be in some manner coherent with the more vital elements of the past.[25]

The monastic life he entered consisted of a daily cycle of prayer to mark the passage from darkness to light. The Divine Office was chanted in Latin five times a day, beginning with Matins and Lauds at 2:00 a.m., followed by a period of rest; Prime and Tierce at daybreak; Sext and None at midday and mid-afternoon; Vespers at dusk; and Compline as night began.[26] Thomas described the power of these transition moments:

> The psalms sung in these various moments of the day-night cycle celebrated the cosmological sequence of dawn, noon, afternoon, evening, and night moments. These moments that gave to life its deep meaning. So, too, the cycle of the year, the solstice moment of Christmas, the resurrection-renewal moment of [Easter] springtime. There still existed a continuity between the cosmological and the human.
>
> (*Goldenrod*, 68)

This continuity between cosmos and human fascinated Thomas. He found it expressed first in liturgical prayer, then in cultural stories or cosmologies

2.6 Priests in the stalls at Immaculate Conception Monastery, Jamaica, New York, where they chanted divine office five times a day.

Photo courtesy of the Passionist Historical Archives

What was striking for Thomas was that, even with all the challenges of the Catholic tradition in the pre-Vatican II era, he was able to sink into the transformative power and grounding energy of daily prayer and seasonal liturgy. He experienced how this ritual placed humans within the dynamics of the universe itself. This realization remained with him his whole life:

> Despite all the trivialization observable throughout the [Catholic] tradition, something immensely significant was still available in this carrying out of the age-old effort of humans to bring human life into accord with the great liturgy of the universe. That the universe itself was the primary liturgy, just as it was the primary scripture, I never doubted.
>
> (*Goldenrod*, 68)

THE INFLUENCE OF BENEDICTINE MONASTICISM

Thomas's desire to participate in such great rotations of prayer and contemplation seems to have been sparked by his early appreciation of the Benedictine monastic tradition. This was transmitted to him through the influential Benedictine Abbey in Belmont outside of Charlotte, North Carolina. This abbey was established by monks from St. Vincent's Archabbey in Latrobe, Pennsylvania, which was itself founded in the mid-nineteenth century from Beuron Abbey along the Danube in southern Germany. Thus, Thomas sensed the long connection to the European Benedictine tradition: "The ancient plainsong of the liturgies going back to the fifth century was to be heard in the Abbey at Belmont. While it cannot be said that this Abbey was capable of giving modern expression to this tradition it did provide some manner of medieval presence to the society" (*Goldenrod*, 44). He savored that historical bonding to fifteen hundred years of European monasticism.

The abbey's influence was widespread in North Carolina, as many of the priests in parishes throughout the state came from this well-respected abbey. Indeed, Thomas's family's church in Greensboro was named after St. Benedict. This fact had an enduring impact on Thomas:

> I have often thought of Benedict, the patron saint of the local Catholic parish. He was the founder of the monastic tradition that had played such a significant

role throughout the course of western civilization from the sixth century. Through this order, the intellectual and cultural traditions of the classical world had been carried through those dark centuries from the sixth through the eleventh century when the medieval period came into its grandeur.

(Goldenrod, 43)

Thomas was intensely aware of the various ways the monastic tradition of Benedict helped to keep Western civilization alive during chaotic times through its liturgical services, monastic organization, agricultural practices, and preservation of intellectual lineages and tradition.

He wrote: "It was this religious tradition that formed, for me, the most vital link with those earlier forces that had given Europe its earliest identity in those traditional centuries from the decline of Rome to the medieval period. Deep in my psyche there was a powerful medieval component" *(Goldenrod, 44)*. Amid the upheavals of the Depression and the two world wars, there was a steadiness and calm in monastic life that gave Thomas a larger context for his creative work.

CYCLES OF NATURE AS SACRED CYCLES

The rituals of medieval monasticism provided a way of participating in an ancient mystical tradition, giving Thomas a sense of belonging to history as well as to something beyond history, something that was vast, mysterious, and meaningful. His cosmological sense began to emerge as he saw how human history is contained within the dynamic unfolding of the Earth and the universe. In many ways, he would spend his life seeking to articulate that monastic experience of being embedded in deep time and vast space.

Thomas sought to be immersed in the immense powers of nature and the cosmos—not so they overpowered him, but rather so that they empowered him. Monastic ritual provided a way of touching the holy, the numinous, the wild. "Religion I always associated with the wild. In church, I was entranced with initiation into the meaning and symbolisms of the various natural phenomena, the manner in which the transition moments in the daily and yearly cycles of nature were sacred moments. I wished for some understanding of the stars in the night sky" *(Goldenrod, 29)*.

These gateways to the divine gave further expression to Thomas's childhood experiences, which were deepened in the monastery: "One of the most ecstatic moments of life was when I learned that prayer in the morning and in the evening was associated with the natural phenomena that this was based on. That dawn and sunset were moments when the deep mysteries of the universe become present to us with special depth of feeling was evident to me from my earliest years" (*Goldenrod*, 29).

Entry into such transformative moments in nature's cycles became a pathway into the larger cosmos. "It was evident to me that this relation of human activity to the cosmological order should be the controlling context and the basic value in the total course of human affairs" (*Goldenrod*, 29). Thomas began to explore an understanding of the cosmos itself as providing a vital context for human life—one that grounds humans both physically and spiritually.

This exploration was later expanded in dialogue with evolutionary science that joined spiritual and scientific perspectives in contemplation of the cosmos. From this dialogue arose an understanding that death and rebirth were present throughout nature and the cosmos, giving rise to exploding stars, dynamic ecosystems, and biodiverse life forms: "This sense of sacrifice and communion were the characteristics that I found throughout the natural world. . . . Human associations alone were inadequate for my own needs. I needed a deeper mode of presence to the mystery of things. It was obviously a pervasive sense of the sacred" (*Goldenrod*, 67). He acknowledged that the sacred "found partial expression in traditional Christian rituals, in eucharistic celebration, in the ideas of sacrifice and communion." But, ultimately for him, the sacred or numinous was all-pervasive, drawing him into an ever-expanding quest for meaning: "I had always had a sense of the deep mystery of things, the numinous dimension of existence. This was my religion" (*Goldenrod*, 67). The quest to enter into this sacred dimension defined his vocation as a religious person.

SHAMANIC VOCATION

Years later, Thomas was able to see more fully what kind of religious personality he was called to be within this monastic context. He was not meant to be simply a contemplative monk or a preacher, as were most of the Passionists. Nor did he see his vocation as only a teacher or an academic, as were priests in other religious orders. Rather, he saw himself as a shamanic type, one who entered deeply into the powers of the universe and Earth and brought back an integrative vision for the community. He sensed that this role was part of his psyche and thus vital for his spiritual journey. He wrote toward the end of his life: "It was the shamanic dimension of my own psychic structure that required that I go into some manner of inner experience in association with the natural world. This was not simply to enter into some form of the spiritual life but to take on a social role. As I envisage it now, this role was closer to the shamanic role" (*Goldenrod*, 54). Thomas realized that his calling was related to his basic orientation toward nature's processes. Because this orientation informed his speaking, writing, and teaching throughout his life, Thomas identified his vocation as shamanic:

> Of the various religious typologies this would probably be the most relevant to my basic orientation. My experience of the natural world was limited at the time. Yet, already I had, it seems, the experience I needed. It was sufficient to awaken in me a mystique of the natural world, the sense of the larger community composed not simply of humans but of the entire universe. This was the ultimate embrace that infolded us all.
>
> (*Goldenrod*, 54)

The understanding that humans are part of a vast universe and embedded in the life of the Earth community became foundational for Thomas. He acknowledged that it was not the number of experiences he had in nature, but instead their depth and lasting impact that shaped him. "The volume of such experiences may not be the determining thing. It may be rather the quality of the experience" (*Goldenrod*, 49).

Expressions of the shamanic personality that Thomas deeply appreciated were oral vision songs and cosmological stories. Later he would see this kind of communication in Native American traditions, but early on he saw the power of oral communication in African American communities. Thomas often remarked on a funeral he attended as a teenager in an African American community in Greensboro. There, the preacher initially read from the Bible at the graveside and then began preaching extemporaneously. That spontaneous preaching showed Thomas the arresting force of language.

Thus, Thomas began to find his way as a shamanic personality, aware of the power of nature, in search of a healing vision, and entranced by the depth of contemplative silence. He gave his life to the rhythms of a monastery and to the challenges of becoming a scholar:

> My path was not that of John Muir or of Aldo Leopold. It was rather closer to the medieval mystics who lived a confined existence. I would perhaps have been a hermit in earlier times. But there was a scholar hidden within me that needed a certain fulfillment. It was the scholar combined with the nature-orientation that defined me in the course of the years.
>
> (*Goldenrod*, 54).

The desire to deepen his life as a scholar later led Thomas to doctoral work at Catholic University in Washington, D.C. The shamanic nature of his vocation never left him, but rather grounded him on the journey ahead. First, he submitted himself to rigorous spiritual and intellectual training in the monastery to hone his skills as both shaman and scholar.

ORDINATION TO THE PRIESTHOOD

By the time his seminary studies were completed, Thomas had earned the equivalent of a bachelor of arts degree, with excellent grades throughout.[27] His final profession in the Passionist Congregation was made on May 30, 1942. On the same day, along with thirty other candidates, he was ordained to the priesthood by Archbishop Thomas J. Walsh at St. Patrick's Cathedral in Newark, New Jersey.

Thomas's mother and youngest brother, Steve, had long planned to attend the ceremony, while another brother, Ben, was ordered to report for final examinations at Belmont Abbey preparatory school near Charlotte, North Carolina. Ben's love for Thomas overcame the problem. Having arranged makeup exams, he hitchhiked up north with a classmate. After a day and a half on the road, the boys slept overnight at a Charlottesville, Virginia, gas station. They showed up quite disheveled the following evening at St. Michael's Monastery in Union City, New Jersey. The monks immediately telephoned Mrs. Berry at the Waldorf-Astoria

2.7 Thomas's ordination in 1942.
Courtesy of Ann Berry Somers for the Berry family

Hotel in New York and put Ben and his friend on a bus to Manhattan. The next day, bathed and refreshed, Ben arrived with his family in Newark at St. Patrick Cathedral to attend Thomas's ordination. Following the ceremony, he received his brother's blessing as a newly ordained priest. Soon afterwards, Thomas returned to Greensboro to say his first Solemn High Mass in his home parish of St. Benedict's Church. His family welcomed him home and celebrated his accomplishments of these fourteen years away. Then they sent him off to the next phase of his life.

THE SOUND OF WAR

Several weeks before Thomas's ordination, his mother received a special award in New York. Elizabeth "Bess" Vize Berry was designated "American Mother of the Year" by the American Mothers' Committee of the Golden Rule Foundation of New York.[28] Cited not only for successfully raising thirteen children and helping establish the Berry Coal Company, Bess was also praised for participation in community civic and social life. At the Waldorf-Astoria luncheon ceremony, Archbishop Francis Spellman awarded Bess Berry her gold medal.[29]

Since the country had entered World War II five months before, on December 7, 1941, Bess's acceptance speech expressed themes of patriotism and sacrifice. During the press conference afterward, she mentioned her other sons' service in the armed forces. Eldest son Jack was in the Naval Reserves; Francis, a fourth-year Georgetown medical student, would be commissioned in June 1942; Jim, a 1940 West Point graduate, served as a North Atlantic squadron commander flying in the offensive over Germany; and Joe was a third-year midshipman at Annapolis.[30] Bess was clearly proud of all her sons, as service for others is what she and her husband had raised them to do.

In the midst of wartime, all of Thomas's brothers distinguished themselves in their military service, as did Thomas in the Cold War period with NATO forces in West Germany. But Thomas's service was ultimately of a different sort. He was headed toward becoming a world historian, first by pursuing graduate studies and eventually by entering university teaching. He needed to immerse himself in history before his own vision for the Earth community could emerge. It was to be a long journey.

CHAPTER 3

Studying History and Living History

How to deal with the ambivalence of life without losing authenticity. This has been the overwhelming problem of my existence. How to respond to this situation without going into a negativism or an inner disintegrating experience, how not to lose the joy of life, how to appreciate the positive accomplishments of the period, how to benefit from the education presented by the society without being absorbed into its illusions; these were the questions from early childhood. I never doubted that there were answers, that they would be communicated somehow through the course of my life, provided I was willing to engage in the quest for understanding.

Thomas Berry, *Goldenrod: Reflections on the Twentieth Century*

GRADUATE STUDIES: GROUNDING IN WESTERN HISTORY AND PHILOSOPHY

Thomas had a keen desire to negotiate the ambivalence of life. To do this, he knew he had to pursue history—both teach it and study it. After his ordination in 1942, and in the midst of the Second World War, Thomas was assigned to teach history at Holy Cross Prep School in Dunkirk, New York. During this year of teaching, his provincial, Carroll Ring, recognized Thomas's broader intellectual potential and encouraged him to apply for graduate study in history at the Catholic University of America in Washington, D.C. He was sent to the university in the fall of 1943. Surrounding Catholic University were many houses of study that were usually owned by a particular religious order. The Passionists did not have such a house, as they were not a teaching order that required graduate studies. Consequently, Thomas initially lived in the dormitory, Caldwell Hall. However, he felt isolated there and soon moved to St. Gemma's, a Passionist residential house in Hyattsville, Maryland.

Thomas planned to study for a two-year master's degree, but he extended his studies until he had almost enough credits for a PhD. Permission was then granted for additional time to complete his doctorate, which he did in 1948. He focused on European cultural history with minors in philosophy and anthropology.[1]

A primary influence on Thomas's graduate education was his adviser and major professor, Friedrich Engel-Janosi, a congenial and cultured Austrian scholar of modern European diplomatic history. After fleeing Austria during World War II, he came to Catholic University in 1941, where he taught in the history department for seventeen years before returning to Vienna.[2] Without access to European archives during World War II, he had turned to historiography, immersing himself in the interpretation of history and the context within which it is written. Thomas later wrote:

> I had the good fortune to study under Professor Frederick Engel-Janosi whose special concern was the manner in which historians had written their account of the human process, the units of human communities they chose to study, their sense of historical periods, their selection of events to narrate, the significance given to these events and the manner in which these gave shape to the human world such as this now exists.[3]

Historiography thus became a major focus of Thomas's work, as he tried to interpret modernity and its challenges. Thus he took courses from Engel-Janosi on European history, philosophy, political theory, and literature.[4] It was Engel-Janosi who stimulated Thomas's interest in China, through his conviction that the future lay with Asia. He introduced Thomas to the thought of Giambattista Vico, which became the subject of his dissertation.

In addition, Thomas studied Indigenous peoples and religions with John Cooper, a past president of the American Anthropological Association. Cooper was an expert on Algonquin and Abenaki cultures of Labrador as well as the classification of South American Indigenous traditions. Cooper provided Thomas with an understanding of "cultural community" as a basic unit of research. He also fostered in Thomas a deep respect for the diversity of Indigenous lifeways. It was Cooper who introduced Thomas to the work of Pierre Teilhard de Chardin (1881–1955), who eventually became a major influence in his thinking.[5]

Cultural History

Thomas later reflected on his move into history: "The years that I spent in historical studies moved me out of the limitations that I had developed in my years of philosophical and theological studies, mostly in classical and medieval thought" (*Goldenrod*, 72). Thomas's graduate studies in history enabled him to enlarge his understanding of the development of cultural history. Under the influence of Columbia University professor Carlton J. H. Hayes (1882–1964), traditional political and military history was gradually being expanded to include cultural history. Thomas was influenced by Hayes's popular textbooks on European history as well as his studies of nationalism.[6] Hayes also encouraged academic departments to move beyond a focus on American history to include Europe. In this spirit, Thomas gravitated toward studies in European history.[7]

Thomas read the works of Christopher Dawson, the British cultural historian noted for his book, *The Making of Europe* (1932). In addition, Thomas absorbed the broad cultural perspectives of two prominent philosophers of world history: Arnold Toynbee (1889–1975) (*A Study of History*, 1961) and Eric Voegelin (1901–1985) (*Order and History*, 1956).[8] These thinkers provided inspiration for Thomas's eventual move toward what he described as the "study of human history and Earth history within the larger context of universe history."[9]

Thomas wrote about his time in graduate school: "During this period I was caught up in my studies with an intensity that would be difficult to describe. I was determined to acquire what knowledge I could in whatever discipline in order to deal with the human-Earth issue in some comprehensive manner" (*Goldenrod*, 90). To this end, after his coursework he wrote his first dissertation, "On the Interpretation of History in a World Religious Context," examining the philosophy of history in Hindu, Buddhist, and Confucian frameworks. He submitted this to his adviser, Engel-Janosi, in November 1947. Having heard nothing from his committee for many months, Thomas finally called Engel-Janosi in March 1948.

He learned that the dissertation had been turned down by his committee as too broad and abstract and as lacking adequate scholarly footnotes and quotations. To the end of his life, Thomas was convinced that his first dissertation was a more significant intellectual contribution to cultural history than the second one, which was hastily written. There was, however, no opportunity to debate the point. Thomas had been accepted for the Passionist mission in China and was scheduled to depart in July 1948.[10]

Several months earlier, in the spring of 1948, when Thomas had returned to teach at Holy Cross prep while finishing his thesis, he had written his provincial asking to serve in China. His motives included long-standing personal and academic interests in China and its history and culture. Moreover, he was keen to work overseas and was dissatisfied with postgraduate prospects. He found teaching history on the high school level tedious, and there was no opportunity within his order for college-level teaching. Lectures by returning China missionaries had whetted his interest in their surroundings and activities. He was eager to experience this for himself.

The Historical Theory of Giambattista Vico (1668–1744)

Thomas was now keen to complete his graduate work before being sent to China. For his second dissertation, he took a thirty-page paper he had written on Vico and divided it into three parts, with twenty-three chapters in total. He expanded the chapters and added Italian quotations, footnotes, and bibliography. To finish his research, he took the train from Buffalo, New York, near where he was teaching in Dunkirk, to the Library of Congress in Washington, D.C. The new dissertation, *The Historical Theory of Giambattista Vico*, was then submitted to Engel-Janosi. Fortunately, the graduate committee promptly accepted it with the proviso that he return to defend it, as was the university's custom.

Thomas writes of this philosopher of history, "Vico was a person who sought a universal range of understanding of the human process."[11] In his central work, *The New Science of the Nature of Nations*, Vico attempted to create a broad cultural history of humanity. He began this history from a Neo-Platonic perspective of universal form, viewing classical Mediterranean civilization as the archetype of all civilizations.[12] This perspective led him toward a theory of the eternal cycles of history in which he saw human culture progressing through three stages: the

Age of the Gods (theocratic); the Age of Heroes (aristocratic); and the Age of Men (democratic).[13] With each age, humans transformed their languages, governance structures, and all facets of life.

Vico agreed with Thomas Hobbes that early humans probably lived in a state of bestiality from which they gradually emerged into a stable society. Vico's sense of cycles led him to assert a "barbarism of reflection" in which this bestiality could recur, often because of the over-refinement of an age. Thus, Thomas found language to describe the darker side of human "progress," even as he recognized broader patterns of history. In these respects, Vico had a profound influence on Thomas's thinking as he sought to identify the contributions and limits of the modern period. In Vico he also found a life direction beyond these limitations:

> Of special relevance to my own orientation was the commitment of Vico to becoming a "homo universalis"—a person whose vision and concerns encompassed the universe. This included a universal historical vision as well as a vision that encompassed the planetary order and even the entire order of the cosmos. In this sense, Vico showed a concern that has been characteristic of indigenous peoples throughout the centuries, their concern for cosmology and their constant awareness that any consideration of the human must be within the larger functioning of the universe itself.
>
> (*Goldenrod*, 72)

This is what Thomas aimed to do with his study of history—first focus on human culture and world religions, then on Earth history, and finally on universe history. Vico's identification of the limits of Enlightenment rationalism was a bass note for Thomas's movement into cosmology:

> Vico established his critique of Francis Bacon and Descartes and Newton, substantially the same persons as William Blake identified in his critique of the enlightenment period. He could not be satisfied with a particular knowledge. In this sense, Vico showed a concern that has been characteristic of indigenous peoples throughout the centuries, their concern for cosmology and their constant awareness that any consideration of the human must be within the larger functioning of the universe itself.
>
> (*Goldenrod*, 72)

Vico created a broad context for Thomas's later study of Native Americans and their understanding of living within a universe.

Dissertation Defense

In early July, Thomas traveled to Washington, D.C., to defend his thesis. The defense fell on the morning of July 3, 1948, the same day he had to catch a train from New York to the west coast for his departure for China. Throughout this defense, Engel-Janosi guided the candidate and deflected troublesome questions, as he believed strongly in Thomas's potential for significant achievement in the future.[14] Thomas would not disappoint him.

After the defense, Thomas hurried to Union Station to catch a train to New York and then on to San Francisco. He made the train with only a few minutes to spare and treated himself to a scotch in the dining car to celebrate. However, in his haste, Thomas had left his dissertation in the taxi en route to the station. This was his only copy, as was common in the age before computers or Xerox machines. There was no time to try to track it down. Fortunately for him and his life work ahead, the massive document was eventually returned to a nearby monastery. He arranged to have a copy sent to his provincial for approval, as was customary, and then to his adviser at Catholic University for deposit in the library. With that done, Thomas was at last off to China.

JOURNEY TO CHINA

The Passionist Congregation had been in China for over twenty-five years providing education and poverty relief. In 1922, it established a mission in northwest Hunan Province, sending six priests to the city of Chenzhou. Other recruits followed, and with them came food, medical assistance, hospital care, and education. Their work was often hampered, not only by the rugged environment but also by famine and sickness, along with bandits and war. In 1929, three Passionist priests traveling on a steep mountain pass were killed by bandits. Nonetheless, during the Sino-Japanese War (1937–1945), despite grave risks for foreigners, 100,000 refugees received care from the Passionists.

The Nationalist Party (Kuomintang) of Chiang Kai-shek held power from 1928 on in the face of severe threats by warlords until they retreated to Taiwan in 1949. First, Chiang's Nationalist Revolutionary army managed to unify much of China in the Northern Expedition, which culminated in 1928. However, this tenuous victory took place largely in the Yangtze River valley area of the north. Then, they fought the Japanese from 1937 until the Japanese defeat in 1945. Finally, they were embroiled in a bloody civil war across China with Mao Zedong's Red Army from 1945 until Mao's victory in 1949. After Mao's takeover of Peking, foreigners faced even greater dangers of house arrest, imprisonment, or expulsion.

In March 1948, amidst the upheavals of civil war, Thomas received his appointment to serve in China. He joined a group of seven other priests, designated as the Fifteenth Passionist China Mission Band.[15] Their departure ceremony was

3.1 Thomas and the Fifteenth Passionist China Mission Band at St. Michael's Monastery in Union City, New Jersey, in 1948, before departure for China.
Photo courtesy of the Passionist Historical Archives

held in Boston at the Cathedral of the Holy Cross on June 30, 1948, with Archbishop Richard Cushing presiding. Ten days later the priests gathered on the dock in San Francisco to embark on the SS *General Gordon*, a converted troop ship from the war. It was a momentous departure, as they didn't know when they would return to the United States or see family and friends again.

It was on that boat that Thomas's life journey was significantly changed. Standing on the deck as the ship pulled out of the San Francisco dock, Thomas noticed a young man waving farewell to his wife on the shore. This was Wm. Theodore (Ted) de Bary, a Columbia University professor who was the first Fulbright scholar to China from the United States. They struck up a conversation, and Thomas writes of the meeting: "Almost immediately we could appreciate each other and the work that we were involved in" (*Goldenrod*, 99). Ted de Bary was impressed with Thomas's seriousness of purpose in traveling to China, especially to study Chinese language and culture. The two men's common interest in Asian religion and philosophy ripened into a lifelong friendship, enhanced by input from Ted's wife, the gifted Fanny de Bary. Thomas reflected later: "This meeting was one of the most significant events in my life, for it was through this association with Professor de Bary that I was eventually able to establish some presence

3.2 Ted and Fanny de Bary in 1942.
Courtesy of Paul de Bary for the de Bary family

in the world of Asian thought traditions" (*Goldenrod*, 99). They would come to share an enduring appreciation of China, especially of Confucianism.

Thomas and Ted de Bary had many hours to talk, as journey by ship was slow. It took three weeks to reach China, with stops in Honolulu, Guam, and the Philippines. In Manila, Thomas was able to visit his sister, Ann (who had taken the religious name Sr. Zoe Marie), who was a Maryknoll nun teaching high school biology. This reunion was especially joyful, as both had entered religious life, uncertain of when they would ever be able to see family members again. From Manila, the boat sailed to Hong Kong. Thomas was struck by the lively business dimensions of the city as well as its international orientation.

Ted de Bary took him to meet with some of the Confucian professors at New Asia University in Hong Kong, which was founded by scholars who were fleeing the mainland because of the civil war. It was these refugee scholars in Hong Kong, along with those in Taiwan, who kept the Confucian tradition alive while it was neglected and persecuted for decades under Mao. That evening, among throngs of onlookers, Ted and Thomas went to see a flower that blooms only one evening a year. They took it to be an auspicious omen. In Shanghai, they visited the Jesuit center at Zikawei, where a large library held records of the Jesuit presence in China over the centuries. Thomas noted: "The city was filled with wandering children begging for rice with a small tin can and a makeshift handle. Many of them were evidently seven or eight years old" (*Goldenrod*, 90).

Thomas's first impressions of Peking were of a city teeming with refugees fleeing the troops clashing in the civil war. One day while traveling through the city, Thomas and Ted de Bary saw refugees from Mongolia huddled together in the drizzling rain in the plaza in front of the French Gothic cathedral. Poverty, destitution, and inadequate housing were widespread in this city of some 2 million people. Chinese paper money was almost worthless because of runaway inflation. When walking through the streets, Thomas would be surrounded by Chinese children, to whom he gave small ribbons he had brought as gifts. With the coming of cold weather in October, Thomas noticed mothers and children sunning themselves in front of their homes for warmth, even while yellow silt blowing out of the north irritated their eyes and penetrated their hair and clothing.

Thomas and Ted managed to get up to the Great Wall at the Nankou Pass, where the railway went through the wall and then north to Manchuria and Harbin. "Some fifteen feet high, the wall was not imposing from its height and yet it was an awesome structure as it wound over the hills. It was a structure that in its full length had been constructed over centuries of time" (*Goldenrod*, 101).

In Peking, surrounded by war and poverty, Thomas settled into language and culture studies at the Franciscan school. There was excellent instruction in the Chinese language by native teachers, but Thomas managed to complete only twenty lessons over three months before evacuation from Peking became advisable. That urgency also prevented Thomas from accepting an invitation to teach at Fu Jen Catholic University. The Communists were moving toward the city and the Nationalist (Kuomintang) troops were retreating. Thomas and his fellow language students had been led to believe that Chiang Kai-shek would prevail through the abilities of Fu Zuoyi, the general of the Northern Nationalist army.

However, as Mao's forces advanced, Peking could no longer be defended. In November 1948, Thomas had to be evacuated. At the same time Ted was evacuated to Nanjing. Thomas caught one of the last flights out of Peking on a *Flying Tiger* cargo plane bound for Shanghai. He spent several weeks there, as the boat that was to bring him back to the States was delayed by storms at sea. He walked the

3.3 Thomas on the Great Wall in 1948.
Courtesy of Ann Berry Somers for the Berry family

streets and observed the hundreds of refugee children living and sleeping in the streets, victims of the civil war. He wrote of two of them:

> This evening a very little girl, not more than 7 years old, sold me a bouquet of faded flowers she had picked from someone's garden in the vicinity—the last flowers of the season, I guess. I gave her a Chinese dollar and she seemed quite happy, though indeed it will barely suffice for her next bowl of rice. Another child came along a little later of the same age walking in the dark and in the rain. She was gathering leaves and little sticks to dry out and use for fuel when the cold weather sets in during the coming weeks. I gave her a Chinese dollar also. As soon as she saw it she dropped the little broom

3.4 Beijing, December 1948: A bewildered old man searches for his son as the new recruits called up by the fast-weakening Kuomintang government march off to defeat.
Henri Cartier-Bresson/Magnum Photos

and basket both, she was so surprised and delighted to have what I gave her. Many of the children will never ask for anything—some even refuse to take anything that is offered them. They prefer to gather the scraps of paper and then sell their basket at the end of the day for the few cents that will enable them to survive.[16]

Finally, in early December, Thomas secured passage on an army transport ship, *Republic*, bound for the American west coast. The boat landed first in Yokohama, and he took the train up to Tokyo. There he witnessed the results of firebombing during the Pacific war, something he would never forget. After a stopover at the Jesuit house at Sophia University in Tokyo, he set sail across the Pacific. He would later correspond with some of these Jesuits who were studying Asian religions. He arrived in Seattle in January 1949 and visited friends in Walla Walla, in Washington State. There he caught a train east to New York, returning finally to the Passionist monastery in Jamaica, in Queens. One of his first visits was to Fanny de Bary to give her news of Ted, as she was patiently awaiting his return from China.

From his experience of Chinese culture and people, Thomas developed an admiration for the endurance, competence, and survival skills of the Chinese under dire circumstances. He was even more keenly drawn to study Chinese culture, history, and language and had ambitious dreams of founding a university and creating a press in China. He shared these ideas in letters with the Passionist missionary Ronald Beaton, who gently discouraged Thomas. He observed that both ideas were unrealistic—founding a university because of the cost involved and establishing a press because of poverty, lack of education, and illiteracy. Rather, Beaton advised: "Write your essays Tom, as you have been considering. You must find an outlet for what you have garnered through blood and tears."[17]

Hoping to go back to Asia, Thomas requested reassignment to China as soon as possible.[18] The provincial recommended that Thomas be encouraged to work with the Miao, a minority group in the south. However, with the victory of Mao's army and the establishment of the People's Republic of China on October 1, 1949, that became impossible. Most foreigners were forced to leave or face imprisonment. Thomas would never return to China, but his life was profoundly changed.

The Ascendency of Maoism

Thomas's view of Mao's rise to power at that time was in line with official American anti-Communist policy, which had little grasp of China's internal political struggles or the corruption of the Nationalist Party of Chiang Kai-shek. As his knowledge of Chinese history, politics, and culture broadened, Thomas would in time adopt a more sophisticated understanding of the causes of the Maoist revolution in light of modern Chinese history. The extent of the imperialist exploitation of the Chinese by Westerners and then by the Japanese was something few Americans had appreciated. As Thomas studied more, he even came to admire some of Mao's goals regarding access to education and health care, as well as equality for women. Indeed, in 1974 he wrote an essay titled "Mao's 'Long March,'" extolling the heroic and mythic push to consolidate the Red Army that took place in difficult terrain in western China from October 1934 to October 1935.[19] However, Thomas also critiqued Mao's autocratic rule once in power. He was exploring the ambiguities in Mao's ideas and actions.

Thomas realized that Mao had created a distinctive style of revolutionary leadership. Mao's new transforming socialist myth guided the Chinese Revolution like a great rising tide. He believed the traditional Chinese feudal order, including Confucianism, had to be destroyed for a new socialist society to be born. He promoted a peasant-based revolution that he felt would result in greater equity, inclusion, and prosperity. This revolutionary ideology became especially clear in 1958 during the Great Leap Forward, with its radical egalitarian ideals. Mao and his followers felt that a truly communist world was beginning to emerge. Even after the Great Leap Forward failed massively and caused widespread famines, Mao launched the Great Proletariat Cultural Revolution in 1966. In this upheaval, the undisciplined forces of youth were set loose to destroy the so-called feudal past, including schools, libraries, and books, as well as religious and cultural traditions. Intellectuals, in particular, were beaten, imprisoned, or sent to the countryside.

Thomas lamented the human cost of the Cultural Revolution. He wondered whether "the controlled transformation of consciousness under the dictatorship of the proletariat is not washing out of the minds of the people much of the noblest part of their heritage along with much that can be considered the dark side of that heritage."[20] Indeed, the traditions of Confucianism, Daoism, and Buddhism were intensely critiqued and intentionally destroyed. Thomas feared the consequences of this destruction and the forced cultural isolation of the Chinese people under Mao. Once again, he was pondering the ambivalence embedded in such historical change as Mao's promise of liberation and progress came at great cost to the Chinese people and their traditions

Western Pragmatism and Democracy with John Dewey

Years later Thomas reflected on why the Chinese embraced Maoist thought over Western democratic principles. He examined the ideas of the philosopher John Dewey (1859–1952) and the influence of his two years of teaching in China from 1919 to 1921.[21] At age sixty Dewey, a professor at Columbia University, became the first foreigner invited to lecture at Chinese universities. Thomas was keen to explore why Dewey's pragmatic thought, especially his promotion of science, democracy, and education, initially had a wide appeal but failed to take hold in China. The failure occurred even though many influential Chinese intellectuals were enamored of Dewey. This was the case with Hu Shih (1891–1962), who studied with Dewey at Columbia and had invited him to come to lecture. Dewey also influenced numerous students during his time in China. In Thomas's view, the greatest impact of Dewey in China was in the area of education.[22] Schools, Dewey noted, were an important instrument of social change and progress.[23] Dewey's notion of "education for living" was a welcome direction for Chinese intellectuals, as it encouraged not just learning but also participation in society.

Because of the large number of Chinese students educated in America after the Boxer Rebellion in 1900, Dewey hoped for the growth of democratic ideals in China. That system, he initially believed, would grow at the grassroots level, a hope dashed in 1921 with the founding of the Chinese Communist Party.[24] Moreover, the nationalist Kuomintang became increasingly authoritarian, and parliamentary democracy never took hold. Both Chinese liberals and communists were anti-Confucian in their thought, while the Kuomintang held to a conservative and outdated form of Confucianism.

The shift away from Confucian ideals, as Thomas noted, was deepened during the May Fourth Movement in 1919, just as Dewey was arriving in China. This rebellion, led by students at Peking University, was in response to the 1919 Treaty of Versailles concluding World War I. In particular, the widespread protest was sparked by a feeling of betrayal regarding the unilateral transfer of the German concessions on the Shandong peninsula to the Japanese. This affront to national sovereignty, and the weak response of the Chinese government, infuriated the younger generation. The students were disillusioned with the Western powers' claims to follow democratic principles.

Among the changes that resulted from the May Fourth Movement was the growth of the "new cultural revolution," where the spoken language became the new written language replacing classical Chinese. Lu Xun (1881–1936), for example, wrote short stories in vernacular Chinese denigrating traditional Confucianism.[25] Adherence to Confucian ideals declined as student rebellion stirred. Chinese intellectuals such as Hu Shih turned away from Confucianism toward Western science and democracy. Such Western modernism sought to replace Confucianism with a new set of civic virtues.[26] While some Chinese initially embraced Western ideas of materialism and secularism, they rejected Western Christian spirituality because of the link between Christian missionary efforts and Western colonialism. The Western legacy was eventually seen as compromised. Thus, following the 1917 Russian Revolution, another revolutionary model arose with Marxist lectures in Peking.[27]

Thomas felt that Chinese intellectuals were attracted to Marxism because it provided motivation that pragmatism or democracy lacked. Communism promised to remake China's ancient civilization and promote a desired renewal. This ideology exploited contradictions in Western liberalism relating to colonialism and its oppression of peoples in the developing world. Chinese students felt betrayed by the Western powers in the Treaty of Versailles and observed that the United States did not join the League of Nations. Western liberalism with its self-serving, nationalist commitments thus did not make much headway among the Chinese. In the final analysis, Thomas contended that the Communist conquest of China was more ideological than military.[28] Thomas was again exploring the ambiguities of ideas and movements. In his judgment, Western liberalism was ineffectual in China because it was not able to articulate a convincing political position that was grounded in the ancient agricultural and cosmological traditions of Chinese culture.[29]

In Thomas's view, there were two other major causes of the failure of Western liberalism: the split between the Nationalists and the Communists during the early years of the new Chinese Republic, after 1928; and the 1937 Japanese invasion during the crucial years when the Republic was still trying to establish its authority. The Republic was weak, and warlords seized much of the country. The disorder in China that Dewey foresaw eventually led either to Japanese military control or to Communist takeover. Mao's victory in 1949 resulted in the proclamation of the People's Republic of China (PRC) and the triumph of communism in its Maoist form.

Back in the United States, in the 1950s the debate raged over the "loss of China" to Mao. The debate was fueled by the ongoing anti-Communist sentiment of the Cold War period and was accompanied by the rise of McCarthyism. In Congress, Senator Joseph McCarthy railed against Communist sympathizers he claimed had infiltrated government, academia, and Hollywood. This was a context for Thomas's next assignment, with the U.S. Army in West Germany. But it would take Thomas several years to reach Europe.

ARMY CHAPLAINCY IN EUROPE

On Thomas's return from China, his superiors reassigned him to teach history, once again at Holy Cross Prep in Dunkirk, New York. He taught there for the next two years, though he was restless and dissatisfied. His superiors were unhappy with his performance as well. Unconventional in his methods, he felt excessively restricted by official course syllabi and often launched into elaborate digressions about other books he was reading at the time. From notes taken during Thomas's classes, a former student recalls learning about Augustine, Dante, Vico, Darwin, Spengler, Toynbee, and Voegelin. With no set text, Thomas welcomed questions from students who were eager to glean something from his broad learning. In a European history course, for example, he contrasted Augustine's *City of God* with Marx's *Communist Manifesto*. Another student remembers Thomas talking to his class about the history of music and how the rhythms and melodies of music reflected the spirit of the times. He discussed, for example, music in the West—from baroque, to romantic, to Viennese waltzes, to jazz and other contemporary music.

While some students enjoyed these digressions, others felt his wide-ranging intellectual style was too challenging. Moreover, some faculty found Thomas's inability to stick to a syllabus difficult to accept. Considered something of a radical and a renegade, he nevertheless managed to instill in many of his students a love of learning. For example, his essay exams always posed questions requiring substantive critical thinking and input from the student, not simply a regurgitation of facts—an approach that was rather revolutionary for its time.

Dissatisfied with classroom teaching in Dunkirk and yearning to return to Asia, in February 1951 Thomas applied for permission to volunteer for the army as a military chaplain. This was during the Korean War, and he was hoping to be sent to Japan or Korea. Instead, he was unexpectedly assigned to West Germany. Ted de Bary tried to discourage him from going and urged him to continue his studies of Asian traditions.[30] However, Thomas didn't have much choice once the army sent him to Chaplain School at Fort Slocum in New Rochelle, New York, and then to Camp Atterbury in Indiana. He began preparations for his new assignment, which would bring him face to face with the challenges of Europe recovering from a devastating war. On July 17, he was appointed to Officers Reserve Corp and made a first lieutenant.

In November 1951, Thomas's battalion was shipped overseas to Europe for stationing in Ellwangen, which was to the east of Baden-Wittemburg in the Jagst river valley. There, during the Cold War years, among approximately 400,000 American and NATO troops, the presence of the enormous Soviet Army garrisoned in East Germany was palpable. In that tense setting, within a divided Germany, Thomas spent the next three years as an army chaplain.

Multiple roles were involved in his work as chaplain and pastoral guide to troops, their American families, and local German villagers. Thomas was deeply involved in parish life, from organizing a choir for Christmas Mass, to preparing people for baptism and marriage, to putting together a church bulletin. Each year, as the National Guard men in his unit were rotated back to the States, Thomas had to work with a new group. The stream of paperwork, the constant mobility of field training, and the lack of regular contact with his men rendered his work ever more challenging. Reliable scheduling of religious services was often impossible, as, for example, field maneuvers were often held during Holy Week.

In 1953, Thomas's duties as chaplain to his battalion were expanded to include the nearby village of Crailsheim. This was a doubling of his responsibilities and left him severely overextended. In spite of the many demands on him, Thomas reached out to both army and civilian populations and, judging from correspondence in later years, made lasting friendships among many German families and American troops. His duties, however, could be physically taxing, as he was often out in the field for maneuvers with his men and living in tents. This way of life gave him little time for reflection or reading.

In a 1952 letter to Ted and Fanny de Bary, Thomas lamented how much he missed his studies. Moreover, he found field duty to be a spiritual desert, a situation he compared with Dante's extended and torturous exile. "Here without my books, without time, without people to talk with, without inner inspiration—almost without any true life of the mind, I drift along in the stream of noise and curses." He confides to the de Barys that "the central attraction toward the life of the scholar remains so strong."[31] With this longing he wrote his parents, begging them to send books.

Nonetheless, he was broadening his horizons in these demanding circumstances. For example, his exposure to the European liturgical movement was valuable in that it convinced him of the need to have Mass in the vernacular language of the country so that people would not be put off by Latin and could follow the liturgy more attentively.[32] This conviction anticipated one of the major changes of Vatican II a decade later that encouraged Mass in the local language rather than in Latin. Moreover, Thomas's German was good, and he appreciated the high quality of local German choirs and musical events. He found delight in their communal celebrations and festivals. He wrote to his sister Ann:

> I am much struck with the European peasant life. Such a life is much the same the world over, but here in Europe it has attained a special richness of cultural development that is remarkably coordinated with the labor of the land. . . . Here too the handicrafts continue to flourish. . . . The religion of the people survives in all its elemental glory and in its public grandeur with processions that are always on the public streets and participated in by the whole community. . . . Their celebrations, too, are more communal, more genuine, more joyful, more spontaneous than ours.[33]

Thomas consistently used what little free time he had to build upon his graduate studies in history and ground himself ever more deeply in classical and contemporary European thought. He traveled widely in Germany, visiting the Passionist monasteries in Pasing and Schwartzenfeld and the noted Benedictine monastery of Beuron. He went to Ulm, where Einstein was born, to observe the rebuilding that was taking place after the destruction of the city in the war.

During these challenging years, Thomas's interest in Dante remained a touchstone for his intellectual and moral imagination. He writes that Dante provided "something to keep a little flame of hope alive, even in this desolate place where all things spiritual wither in [a] world of metal and machines, where everything human is crushed under rolling wheels and marching feet."[34] For Thomas, Dante served as an ideal of the scholar, visionary, and mystic articulating a comprehensive vision of his age. Of the poet's influence he later wrote:

> Perhaps Dante can be considered the most learned person in the course of western civilization in his knowledge of persons and historical events, of mythological characters, of Biblical personalities, of the entire course of political, religious, and cultural history of Rome and the centuries leading up to the thirteenth century. That he could tell the human story and provide moral evaluation of persons and actions throughout the course of human history as was known at the time; that he could tell this in poetic expression with superb skill, all of this is a treasure of culture, of learning, of religious faith that is overwhelming.[35]

Throughout his life, wherever he found himself, Thomas sought to organize an adult study group on Dante's *Divine Comedy*, and so he did with his battalion.[36]

He also followed Dante's life in his travels. To this end, he went twice to Italy, in spring 1952 and fall 1953. He was particularly drawn to Florence, where Dante had lived, and where the Tuscan vernacular language influenced the emergence of modern Italian. In a letter to the de Barys, he describes a few days he spent there, staying in a room by the Arno River, visiting the Italian Dante Society, enjoying the art of Michelangelo, Giotto, and Cimabue, and offering Mass under a Crucifixion scene by Giotto.[37] In fall 1953, during a twelve-day trip to Italy, he visited Dante's tomb in Ravenna,[38] attended a papal audience at Castel Gondolfo outside of Rome, and visited the museums and churches of Florence, Venice, Padua, and Verona.[39] That same year he visited Belgium and Holland.

3.5 Statue of Dante Alighieri by Enrico Pazzi. Located next to the Basilica of Santa Croce in Florence, Italy.
iStock by Getty Images

Thomas sought contact with living scholars as well. While on leave from his chaplaincy and traveling to Zurich for an international affairs conference, he met the noted Catholic philosopher and existentialist Gabriel Marcel (1889–1973). Thomas was especially interested in his book *Creative Fidelity*, in which he focused on "communion," or communication among others across the solitary subjectivity of existentialism.

In February 1954, Thomas visited the British cultural historian Christopher Dawson at his home in Devon in southwest England. In his books, *The Age of the Gods* (1928), *The Making of Europe* (1932), *Religion and Culture* (1948), and *Religion and the Rise of Western Culture* (1950), Dawson emphasizes the importance of Christianity in the formation of European culture. Thomas responded positively to his argument that the foundation of every culture was shaped by religion. During Thomas's visit, the two discussed the consequences of World War II, the Korean War, and the postwar period.[40] Thomas was optimistic that Germany was in a new era of cooperation and that European unity was more possible. He reflected:

> The troubles of attaining a true unity of Europe are almost too much for com-
> prehension. Yet that is the first and most important work of all. I think that

is progressing in a "satisfactory" manner. Still the hardest difficulties remain unsolved. Concerning Germany's position as a source of danger for Europe I am more optimistic than most others. I think myself that the country is too broken and too deeply wounded in every way for Germany to become any real threat in the next few generations. It is a turning point in modern history in that sense.[41]

In 1954, Thomas also visited Cairo and Jerusalem, the latter still under Jordanian control. The trip to the Holy Land both deepened his classical and biblical perspectives and reminded him of how much he yearned to return to his academic studies and pursue his interest in Asian religious traditions. Corresponding regularly with his provincial during the European years, Thomas continued to lobby for an assignment in Asia, now having Japan in mind. In April 1954, when his unit was transferred to Nuremberg, he suddenly found himself superfluous, as two Catholic chaplains were already serving there. Having earlier decided not to reenlist in the army, he was sent back to the States in late June and honorably discharged as first lieutenant on July 16, exactly three years after he entered. He sought to move forward in his life path, but it was not to be without significant struggle.

CHAPTER 4

The Struggle to Teach

For the first time we are bringing the world spiritual traditions into a common human heritage. This is not only a study; it is a creative spiritual process. Those studying the world religions are themselves creating this common spiritual heritage. One of the great tasks to which our age is called is that of giving spiritual shape and substance to the world society now in the process of formation. This new vision of the past is a creation of the present with infinite consequences for the future.

Thomas Berry, *Religions of India: Hinduism, Yoga, Buddhism*

"THE BEST EDUCATED DOORMAN IN JAMAICA"

On returning from Germany in the summer of 1954, Thomas aspired to bring his studies and overseas experiences into fuller expression through teaching and writing. He had seen something of the world during his time in China and Germany and now wished to integrate those experiences with his studies of history, culture, and religion. But after three years as an army chaplain with the NATO forces in Europe, he found himself in something of a quandary. Forty years old and eager to serve in Asia or teach at a university, Thomas was denied both opportunities. Instead, he was sent to Immaculate Conception Monastery in Jamaica, Queens, in New York City. Thomas was considered too freethinking to return to seminary education, which was dominated by orthodox ideas. Moreover, few overseas appointments were available, and when one was offered,

4.1 The church at Immaculate Conception Monastery, Jamaica, New York.

Photo courtesy of the Passionist Historical Archives

he was denied permission to accept. His religious superior, Father Ernest Welch, stood in his way of both teaching and overseas work.

Thomas's family was sympathetic to his plight.[1] A letter to his sister Ann reports that Thomas's superior denied him permission to work and study in Japan. He had been invited there by Fr. Joseph Spae, a longtime Belgian missionary in Japan who was a noted Asian scholar and the director of the Oriens Institute for Religious Research in Tokyo. Thomas describes the situation: "My hopes of further mission work in Japan have again been disappointed. I had been invited by Father Spae, who is in charge of the entire mission program under the hierarchy; but superiors here did not permit me to go. Thus I remain praying and preaching, studying and writing; in truth accomplishing little."[2] In another letter to Ann, Thomas expresses frustration with the lack of direction in his studies: "I keep scribbling now and again. Too bad I am involved in such vast areas of study. 'Twere simpler to be a specialist in some little area of study— or to be a poet. The worse curse of all is to [be] a historian interested in the whole world of nations from creation till today."[3]

Because of his broad interests and independent thinking, Thomas was considered unsuited for conventional parish work or preaching. Yet the order had to find a place for him. The Passionists were not historically a teaching order and had no schools or universities as did other orders, such as the Jesuits. Moreover, they were unwilling to allow Thomas to teach at an institution outside the Passionist seminaries. Instead, at the monastery in Jamaica, Thomas served as confessor and spiritual director to other monks. At the same time, he was assigned the "Front Door and Parlor Apostolate." Commonly referred to as "doorman," the monk in this position was available to meet in the monastery parlor with those seeking counseling or confession. Among those Thomas assisted was a homeless woman with a brain tumor who stayed at the Salvation Army and wrote moving poetry about her suffering. Through letters to her doctor and social service agencies, Thomas helped her obtain needed hospitalization and brain surgery. In short, Thomas responded to the needs of visitors who came to the door, heard confessions, and filled out requests for Mass cards. Years later, he would reflect on how much he learned about people during this period. Yet, while Thomas obligingly assisted those who sought him out, he was longing for more intellectually stimulating work.

On a visit to Ted and Fanny de Bary's home in Tappan, New York, Thomas was discussing his situation one evening over dinner. Ted observed that Confucius also became a gatekeeper because he couldn't obtain a position as a teacher or adviser to a state. Thomas was consoled by this notion and would humorously call himself "the best educated doorman in Jamaica."

While Thomas was living in Jamaica, seminary students were warned to stay away from him because he was too progressive in his thinking. However, some students, such as Steve Dunn, would go to his room for confession and then have the benefit of extended conversations with him. Steve was profoundly moved by those encounters. Indeed, he later became a major supporter of Thomas's work in Canada while Steve taught at the University of Toronto and organized conferences in Port Burwell on Lake Erie.

A VOCATIONAL CRISIS

Thomas became increasingly frustrated with his situation, and by 1957 he considered leaving the Passionist order and becoming a diocesan priest in North

Carolina. The issue came to a head when his superior, Father Welch, refused permission for Thomas to accept an invitation to teach at Seton Hall University during the 1957–1958 academic year, saying that such teaching was considered outside the scope of the order's rule.[4] In late May, Thomas appealed to Father Malcolm Lavelle, the superior general of the Passionist Congregation in Rome, for a reversal of this decision.[5] He also wrote Father Welch announcing his desire, in the event of continued opposition to the Seton Hall appointment, to leave the order.[6] At one point, he was so frustrated that he said to Welch, "You can do what you want, but I'm going to teach." Seeking a benevolent patron, he even contacted Bishop Vincent Waters of the Diocese of Raleigh, North Carolina, requesting his support to serve as a diocesan university chaplain. There were not many such positions available, and while Waters was sympathetic, he also indicated, "You will do as you are told if you come to this diocese."

By July, however, Thomas received some good news from Rome. The superior general in Rome authorized an exception, allowing Thomas to teach.[7] Thomas thus was able to accept an adjunct appointment in Seton Hall University's new Institute of Far Eastern Studies on the campus in South Orange, New Jersey. He was determined to set this difficult period behind him and move into university teaching. Thomas was the first member of the Passionist order to teach at an institution other than its own monasteries. However, he was urged to "walk warily" by a fellow Passionist and friend, Father Robert Wilken, who wrote: "If this experiment doesn't work out well . . . the failure will be cited for years. . . . So for all sorts of reasons I sincerely hope that your work at the school will be so obviously satisfactory in every way that the critics will be left speechless and, in fact, a trend might be inaugurated."[8]

Thomas benefited at this time from the American Catholic Church's gradual relaxation of its strictures, thanks to the writings of the Jesuit John Courtney Murray and the Catholic University historian John Tracy Ellis. Over the next several decades, Thomas would continue to face conservative opposition or lack of understanding. American Catholic provincialism and anti-intellectualism prevailed in many quarters, including his own order. Nonetheless, he persisted in his teaching, shrugging off obstacles. In doing so, he opened up a path for some in his order to teach. Most importantly, he helped to pave the way for others outside his order to study Asian religious traditions and history before this area of study had become more widespread.

SETON HALL UNIVERSITY: INSTITUTE
OF FAR EASTERN STUDIES

In the postwar period, the need for a better understanding of Asia and other parts of the non-Western world was becoming more widely recognized in the United States. To improve foreign policy decisions, international studies programs were being established in the 1950s at American colleges and universities. During this period, the teaching of Asian cultures, religions, history, and languages was encouraged. Indeed, one of the more positive outcomes of World War II was that a whole new area of Asian studies arose in higher education that had been virtually absent before the war. As Thomas observed:

> The study of so-called "non-western religions" was still relatively new in colleges and universities in North America, except at some of the Ivy League universities. The effort to study language and texts of the Asian traditions was largely a function of the post World War II era when scholars who were trained in the Army and Navy language schools set up departments of Asian studies. In this way, the Asian religions began to be taught in such departments as well as in religious studies departments. These were distinct from theology departments or seminaries that focused primarily on Christianity.[9]

Thus, Seton Hall's pioneering program in Asian studies was established in response to the Pacific War and in the context of the Cold War. In 1952, in the midst of the Korean War, the university created an Institute of Far Eastern Studies with a distinguished advisory board of Asian leaders.[10] Thomas's teaching was part of this larger academic trend toward understanding Asia.

Focused on China, the Seton Hall program required three areas of study: cultural history, spoken and written language, and thought and interpretation. During his years at Seton Hall, from 1957 to 1961, Thomas taught two courses a semester as well as summer school. In the first semester, his classes on Asian religious traditions and the history and culture of Japan drew only one or two students, but in time he attracted large enrollments.

Still living at the monastery on Long Island, Thomas made the two-hour commute by bus and train to the Seton Hall campus. That travel time was

Institute of

Far Eastern Studies

Seton Hall University
Newark, New Jersey

4.2 Seton Hall, Institute of Far Eastern Studies brochure.
Courtesy of Archives & Special Collections Center, Seton Hall University

augmented in 1959 when he began studying Sanskrit at Columbia University. He also continued his Chinese language studies with a tutor. While Thomas's knowledge of Chinese was not sufficient for exclusive concentration on original texts, he worked ably with translations:

> I was never entirely proficient in the Chinese language, since I had begun my studies of the language too late in life and at a time when I was involved in other studies. Thus, it was my appreciation of the thought tradition itself that enabled me with a minimum of Chinese textual knowledge to provide some appreciation of the meaning of the tradition. If I was deficient in the language, those proficient in the language were frequently deficient in their capacity for intellectual insight into just what the texts were saying. I was able to make the scholarship of others more effective by my capacity for interpretation within the thought and spiritual traditions of the west.

(*Goldenrod,* 89–90)

At Seton Hall Thomas came to know a number of leading Asian scholars, including John C. H. Wu, a distinguished international lawyer and the author of the first draft of the 1933 Chinese Constitution. Wu also served on the Permanent Court of Arbitration in the Hague. In addition, he wrote a book titled *Beyond East and West* (1951) and published an English translation of Lao Tzu's *Tao Te Ching* (1961). As an Asian scholar, he inspired many American Catholic thinkers, among them Thomas Merton (1915-1968), whose translation of the writings of the Taoist Chuang Tzu is dedicated to Wu. Overall, Thomas's growing competence in Asian traditions and languages, his acquaintance with Asian scholars, and his marked classroom success strengthened his sense of direction and purpose during these years. The Seton Hall experience thus provided a major step forward in his intellectual path.

"OUR NEED OF ORIENTALISTS"

In 1958 Thomas announced his intention to work on a book to be entitled *The Orient: The Need for Catholic Understanding*.[11] It was, however, during this time that his sister Zoë Marie, a Maryknoll nun, was being treated for breast cancer. He made many visits to see her in Maryknoll, New York, before she passed away that same year at the tender age of thirty-five. Years later, the other nuns would comment on how touching was his devotion to his sister.

Thomas had many other obligations in his teaching as well, and thus the book on the "Orient" was never written. However, he had already published several articles on this topic. One of the first was his piece "Our Need of Orientalists," published in *World Mission* in 1956. The term *Orientalists* was part of the accepted academic terminology of the day; it was eventually changed to *Asian scholars*.[12] At this time Thomas was trying to rethink the role of missionaries in understanding and respecting other cultures.

While lamenting the modest state of Chinese studies in the United States and the comparative lack of Catholic Orientalists, in this article Thomas pointed out differences between missionaries, missiologists, and Orientalists. The first, he notes, are workers on the ground, the second are theologians framing the purpose of Christian missions, and the third are scholars of the cultural context of missionary activity. He concluded that the work of all three is needed.

Reflecting on his China experience, Thomas called for the establishment of a well-educated group of American Catholic Asian scholars who could conduct missionary work from an informed perspective. He envisioned a thorough study of Chinese culture, language, religious traditions, history, and social structures as foundational for such missionary work. Such a background, he believed, would enable missionaries to reach Chinese people through their own culture and to integrate Catholicism with their native traditions. This is what the Jesuit Matteo Ricci did in Ming China from 1583 to 1610 when he studied Chinese and learned to read the classical texts of Confucianism. In more recent times this has been called "inculturation," something Thomas recognized sixty years ago as crucial in cross-cultural religious exchanges. In this regard, he agreed with those missionaries who also realized that transmitting Christianity into non-Western cultures required study and empathy, not simply a strident imposition of doctrines, rules, and rituals.

Noting the failure of Western Christianity to make significant inroads in China, Thomas raised the question of why communism succeeded where Christianity faltered. He compared Ricci's labors in China, including contact with the imperial court, with the efforts of Vladimir Lenin (1870–1924), whose writings on behalf of communism inspired Mao Zedong. Part of the answer, in Thomas's view, was that Ricci's innovative work in cultural relations was discontinued because of conflicts with Rome, especially because of the "rites controversy," in which the Vatican disagreed with Ricci and other Jesuits who argued that the long-term Chinese practice of veneration of the ancestors should be permitted, not discouraged.[13] In forbidding such veneration of ancestors, Catholicism lost adherents in China, as this practice was deeply embedded in Confucian culture.

Another early essay expressing Thomas's interest in Asian scholarship, "Oriental Scholarship: A Challenge to Catholic Scholars," appeared in *World Mission* in 1957. In it Thomas surveyed the status of Asian studies at leading American universities and pointed to corresponding deficiencies at Catholic universities:

In our Catholic Universities in America, we had no tradition of any professional level of scholarship in any field of Asian Studies. We had for years been in China, certainly since the early 1920s but this had led to no interest in the field of Catholic thinking. Meanwhile, the entire intellectual life of the country was being affected by the incoming presence of Asian thought and Asian Spirituality. Persons such as Vivekananda had been an influence in America since his speech given at the World Parliament of Religions in Chicago in 1893. So, too, Daisetz Suzuki had been a teacher of Zen in this country since the end of the 1920s when he had written his earlier volumes of his three volume series *Essays on Zen Buddhism*.

(*Goldenrod*, 92)

He observed that these Asian studies should particularly interest Catholic scholars because of the need for better understanding and dialogue between Asian and Western religions. To this end, he regularly reviewed newly available English translations of Chinese, Japanese, and Indian classics. For the next quarter century, this endeavor to study and teach Asian religions became a primary focus for Thomas, first at Seton Hall, then at St. John's University, and finally at Fordham. During this period, he was committed to promoting understanding and dialogue among the world's religions, decades before this effort became more mainstream.[14] But first, he felt a need for grounding in the history and texts of other religions.

COLLABORATION AT COLUMBIA

In 1961, Ted de Bary invited Thomas to participate in the newly established Columbia University Seminar on Oriental Thought and Religion.[15] He readily accepted the invitation and continued to attend these meetings throughout his subsequent teaching years. Thomas was thus assured of scholarly dialogue with peers in the field of Asian religions. The group met once a month in the late afternoon on Friday at Columbia University. Other early participants included Frederick Underwood, a specialist on Buddhism at Columbia; Wing-tsit Chan, a leading scholar and translator of Confucian texts; Yoshito Hakeda, a Columbia professor of Chinese and Japanese Buddhism; and, for a brief time, Robert C. Zaehner, an Oxford don who focused on Indian and Iranian religions and who was visiting Columbia.

Thomas presented papers to the seminar on various topics in Confucianism and Buddhism, all of which were well received.[16] Ted de Bary told the story that

4.3 Columbia University, Kent Hall, where the East Asian Department is located and where Ted de Bary spoke with Professor Hakeda about Thomas's paper on Shingon Buddhism.
Mary Evelyn Tucker

one evening, while Thomas was delivering a paper on the esoteric school of Shingon Buddhism in Japan, de Bary saw tears running down Professor Hakeda's face. The next day when de Bary saw him in the hall, he quietly asked him why he was so moved at the seminar. Hakeda replied that in listening to Thomas's paper, "I felt as if I was hearing my old master in Japan speak." Before coming to Columbia to teach, Hakeda had studied for ordination as a Shingon Buddhist monk on Mt. Koya, the sacred Buddhist mountain in central Japan. Thomas's insight into Buddhist texts and teachings had moved even a highly learned Buddhist monk and Columbia professor.

In 1961, the same year the Columbia seminar began, Thomas published the lead essay in the first issue of the scholarly journal *International Philosophical Quarterly*. Titled "Oriental Philosophies and World Humanism," it highlighted in broad strokes the spiritual characteristics of Hinduism, Buddhism, Confucianism, Taoism, and Zen.[17] In describing the original impulses of the principal Asian systems of thought, Thomas highlighted their spiritual essence and avoided the layers of complexity that tend to obfuscate rather than clarify. A few examples will illustrate his phenomenological method, which he later supplemented by discussing the development of the particular tradition.

> Of Hinduism: "Hinduism is founded in a most intensive experience of divine being. It is an experience of the One beyond all Multiplicity. . . ."[18]
>
> Of Buddhism: "Buddhist thought originates in an unusual experience of the sorrows of time. No abiding reality is here, no lasting peace, no fit condition for human life. The first and final wisdom is to recognize the insubstantial nature of all things."[19]
>
> Of Confucianism: "Confucian thought originates in the experience of an all-embracing harmony of the cosmic and human orders of reality. This intimate relationship between the cosmic and the human is expressed and perfected in an elaborate order of ritual and etiquette which, in a certain manner contains and harmonizes both the cosmic and the human."[20]
>
> Of Taoism: "Taoism arises from an experience of the dynamic force immanent in the universe which gives order and life and meaning to all reality and which in China is known as the Tao. This experience is not radically different from that which produced the Confucian tradition of thought, but while the Confucian scholars gave their attention to the moral qualities of the Tao and to the social and political structure of society, the Taoist visionaries turned to the contemplation of the Tao itself and the mysterious manner in which it wrought the succession of changes in the universal order of things."[21]
>
> Of Zen: ". . . the total effort of Zen is to keep the intellectual and cultural life of humans in a state of elemental simplicity with all the vigor that is associated with the spontaneous and instinctive."[22]

Thomas participated in the major scholarly organizations in Asian studies. In 1964, the American Academy of Religion began a section on History of Religions, which was changed to Asian Religions in 1968. That same year, the Society for Asian and Comparative Philosophy was founded to expose Western philosophers to the rich traditions of Asian thought. Thomas later served on the board in 1974 and 1975. He also participated in a panel of the Association of Asian Studies, where he delivered a paper entitled "Affectivity in Classical

Confucianism."[23] His scholarly endeavors were recognized in December 1968, when he was invited to join the Catholic Commission on Intellectual and Cultural Affairs.

During the 1960s Thomas worked on a book on Buddhism and was immersed in the various schools of Buddhist thought. He had been invited by the editors of the multivolume *Twentieth Century Encyclopedia of Catholicism* to write a monograph on Buddhism as part of a series on non-Christian beliefs. The book includes sections entitled "Early Buddhism (Theravada)," "The New Buddhism (Mahayana)," and "The Expansion of Buddhism (across Asia and to the West)." This endeavor brought together nearly twenty years of studying, teaching, and reflecting on Buddhism and other Asian religions.[24]

One of the most moving sections of the book is Thomas's discussion of redemptive suffering through the saintlike bodhisattva figure. He quotes Shanti Deva on the ability of the bodhisattva to absorb the sorrows of the world.

> May all that are sick of body and soul in every region find oceans of bliss and delight through my merits. Whilst embodied life lasts on, may they never lack happiness, and forever may the world win the joy of the Sons of Enlightenment. . . . As long as the heavens and the earth abide, may I continue to overcome the world's sorrows. . . . May all the world' suffering be cast upon me, and may the world be made happy by all the merits of the Bodhisattva.[25]

This redemptive suffering is similar to the commitment in Christianity, and especially of Thomas's religious order, to bear the sufferings of others. Thomas also shows how the bodhisattva becomes identified with the whole universe in a self-sacrificial act of consciousness awareness and generous giving:

> I will cease to live as a self, and will take as myself my fellow-creatures. We love our hands and other limbs, as members of the body; then why not love other living beings, as members of the universe? . . . Make thyself a spy for the service of others, and whatsoever thou seest in thy body's work that is good for thy fellows, perform it so that it may be conveyed to them.[26]

In the late 1960s, Bruce Publishing Company invited Thomas, as a follow-up to his Buddhism monograph, to write a book entitled *Religions of India*.[27]

In this book Thomas presents the historical development, sacred texts, and ritual practices of India's major religious traditions, namely, Hinduism, Yoga, and Buddhism. He also articulates their spiritual significance for the contemporary period. These traditions, Thomas observes, now belong to the cultural and spiritual heritage of all humans and will contribute to the future shaping of world spirituality: "Hinduism, Yoga, and Buddhism are no longer merely Indian traditions . . . they are world traditions. . . . Now they are part of the universal human heritage; even the creative aspect of these traditions is no longer an exclusive concern of India."[28] Thomas realized that these diverse traditions hold rich resources for healing the spiritual deficiencies of Western culture and its excessive faith in secular goals and material progress.

Thomas also recognized that these spiritual paths need to be part of the multicultural global inheritance of humanity. Despite the forces of fundamentalism, which resist interaction with other religions, he acknowledged the currents of interreligious dialogue that were emerging around the world:

> The global spiritual past is the only adequate context for present understanding of the human even though this effort at universal awareness is thwarted by exclusivist attitudes that still exist in the world. Even now, however, the futility of such exclusivism is widely recognized. All live currents of thought seek to encompass the full human dimensions of the human.[29]

He felt that this dialogue would grow because these religions have universal implications for all humans in their struggle with suffering and loss, diminishment and death, along with celebration and ritual, rejoicing and renewing. Thomas argued that the human community needs the multiple perspectives of the world's religious traditions:

> Within this larger world of mankind the multiple spiritual and humanist traditions implicate each other, complete each other, and evoke from each other higher developments of which each is capable. These traditions implicate each other, for each has a universal mission to humankind. Each is panhuman in its significance.[30]

Thomas's insights into world religions were appreciated at Columbia, and during the 1960s and 1970s he would occasionally teach courses there at the invitation of Ted de Bary. This teaching began with a class on the *Bhagavad Gita* in 1963 and concluded in 1976 with courses at Barnard on American Indian religions and on contemporary spirituality. They were path-breaking classes and well attended. Students and friends would frequently take Thomas to dinner afterwards to continue the discussion.

ASIAN ART

Thomas also appreciated the variety and depth of Asian art. In 1965, he published a survey article entitled "Asian Art" for the *Encyclopedia Americana* in which he remarked on the sensual portrayal of the body in Indian art, as well as its devotional spirituality and warm portrayal of human life.[31] He highlighted the Hindu-inspired temples of Angkor Wat in Cambodia and the Buddhist temple art of Borobudor in Java.

Thomas also conjectured that the ancient bronze vessels of China's Shang dynasty, with their fantastic depictions of *tao tie* dragon masks, may represent a balance of two major elements, the wild and the serene. He maintained that Buddhist spirituality and Chinese humanism came together in the intensely compassionate expressions of the Maitreya bodhisattva statues. Thomas also considered Chinese landscape paintings to be a highpoint of a refined sensibility regarding nature—misty mountains and rushing waterfalls in which the human is a modest, but integral, part. In commenting on Chinese landscape paintings in relation to the Buddhist concept of *sunyata*, Thomas would often remark, "India invented the idea of nothingness or emptiness and China painted it."[32] He also celebrated similar sophisticated expressions in Japanese art, particularly in Zen Buddhist paintings and temples.

Thus, Thomas had the ability not only to study and explicate Asian scriptures but also to see how their spiritual teachings were expressed in painting and sculpture, temples and shrines, and Zen gardens and tea ceremonies. His library was filled with books on Asian art, and he would use these in his teaching.

ST. JOHN'S UNIVERSITY: INSTITUTE FOR ASIAN STUDIES

In 1960, Paul Shih, a professor at Seton Hall, was invited to St. John's University in Jamaica, New York, to create an Institute for Asian Studies. He arranged for Thomas to be hired as an instructor in the program in 1961. Thomas was initially part-time, and two years later he became full-time. Only five blocks from his residence at Immaculate Conception Monastery, the university's location was far more convenient for him than Seton Hall. By 1965, he had advanced to the position of adjunct associate professor in Asian history and religion.

Founded in 1870 by the Vincentian order, St. John's University was primarily a commuter institution with three campuses in Queens and Brooklyn. From a

4.4 St. John's University quad, circa mid-1960s.
Courtesy of St. John's University Special Collections and Archives, Queens, N.Y.

small college in Brooklyn, it became the largest Roman Catholic university in the United States. Within a decade, from the mid-fifties to 1966, its enrollment grew from 6,000 to 13,000. Largely the product of local parochial schools, the student body was deferential to clerical authority, and the Vincentian administration was known to be authoritarian.

The university's rapid growth and its conservative tendencies seriously strained relations between the faculty and the administration over academic freedom. In addition, the faculty protested the lack of a faculty senate, the absence of a clear tenure policy, inadequate retirement and insurance benefits, low salaries, and clerical administrative domination. Tensions became heated in the spring term of 1965. Well publicized and with media present, the first major protest and walkout occurred at a faculty meeting on March 6, 1965. On March 19, Father Joseph Tinnelly, former dean of the St. John's law school, was appointed by the administration as arbitrator.[33] Two days later, Thomas went to Tinnelly and offered to help mediate the dispute as a neutral party.[34] His efforts were in vain. While still attempting to serve as mediator, he was asked to address a lunch of faculty and administrators. His topic was the nature and functioning of a Catholic university. A tape recorder had been placed on a piano to record the talk, but after the presentation a dean came up and confiscated the recording. Thomas and other faculty members were not pleased. During this tumultuous period, Thomas's father, William Nathan, passed away from heart troubles at the Maryfield Nursing Home in High Point, North Carolina.

At the end of the fall term in 1965, tensions had reached a boiling point. On December 15, 1965, President Rev. Joseph T. Cahill fired thirty-one faculty members.[35] Thomas was among those dismissed. A faculty strike was called against the administration. Although Thomas was not a member of the St. John's chapter of the United Federation of College Teachers (UFCT), which called the strike, and despite his intentions to remain neutral, he was gradually drawn into the conflict.

This was the first time in the history of American higher education that faculty openly revolted against an administration.[36] The action raised serious concerns about the nature of Catholic university education and severely strained relations between religious and secular faculty. Immediate issues to be addressed were those of academic freedom and due process for the fired faculty members. Censure of the university arose from other academic organizations. The American

Association of University Professors (AAUP) condemned St. John's administrative action at its spring 1966 annual meeting. In December the Middle States Association of Colleges and Secondary Schools announced that St. John's was on probation and must demonstrate why it should not lose its accreditation.[37]

The problem at St. John's clearly stemmed from a difference of opinion about what constitutes a Catholic university: Would there be genuine academic freedom or simply clerical control? This became the core issue of the St. John's strike. John Tracy Ellis of Catholic University had raised this problem in his 1956 book, *American Catholics and the Intellectual Life*. In the eyes of many, the university was basically an extension of the New York City parochial school system, its atmosphere marked by "formalism, authoritarianism, clericalism, moralism, and defensiveness."[38] The entrenched views of clerical hierarchy and control would take years to sort out. American Catholic higher education was breaking out of the conservative strictures of the pre–Vatican II world. Faculty were desiring genuine academic freedom, and Thomas was caught in these winds of change.

THE PASSIONISTS' RESPONSE

Meanwhile, Thomas had to address the reactions of his own order to these issues. Thomas's dismissal from St. John's raised difficult issues with his provincial and the superior general of the Passionist Congregation in Rome. Indeed, it nearly lost for him the opportunity to continue university teaching, and Thomas was already breaking new ground in that regard within his order. Moreover, the vow of obedience was taken very seriously in religious orders, especially in pre–Vatican Council II years. A priest, such as a Passionist, had to ask permission of his superior before accepting a teaching assignment; buying books or audio equipment, such as a tape recorder for foreign language study; or making living arrangements away from the monastery for study or teaching. Publication of articles and books required prior approval of the Congregation's censor. Gradual relaxation of such strictures in the American Catholic Church resulted from Vatican Council II reforms introduced in the early 1960s.

During this period, Thomas had particular problems with his immediate superior, the provincial Father Gerard Rooney. Rooney may have been pressured by Vincentian authorities at St. John's. In any case, Thomas had to fight to continue his teaching career. His liberal ideas about the nature of a Catholic university as a place of open intellectual discourse and his alleged involvement with faculty protestors at St. John's had apparently caused the Sacred Congregation of Seminaries and Universities at the Vatican to request his removal from teaching. The Passionist order agreed to this request on November 23, 1965. A month later, in a letter of December 20, 1965, to the superior general of the Passionist order in Rome, Father Theodore Foley, Thomas defended himself against what he considered false charges and argued that he should be allowed to continue his teaching.[39]

What followed was a testy exchange of letters between Thomas and his provincial, Rooney, regarding Thomas's academic future and the degree of freedom and autonomy that was consistent with his vow of obedience.[40] On December 27, 1965, Rooney, who had good intellectual credentials, sent Thomas an extensive letter of critique. Thomas replied with a long letter on January 1, 1966, defending his freedom to teach and to enter into contract negotiations without prior notification of his provincial. Chafing at Rooney's narrow interpretation of the vow of obedience, Thomas denounced the "short leash" on which he was being held. As a scholar, he insisted on his right to make study and lecture arrangements without prior notification to his superior. To Rooney, he wrote: "While I am willing to accept my removal from St. John's as a fact, I am not willing to accept this as a justified action on the part of the authorities concerned. Nor am I willing to accept as a result of this decision anything that would restrict my teaching at other universities."[41] In particular, he insisted on his right to confront his accusers directly and respond to charges brought against him. His purpose, Thomas insisted, was to uphold, not undermine, the welfare of the Church and of Catholic higher education in America.

Fortunately for Thomas, his forthright personal defense resulted in complete exoneration and the reinstatement of his permission to teach. In a letter dated January 18, 1966, Theodore Foley, superior general of the Passionist Congregation, reversed the Congregation's earlier decision to remove Thomas from teaching and transfer him to another type of work. Grounds for the charges against him were easily disproved. Aside from offering to mediate the St. John's strike, Thomas was not actively involved with the strikers and had never taught anything contrary to church doctrine. In the end, the only caveat was that Thomas must still request his provincial's approval before undertaking teaching commitments or research projects.[42]

In this case, as in Thomas's earlier dispute with the local provincial, the superior general in Rome supported him and seemed to appreciate the larger global perspective that Thomas was trying to articulate for the Church and its relations with other religions. The St. John's strike took place against a backdrop of the final session of Vatican Council II, which issued important statements regarding the Church in the modern world, including more open-minded decrees on the relationship of the Church to non-Christians, Christian education, religious liberty, priestly formation, the bishop's pastoral office, renewal of religious life, ministry and priestly life, and the apostolate of the laity.

During this time, inspired by the spirit of Vatican II and his own studies of Asia, Thomas cultivated a wider and freer view of his role as a scholar and teacher. He was clearly moving in new directions. Indeed, after having been caught up in events at St. John's and unjustly implicated in them, Thomas would find his dismissal a blessing in disguise. He was soon offered the opportunity to join the theology department at Fordham University in the Bronx, which he readily accepted, as he was eager to continue his teaching and writing in a more hospitable environment. Here, he could take up his broader aspiration: "One of the great tasks to which our age is called is that of giving spiritual shape and substance to the world society now in the process of formation. This new vision of the past is a creation of the present with infinite consequences for the future."[43] Fordham, where he would teach, and the Riverdale Center, where he would live, opened up a space that was conducive for creative thinking in the next phase of his life path.

CHAPTER 5

From Human History to Earth History

Strangely enough, the very forces moving various cultures and religions out of the traditional into the modern world are exactly the forces enabling each tradition to recover contact with its most pristine forms and ancient literatures. Thus these traditions live more deeply in the past even as they move into the present and future. Each tradition is made more complete with itself, more integral with its primordial moments. From this earliest period, the historical movement of religions and cultures has been converging toward multiform global expression in which each finds its place and each is in some manner present to the entire society.

Thomas Berry, "Religions in the Global Human Community"

Fordham became an important setting for the growth of Thomas's thinking and teaching on world religions and ecology. There he would eventually focus on how the world's religions in the late twentieth century were converging. While such encounters had been taking place throughout history, the particular global challenges that religious traditions were facing presented new opportunities for change. Religious traditions were being called to participate in interreligious dialogue and to address the planetary crisis of ecology and justice. The arc of history was being enlarged, as contact between various religions around the planet became ever more visible and inevitable.

The context for this study was the 1960s civil rights, anti–Vietnam War, feminist, and environmental movements. College campuses were ripe with unrest, especially regarding the Vietnam War and the draft, as well as the policy of segregation of African Americans. The free speech movement in 1964–1965 at Berkeley had already ignited student activism at other universities. A year after Thomas arrived at Fordham, classes were suspended on December 6, 1967, to explore the moral issues regarding the Vietnam War. The following spring, Columbia University exploded with student protests opposing the war and a proposed gym to be built in Harlem. Martin Luther King was assassinated in the spring of 1968, and riots ensued across the country. Thomas made his way forward in the midst of these disruptive forces, generally being supportive of student concerns. He was also empathetic regarding women's issues and always had a strong following of women among his students and friends. He affirmed women's intuitive ways of knowing and encouraged their voices in academia and beyond. His article on patriarchy was a watershed piece in the historical understanding of male dominance.[1] There he strongly affirmed women's intellectual perspectives, leadership capacities, and moral authority.

THE CALL TO FORDHAM UNIVERSITY

After learning of Thomas's dismissal from St. John's University, Christopher Mooney, S.J., the chair of Fordham's theology department, received a phone call from Beatrice Bruteau urging him to consider hiring Thomas. Mooney replied that he had already done so. Bruteau was a gifted graduate student in philosophy at Fordham and the assistant director of the Cardinal Bea Institute of Spirituality, headed by Mooney. She was also the founder and coordinator of Fordham's Teilhard Research Institute. Two years earlier, at Fordham's 1964 Teilhard Conference, she and others had been deeply impressed by Thomas's lecture "The Threshold of the Modern World." His reputation for original thinking had preceded him.

Moreover, Thomas was keen to move into an intellectual environment where he could thrive without fear of reprisal or censorship. Thus, when Chris Mooney called with a job offer, Thomas promptly accepted, pending permission from his superior. He was eager to get on with his life work after the upheavals he had experienced at St. John's University. Fordham was, by and large, a good fit for his desire to expand his teaching, especially of Asian religions. He wrote to Mooney: "This Oriental field is vast, vast, vast! There is almost no end to it. Always the feeling is that a person has not even begun, even after years of work in the field."[2]

Thomas spent thirteen productive years at Fordham, from the fall of 1966 through the spring of 1979.[3] During this significant period of academic achievement, he created the History of Religions program in the theology department. From Thomas's new home at the Passionist retreat center in Riverdale, Fordham's Rose Hill campus was a convenient fifteen-minute drive. In addition to teaching, he began to establish a place of learning and reflection at the Riverdale Center for Religious Research. This center flourished during the Fordham years and well beyond, until he retired to North Carolina in 1995.

In moving to Fordham, Thomas was joining a well-known Jesuit university and a competent faculty. Founded in 1841, Fordham was the oldest Catholic institution of higher education in the Northeast, with an enrollment of some six thousand students. During the dynamic 1960s and 1970s, it was reshaping its identity from a predominantly Jesuit establishment to a more pluralistic, modern urban Catholic university. As Fordham began transforming its theology department from a place of traditional Catholic orthodoxy to a broader intellectual center of research and teaching with promising graduate students, Thomas became a vital part of these changes. His presence ensured that attention would be given to the religious traditions of Asia.

5.1 Fordham University, Duane Library, named after Fr. William Duane, S.J., president of Fordham from 1924 to 1930. Thomas and his students used this library frequently.
iStock by Getty Images

Colleagues in the theology department included Ewert Cousins, a scholar of medieval Christian mysticism, especially Bonaventure; John Heaney, a specialist in theology and psychology; Joseph Mitros, S.J., a Christian theologian, and Byron Schaeffer, a biblical scholar. Ewert Cousins was a valuable colleague and an avid supporter of Thomas's work. Having a strong interest in comparative religions and interreligious dialogue, Ewert directed a large multiyear project on world spirituality in which Thomas participated. This project involved international conferences and edited books on all the world's religions.[4] Thomas served on the board of editors and advisers along with leading theologians and historians of world religion.

Thomas and the History of Religions program could also draw upon the expertise of Norris Clark, S.J., and Father John Chethimattam in the philosophy department. Jose Pereira, a Portuguese-Indian professor from Goa, joined the History of Religions program in 1974 and directed dissertations on Hinduism. After a productive period with Christopher Mooney, Thomas worked with several subsequent chairs of theology.[5] While not all the chairs appreciated the importance of the History of Religions program, the many students who flocked to it clearly did. They recognized Thomas's immense learning, but also his willingness to keep on learning. They could see that he loved to engage in debate and dialogue that would clarify ideas. Most of all, they appreciated his welcoming manner, his joyful spirit, and his wry sense of humor.

ESTABLISHING THE HISTORY OF RELIGIONS PROGRAM

By the time he arrived at Fordham, Thomas had been studying the religions of the world for nearly two decades and had been teaching Asian religions for nearly ten years. His immersion in the world's religions continued to deepen at Fordham. During this period, as previously mentioned, Thomas collaborated with his colleagues to create a distinguished History of Religions doctoral and master's program. His reputation as a scholar, teacher, and original thinker grew rapidly. Indeed, students came from other universities to study with him, some of them turning down offers from Yale and Columbia. It was the only such program at any Catholic university in North America and has never been replicated.[6]

When Thomas initiated the History of Religions program, his approach defined the direction of the master's and doctoral degrees. He emphasized cultural-historical contexts, language proficiency, scriptural studies, and wisdom teachings. The emphasis on wisdom teachings was unique in academic settings. Other History of Religions programs at secular universities generally focused on textual, historical, and philosophical approaches and tended to ignore mystical traditions, experiential practices, and spiritual exercises. Thomas helped students see the contemporary relevance of the world's religions.[7] He felt that each student, while becoming a specialist in one tradition, should also have a broad understanding of the world's religions. He did not adhere to a theological approach that examined these traditions in relation to Christianity. Rather, he encouraged a rigorous study of their historical unfolding, scriptural and commentarial base, and meditative and ritual practices. Only then, he felt, could substantive dialogue occur. During this period he corresponded with many scholars of Asian religions, some of whom he hoped would come to teach at Fordham.[8]

In carrying out Christopher Mooney's mandate to develop this new curriculum, Thomas articulated three goals for the History of Religions program:

1. Students should have a comprehensive sense of human religious life.
2. They should have a sense of the historical and intellectual development of Christianity.
3. They should demonstrate competence in one nonbiblical religion, reading its scriptures in the original language; or show advanced understanding of the intellectual relevance of a non-Christian religion or an Indigenous tradition, using anthropological studies and with special reference to symbols.

The program drew on other classes in the theology department, but Thomas's courses were the centerpieces. They included over twenty different graduate courses on Asian and comparative religion studies, with special emphasis on Hinduism, Buddhism, Confucianism, and Daoism. He also taught classes on the understanding of symbols, drawing from the work of the historian of religion Mircea Eliade and the depth psychologist Carl Jung.[9] His courses on American Indian religions were some of the first ever offered at a Catholic university.

He had an extensive collection of books on Native American studies and devoted a room on the second floor of the Riverdale Center to this collection. Five students wrote their theses on this topic. A brilliant and broadly knowledgeable professor, Thomas directed or was a reader on more than twenty dissertations on a wide range of topics.[10] He spent a significant amount of time mentoring his PhD students and writing letters of recommendation for them. Almost all of these students went on to successful careers in teaching, interreligious dialogue, or religious environmentalism.

UNDERSTANDING AND DIALOGUING WITH OTHER RELIGIONS: VATICAN II

The historical study of each of the traditions remained central for Thomas, as did the articulation of their deeper significance for the contemporary period. He taught and wrote about how the insights of these traditions helped to navigate the challenges of modernity. Each Asian tradition made a contribution: the Buddhist response to suffering, the Hindu recognition of Oneness, the Confucian understanding of humaneness, the Daoist sense of life's flow, and Shinto's appreciation for the sacred quality of nature. Each tradition was also being transformed in the face of modernity. As Thomas highlighted their traditional teachings and practices, he also noted how they were adapting these forms for a new moment in contemporary history.

This adaptation of tradition and modernity is what Catholicism was also struggling to do with the changes inaugurated with the second Vatican Council (1962–1965). In initiating the Council on January 25, 1959, Pope John XXIII called for an "aggiornamento," an updating of the Church to meet the challenges of modernity. It was time to "open the windows [of the Church] and let in some fresh air."[11] From its commencement on October 11, 1962, to its conclusion on December 3, 1965, the Council did exactly that. For example, the Council statement on *The Church in the Modern World* begins with a renewed commitment to Christian humanism: "The joys and hopes, the grief and anguish of the people of our time, especially of those who are poor or afflicted, are the joys and hopes, the grief and anguish of the followers of Christ as well. Nothing that is genuinely human fails to find an echo in their hearts."[12] In this spirit, the Council encouraged the pursuit of justice and human rights. Indeed, liberation theology, which advocated for the poor, began to flourish in Latin America in response to these directives.[13]

The Council also made radical changes in the liturgy by shifting the language of the Mass from Latin to the local vernacular and turning the altar around to face the congregation. It promoted the change of religious dress from medieval habits to modern dress. It affirmed the importance of individual conscience and gave bishops more authority. It also encouraged ecumenism among the Christian churches. Most notably, it opened the door to dialogue with other Christian denominations as well as other religions. This new openness required an understanding of, and respect toward, non-Christian religions, which had not been part of the education of priests, nuns, or laity. The Council's new outlook explained why the History of Religions program at Fordham was so timely and so well received by the students. Thomas arrived there in 1966, just a year after the Council was concluded and when the new documents were being read and implemented at universities such as Fordham. His decades of study, writing, teaching, and travel prepared him for this moment; he could now create a robust curriculum in world religions that could become an informed basis for substantive interreligious dialogue. During the late 1960s he was frequently asked to speak on this topic of dialogue at other Catholic universities.[14]

Many of Thomas's students engaged in such dialogue after obtaining their degrees. Those who went on to do significant and sustained work in ecumenical and interreligious dialogue included John Borelli at the U.S. Conference of Catholic Bishops and later at Georgetown University; William Cenkner, O.P., at the Catholic University of America, where he served as dean of the School of Religious Studies; Monsignor Ettore Di Filippo at the Permanent Observer Mission of the Holy See to the United Nations (1965–1983); and Archbishop Felix Machado at the Vatican as undersecretary in the Pontifical Council for Interreligious Dialogue from 1999 to 2008.[15] All of these individuals were inspired to do their path-breaking work because of classes with Thomas at Fordham.

Important in Thomas's career was a long and productive relationship with Monsignor Ettore Di Filippo.[16] Having studied under Thomas in the History of Religions program, Di Filippo later arranged for him to participate in conferences and retreats of the Vatican Mission to the United Nations. In 1973, Catholic delegates to the UN were hosted at Riverdale Center. Other collaborations followed.[17] It was Di Filippo who introduced Thomas to Robert Muller, who was, for forty years, under-secretary-general of the United Nations. This contact resulted in numerous speaking engagements and an invitation for Thomas to comment on the UN "World Charter for Nature," which was adopted by member nation-states on October 28, 1982.[18]

RELATIONS OF THE CHURCH WITH NON-CHRISTIAN TRADITIONS

Thomas's appreciation for the uniqueness of each religious tradition, so evident in his teaching, was unusual for its time. During this post–Vatican II period, the Catholic Church was moving away from its traditional claim that there was no truth or salvation outside the Church. Instead, in the 1965 Vatican II document, *Nostra Aetate* (In Our Time), it proposed a new opening to other religions.[19] It describes in sympathetic language some of the teachings of Hinduism and Buddhism:

> Thus in Hinduism, men contemplate the divine mystery and express it through an inexhaustible abundance of myths and through searching philosophical inquiry. They seek freedom from the anguish of our human condition either through ascetical practices or profound meditation or a flight to God with love and trust. Again, Buddhism, in its various forms, realizes the radical insufficiency of this changeable world; it teaches a way by which men, in a devout and confident spirit, may be able either to acquire the state of perfect liberation, or attain, by their own efforts or through higher help, supreme illumination. Likewise, other religions found everywhere try to counter the restlessness of the human heart, each in its own manner, by proposing "ways," comprising teachings, rules of life, and sacred rites.
>
> The Catholic Church rejects nothing that is true and holy in these religions. She regards with sincere reverence those ways of conduct and of life, those precepts and teachings which, though differing in many aspects from the ones she holds and sets forth, nonetheless often reflect a ray of that Truth which enlightens all men.[20]

Here the Church affirmed, for the first time, that there is a ray of light in other traditions. Thomas would laugh and say, "My goodness, it's not simply a ray of light, but floods of light!"[21]

Nostra Aetate proceeds to encourage interreligious collaboration:

> The Church, therefore, exhorts her sons, that through dialogue and collabo-
> ration with the followers of other religions, carried out with prudence and
> love and in witness to the Christian faith and life, they recognize, preserve
> and promote the good things, spiritual and moral, as well as the socio-cultural
> values found among these men.[22]

The document also forbids discrimination based on religion: "The Church
reproves, as foreign to the mind of Christ, any discrimination against men or
harassment of them because of their race, color, condition of life, or religion."[23]

Thomas had already been studying other religions for many years when *Nostra Aetate* was issued. Now he felt he could encourage others to build on church
teachings in this regard and thus created the unique History of Religions program at Fordham. However, after Thomas's retirement, the program was diminished and soon after was discontinued because conservative forces within the
theology department and the university chose not to hire replacement faculty
who could carry on the program. Regrettably, the university did not understand
the significance of the history of religions and its attraction for students. The
provost at the time told a graduate student who was concerned about the future
of the program, "We don't need classes on other religions; we need more courses
on Jesus in the theology department." The emphasis on Catholic theology, church
history, and biblical studies remained, while the call of Vatican II to engage with
the world's religions was left behind.[24]

PERSONAL ENCOUNTER WITH THE WORLD RELIGIONS:
THE ROSE WINDOW

In appreciating other religions, Thomas proposed the image of the Gothic rose
window as an organizing symbol. The center represented the religious tradition
in which one is born, while the outer petals represented the other religions of
the world. Some students would raise the question: What if a person had no
formal religious training or tradition? Did that eliminate the role of the central
window? "Not really," Berry would counter, "because no one chooses where they
will be born, but they receive some cultural formation in the ethical and religious

values of their society." From this perspective, nonpracticing Jews, Christians, or Muslims still participate in their culturally accepted values within families, societies, and countries. Perhaps, Thomas conjectured, one would reject or resist those values, but they still provided the context that he likened to that central window. The outer petals, then, emphasized for him the magnificent diversity of human religious expressions.

Thomas suggested that a central task of humans in the contemporary period of global encounters between cultures and traditions is to relate one's basic natal orientation to the diverse religions of the world. The challenge, of course, is how to connect the deep and often unconscious commitments of one's own culture to the diversity of traditions imaged in the outer rose petals of those Gothic windows. Some individuals, Thomas would lament, turn inward and seize upon the strength and inner purpose of the central window, namely, the religious teachings of their youth. These practitioners often reject the outer windows as totally Other, disorienting, or false. There are also individuals who become so fixated by the outer windows that they move from one spiritual practice to another, or from one religious expression to another. Giving themselves over to the allure of the exotic, they diminish and often lose the stability of their own formative cultural vision. The task, as Thomas saw it, is to balance this tension and to explore through the history of religions what the religions of the world might bring to personal creativity, spiritual growth, and intellectual understanding.

Thomas's calm and deliberate manner oriented students to this type of exploration. His serious consideration of religious scriptures, traditions, and rituals conveyed to students not simply the need to know the historical and cultural context in which these religions were embedded, but more importantly the depth of insight into the human condition that they provided for individuals and communities. The study of these traditions became a basis for his later intellectual turn toward an integrating story that positioned the human within the larger community of life.

GLOBAL ENCOUNTER OF THE WORLD RELIGIONS: SECOND AXIAL AGE

While Thomas taught the unique history of each of the world's religions, he also began to articulate the multiform global dimensions of these traditions. Thomas felt that their symbolic forms, their spiritual practices, and their wisdom were becoming, as never before, the common inheritance of the human community. This coming together was due to communication and travel, as well as new translations of scriptures and commentaries.

The increase in translations after the war was particularly fostered by Ted de Bary at Columbia University Press with the Sourcebooks of Indian, Chinese, and Japanese Traditions, along with the Translations from the Asian Classics series. De Bary also published several books on how to teach these texts, among them the volumes entitled *Approaches to the Oriental Classics*. Thomas contributed two articles to these volumes.[25] It is one of the great ironies of history that out of the conflict of the Pacific war there emerged a better understanding of Asian cultures and religions. Many of the scholars learned East Asian languages in the army and navy language schools, and they were prepared to make translations of texts that were not available earlier. Most dissertations under de Bary were translations and commentaries of Chinese or Japanese classics, while Thomas encouraged his doctoral students to explicate and reflect on Asian texts that were already translated.[26] Both of these approaches made significant contributions to the newly emerging fields of Asian religions and Asian studies.

The intermingling of the religions, both historically and in the present, became a critical dimension of Thomas's studies and teaching. The contemporary encounters between the world's religions, as he saw them, represented a new phase in human culture and civilization, what he called a second Axial Age.[27] In using this term, he was building on the idea of the German philosopher Karl Jaspers, who proposed that the Axial Age was a pivotal time in which key spiritual ideas appeared simultaneously in various areas of the world. Jaspers pointed to the rise of the world's religions in the sixth century BCE in the great river valley civilizations of the Yellow River in East Asia and the Indus in South Asia, as well as in Persia, Israel, and Greece in West Asia.[28] Axial Age religions and thinkers included Confucianism and Daoism in China, Hinduism and Buddhism in India, Zoroastrianism in Persia, the Jewish prophets in Israel, and the philosophers in Greece. Now, some 2,500 years later, Thomas observed that the world religions were meeting and creating a new planetary phase of their unfolding.

Following Jaspers, Thomas highlighted the transformation of traditions across great expanses of space and time in the first millennium CE, including the movement of Buddhism from India to China, with the Buddhist tradition changing in each cultural context. He helped his students to see how trade in ideas and goods occurred across the Silk Road from Persia and China to Japan. He identified interactions that would result in creative forms of syncretism, such as those between Buddhism and Daoism in China and between Buddhism and Shinto in Japan. All of this teaching brought to life how religions respond to contact with new regions, ideas, and peoples. For Thomas, these stories of encounter and exchange were fundamental to the way history unfolds, the way people adapt, and the way cultures change through both conscious and unconscious processes.

Thomas's interest in such changes and adaptations became more focused as the ecological crisis began to preoccupy him. He brooded over not only how these religious and cultural traditions might respond to threats to their own survival from the rapid onslaught of modernity and technology, but also how they might deal with the diminishment of the planet's life systems. Thomas noted that the multireligious civilization emerging in the present period clearly needs to develop interreligious dialogue, but also interreligious cooperation, to meet the ecological and social challenges that threaten the future of the Earth community. Without the spiritual insights and cosmological perspectives of religious communities, humans will falter and lose their way. This, he noted, is part of the challenge of the meeting of the world religions in the current Axial Age. Indeed, Thomas's ideas inspired the Harvard conferences entitled World Religions and Ecology (1996–1998) and subsequently the Forum on Religion and Ecology, which was based at Harvard from 1998 to 2006 and at Yale from 2006 to the present.[29]

CONTEMPORARY SPIRITUALITY

Thomas's concern for greater understanding of other religions was later complemented by his keen interest in new modes of spiritual development in the West. This interest began as a concern for spiritual formation and training in his own order, which he found outdated.[30] Stressing the need for creative thinking to combat theological sterility, Thomas considered the Congregation "intellectually still imprisoned in medieval scholastic a priori theological processes with no true feeling for the world of reality."[31] In his eyes, the Passionists resembled "the farmer who spends all his time examining the seed and studying techniques of sowing but who never bothers to examine the soil."[32] Too much attention was given, he believed, to developing a praying and preaching community and not enough to producing a thinking community.[33]

Thomas gradually expanded his exploration of spirituality to address the needs of the larger society. In the summer of 1974, at the Chautauqua Institution along Lake Erie in upstate New York, he gave the Edwin P. Booth Memorial Lectures on "Contemporary Spirituality." In the fall, these lectures morphed into a fourteen-week course at Barnard College. This class was later taught at Fordham, as Thomas sought to describe new means and methods of spiritual renewal. It included such engaging topics as Stopping the World, The Journey Symbol, The Demonic Obstacle, Depths of the Unconscious, Meditation, Psychedelic Experience, Mandala and Mantra, The Spiritual Guide, The Dionysian and Apollonian, Cosmic Connection, Power, Spiritual Rebirth, Technology and Spirituality, and The Human Future.[34]

Thomas maintained that traditional Christian spirituality no longer adequately addressed the pressing problems of the modern world because it tended to emphasize individual redemption out of the world, to the neglect of

5.2 Thomas at one of his many speaking engagements in the 1970s.
Gretchen McHugh, courtesy of J. Murray McHugh

the Earth. With a broader spirituality, he felt that a new consciousness could emerge in the West, thus deepening global environmental awareness and a sense of responsibility for the Earth community. Thus, he spoke of the call for an interior journey to one's authentic self, which would result in a newly awakened spiritual consciousness.[35] In his concluding class on "The Human Future," Thomas declared that "one of our most urgent needs would seem to be an effective myth of the future."[36]

CLASSES AT FORDHAM

Classes with Thomas typically alternated between lecture and discussion. He distinguished his lecture courses from seminars, which involved student participation and individual paper projects. Thomas encouraged exchanges between instructor and student, as well as among students. Throughout his teaching days, he fostered lively conversations. It was not unusual to find him after class with his students at the local Howard Johnson's restaurant continuing the conversation over coffee and a grilled cheese sandwich. With the loosening of religious dress and community life after Vatican II, Thomas put aside his clerical habit and wore a suit or a brown corduroy jacket, tie, and slacks.

Thomas was constantly helping his students with both academic and personal challenges. One graduate student, Amarylis Cortijo, recalled years later how she went to talk with Thomas to consider what program might be best for her. Although registered for courses in a different field in the theology department, she had not yet purchased the books. Thomas discussed her program and then took her to the bookstore, where he proceeded to buy her many of the different religious scriptures. By the time the conversation was over, she had not only an armful of books but also a clear idea of her direction in studying the history of religions.

Another student recalled a first meeting with Thomas in his office in the theology department in Collins Hall at the beginning of the fall semester of 1968. Since Thomas was not wearing religious garb, the student wondered what term he should use to address him. Giving vent to his nervousness, the student asked: "Should I call you Father, Doctor, or Professor?" Thomas replied with a smile, "You can call me whatever you like." From that moment forward, the student recalls feeling an ease and attentiveness with Thomas that matched what others also felt.

Thomas's generosity was evident in the Fordham cafeteria, where he would often buy students a meal. At the Rathskeller he would enjoy endless cups of coffee while students drank beer and carried on animated discussions of different religious scriptures. One time, after a class on Chinese Classical texts, a group went to the Rathskeller with Thomas and focused on the *I Ching* or *Book of Changes*. They marveled at the wisdom in that text, which seemingly responds so personally to an individual's question. With successive throws of yarrow stalks or three coins a particular hexagram emerges and conveys a teaching. Soon the students mastered the technique and formulated serious questions, throwing coins and building hexagrams. On that occasion, and many more, Thomas would gently and persuasively move the students from their fascination with the divination process to the more profound and subtle meanings of the text itself. He was able to use various approaches to understanding religious traditions as serious guides to life's questions, tensions, and joys.

In the spring of 1975, Thomas offered an unusual seminar entitled "Music and Dance in Ritual."[37] The class took an unexpectedly delightful turn when Monsignor Ettore Di Filippo arranged for the students to visit the conductor of the New York Philharmonic, Leonard Bernstein, in his New York apartment on Fifty-Seventh Street. Di Filippo served in the Office of the Permanent Observer of the Holy See to the United Nations and had made it possible for Bernstein's *Mass* to be transmitted through the Vatican diplomatic mail directly to Pope Paul VI. This visit was a return for that favor. Bernstein began by asking each student for his or her name and particular interest in the study of music and religion. He then responded to questions ranging from his intuitions while composing music to his emotional engagement with a musical score as a conductor. Particularly memorable was Bernstein's acknowledgment that, while conducting Beethoven's symphonies, twice he sensed that he had become Beethoven. He said, "I felt so sad for those who came up to congratulate me on the performance because they didn't know who I was." The exchange between Thomas and Bernstein was especially lively when they discussed Bernstein's teaching style during his televised lectures in the 1950s. In this conversation, Thomas explored Bernstein's capacity to move between the sensibilities of his musical persona to the articulation of themes and patterns in symphonic scores.

In Thomas's classroom, students first read original texts in translation and then studied different interpretations of those texts. Thomas painstakingly elaborated the subtle nuances of the great synthesizing scholars, such as Thomas Aquinas in Christianity, Moses Maimonides in Judaism, Shankara in Hinduism, and Chu Hsi (Zhu Xi) in Confucianism. He would assign different students to make presentations on these texts, encouraging them to assess their intellectual and spiritual significance. They would then explore together the commentaries on these texts. Under his tutelage, the various schools of thought in the religions of South Asia, East Asia, and West Asia (the Middle East) were examined, including their historical complexities and changes.[38]

Early on in the program, before the Sanskritist Jose Pereira was hired, Thomas taught students Sanskrit so that they could encounter the intricate grammatical turns of the original language of Hindu texts, such as the *Bhagavad Gita,* "The Song of the Lord." They began to learn how different traditional schools of Hinduism developed rich spiritual understandings of this classic text. They also explored Gandhi's modern interpretation of the text. At the same time, they brought comparative approaches to the different wisdom teachings, devotional strains, and yogic techniques developed in accordance with the *Gita.*

Thomas's style of lecturing varied over the years of the History of Religions program. He often handed out mimeographed sheets that students could use as an outline to follow his lectures. These sheets presented lists of religious personalities, seminal historical developments in a tradition, or symbols for spiritual teachings. In seminars he would guide students into scriptures and commentaries on chosen topics within a tradition and help them prepare for giving classroom presentations and leading discussions. In these ways, Thomas not only deepened the knowledge base of the students, but also assisted them in the techniques of teaching so that they might be more engaged teachers after they received their doctoral degrees.

Thomas was in great demand in many areas besides teaching. He was constantly writing letters of recommendation for students, advising them on their papers and dissertations, and responding to inquiries regarding Asian religions. Moreover, he was frequently asked to review books and write articles, and he spoke widely. His correspondence reflects how many people he was in touch with in the United States and around the world and how many people he tried to assist.[39]

FROM HISTORY OF RELIGIONS TO COSMOLOGY
OF RELIGIONS

The years at Fordham were marked by the comprehensive program of studies Thomas created. In the late 1960s, he emphasized the spiritual and dialogical significance of the world's religions, both historically and in the present. Then, from the early 1970s on, he expanded into an exploration of the cosmology of religions. As Thomas said: "All religious expression by humans should be considered participation in the religious aspect of the universe itself."[40]

He became increasingly fascinated with how religions are cosmological systems that orient humans to their place in the universe and on the Earth. He realized that the large questions of where we have come from, where we are going, and why we are here are not simply theological questions, but rather cosmological ones. How humans see themselves embedded in an unfolding universe and in dynamic Earth processes is what interested him. This concern is expressed in religious traditions in a variety of ways, including seasonal celebrations such as the agricultural rites in the autumn or Solstice, Christmas, and Hanukkah in the winter. Thomas wrote:

> In the immediate future, our religious concerns will, I believe, be more cosmological. They will be more sensitive to the universe as the primary religious mode of being and to ourselves being religious through our participation in the religion of the universe. There will, I believe, be an emphasis on the planet Earth and on the universe itself as a single sacred community.[41]

Thomas's long intellectual journey from the study of history, to the teaching of history of religions, and finally to the cosmology of religions was becoming clear. He felt there was still more to explore for students, scholars, and practitioners:

> We are moving from a theology of religion and an anthropology of religion to a cosmology of religions. This is the direction where, I think, religious studies will inevitably go in the future. In earlier times, our religious inquiry was theological: it was organized around questions concerned with the existence and nature of God and the relations of creature to God. Later, our religious

concerns were largely anthropological, ministerial and spiritual, organized around such studies as the sociology and psychology of religion and the history of religions.[42]

Thomas realized that the various approaches of religious studies didn't take into account the power of science, especially as it was emerging in evolutionary cosmology and biological ecology. Something was lacking that Thomas wished to address so as to help people meet the growing environmental challenges:

> Because none of these forms of religious consciousness has been able to deal effectively with the evolutionary story of the universe or with the ecological crisis that is now disturbing Earth's basic life systems, we are being led to a cosmological dimension of religion both by our efforts at academic understanding and for practical issues of physical survival on a planet severely diminished in its life-giving capacities.[43]

Some years later the inability of religions to deal with evolution and ecology became even more visible. At a College Theology Society meeting at Loyola Marymount University in Los Angeles, a heated discussion took place between Thomas and a distinguished group of theologians.[44] The participants included the comparative theologian Raimon Panikkar, the liberation theologian Jon Sobrino, and the liberation philosopher Enrique Dussel. Panikkar spoke eloquently about a spiritual life involved with a transcendent divine presence, Sobrino invoked the horrors of injustice perpetuated by military regimes in Central America, and Dussel called for communities of justice and networks of peace to be built. While respecting the perspectives of each speaker, Thomas noted that without a healthy planet all human hopes and dreams would be thwarted. He acknowledged the immense suffering present in history but called for a new perspective of ecological awakening and planetary justice. It was an arresting discussion that lasted late into the evening.

The need to respond to the environmental crisis opened up Thomas's thinking to embrace not only religious cosmology, but also evolutionary cosmology. He saw that what the religions offered to their followers was a cosmological interpretation of life—its emergence, its purpose, and the human role in it. But he was also aware that with the science of evolution something new was possible, namely, the articulation of a broader cosmological narrative of 14 billion years during which the cosmos and Earth unfolded. When told as a story, this had the potential to be not only engaging, but also life changing. These insights were the first glimmers of his transformative essay entitled "The New Story" that emerged during his Golden Year.

THE GOLDEN YEAR

In 1977 Thomas Berry extended invitations to three graduate students to work on their doctoral dissertations while living with him at the Riverdale Center for Religious Research. John Grim and Valerio Ortolani, S.J., came in the summer of 1977. They were joined by Brian Brown as the fall semester began. Thomas called this his Golden Year. It was a time when he was moving toward retirement from Fordham and was engaged in increased travel to give talks that explored his latest thinking. He would develop these talks into longer essays after discussions at the Center. These essays were then collected in the blue-bound Riverdale Papers. Thus, it was a special time for intellectual camaraderie among the like-minded graduate students and visitors at the Center.

5.3 Thomas Berry in the 1970s.
Lou Niznik, courtesy of Jane Blewett

In the day-to-day activities, John Grim and Brian Brown typically shopped for food, prepared meals, and washed the dishes. Often joining the group for meals were other graduate students. While breakfast was taken individually at the Center, both lunch and dinner were times of extended discussions of Thomas's planned lectures and of the writing progress of the three students. The dissertations themselves indicated the range of Thomas's scholarly readings and studies: Ortolani was working on eco-psychology; Grim on comparative shamanisms and healing practices; and Brown on the Buddhist concept of the Tathagatagarbha, a womblike potential for enlightenment in all sentient beings.[45]

The memorable events of this time together were the intense intellectual exchanges at mealtimes, sometimes with guests who gave talks at the Riverdale Center. The sun porch room with its dappled light next to the great red oak was the site of many gatherings. During this year, Thomas's ideas on ecology began to develop further. A recurrent topic for discussion was the degradation of the environment and the inability of major sectors of our societies— educational, religious, political, legal, or economic—to address these issues sufficiently. To ease the intensity of these conversations, they would often listen to classical music after dinner. Thomas especially enjoyed Beethoven's *Archduke Trio Concerto* and Mozart's *Magic Flute*. On Good Friday, the students would come together to listen to Bach's *Passion* and share a vegetarian meal of ratatouille. The sunset over the Hudson River was a fitting backdrop for these nourishing gatherings.

At the end of the Golden Year, on December 17, 1978, Brian Edward Brown wrote a poem to commemorate his time at the Riverdale Center, before he departed to be married to another of Thomas's students, Amarylis Cortijo, in Puerto Rico:

> "Oh Watchman, What of the Night?"
> Unfinished thesis, finished for the night
> I wander down stairs in this house that has been my home.
> I have known its silence before in a year of nights
> and have haunted its rooms often at this hour of favored quiet.
> But tonight, like an improper Buddhist, I stand warmed
> by the memories of enchanted months, shamelessly, flagrantly moved by
>   their passing.

The red-tiled entrance, lit for the night,
reflects now the images of how many departures . . . for the Seychelles
     and Los Angeles,
for Toronto and Louisville, for Washington and Greensboro, Detroit
     and San Francisco.
What enthusiastic journeyings of happy goodbyes!
The casual corduroy prophet of earth's wisdom and heaven's goodness,
of passports forgotten, of a bag with only books, of detachment's mirth at
     the prospect
of the challenge and the relish of the audacious phrase.

To the left, in the great, dark-wooded room
the Chinese and Christian fathers sit in their shelves of green and purple,
exchanging the muted silence of their common mystery.
A paneled hugeness—it is empty now of its May-time volumes, the
     scattered lore of
a universe piled deep and wide across its table, awaiting the magic distil-
     lation that
would become June's conference.

And its ceilinged solemnity still pales at the revered Benedictine of
     a summer's eve,
impervious to the gentle demands of an immense magnitude,
the spirituality of starry energies eclipsing the
shameful boundaries of so impoverished a monasticism.

A few steps beyond, and China and Japan expansively lie before me,
along their wall of moonlight. While the Hindus and Buddhists are
     patient in an
appropriate modesty, sharing shadowy space with myths and symbols,
     Dante and Blake.
It is a room of rare texts and of Brittanic knowledge, yet somehow,
only the antechamber, the passageway to the site of my most attentive
     scholarship,
my most frequent inspiration, my warmest and most constant laughter.

Multi-glassed prism, reflecting onto rock and river,
I have known such a gladness in you
That will warm me in my going and lure me to my return.
    I have sat at your table of frequent polishings and only reticent shines
    through lunches and dinners of quartets and sonatas, concertos
    and symphonies, hearing beyond these-only-partial strains, the
    song of the spheres, the wondrous movements of time's
        transformations,
    through the voice of earth's sage, my spirit's father, my heart's friend.

Greenhouse porch of my imagination's growth, I have sat dumbly
for a year like one of your potted plants, content merely to listen with
geologians and bishops, technicians and planners, contemplatives and
        artists,
engineers and scientists, dearest friends and fellow students.
    Content to root in my mind's soil
    the vision and the challenge, the perspective and the approach,
    to be schooled in the responsibility and energized by the tireless
        dedication.
Though you have been a room of the most sublime idea and critical
        thought,
of the most sober evaluation and urgent quest,
I shall stand in the breeze of the Caribbean night
still smiling with the constant laughter of your year's grace.

The sky is pale with moon and stars, and as I turn to go,
instinctively I hear the question of night's sentinel, holding its branches
        protectively
for this house that has been my home. A question posed nightly as
        I stood for a year
and shared its rooted stillness, before sleep,

    "Oh watchman, what of the night?"

A time of memories and their tears,
of ideals and enthusiasms,
of deepest admiration and warmest gratitude,
of affectionate welcomes,

          and happy goodbyes.

CHAPTER 6

From New Story to Universe Story

In 1970 I established the Riverdale Center for Religious Research in the north-west corner of New York City along the east bank of the Hudson River, a center dedicated to the study of the more comprehensive forces determining the course of history. While this center began as a concern for the cultural formation of the human and the inter-relation of cultures with each other, it shifted in a few years toward a study of the devastating impact of industrial culture on the survival of the planet and on the future of the human. Human-Earth relations became the essential issue. It was immediately apparent that any damage or any loss of the outer world of nature was a loss to the inner world of the human. A desolate outer world immediately produces a desolate inner world. The loss of the primordial forest is a loss of the soul in the human, since the way to the sacred is through the place of our dwelling.

Thomas Berry, An Appalachian View

RIVERDALE CENTER FOR RELIGIOUS RESEARCH

The Golden Year from the summer of 1977 to the summer of 1978 was a highlight of Thomas's many years of teaching, writing, and speaking. Much of this was made possible by the integrated setting of home and hearth that he created at Riverdale, where a community of people emerged who were inspired by the beauty of the setting and the efficacy of the ideas that were born there.

6.1 Riverdale Center for Religious Research and the great red oak in winter.
Gretchen McHugh, courtesy of J Murray McHugh

With the move to Fordham in 1966, Thomas came to live that summer in the newly built Passionist Retreat House on Riverdale Avenue in the Bronx.[1] It was a large institutional building next to the Hebrew Home for the Aged, a Jewish retirement home. Up the street, to the north, was Mt. St. Vincent College, where Thomas would occasionally lecture. A half mile to the south was Wave Hill, the former Toscanini estate, where the ecologist Rene Dubos founded a Center for Human Environment.[2] In 1971, Thomas began to hold his June conferences at the retreat house, as it could easily accommodate the hundred people or so who attended. Set on fourteen acres overlooking the Hudson River, it was an inspirational venue for conferences and gatherings of students.

Next to the retreat house was a striking four-story Victorian home owned by the Passionists.[3] After several years of asking, in 1970 Thomas was granted permission and funding by the Passionists to establish a research center there.[4] With the help of some members of the order, the first two floors of the house were renovated to accommodate his library and conference space, as well as overnight visitors. The third floor had rooms for those who lived at the Center.

In the summer of 1974, Thomas moved in with his books while the renovation was being completed.[5] He had a feeling of enthusiasm and great anticipation with this move. In the early years he received indispensable administrative assistance from Passionist Brother Dan Sheridan, who was also a History of Religions PhD student at Fordham. Later, Passionist Brother Conrad Federspeil lived at Riverdale for fifteen years and helped Thomas in a variety of ways—caring for the property, planting trees, creating a passive solar porch, and cooking meals.

Thomas named this house the Riverdale Center for Religious Research. It was situated on a knoll facing west, with splendid views of the Hudson River and the Palisades beyond. These rock cliffs, 200 million years old, gave depth to Thomas's musings on geological time and the age of the Earth. As the sun set behind these cliffs, a soft orange glow spread over the house and filled the sun porch where visitors gathered for food and conversation. Held in a liminal moment of ancient rock, flooded with shimmering light, these gatherings reverberated with the rippling river reflections below.

6.2 Brother Conrad Federspeil lived at the Riverdale Center from 1979 to 1995.
Gretchen McHugh, courtesy of J. Murray McHugh

THE GREAT RED OAK

Just off the sun porch, behind the house, stood a four-hundred-year-old red oak. Thomas would often muse that Henry Hudson could have seen this tree when he sailed up the river in the sixteenth century. The oak was a captivating presence, drawing people to marvel at its age, its size, and its beauty. The trunk was so large that it required seven people to circle it. Its branches stretched nearly the breadth of the building, some sixty feet wide, and it towered over the house. From the fourth-floor attic, there was a small balcony perched in the high reaches of the red oak branches. In the summer, its shade was a welcome balm for visitors; in the fall, the squirrels gathered its acorns for storage; in the winter, its stark silhouette against the snow inspired many a poem; and in the spring, it invariably attracted nesting birds. Its location behind the Riverdale Center provided a setting for magnificent views of the river and its ever-changing currents.

The red oak became a guardian spirit for the Center and an inspiring presence for Thomas. In later years, he saw that its health was ensured by expert arborist care and its massive branches were held steady by cables. Many gatherings

6.3 Looking up through the great red oak.
Judith Emery

took place under those branches, sometimes prompted by a celebration, such as a student's birthday or a child's baptism.[6] There was a bench near the tree where Thomas often sat to view the Hudson. There, visitors would draw up chairs to reflect with him, accompanied by a mug of coffee in the afternoon and a glass of wine in the evening. Watching the sunset was a favorite pastime for Thomas and his students. The inspiration provided by the venue and the vista was palpable for all who came out of the flurry of New York City or from other parts of the country or the world. Being at the Riverdale Center gave some sense of how the built and natural environments blended into one another. Not only the massive red oak tree, but in time many beautiful trees and bushes were planted on the property by Brother Conrad. Together Thomas and Conrad identified the species of all of the trees. The oak, in particular, provided a feeling of endurance for the work ahead. Thomas dedicated his first book on the environment, *The Dream of the Earth*, to the great red oak, recognizing that the book's essays were written under its sheltering branches.

A BEACON

With the red oak as a guardian spirit, the house grew into a vibrant intellectual center with Thomas at its heart. It became a beacon for travelers from North America and abroad, for academics and writers, and for innovative environmentalists and spiritual seekers. With Thomas's gracious welcoming presence, students and professors were housed, meetings and lectures were held, and lunches and dinners were hosted. Conversation and laughter filled the sun porch, and silence pervaded the library. The restorative rhythms of reflection and conviviality pervaded the rooms, touching those who lived or gathered there.

The Riverdale Center was a sanctuary for Thomas, as it provided both times of quiet and moments of companionship. His earlier monastic life now blossomed into the intermingling of silence and speech, reading and lecturing, and writing and publishing. All of this took place within the magnificent context of the deep geological time of the Palisades and the flowing estuary space of the Hudson River. It was in this house, abundant with books, and in this bioregion, redolent with history, that Thomas's most creative writing occurred. He describes his vision of the Center:

> The atmosphere created at the Center is not that of a meditation community, nor is it that of abstract intellectual analysis; it is rather an atmosphere of depth reflection on the great mysteries of reality and how humans are being spiritually transformed by their experience of these mysteries. The resources available here foster both a critical-analytical mentality of intense intellectual activity as well as a communion of the rational mind with the depths of the unconscious as this is revealed in religious symbols as well as in the arts and in literature.[7]

THE RIVERDALE LIBRARY

Thus, Thomas established the Riverdale Center as a place for reflection on history—human, biological, geological, and cosmological. The library of nearly 10,000 books signaled the breadth of his explorations. He had gathered the books over several decades of teaching and writing with help from scholars in Asia, North America, and Europe, and he continued to add to the collection during his nearly thirty years in Riverdale. The majority of the volumes were on human cultures as expressed in religion, art, symbols, and texts. The range was breathtaking: the Church Fathers and the Chinese sages in the front conference room; primary scriptures from South Asian religious traditions and arts in the seminar room; Western history, theology, and psychology in the hall; Native American writers and ethnographies upstairs. Many of the classical texts were in their original languages of Latin, Sanskrit, or Chinese. Reference works were also available, including encyclopedias, dictionaries, bibliographies, and histories. The workroom on the first floor was lined with books on ecology and cosmology, which Thomas read voraciously. He was integrating his study of the cosmology of religions with his readings on life systems and processes in the universe, including books on science and technology. He was rethinking the human story as embedded in the larger evolutionary story of Earth and the universe.

In a founding document about the Riverdale Center, Thomas wrote:

> Our method of study is principally the cultural-historical method. We wish
> to establish an awareness of human spiritual development. Back of the human
> venture, however, there is the living process of the Earth itself. Thus we wish
> to associate our work with the study of the Earth, with the emergence of
> life, the appearance of humans, the cultural formation of traditional societies,
> with the recent scientific-technological revolution in human affairs, and with
> the ecological equilibrium, which is being sought in the future.[8]

THE RISE OF ENVIRONMENTALISM

It was at Riverdale that Thomas enlarged his study of world religions and cultures to include the study of ecology and cosmology. He began to see human cultures within the context of ecosystems and bioregions as well as within geological
and cosmological time. In addition, his readings in ecology moved him toward
a deepening concern for the environment. He had already been pondering the
alienation of humans from nature that he had observed much earlier:

> While I was living in Jamaica, Long Island, during the 1950s, I was extending
> my concern for the loss of the natural world that was taking place. I gave a
> talk at this time to a group of scholars concerned with science and philoso-
> phy at a conference center outside of Pittsburgh. I had been much concerned
> with the alienation of human life from contact with the natural world. One
> of my moments of realization of how different my thoughts were, was when
> I pointed out that human alienation from the natural world could only lead
> to increasing mental and emotional stress, with all the emotional and moral
> breakup and social disturbance that this would involve, as well as intellectual
> alienation from the more intimate experience of the natural world that was
> at the base of all human thinking.
>
> Excessive releasing of human affairs into the control of scientific and tech-
> nological processes would end in an intellectual as well as a human impasse.
> The almost universal negative response of the group was something of a shock
> to me. I was seen as anti-science, anti-technology. The person who supported

me most fully was Ernst Winter, an exceptional person, the first person I ever met who had seen the need of restoring the earlier peasant village contact with the land. He had written his dissertation at Columbia University on the peasantry of Europe and their place in the social-political life of Europe.

Winter's concern with the soil was something more than academic, since he was at the time growing the greater amount of the food that his family was eating by gardening a two-acre plot of land on the west bank of the Hudson River in the New City area not far from Nyack, New York. At the same time he was directing the political science department at Iona College in New Rochelle.

After I had spoken, we talked for some time and he took me over to a wheat field nearby where he showed me the corn that looked so healthy from a distance, but if looked at up close a person could see that the growth in its leafing was defective. He later showed me a book written in German that was making the point that the chemical poisoning of the land was a dangerous process that would eventually have serious consequences for humans. (*Goldenrod*, 85–86)T

Thomas was thus drawn to address the growing ecological crisis as he saw its destructive effects on humans and ecosystems: pollution of air, water, soil; toxicities seeping into the tissues of all species; biodiversity loss on a massive scale; climate change resulting in rising seas. Rachel Carson's book, *Silent Spring*, marked a significant turn toward environmental awakening in 1962, and the Santa Barbara oil spill in 1969 heightened environmental activism. As Thomas was establishing the Riverdale Center in 1970, the first Earth Day was held and the U.S. Environmental Protection Agency (EPA) was created. Two years later, the first United Nations Conference on the Human Environment took place in Stockholm. The Clean Water, Clean Air, and Endangered Species Acts were all passed at this time. There was a growing response by government and civil society to these problems, but Thomas sensed that something more was needed:

So, after the Center was founded, the focus of attention shifted to the ecology issue. Already, I was studying the manner in which the various traditions established their human rapport with the natural world. By 1972, when the Stockholm Conference had been held, I saw this as the immediate and comprehensive purpose of the Center. This was the year also when the book *The Limits to Growth* appeared and the statement was made quite plainly that exponential rates of growth in using the resources of the Earth could not long continue. These developments occurred exactly ten years after the book of Rachel Carson entitled *Silent Spring* and its identifying the damage that DDT was doing to the life systems of the planet, especially to the bird species.

(*Goldenrod*, 98)

Some two decades later, Thomas was to become acquainted with members of the Club of Rome, a distinguished group of leaders who published *The Limits to Growth*. He was also invited by the systems theorist Ervin Laszlo to be part of the Club of Budapest. But first he focused on the challenge of living locally.

BIOREGIONALISM AND THE HUDSON RIVER VALLEY

During this period, Thomas participated in the shaping of the bioregional movement. This movement was conceptualized at the UN conference in Stockholm and launched in San Francisco when Peter Berg and Gary Snyder formed the Planet Drum Foundation in 1973. They encouraged reinhabiting local regions, as Snyder was doing in the foothills of the Sierras near Nevada City, California. Across North America, various bioregional groups grew up as watersheds, woodlands, and mountains became defining places for forming natural ecological communities. Thomas gave eloquence and depth to this movement in his talks and his writing. He defined a bioregion as

an identifiable geographic area of interacting life systems that is relatively self-sustaining in the ever-renewing processes of nature. The full diversity of life functions is carried out, not as individuals or as species, or even as organic beings, but as a community that includes the physical as well as the organic components of the region. Such a bioregion is a self-propagating, self-nourishing, self-educating, self-governing, self-healing, and self-fulfilling community. Each of the component life systems must integrate its own functioning within this community to survive in any effective manner. [9]

Thomas was much influenced by bioregional historians, artists, ecologists, and activists, especially those committed to telling the story of the Hudson River valley.[10] In the nineteenth century, the Hudson River School of artists, which included Thomas Cole, Albert Bierstadt, and Frederick Church, painted the beauty of the river and its environs as an expression of the sublime in nature. This romantic view resonated deeply with Thomas. While he lived at the Riverdale Center, the river was the focus of several environmental struggles, including concern over a proposed plant on Storm King Mountain, PCB pollution by General Electric, the Indian Point nuclear power plant, and rebuilding the West Side highway in New York City.

Environmental organizations, such as Scenic Hudson and Riverkeeper, were established to protect the river. Scenic Hudson led a seventeen-year legal battle to stop Consolidated Edison from building the world's largest pump storage hydroelectric plant on the face of Storm King Mountain, a place of iconic beauty along the river. The suit, which ushered in the era of citizens' environmentalism and the role of environmental law, was won in 1981. Two years later, John Cronin became the first Riverkeeper, a position that is now replicated on hundreds of rivers. Others, such as Robert Kennedy Jr., took legal action against polluters of the river. Both Kennedy and Cronin came to know Thomas and were deeply inspired by his bioregional vision.[11]

Working with these groups and individuals who were protecting the river, Thomas helped to create a Hudson River bioregional "bundle." This was a collection of published materials and maps that celebrated the spirit of the Hudson River by drawing on the medicine bundle traditions among Native peoples of the North American continent. Such traditions brought together in a cloth or skin bundle elements such as plants, stones, seeds, or feathers for healing.

In 1979, just as Thomas was retiring from Fordham, David Haenke issued a call for the first North American Bioregional Conference.[12] This was held in the spring of 1984 in the Ozarks near Excelsior Springs in Missouri.[13] Two hundred people gathered from all over the United States. Thomas was active in the planning of the conference, and the Riverdale Center was a cosponsor. For his keynote talk, Thomas delivered his paper on bioregionalism to great critical acclaim.[14]

THE RIVERDALE PAPERS AND *THE DREAM OF THE EARTH*

In response to invitations to give talks or attend conferences, Thomas began writing papers on the growing ecological challenges. These were then typed by his assistant Eileen Doyle, mimeographed, and bound into blue-covered books called the Riverdale Papers. They became a treasure trove of original insights and synthesizing perspectives. Multiple versions of his essays emerged during these years, as Thomas revised them for different talks and updated them with his latest ideas. For example, the "Twelve Principles" were arranged in different sequences and altered. In 1984, when Thomas turned seventy, his students purchased his first computer with funds they raised with help from his supporters, led by Fanny de Bary. The number of versions of the essays increased as they became easier to change or adapt for different contexts.

Thomas would give these Riverdale Papers away to visitors or accept a small fee for mailing them to people. People were hungry for his interpretive framework, which attended to both local and global communities. His ideas were expressed most succinctly and eloquently in essay form rather than in longer monographs or systematic tomes. He wished to avoid a scholarly approach that was burdened with academic language, theories, or footnotes. Rather, he spoke directly to the imagination, envisioning possibilities of another way forward.

Early versions of some of these essays were edited by the dedicated secretary of the Teilhard Association, Winifred McCulloch. These were published in the *Teilhard Newsletter*, later called the *Teilhard Perspective*. It was during these Riverdale years that the journal *Cross Currents* was being edited by Joseph and Sally Cunneen and William and Mary Louise Birmingham, who published some of the well-known contemporary European thinkers, making them accessible to an American audience. As admirers of Thomas's ideas, they were also helpful in publishing a number of his early essays in *Cross Currents* (*Goldenrod*, 86).[15]

For nearly three decades at Riverdale, Thomas's essays grew into eleven blue books. These were eventually edited and published in his iconic monographs: *The Dream of the Earth* (1988), *The Great Work* (1999), *Evening Thoughts* (2006),

The Sacred Universe (2009), and *The Christian Future and the Fate of Earth* (2009).[16]
The Dream of the Earth, originally published by the Sierra Club, was his first book
on the environment. In many ways this became a signature volume with some
of Thomas's key visionary essays: "The Earth Community," "Creative Energy,"
"The Ecological Age," and "The New Story." In addition, Thomas included papers
on such topics as economics, technology, bioregionalism, and patriarchy. Theory
and practice were blended; bold vision and practical work were interwoven.
The publication of this book was celebrated at Riverdale and well beyond. It
sold over 100,000 copies, went into multiple reprints, and received a Lannan
Literary Award in 1995. In a reprinting in 2015, leading environmentalists provided endorsements:

> "With this classic book, Thomas Berry broke crucial new ground in the
> human relationship with the planet. Its ripples will spread for generations
> to come."
>
> —Bill McKibben, author of *Hope, Human and Wild*

> "*The Dream of the Earth* is a landmark. There is no wiser or more hopeful guide
> through the years ahead."
>
> David Orr, creator of Adam Lewis Center, Oberlin College

> "Thomas Berry brings us into the presence of the entire cosmic order, of
> body-earth-body, and with his hand on the pulse—on ours and on what he
> calls 'the basic structure and functioning of the Earth,' we re-find the deep
> interior, the 'Everywhere'."
>
> —Gretel Ehrlich, author of *Facing the Wave*

> ". . . . a profoundly important and contemplative vision of how we should
> relate to this privileged planet which nurtured the rise of civilization. . . ."
>
> —Thomas E. Lovejoy, Blue Planet Prize Laureate 2012

Part of the iconic nature of *The Dream of the Earth* is Thomas's comprehensive
historical perspective and his insight into present challenges. These essays are

6.4 Thomas Berry at Riverdale.
Gretchen McHugh, courtesy of J. Murray McHugh

accessible to a broad public as well as engaged scholars—a combination that is as original as it is rare. This book is not a science or policy book, but rather one that draws on the sciences, the humanities, and the social sciences for fresh insight. "The New Story," in particular, became a basis for further work, namely, *The Universe Story* book and *The Journey of the Universe* film and book.[17]

A NEW STORY EMERGES

It was in 1978 that Thomas first published his path-breaking essay "The New Story" where he called for a coming together of science and the humanities to narrate the great epic of evolution. Much of Thomas's later writings arose out of this essay, which was in response to "the devastating impact of industrial culture on the survival of the planet and on the future of the human."[18] For Thomas, renewed human-Earth relations became the essential challenge. He sought to articulate a comprehensive evolutionary context for these relations. However, he recognized that many people, including scientists, were unable to experience or articulate a sense of connection to the Earth:

> I could now identify the pathology of the modern western world as its inability to relate to the natural world. My generation, the generation born in the earlier years of the twentieth century, had been locked within itself without any feeling for or intimacy with the surrounding universe. That scientists could be so completely unmoved by the magnificence of their own discoveries, this was and remains to me, an inexplicable phenomenon. Perhaps scientists have had such difficulty detaching themselves from the fixations of traditional views that they have felt it important to say, as one scientist [Steven Weinberg] has said after writing one of the most profound books ever written on the earliest moments of the universe, that the more we understand the universe, the less point it seems to have.[19]

For Thomas, however, the powers of the natural world were ever present; the allure of the cosmos penetrated his psyche. He understood the interior presence of things.[20] He was enveloped in the universe, pervaded by its dynamic forces. Captivated by a desire to speak of the livingness of things, he yearned to give voice to the flow of evolutionary time. He wrote: "With all the inadequacies of any narrative, the epic of evolution does present the story of the universe, as this story is now available to us out of our present experience. This is our sacred story. It is our way of dealing with the ultimate mystery whence all things come into being."[21]

The epic story of evolution began in the Riverdale years with Thomas's initial call for a "New Story" in 1978; it was articulated by Thomas with Brian Thomas Swimme in *The Universe Story* in 1992. This book brought fulfillment to Thomas's early desire, even as a young person, to respond to the challenges of economic growth and unrestrained progress in the newly industrializing South. Something was needed to move away from the allurement of consumerism. A new story could help humans participate in the dream of the Earth. Through Thomas's decade of creative work with Brian, an integrating epic of evolution became available for restoring the Earth community.

> This was the culmination of my childhood concern for the beauty and grandeur and wonder of the world. My study of indigenous peoples and their remarkable sensitivity to the surrounding universe, my study of the great classical civilizations, my study of western culture: all conformed to the same understanding—the immersion of the human in the world of nature was also immersion in the world of the sacred. Every being of planet Earth, even of the entire universe, was participant in the grand liturgy of the universe that I had for so many years celebrated in my earlier years of monastic seclusion.[22]

It was during this period at Riverdale that Thomas's mother passed away, in May of 1980. She had been a guiding force in awakening his sense of awe and beauty as a child. Now this sensibility was giving birth to a healing story for future generations.

BECOMING A "GEOLOGIAN" IN THE ECOZOIC ERA

It was also at this time that Thomas gradually moved from identifying himself as a cultural historian to something more encompassing. His graduate school focus had been on Western cultural history, and his later studies included Asian and indigenous cultural history and traditions. People who were unfamiliar with his intellectual breadth wanted to describe Thomas as a theologian, but he insisted that his studies and his approaches were not sectarian or shaped by one perspective, such as that of a theologian who is dedicated to the study of the Christian tradition. Nor was he committed to framing his sense of the sacred in categories drawn solely from Christian theology. He was trying to see himself as part of a narrative that was much larger than two thousand years of Christian history and religion. He wanted to be immersed in deep time, what Loren Eiseley called "The Immense Journey."[23] One event that marked this shift took place as he flew back from a conference in the Seychelles in 1978. Flying 30,000 feet above the Nile River and reflecting on the depths of evolutionary time, he came to call himself a "geologian."

In this respect, the geology of the Hudson River bioregion in which Thomas lived also helped to shape his thinking about the significance of evolutionary time and geological eras. He observed how the majestic Palisade cliffs were formed at the end of the Triassic period 200 million years ago when molten magma was thrust upward into sandstone. This material cooled as it came to the surface. Water gradually eroded the softer sandstone, forming the column-like structure of the rocks visible today. Thomas noted that the great geological upheaval at the end of the Triassic gave rise to an extinction period that was considered the most severe such period after the Permian extinction 250 million years ago, also called the "Great Dying."

Thomas would brood on these explosive movements in Earth's history, the destruction of life out of which new forms eventually emerged. He mourned the current extinction period during which biodiversity was rapidly being lost around the planet. Thomas sensed that this sixth extinction period would, like the five other mass extinctions, alter the course of evolution for all time and result in the loss of irreplaceable beauty and wonder.[24] He also lamented the potential weakening of the genetic inheritance of life by such an extensive winnowing of biodiversity.

This sixth extinction is not due to geological disruptions, but rather to human overreach: the rapid population explosion, the increased extractive capacities of human technologies, and a massive rise in global consumption. Early on Thomas had seen the callous disregard for bioregions and the soaring extinction rate of life forms in the contemporary period as marking the end of a geological era. The Cenozoic period, the last 65 million years of Earth's history when life blossomed into abundant forms, was now being transformed into a new period due to human impact. Thomas made this observation several decades before discussions began about the "Anthropocene era," which is said to mark the end of the Holocene, namely, the last 10,000–12,000 years of human cultures.[25]

Thomas's response to this large change was to indicate that humans could still recover human-Earth relations in a mutually enhancing way. He coined the terms *Ecological age* and, later, *Ecozoic era* to reflect his hope that humans would awaken to their disconnection from Earth processes and reestablish ways of living that would ensure the flourishing of life. He knew he would have to journey into deep evolutionary time to bring back a healing vision for this new era. And he sensed he would be able to do this when he met Brian.

MEETING BRIAN THOMAS SWIMME

When Thomas returned from Chicago in the deep winter of 1981, he walked into the Riverdale Center and announced with a twinkle in his eye, "I have met my Plato." He had discovered someone who could record his dialogues and teachings and thus make them available for posterity. Brian was a younger scholar in science who immediately understood Thomas's idea of the need for a story of evolution. Brian was equally frustrated by the inability of academia to respond to the growing ecological crisis. A year before, he had left a tenure-track job in the Pacific Northwest because he saw that science was being co-opted for research that had primarily commercial or military purposes. He wanted no part of it. Like Thomas, he felt that universities were, by and large, inadvertently preparing students to participate in the disruption of the ecosystems that had evolved over billions of years, producing an astonishing florescence of life forms. He also sensed that a new story was needed.

Thomas wrote about his first encounter with Brian: "Immediately we seemed to understand each other and were able to contribute significantly to each other in our thoughts concerned with the origin, structure, and functioning of the physical universe and the role of the human in the universe."[26] He reflected on Brian's unique qualities:

> While my meeting with the thought of Teilhard was decisive in my life what I gained from him did not come to its full expression in my own mind until my meeting with Brian Swimme. . . . Brian was far more advanced in his cosmological thinking than was Teilhard although he found it not difficult apparently to accept those basic views of Teilhard that I had adopted.
>
> (*Goldenrod*, 65 and 66)

Shortly after their winter meeting in Chicago, Thomas invited Brian to come to study with him for the academic year 1982–83. Thomas reflected many years later: "That Brian agreed to come was indeed a fateful decision for me, possibly for both of us" (*Goldenrod*, 66). That summer Brian moved east, settling into an apartment in Mt. Kisco, New York, with his wife, Denise, and their young son, Thomas, who had been named after Thomas. This locale was within easy reach of the Riverdale Center, where Thomas and Brian met each week. Brian absorbed the books Thomas gave him, and they began discussing ways to move forward with their shared concerns. In June 1983 their collaboration blossomed into a jointly delivered Riverdale summer conference on this New Story. From then on they began giving talks across the United States and Canada, from the Cathedral of St. John the Divine in New York, to the Centre for Ecology and Spirituality at Port Burwell in Canada, to the Institute for Culture and Creation Spirituality at Holy Names College in Oakland, California, to the California Institute of Integral Studies in San Francisco.

Over the next decade this collaboration resulted in the first telling of the epic of evolution in *The Universe Story*.[27] It was a partnership born of deep concern for the world's environmental challenges and with a shared conviction that story is what moves people to change. Thomas recognized that all of the religions of the world tell their stories as cosmologies. These cosmologies arise not from some abstract realm, but from intimate human interactions and the Earth systems themselves. They give humans a sense of belonging and purpose, providing reflections on such basic questions as: Where do I come from? Why am I here?

6.5 Thomas Berry and Brian Thomas Swimme at the Field Museum in Chicago at the Epic of Evolution Conference in 1997, sponsored by the American Association for the Advancement of Science.

Courtesy of Brian Thomas Swimme

What can I contribute? For Brian and Thomas, these questions became an under-lying basis for their ongoing Socratic dialogues. They sought a "functional" cos-mology that would give humans an integral vision of how they could participate in the healing of the Earth. In using the term *functional*, they were suggesting that this story would inspire people to engage in the Great Work of transformative ecological and social change, such as by developing organic farms, eco-cities, eco-logical economics, or environmental education.

SAN FRANCISCO VISITS

Brian moved back to California in the summer of 1983 to teach and write, and Thomas traveled several times a year to the San Francisco Bay area to visit Brian and give lectures. They spent hours talking together in the sunlit beauty of Walnut Creek near Brian's home. From morning coffee and breakfast to evening wine and dinner, they ranged across a wide variety of topics reflecting on our historical moment.

On these visits, Thomas shared his ideas with graduate students at the Insti-tute of Culture and Creation Spirituality (ICCS) at Holy Names College in Oakland, where Brian was teaching. Thomas thus had the opportunity also to be in dialogue with Matthew Fox, who directed the Institute.[28] Matt was an original thinker, a dynamic speaker, and a prolific writer on creation centered spirituality. Thomas and Brian's work on cosmology became a critical part of the Institute's curriculum.

After Matt moved on in 1991, the Institute was directed by Jim Conlon, a Canadian priest inspired by Thomas's work. Jim continued to engage Thomas and Brian for talks and organized lively summer sessions on the universe story.[29] When Brian began to teach at the California Institute of Integral Studies (CIIS) in San Francisco in 1989, he worked to create a Center for the Story of the Universe (CSU) with his close college friend, Bruce Bochte. Thomas spoke there frequently as well, reaching new audiences. Over a decade of these lectures, Thomas came in touch with many well-known thinkers and environmentalists in the Bay area, such as Charlene Spretnak, Joanna Macy, Theodore Roszak, and Duane Elgin, who became influenced by his ideas.

SOCRATIC DIALOGUES RECORDED

Even though San Francisco is a creative wellspring of people and projects, Brian often reflected that it was his year in New York that nurtured him into his various innovative endeavors. He found the vibrant intellectual community at the Riverdale Center to be unique, indeed unsurpassed. Because of this experience, he was able to realize the shared dream of delivering his Socratic dialogues with Thomas to a larger audience. Two years after meeting Thomas, he did this with his first book, *The Universe Is a Green Dragon*. In it, he recreated some of the illuminating conversations he had with Thomas at the Broadway Diner in Riverdale.[30] Thomas reflected on this book: "The lyric style of the writing, the intimate communication to the reader, the vision of the universe expounded, the clarity and authenticity of the scientific data, all these qualities of the little book established Brian as someone with unique competence in presenting the mystery and the magic of the universe that we experience all about us" (*Goldenrod*, 66) Brian was able to articulate in an engaging style many of Thomas's insights into the nature of the universe:

> To live in an awareness that the powers that created the Earth reflect on themselves through us. That's why we are discussing the night sky, the sea, and the land. Each of these reveals cosmic powers that we are to have and become. We are to live as alluring and remembering activity, as shimmering sensitivity.[31]

Brian further explicated and developed Thomas's "Twelve Principles of the Universe" in a widely acclaimed video series, *The Canticle to the Cosmos* (1990). Brian's twelve lectures in this series reached thousands of people in North America and abroad. They planted the seeds for Thomas's ideas to be more readily understood, and they became a foundation for *The Universe Story*. Filtered through Brian's scientific knowledge, poetic sensibilities, and infectious enthusiasm, this new understanding of cosmology was becoming more widely available.

In January 1990, this collaboration resulted in an animated gathering at Santa Sabina conference center in San Rafael, California.[32] A group of twenty-seven people were given a first draft of the *Universe Story*.[33] Then, for several days they discussed the manuscript while Brian and Thomas took notes and responded. This was an enlivening moment for all the participants. Indeed, at the conclusion Thomas reflected, "This is the first time in a long time that I have felt some signs of hope for our future." Something new came into being at Santa Sabina.[34] Yet it would take Thomas and Brian another two years to revise the manuscript for publication.

The Universe Story took a decade to write and shifted the contours of thinking about evolution as a story, not simply as a series of mechanistic or random events. To do this work required not only intense research with scientists, but also dialogue with other colleagues and supporters. Indeed, conversation partners arose in various communities, which then became key incubators of these new ideas. These included the Riverdale Center, Port Burwell, Genesis Farm, and the Cathedral of St. John the Divine. Riverdale was a place for a monthly lecture series and an annual June conference, Port Burwell in Canada was a summer venue for Thomas to speak and interact, Genesis Farm was a setting for grounding these ideas in a local Earth Literacy center, and the Cathedral was a place where an eco-spiritual community was born through the arts, music, and liturgy.

TEILHARDIAN CONTEXT

Fundamental to telling this cosmological story was the evolutionary worldview of Pierre Teilhard de Chardin (1981–1955), who inspired both Thomas and Brian.[35] Teilhard's reflections on the human as arising from the evolution of the universe and the Earth created a new context for considering the direction and purpose of human life. An understanding of this expanded framework, as described in chapter 10, is what Thomas and Brian hoped to awaken with *The Universe Story*, which is told within a Teihardian evolutionary perspective and woven with the threads of a mythic story.

Thomas noted, "The three main teachings of Teilhard that influenced me most profoundly were: that the universe from its beginning had a psychic-spiritual as well as a physical-material dimension; that the human story and the universe story are a single story; that western religious thinking needed to move from an almost exclusive concern for redemption to a greater emphasis on creation."[36] This insight implied that matter and spirit evolve together; that humans arise from within evolution; and that care for the Earth, rather than escape from it, is essential.

TEILHARD LECTURE SERIES AT RIVERDALE: 1978–1993

It was during the Riverdale years that a close-knit community emerged in which this cosmological thinking could develop. For fifteen years, a monthly Teilhard lecture series was held at the Riverdale Center, organized by Mary Evelyn Tucker and John Grim. The speakers ranged from distinguished scientists, such as Norman Newell from the American Museum of Natural History, to environmentalists and activists, such as Niconar Perlas from the Philippines.[37] During the year he spent in New York studying with Thomas, Brian assiduously attended these lectures and spoke at one of them.

The lecture series soon created a lively community around Thomas Berry that supported and reflected on his emerging ideas on the universe story. Each Saturday afternoon a lecture was followed by a potluck supper, which gave newcomers a chance to meet people and graduate students an opportunity to share their ideas in an informal setting. Every November, Thomas was the speaker, and afterwards the group would celebrate his birthday. These gatherings added to the strong bonding that developed among Teilhardians and the Fordham graduate students. Indeed, more than a few marriages emerged from these years together. Several couples went on to teach, practice medicine, or do environmental work.

The Riverdale community expanded each June when Thomas would give a two-day conference at the Passionist retreat house next door. These conferences were open to the public, and usually a hundred people attended. Topics included the following: The Spiritual Significance of the Counter Culture, 1971; Transformation Symbolism, 1972; The Writings of Carlos Castaneda, 1973; Visions of the Future, 1974, Contemporary Spirituality, 1975; Energy: The Cosmic Human Process, 1976; New York as Sacred City, 1977; The Lower Hudson River Basin as Bioregional Community, 1978; and the New Story, 1983. The conference room table at the Riverdale Center was covered with books for months in advance as Thomas prepared his lectures. People would come from great distances to hear him speak and to interact with him at meals. Watching the sunset over the Palisades before the evening lecture was always a highlight.

HOLY CROSS CENTRE COLLOQUIA: 1979–2000

Another supportive community developed in Canada. For four days each July from 1979 to 2000, Thomas would travel to the Passionists' Holy Cross Centre for Ecology and Spirituality, located in Port Burwell on Lake Erie in Ontario, Canada, on a beautiful fifty-five-acre site with a woodlot, meadow, and beach. In Thomas's early visits to Port Burwell, he led two small retreats, the first for the staff of Holy Cross Centre in 1979 and the second for Centre associates in 1980.[38]

Based on the appeal of these retreats, a decision was made to hold an annual summer colloquium on the topic of ecology and religion, which took place for the next two decades until 2000. At each colloquium, Thomas interacted with theologians, intellectuals, artists, environmentalists, and other public figures on a broad range of issues. Like the Riverdale Center, this was a perfect summer environment for Thomas to continue to develop his ideas. In a relaxed lakeside setting, people gathered for several days of talks and discussions. Stephen Dunn, with the help of Cenacle Sister Anne Lonergan, organized these colloquia and hosted visitors from across Canada, the United States, and abroad. Dunn, who had met and been inspired by Thomas during their time together at Immaculate Conception Monastery in the mid-1950s, was now a professor of theology at St. Michael's College at the University of Toronto and had become a major supporter of Thomas's work. Indeed, he was one of the few Passionists to understand the significance of Thomas's ideas early on. People gathered at Burwell from across North America and from Ireland, England, Australia, Korea, and the Philippines. International students also came from the University of Toronto program in theology and ecology that Steve had created.

A high point of this series was in 1986, when Brian Swimme and Thomas spoke on this New Story to more than a hundred people. Twice that number gathered with Thomas and Brian in 1993 to celebrate the publication of *The Universe Story*. Another landmark colloquium was in 1990, when Thomas was in conversation

6.6 Stephen Dunn, C.P., with Jai-Don Lee receiving his PhD at the University of Toronto in 2004. Father Lee has pioneered the work of Thomas Berry in Korea, especially through translations of his writings.

Dennis O'Hara

with Thomas Clarke, S.J., a prominent author in the field of social justice and liberation theology.[39] This is one of the few times that Thomas spoke about the theological implications of his thinking, as he wanted his ideas to be available to a wide range of people beyond Christianity. These conversations were published in 1991 as a book and a video series titled *Befriending the Earth: A Theology of Reconciliation Between Humans and the Earth.* The video series helped to make Thomas widely known in Canada, especially when it was aired on cable television. Thomas always returned to Riverdale reenergized from his presentations and discussions at Port Burwell.

Thomas also helped to inspire the Ecology Project at the Ignatius Jesuit Centre in Guelph, Ontario, which organized retreats on the mysticism of the Earth as linked to Ignatian spirituality. In addition, the Stations of the Cosmos were created there and were dedicated to Thomas on May 30, 2009, the day before he died.[40] They were based on the Stations of Our Cosmic Earth, which were originally created at Port Burwell and were then moved to St. Gabriel's Church in Toronto.

St. Gabriel's became the first green church in Toronto. Steve Dunn and Pastor Paul Cusack, C.P., were instrumental in helping the Passionists build this church at their parish in Toronto. The architect, Roberto Chiotti, was inspired by Thomas Berry's vision of an emerging Earth community.[41]

GENESIS FARM: 1980–PRESENT

Closer to home, a vibrant community that fostered Thomas's ideas was Genesis Farm in New Jersey, which arose out of the broad studies and visionary thinking of the Dominican sister Miriam Therese MacGillis. Miriam was introduced to Thomas during Easter week 1977 at a meeting at Maryknoll, New York, which was organized by Patricia and Gerry Mische, directors of Global Education Associates.[42] After hearing Thomas's talk, Miriam knew her worldview was forever changed. His lecture was titled "Contemplation and World Order"; Thomas turned this phrase around by asking the question: "What world order are you contemplating?" Miriam recalls the moment:

> That presentation . . . totally revolutionized my life. There were no books or films or websites in those days to which anyone could go for further study. We got in touch with Thomas who would kindly send us copies of papers he was developing and which he put together as the beginnings of the *Riverdale Papers*. . . . I devoured every one I could get my hands on. That was all there was.[43]

She began to study with Thomas at the Riverdale Center in 1978, the year he published his New Story essay.

Two years later, Miriam founded Genesis Farm in the beautiful bioregion of the Delaware Water Gap.[44] The farm had been donated to her order, the Dominican Sisters of Caldwell, New Jersey. They supported Miriam in establishing an ecological learning center in Blairstown on 226 acres of preserved farmland. The facilities to conduct programs and welcome visitors include two guest residences, a library and media and resource center, an art studio, and staff offices. In addition, two straw bale houses were built to model sustainable living. Genesis Farm and local community members founded the Community Supported Garden, which has over three hundred members. All of this was done with a commitment to both bioregionalism and the universe story. Thomas visited and lectured at Genesis Farm on numerous occasions and provided the intellectual and spiritual framework for Miriam's work there. She describes the mission in this way:

> Genesis Farm is dedicated to understanding the Universe and Earth as a single, unfolding process. The scientifically based story of the Universe offers profound insights into our public, personal and spiritual lives. Through its educational programs and its commitment to action, Genesis Farm has offered diverse and innovative experiences that inspire a comprehensive approach to personal and social change.[45]

Over the ensuing decades, people came from local towns and every continent on the planet to immerse themselves in Earth literacy at Genesis Farm. Many participated in the residential learning courses, which taught the science of the Universe Story and its varied implications for social change, ecology, and spirituality. Along with Miriam, Larry and Jean Edwards were key teachers of these courses. A large number of Earth Literacy graduates went on to found successful nonprofits and ecology centers of their own.[46] Miriam also worked to shape a master's degree in Earth Literacy, a program that was based at Miami Dade Community College and that was offered in cooperation with St. Thomas University in Miami. Students came for a period to study at Genesis Farm.[47] The Farm also offered seasonal rituals, workshops, film showings, and study groups that took place year-round. It was a major supporter and catalyst for locally based organizations that formed and thrived over the years, including the Ridge and Valley Charter School, which was founded based on the Universe Story.[48]

Genesis Farm was a unique place where Thomas's ideas could be grounded in the context of eco-literacy and extended in the framework of the evolutionary story. Miriam described it as follows:

> Genesis Farm, where I live and work in the Delaware River water basin is committed to Berry's understandings of the need for a new cosmology to transform traditional western thought and its impact on our economic, religious, governmental and educational institutions. He suggested that their wisdom needs to be infused and radically integrated with the scientific discovery

6.7 Miriam MacGillis and Thomas Berry at the tenth anniversary of Genesis Farm in 1990.
Photo courtesy of Miriam MacGillis

of an evolving Universe, with the human species as being one of its expressions—one that is capable of reflecting on itself as a member of the Earth community; one that is capable of realizing a deeper identity of itself and of correcting its present deadly spiral toward self destruction. His thoughts are a powerful context for activism.[49]

THE CATHEDRAL OF ST. JOHN THE DIVINE: 1975–1997

Thomas also found a special home at the Episcopal Cathedral of St. John the Divine near Columbia University in New York. This was in large measure due to the welcoming spirit of the dean, James Parks Morton, who led the Cathedral for twenty-five years from 1972 to 1997. Morton was educated at Harvard and began his work as a priest in Jersey City, focusing on ministry to the poor. He had a spiritual awakening while watching the first moon landing on television in 1969. Along with many others, he saw the Earth as a beautiful blue planet in the vastness of space and was moved to bring an ecological consciousness into the heart of his theology.

It was three years after Morton became dean that he met Thomas Berry, in 1975. Morton was immediately attracted to Thomas's ideas and frequently invited him to speak at the Cathedral. Indeed, Thomas became an honorary canon there in 1977. Nearly twenty years later, on October 2, 1994, he was honored for his approaching eightieth birthday at the Cathedral as homilist during the *Earth Mass* and then during the late afternoon prayer service, Evensong. A dinner and testimonials followed at the nearby Symposium restaurant. Thomas's memorial service was also held at the Cathedral, on September 23, 2009. Over a thousand people attended.[50]

It was in large part due to Thomas's influence that Jim Morton came to be known as the "Green Dean" and the Cathedral as an epicenter of eco-spiritual thinking in New York. Many sermons, liturgies, and conferences focused on the Earth took place there. This was a period of awakening to the environmental devastation that was already taking place regarding ecosystems and species. The urgency of an adequate response became a central theme of Thomas's talks at the Cathedral.

6.8 Thomas Berry and the Very Rev. James Parks Morton at the Cathedral of St. John the Divine.

Gretchen McHugh, courtesy of J. Murray McHugh

In 1980 a gifted musician, Paul Winter, and his Paul Winter Consort became artists-in-residence at the Cathedral. Paul was much influenced by Thomas's ideas and welcomed his frequent presence at the Cathedral. He also resonated deeply with Brian Thomas Swimme's work, especially his dialogues with Thomas as related in *The Universe Is a Green Dragon*. In early 1981, Jim Morton invited Paul to compose a contemporary Mass for the Cathedral. That spring Paul went to England to meet James Lovelock, originator of the "Gaia Hypothesis," to explore how this could reflect the idea that the Earth is a single organism. Paul then set out to create a work that was both ecumenical and ecological, one that would embrace all the voices of the Earth. He reflected, "I wanted to feel the Earth-power of percussion in harmony with the serene voices of the choir, and to share with the congregation that spirit of celebration we know with our concert audiences."[51]

The *Earth Mass* (*Missa Gaia*) premiered on Mother's Day, May 10, 1981, celebrating the fecundity of Mother Earth and all her species. David Brower, then president of Friends of the Earth, gave the homily. The Mass was recorded that September on two nights in the Cathedral and was performed on the feast day of St. Francis, October 4, to honor the beginning of the year marking the eight-hundredth anniversary of St. Francis's birthday. Thomas was at the October performance and attended frequently in subsequent years, as it became an annual event celebrating St. Francis.

In 1985, the suggestion was made by two people involved in dramatic productions at the Cathedral—Lavinia Currier, a filmmaker inspired by Thomas, and Jon Michael Tebelak—author of "Godspell"—that St. Francis Day become more of a pageant and that animals be included. So in October 1985, near the end of the Mass, the great bronze doors of the Cathedral were opened and a grand procession, led by an elephant, camel, and llama and including some thirty different animals, came flooding into the Cathedral and formed a circle around the altar in the Crossing to receive the blessing of the bishop. In following years, people were invited to bring their pets, as well, for the traditional Blessing of the Animals.

For nearly forty years, Paul Winter and his Consort have celebrated the *Earth Mass* at the Cathedral each October to honor the feast of St. Francis, patron saint of animals and ecology. Paul also developed celebrations for the summer and winter solstices, which Thomas would often attend. These remarkable performances of music and dance feature the songs of whales, wolves, and birds. A highlight of the winter solstice event is when a huge gong rises with its player one hundred

6.9 Paul Halley, Paul Winter, and the Very Rev. James Parks Morton in front of the great bronze doors of the Cathedral of St. John the Divine in New York (1982) at the time of the recording of *Earth Mass*. The panels are titled (left to right) "Creation of Light" and "Creation of the Waters." A whale is visible in the right panel.
Beverly Hall

feet into the vault of the Great Choir at the back of the nave, signaling the return of the sun. It was at a solstice performance in December 1983 that Thomas composed the poem "Morningside Cathedral," celebrating the wolf howl as a primal call to reinvigorate the sense of the sacred:

> The meaning of the moment
> and the healing of the wound
> are there in a single cry
>
> A throat open wide
> for the wild
> sacred sound . . .
> A Gothic sound—
> come down from
> the beginning of time.[52]

INSPIRING CHANGE

Thomas's vision of the healing of the Earth in a wounded world was beginning to inspire changes in music and the arts, in education and religion, and in law and economics. The Riverdale years were key to effecting these changes. They were marked by Thomas's transition from teaching the history of religions at Fordham to teaching Earth history and Earth literacy. Thomas moved from the cosmology of religions, to the cosmology of the universe; from being a historian of religions, to being a geologian. His numerous decades of reading and reflecting, brooding and meditating, came to fruition during these years, especially with his collaboration with Brian Thomas Swimme.

CHAPTER 7

Evoking the Great Work

We have, it seems, an immediate, a particular work or profession whereby we ful-
fill our role in the social order, obtain our living, and support our families. Within
this context we carry out the Great Work to be done in the larger historical order;
establishing a way of life, developing a nation, establishing ideals that make life
meaningful, articulating visions of beauty, defending a country, building a world
of aesthetic beauty and magnificence. Composing great music, establishing a reli-
gious tradition. Everyone participates in such Great Work. The particular work is
best understood in the light of some Great Work, while every Great Work has its
support and manifestation in particular work. Ultimately, in my view, it is the
Great Work that validates and ennobles all particular work.

Thomas Berry, *Goldenrod: Reflections on the Twentieth Century*

FROM NEW STORY TO THE GREAT WORK

In 1994, at his eightieth birthday party at the Symposium restaurant in New York, near the Cathedral of St. John the Divine, Thomas announced in an impromptu speech after dinner, "I am moving from the New Story to the Great Work to assist in laying the foundations of the Ecozoic Era." He later reflected: "At this time I began to understand my life as a dedication to some Great Work, first to identifying the destructive tendency of my times in its misunderstanding of the Great Work to which it was called; then to the authentic Great Work of shaping a viable world for the future" (*Goldenrod*, 50).

In saying this, Thomas was drawing on the extensive references to "Great Work" in the alchemical tradition of medieval Europe. The phrase implied that elements could be transmuted from the mundane to the precious. Thomas was also aware of the Jungian interpretation, in which the "Great Work" was an integration of the conscious and unconscious dimensions of the human psyche. In the contemporary period, Thomas wrote of the Great Work as part of the task of key sectors in society, such as religion, law, education, and economics, to create a flourishing future. He helped to articulate principles and encourage strategies for transformation in these areas by calling for new modes of human-Earth relations. What follows is a description of three major projects that engaged him in the Great Work and that still thrive in the present: the American Teilhard Association, Religion and Ecology, and Earth Jurisprudence. This work was set within the context of a Teilhardian cosmology that encouraged human participation in a vibrant Earth community.

The French Jesuit paleontologist Pierre Teilhard de Chardin (1881–1955) was a major influence on Thomas's thought, especially with regard to the dynamics of evolution and the activation of human energy.[1] Teilhard's vision of human participation in the epic of evolution led him to validate the importance of human action through work.[2] He was keen to affirm the contribution of humans to "building the Earth" through research and education, as well as through fulfilling necessary daily tasks. The term *great work* was used by Teilhard in his first religious essay, "Cosmic Life," where he writes: "The true summons of the cosmos is a call consciously to share in the great work that goes on within it; it is not by drifting down the current of things that we shall be united with their one, single, soul, but by fighting our way, with them, towards some term still to come."[3] This essay was drafted in 1916, when he was a stretcher-bearer in World War I, witnessing massive loss of life. This perspective of human vocation as linked to a cosmic calling contributed to Thomas's writing about the Great Work.[4]

THE AMERICAN TEILHARD ASSOCIATION

Teilhard lived the last years of his life at the Jesuit residence at St. Ignatius Church on Park Avenue and Eighty-Fourth Street in New York City. Thomas never met Teilhard, as these were the years when he was serving as a chaplain in

Germany from 1951 to 1954. Teilhard accepted an appointment at the Wenner Gren Foundation in 1951 and did his paleontological research there and at the American Museum of Natural History. He lived quietly until his death in New York on Easter Sunday, April 10, 1955. He was buried in Poughkeepsie at the Jesuit novitiate, St. Andrew-on-Hudson.[5]

With the publication shortly after his death of his seminal work—*The Phenomenon of Man*—in several languages, Teilhard's ideas on evolution found a receptive audience.[6] Indeed, Fordham University emerged as a critical center of his thought. In 1962, in conjunction with a group of scientists, Robert Francoeur, a graduate student at Fordham, organized an informal American Teilhard de Chardin Association to promote Teilhard's legacy. In 1964, Beatrice Bruteau, vice president of the Association, proposed the formation of a Teilhard Research Institute at Fordham University to sponsor lecture series and workshops.[7] Her proposal resulted in the dynamic and well-attended Teilhard Conference in August 1964. It was there that Thomas delivered his paper "Threshold of the Modern World" to critical acclaim. This conference was the first event in the United States to explore Teilhard's work.

7.1 Teilhard's grave at the former Jesuit Novitiate, now the Culinary Institute of America.

Teresa Berger

In 1967 an independent group, including Thomas, created a more formalized Teilhard organization with a group of interdisciplinary scholars as officers. In 1974, the Institute's name was lengthened to the American Teilhard Association for the Future of Man because the board felt the Association should have a broader focus than Teilhard himself. The concern of the Association, especially as articulated by Thomas, was to give expression to the implications of Teilhard's ideas for a viable future. It has held to this mission ever since.

In 1973, the Association moved into a building owned by St. James's Church at 867 Madison Avenue. There, the Association assembled a library and held a lecture series in which Thomas frequently spoke. After several years, because of the financial burden of the rent, Thomas offered to house the Association at the Riverdale Center for Religious Research. In 1978, John Grim moved the files and archives to Riverdale. The Association remained there until Thomas retired to Greensboro in 1995.[8]

Twenty years after Teilhard's passing, in 1975, Thomas was elected president of the Association and remained in that capacity until 1987, when John Grim became president.[9] Thomas continued to serve as an active member of the board until his death. Mary Evelyn Tucker was elected vice president in 1979 and was later joined by Brian Thomas Swimme in 2005. Grim and Tucker have led the Association for more than three decades, ensuring that Thomas's work would have a larger Teilhardian context in which to thrive.

The Teilhard Association's annual meeting has been held in New York City for some fifty years, most frequently at Union Seminary at Columbia University.[10] This gathering consists of a board meeting, a noon lunch, and a featured speaker. It is an occasion for Teilhardians to renew ties and commitments to the Great Work. It is an energizing event, held in the spring when the buds and blooms are first appearing. Fanny de Bary would bring flowers from her home and arrange them for each table, ably assisted by Jayne Ann McPartlin, who has carried on the tradition. In addition to Thomas, annual meeting speakers included the esteemed biologists Theodosius Dobzhansky and Edward Dodson, the anthropologist Margaret Mead, the physicist Robert Jastrow, and such Teilhardian scholars as Thomas King and Karl and Nicole Schmitz-Moorman.[11]

The Association has made scholarly contributions by compiling a Teilhard bibliography and by creating a biannual newsletter (*Teilhard Perspective*), short essays (*Teilhard Studies*), and a website.[12] The *Teilhard Studies* began in 1978 with

7.2 After the American Teilhard Association meeting in 1993, outside Union Theological Seminary in New York City. Included in the photo are (left to right): Front row: Hank Perrine, Judy Emery, Thomas Berry, Greg Giordano, Beatrice de Bary Heinrichs, unknown; Back row: Brother Conrad Federspeil, Brian Brown, Mary Evelyn Tucker, John Grim, Ken Dupuy, Gwen Dupuy, Kateri Dupuy.

Gretchen McHugh, courtesy of Brian Brown, Amarilys Cortijo, and J. Murray McHugh

the publication of Thomas's essay "The New Story," which shows the influence of Teilhard on his thinking. Thomas admired Teilhard's comprehensive vision, especially his synthesis of evolutionary science in *The Human Phenomenon*. He also had some disagreements with Teilhard, which he expressed in a 1982 *Teilhard Study* called "Teilhard in the Ecological Age." The Association compiled a selection of the *Teilhard Studies* titled *Teilhard in the 21st Century: The Emerging Spirit of Earth*.[13]

TEILHARD CONFERENCES

In its early years, the Association organized an important ecumenical conference entitled "Hope and the Future of Man" held at Riverside Church on October 8–10, 1971. This conference brought together noted theologians from North America and Europe, such as Johannes Metz, Jurgen Moltman, and Walter Pannenberg, who spoke before an appreciative audience of twenty-five hundred people.

Four years later, a major conference focusing on Teilhard and Carl Jung was organized by Reverend Dr. Franklin (Skip) Vilas, who was president of the Jung Society, and Thomas, who had just become president of the Teilhard Association. This event commemorated the twentieth anniversary of Teilhard's death in 1955. It was held at International House on Riverside Drive at Columbia University on November 14-15, 1975, and attracted five hundred people. The keynote speakers were Teilhardians Thomas Berry on the "Symbol of the Cosmic Person" and Jean Houston on "Ecology of Inner Space," along with Jungian analysts Edward Whitmont on "Masculine and Feminine in Cultural Evolution" and John Perry on "Eros and History."[14]

Another significant conference took place in 2005 to celebrate the fiftieth anniversary of Teilhard's passing, again with Reverend Vilas's help. This included numerous events in New York, highlighted by one at the United Nations on April 8 with over one thousand people in attendance. Titled "The Spirit of the Earth: Global Spirituality and Sustainable Development," it was sponsored by the American Teilhard Association, the French Mission to the United Nations, the United Nations Environment Programme, and UNESCO.[15] The following day a large celebration took place at the Cathedral of St. John the Divine that was attended by some fourteen hundred people. It was a tribute to Teilhard's influence that fifty years after his death so many people would gather to reflect on his ongoing significance.

Until the end of his life, Thomas took a keen interest in Teilhard's thought and its implications for the modern world. In particular, he felt that the perspective of evolutionary time could engender a zest for life that would inspire the transformative work needed for a flourishing future for the Earth community.

JOURNEY OF THE UNIVERSE

In order to implement Thomas's fundamental insight into the need for a New Story of evolution, and in alignment with his Teilhardian perspective, Brian Thomas Swimme, Mary Evelyn Tucker, and John Grim developed the *Journey of the Universe* project. In 2011 a book by that name was published by Yale University

Press and a documentary film was released that was dedicated to Thomas Berry. The film won an Emmy and was broadcast for three years on public television in the United States. The accompanying *Journey Conversations* deepen the story with interviews from twenty scientists and environmentalists. These are intended to connect the Great Story to the Great Work through conversations with people working in such diverse areas as education, economics, permaculture, eco-cities, race studies, and the arts. Many of the interviewees credit the universe story and Thomas Berry as being an inspiration for their engaged work on the ground.

In November 2014, Tucker and Grim organized a conference at Yale to celebrate the hundredth anniversary of Thomas's birth and the fifth anniversary of his death. From this conference a book was published, titled *Living Cosmology: Christian Responses to* Journey of the Universe.[16] To make the *Journey* film, book, and conversations available to a worldwide public, massive open online courses (MOOCS) were released from Yale/Coursera in the fall of 2016. These were translated into Chinese a year later. They include a course on Thomas Berry's life and thought as a key influence on the project.

7.3 Mary Evelyn Tucker, John Grim, and Fanny de Bary with Thomas Berry.
Gretchen McHugh, courtesy of Mary Evelyn Tucker, John Grim, and J. Murray McHugh

RELIGION AND ECOLOGY

Thomas also made extensive contributions to the Great Work through his involvement with the emerging field of religion and ecology, especially through his writings on the cosmology of religions.[17] These reflections began while he was at Fordham and Riverdale and continued to unfold in his later writings. They came to fruition when he participated in the Harvard conference series on World Religions and Ecology from 1996 to 1998. Organized by Mary Evelyn Tucker and John Grim, these were the first conferences to focus on views of nature and environmental ethics from the perspective of world religions. They were inspired by Thomas's concern for the growing worldwide environmental and climate crises. Thomas and the conference participants acknowledged that science and policy were crucial in addressing environmental problems, but religious and ethical perspectives were also necessary. The series would not have been possible without the extensive training in world religions that Thomas, Wm. Theodore de Bary, Tu Weiming, and others had imparted to Tucker and Grim. Tu Weiming hosted most of the opening dinners at his home in Cambridge. With the work of many scholars, ten edited volumes were published from these conferences on the ecological dimensions embedded in the religions of the world.[18]

Thomas was the lead speaker at the concluding conference at the American Academy of Arts and Sciences in Cambridge, Massachusetts, in September 1998, along with the Harvard biologist E. O. Wilson. He was also a keynote speaker at the Harvard symposium on religion and nonhuman animals in 1999. The collection of papers from this meeting is titled *A Communion of Subjects*,[19] drawing on Thomas's frequently cited statement: "The universe is not a collection of objects, but a communion of subjects."[20] This book is the first interdisciplinary study of the conceptualization of nonhuman animals in world religions. Thomas was an inspiration to many in the emerging field of religion and animals, such as Paul Waldau, one of the founders.

Religion and ecology, then, inspired by Thomas's perspectives, is an emerging area of study, research, and engagement that is in dialogue with multiple disciplines focused on the environment. This field of study responds to both historical and contemporary quests for understanding the interrelationships of humans, the Earth, the cosmos, and the sacred. The field involves studies of such topics as the ways in which environments have shaped and been shaped by human culture, the symbolic expression of nature in myth and rituals, and the understanding of ecology as displayed in traditional religious practices in the context of agriculture, commerce, fishing, or hunting. It also highlights environmental justice issues that have often been overlooked in environmental studies.[21] In short, it explores the complex and varied systems of human-Earth relations as expressed in religious traditions, which Thomas had begun to articulate in the History of Religions program at Fordham.

As Thomas observed, religions are often thought to concentrate primarily on divine-human relations that aim at liberation from earthly travails. He was concerned that such emphasis on salvation outside the world left the Earth open to exploitation. In relation to Christianity, Thomas urged the tradition to move from an exclusive concentration on redemption to one focused on creation.

Religions are also understood to emphasize the importance of social and ethical relations between humans. However, Thomas encouraged those in the field of religion and ecology to investigate the interactions of humans as individuals and as communities with the natural world and the universe at large. For Thomas, this focus underscores the many ways that humans locate themselves by means of religious cosmologies within a universe of meaning and mystery. It explores the varieties of human interactions with nature, whether those interactions reflect reciprocity or respect, domination or manipulation, or celebration or submission. For Thomas, human interaction with the sacred repeatedly occurs in, and through, nature and the larger cosmos.

Indeed, Thomas notes that religious practitioners recognize that simultaneously with ongoing seasonal and geological changes there is a wholeness and a holiness in the Earth.[22] Religions seek to integrate their intricate symbolic and ritual structures with these life processes. As Thomas observed, life, death, and rebirth in the natural world are frequently symbolized in religious traditions. This alignment of the passage of human life with natural systems constitutes a profound dynamic of religious energy expressed in cosmological myths, symbols, and rituals. Along with this alignment, numerous scriptures include injunctions against overuse of land and species. Thomas underscored how this interweaving of cosmological religious thought and environmental ethics can be explored in the study of religion and ecology.

As an emerging field, Thomas realized that religion and ecology is still defining its scope and limitations. The field embraces descriptive and historical studies as well as prescriptive and constructive theologies. Most scholars in the field do not presume that environmentally friendly scriptural passages imply environmentally sensitive practices. Moreover, scholars acknowledge the vastly different historical contexts in which religious traditions have evolved. Nonetheless, Thomas and other historians of the world's religions have suggested that concepts and practices from these traditions can be integrated into discussions of current environmental policy and ethics. These need to be retrieved, reevaluated, and reconstructed.[23]

Thomas and others have acknowledged the promise and problems of religions in relation to ecological challenges. The ideological control of religions and the oppressive dimensions of religious institutions are widely recognized. Yet many religious leaders, laity, and scholars, as well as some environmentalists, believe that religions offer intellectual energy, symbolic power, moral persuasion, institutional structures, investment leverage, and a commitment to social and economic justice that may contribute to the transformation of attitudes, values, and practices for a flourishing future. Scholars also recognize the challenges of historical complexities, the inevitable gaps between ideas and practices, and the extremes of either idealizing or dismissing particular religions. In this regard, academics have written about the dangers of romanticizing the "noble savage" or "noble oriental." Correctives to such idealizations can be found in environmental history. These historical studies help to shed light on the actual environmental practices of various cultures that have been influenced in part by their religious traditions.

A specific outcome of the Harvard conferences was the formation of the Forum on Religion and Ecology, first located at Harvard in 1998 and then brought to Yale in 2006. Founded and directed by Tucker and Grim, its aim is to create a new academic field of study that has implications for environmental policy and practices. To this end, the Forum has organized a dozen more conferences, published books and articles, and developed a comprehensive website on world religions and ecology.[24] It also sends a monthly newsletter via email around the world. As Thomas suggested, the Forum recognizes that religions need to be in dialogue with other disciplines (e.g., science, economics, education, public policy) in seeking comprehensive solutions to both global and local environmental problems.

Twenty years ago, religion and ecology was neither a field of study nor a force for transformation. Over the past two decades, this new field of study has emerged within academia, with courses being taught at colleges and high schools across North America and in some universities in Europe. At the University of Toronto, for example, the Elliott Allen Institute for Theology and Ecology, inspired by Thomas's vision, has been contributing to this area since 1991 with a remarkable range of PhD students.[25] Yale Divinity School now has a concentration in this area for its Master of Arts in Religion (MAR) students, and it also offers a broader joint-degree program with the Yale School of Forestry and Environmental Studies. The University of Florida has a PhD program in religion and nature, and there are two journals being published in this area.[26] Moreover, a new force of religious environmentalism is growing in churches, synagogues, temples, and mosques around the world. Now every major religion has statements on the importance of ecological protection, and hundreds of grassroots projects have emerged. Thomas Berry's teaching and writing have played an active role in these developments within and among the world's religions.

Thomas's influence on the papal encyclical *Laudato Si* is also noteworthy. The repeated phrase in the encyclical, "Cry of the Earth; Cry of the Poor," comes from the title of a 1995 book by leading Latin American liberation theologian Leonardo Boff. This book is in the series on Ecology and Justice that, in the spirit of Thomas, "seeks to integrate an understanding of Earth's interconnected life systems with sustainable social, political, and economic systems that enhance the Earth community."[27] Boff was deeply influenced by Thomas's suggestion to him in the 1980s that one cannot work for the liberation of people without also including the Earth. Thus, Boff eloquently framed his arguments for a "holistic ecology" in the context of the universe story in his writing and speaking.[28]

In the encyclical, Pope Francis calls for an "integral ecology," a term that Thomas used first in 1995.[29] This is intended to bring together concern for both people and the planet. In line with Thomas's earlier thinking, the pope makes it clear that the environment can no longer be seen as only an issue for scientific experts, or environmental groups, or government agencies alone. Rather, he invites all people, programs, and institutions to realize that these complicated

7.4 Thomas Berry at Riverdale.
Gretchen McHugh, courtesy of J. Murray McHugh

environmental and social problems require integrated solutions beyond a "technocratic paradigm" that values an easy fix. This emphasis echoes Thomas's early critique of the "technological trance" that blinded people to the problematic side of technology or made them think within a limited framework for solutions.

In short, Thomas had a significant influence on the emergence of religion and ecology as a field within academia and a force within the larger society. This was a noteworthy contribution to the Great Work of eliciting viable human-Earth relations.

LAW: EARTH JURISPRUDENCE

Thomas also suggested that law needed to be included in discussions about creating a flourishing future for the Earth community. One of Thomas's major contributions to the Great Work was his articulation of the principles and philosophy of Earth Jurisprudence. He originated the term and explained its key concepts over many years.[30] A Gaia Foundation report acknowledges: "Earth Jurisprudence is the term first used by cultural historian Thomas Berry to name the philosophy of governance and law, in which the Earth, not human interests, is primary. It accepts that humans are born into an ordered and lawful Universe, to whose laws we need to comply if we are to be a benign presence on Earth."[31]

Thomas had an interest in jurisprudence from the time of his doctoral thesis on Giambattista Vico, who felt that jurisprudence provided the surest insight into the mores, customs, and worldview of a people.[32] In 1988 in *The Dream of the Earth*, Thomas noted: "The [contemporary] legal system is especially deficient in its inability to deal with questions of human-Earth relations."[33] He acknowledged the need to understand the integrity of ecosystems and to protect the inherent rights of all living beings.[34] In 1999 in *The Great Work* he wrote:

> Especially as regards law, we need a jurisprudence that would provide for the legal rights of geological and biological as well as human components of the Earth community. A legal system exclusively for humans is not realistic. Habitat of all species, for instance, must be given legal status as sacred and inviolable.[35]

Finally, in 2006, Thomas's major statements on Earth Jurisprudence were published in *Evening Thoughts*: "Legal Conditions for Earth Survival" and "Ten Principles for Jurisprudence Revision."[36] Thomas developed these ideas over several decades in conversation with others.

As Thomas saw it, even the United States Constitution is fundamentally flawed because it reserves all rights for humans and recognizes none for nature. For Thomas, the deficiency cries out for a fundamental transformation of our modern ideas of law. At the heart of this transformation, he noted, is the shift from a human-centered to an Earth-centered understanding of our relationship with the larger community of life. A profound change in perspective, he felt, would enable humans to recognize and protect the rights of the natural world. The legal scholar and historian of religions Brian Brown has called this the revolution of law from a focus on order to a focus on justice. Brown writes: "The self-regard of human law, long propertised and extensively commercialized, has rendered it insensible and mute to the cataclysm that terminates the Earth in its florescence."[37]

ARTICULATING A PHILOSOPHY OF EARTH JURISPRUDENCE

Given that the prevailing jurisprudence system does not protect other species or components of the living Earth, Thomas asked what a different system would look like. He pointed to various sources of inspiration, namely, nature itself and indigenous peoples' understanding of law. The starting point, he said, is recognizing that the laws of the Earth are primary. They govern life on the planet, and human laws should be derived from them. This is clear for indigenous peoples, whose languages, customary laws, and governance systems are rooted in the understanding that nature regulates the order of living processes in which humans are embedded. Thus, to maintain the health and well-being of people and the planet, humans need to comply with the dynamics of nature. For indigenous peoples, the relationship between land and species is regarded as sacred and involves reciprocity.

That nature has rights within this worldview is not difficult to affirm because all components of life are interdependent and have an inherent right to exist. But since the language of rights evolved in a modern context, Thomas felt that humans need to acknowledge these biases in recognizing rights in a more-than-human context. These biases include a modern anthropocentric perspective, the objectification of the natural world, a view of the world as inert or even dead, and the assumption that humans, as the dominant species, can simply "use" nature in the current industrial system.

Thomas was inspired early on by Christopher Stone, a law professor at the University of Southern California. Stone was one of the first to call for judicial reform with his groundbreaking book in 1974, *Should Trees Have Standing? Towards Legal Rights for Natural Objects.*[38] Stone argued for the rights of natural objects (trees) or ecosystems (forests, oceans, rivers) to have legal standing and to be represented by guardians that protect them, just as corporations and charitable trusts have legal representatives. He felt that these natural objects or systems should be recognized for their own worth and dignity, not merely their benefit to humans.

Thomas drew on this position regarding the inherent value of nature and of natural processes: "Every being has rights to be recognized and revered. Trees have tree rights, insects have insect rights, rivers have river rights, mountains have mountain rights. So too with the entire range of beings throughout the universe. All rights are limited and relative."[39] Thus Thomas emphasized that "every component of the Earth community, living and non-living has three rights: the right to be, the right to habitat or a place to be, and the right to fulfill its role in the ever-renewing processes of the Earth community."[40] This position has been foundational for many of those involved in formulating and making operational an effective rights-of-nature approach rooted in Earth Jurisprudence.[41] Similar perspectives have arisen in the contemporary period with the scientific understanding of the interdependence of Earth systems, particularly in ecology. Thus, by drawing on both indigenous and scientific knowledge, Earth Jurisprudence is responding to the needs of the larger community of life.

EMERGING DEVELOPMENTS OF EARTH JURISPRUDENCE

Groundwork for the articulation of Earth Jurisprudence emerged with the United Nations' World Charter for Nature in 1982. This was further developed with the Earth Charter issued in 2000 and the Universal Declaration of the Rights of Mother Earth in 2010. Thomas was especially appreciative of the World Charter for Nature. He felt it embraced a dynamic biocentric perspective, and he built on this in his early articulation of the rights of nature.

In this spirit, in 1984, Thomas urged the Gaia Foundation in England to commit to the protection of biological and cultural diversity, the restoration of healthy ecosystems, and the support of indigenous peoples, especially in the Southern Hemisphere.[42] Inspired by a workshop led by Thomas more than a decade later at Schumacher College in 1996, the Gaia Foundation launched an Earth Jurisprudence initiative.[43] This initiative involved a commitment to explore, develop, and promote pathways to affirm that Earth-derived law take precedence over human law to protect the well-being of all components of the Earth community.

In April 2001, the Gaia Foundation and Andrew Kimbrell, founder of the Center for Food Safety, organized a conference with Thomas Berry at the Airlie Conference Center outside Washington. A group of people involved with both law and with indigenous peoples came together from South Africa, Colombia, Britain, Canada, and the United States.[44] One of those in attendance was the South African lawyer Cormac Cullinan, who was inspired and encouraged by Thomas and the Gaia Foundation to write his path-breaking book, *Wild Law: A Manifesto for Earth Justice*, which was published in 2002.[45] In the foreword, Thomas calls for explicit legal protection of the larger Earth community. In December 2002, Thomas delivered this message in his plenary talk to an international conference on Earth Jurisprudence at Pace University Law School and its Academy for the Environment. Robert Kennedy Jr., an environmental lawyer at Pace, was particularly influenced by Thomas's thinking. The following year, in October 2003, Thomas delivered the E. F. Schumacher Lecture in Great Barrington, Massachusetts, titled "Every Being Has Rights," which was received with enormous appreciation.[46]

In 2002, an African regional network was formed—the African Biodiversity Network—with one of its major priorities being to revive indigenous knowledge systems and their Earth Jurisprudence underpinning; this network was inspired by Thomas and supported by the Gaia Foundation.[47] In 2005, the Nobel Laureate, Wangari Maathai, and her legal adviser, Ng'ang'a Thiongo, campaigned, as advised by Thomas, to incorporate an Earth Jurisprudence preamble in the new Kenyan constitution.

In the fall of 2006, a major step forward in institutionalizing Earth Jurisprudence occurred with the creation of a Center for Earth Jurisprudence (CEJ) at the Schools of Law at Barry University and St. Thomas University in Florida. Sr. Patricia Siemen, an environmental lawyer and professor, was the founder and first director. Drawing on Thomas's ideas, she has written on Earth Jurisprudence in a cosmological perspective.[48] The establishment of the Center was inspired by "the processes and laws of the natural world that sustain all life forms, the writings of Thomas Berry and other environmental philosophers, lawyers and scientists, and the reverence and care for all of creation."[49] In April 2007, the Center sponsored a conference called "Defining the Field and Claiming the Promise" at St. Thomas University School of Law in Miami. Two of the keynote speakers were influenced by Thomas, namely, Cormac Cullinan and

Liz Hosken of the Gaia Foundation, along with Thomas Linzey, cofounder of Community Environmental Legal Defense Fund who has made significant contributions to this movement.[50]

In 2008, the Center for Earth Jurisprudence created the Earth Law Center. Its first executive director, environmental attorney Linda Sheehan, advanced the passage of new rights of nature laws, advocated for rights of rivers to flow, held local rights of nature tribunals, promoted rights of nature before the United Nations, developed and taught an "Earth Law" class at Vermont Law School, and offered specific strategies to address the growing number of "co-violations" of nature's rights, human rights, and the rights of indigenous peoples.[51]

MILESTONES IN IMPLEMENTING EARTH JURISPRUDENCE

Thomas's notions of the rights of nature required that the dominant legal philosophy and principles be transformed and widened to include the whole Earth community of which humans are a part. He often spoke of the need for principles, strategies, and tactics for transforming individuals, societies, and institutions. He and others realized that strategies and tactics leading to the enactment of the rights of nature would be difficult, but contrary to expectations, several significant breakthroughs have occurred. These began the year before Thomas died and have continued since.

In 2008, Ecuador adopted the rights of nature into its new constitution. Article 71 reads, "Nature, or *Pachamama*, where life is reproduced and occurs, has the right to integral respect for its existence and for the maintenance and regeneration of its life cycles, structure, functions and evolutionary processes."[52]

In 2009, the United Nations General Assembly proclaimed April 22 as International Mother Earth Day. In so doing, member states acknowledged that the Earth and its ecosystems are our common home. The same year, the General Assembly adopted its first resolution on Harmony with Nature.[53]

On April 22, 2010, the World People's Conference on Climate Change and the Rights of Mother Earth in Cochabamba, Bolivia, approved the *Universal Declaration of the Rights of Mother Earth*. Over thirty thousand people attended, representing more than a hundred nations. The vast majority present were indigenous peoples, especially from Latin America.[54] As a follow-up, in September 2010, individuals and organizations from four continents gathered in Patate, Ecuador. Out of this four-day meeting, the Global Alliance for Rights of Nature was formed.[55]

In December 2010, the first indigenous president of Bolivia, Evo Morales, and Bolivia's Plurinational Legislative Assembly established the Law of the Rights of Mother Earth. The law defines Mother Earth as "a dynamic living system comprising an indivisible community of all living systems and living organisms, interrelated, interdependent, and complementary, which share a common destiny."[56] It calls on all people to "respect, protect and guarantee the rights of Mother Earth," which is considered sacred in the worldview of indigenous peoples and nations.

Several other watershed moments have emerged in the rights of nature movement. At its 2016 meeting in Hawaii, the International Union of the Conservation of Nature (IUCN) adopted a resolution calling for no development or extractive industries in Sacred Natural Sites and Territories and the recognition of customary governance systems. The IUCN in 2012 also committed to the rights of nature in its Resolution 100 and included action on rights of nature in its 2017–2020 work plan.

In New Zealand, the Whanganui River was the first in the world to receive legal personhood through a law passed on March 16, 2017.[57] This was followed on March 21 by court recognition of legal personhood for the Ganges and Yamuna Rivers in northern India.[58] Rights of nature legal provisions also now exist in Colombia, Mexico, and dozens of municipalities in the United States and are being debated in a number of other nations. Education in Earth Jurisprudence is also emerging.[59] In April 2018, the Colombian Supreme Court ruled that stronger efforts must be made against deforestation in the Amazon and the country as a whole must be protected from the effects of climate change. In this ruling, the Colombian Amazon is granted personhood and thus is regarded as an entity with rights. This is the first such ruling in Latin America.[60]

Thomas's contribution to this growing movement was his articulation of the principles of Earth Jurisprudence. These ideas have influenced many individuals and organizations working to promote the rights of nature both in theory and in practice. Thus, in the areas of law and religion, as well as in other fields such as education and economics, agriculture, and bioregionalism, Thomas made significant contributions to the Great Work. His Teilhardian evolutionary context has been vital to this effort. As Thomas made his transition from Riverdale back to Greensboro, he continued to inspire other creative projects.

CHAPTER 8

Coming Home

Each of us is as old as the universe and experiences our greater self in the larger story of the universe. So we are as old as the universe and as big as the universe. This is our great self. We survive in our great self. Our particular manifestation is distinct from our universal presence to the total process. We exist eternally in our participation in the universe's existence.

Thomas Berry, *Selected Writings on the Earth Community*

Thomas began to contemplate moving from New York back to his hometown of Greensboro, North Carolina, in the autumn of 1994. This move would require over a year to complete, as there were many details to attend to in closing the Riverdale Center. It had been a sanctuary for so many visitors for over two decades and a special place for Thomas to write and think. Yet it was not easy to sustain at this point in his life. In his eagerness to start the moving process, he suggested that the attic, where his letters and writings were stored, be swept clean and everything thrown out. Fortunately, Brother Conrad Federspeil, who assisted Thomas at the Center, let Mary Evelyn Tucker and John Grim know of Thomas's plan, and they prevailed upon him to let these materials be packed for mailing south. The materials eventually made their way back north a few years later after the Thomas Berry Archives were established at Harvard.

Another major concern was Thomas's large library of ten thousand books. What had been for so many students a source of intellectual inquiry, spiritual inspiration, and cultural awakening was beginning to weigh on Thomas. No person or institution had come forward to take the whole library. This was to be expected, as the library held such a diversity of religious scriptures and academic disciplines that it was challenging to imagine any individual person or institution thinking so broadly about religion or environmental issues.

Gradually, John and Mary Evelyn developed a plan that appealed to Thomas. They proposed inquiring among Thomas's former graduate students who were teaching to see if they or their university library would benefit from a selection of the books. The response was immediate, and scholars were grateful to receive part of such a valuable collection. From September through December 1994, the threesome selected and packed books for shipping to colleagues around the United States and Canada. John, Mary Evelyn, and Thomas would conclude each weekend of packing by having dinner and margaritas on the porch. As the sun set over the Hudson River, they reminisced over the many years they had spent working together. What began as a burden—the distribution of books—was transformed into four months of thoughtful and joy-filled gatherings. This memorable experience prompted reflections by John Grim that were written the day after the packing was completed:

THE SONG OF THE LIBRARY
JANUARY 3, 1995

The great work has always been
transmutation.
From the first movement of the
formative fireball
an inner silence has prepared us
for contemplation,
an expansive abyss has challenged us
to engage
the ten thousand things.
Reading flows across these realms of visual brooding
beyond the word to touch the soundless presence.

Now, the time of the ten thousand books
by the Hudson River
in the shadow of the great red oak
transmutes with the palisades' sunset,
with the community gatherings,
with the glorious year,
with the joys and sorrows,
of the crucible of life.
Into another harmony, held by hands
in other places.

Ecclesiastes wrote,
books involve endless hard work,
and much study
wearies the body.
There is no end of books.
"Put that book on the shelf!"
the storyteller said.
Here, at the Center of immensities
these books have sat on the shelf
for over twenty years
working their magic with bodies
and minds eager to encounter
the generative tumult of the universe story.

The storyteller and his marvelous
collection of writings and books
interpenetrate narrative and event.
As the Avatamsaka Sutra says:
"For unreckonable vast eons
they travel constantly through the ten directions
infinitely.
Their knowledge of enlightening means is infinite,
Their knowledge of truth is infinite,

Their knowledge of spiritual power is infinite,
Their miracles in each mental instant
are infinite."

Looking out from the sun porch
at the juncture of these volumes of time,
reading this many treed place,
hearing the ever-renewing song
of the trickster-transformer,
gravity pours into me.
Will wine ever hold bouquet again?
Can a margarita bring your sunset smile
after the books are packed,
the boxes mailed?

This great work has tipped,
tasted, and delighted us
ever lithesome as we walk the rooms.
Never empty, infinite in their fullness.
Echoing the beauty of a healing chant.
The door does not close,
the thoughtful laughter never ends,
just a light and shadow change
in the journey.[1]

And on New Year's Eve 1994, Mary Evelyn Tucker wrote "Reflections on Sending Out a Library":

The books are everywhere. . . . They have lived for many years in the shadow of the Great Red Oak, across from the two hundred million year old Palisades, beside the continual flow of the Hudson River. They have been loved and read by many a student, a seeker, a researcher, a teacher. They have circulated through numerous hands, felt many eyes upon them, and been the source of inspiration and creativity more than once. This is the library of the Riverdale Center; this is Thomas Berry's extraordinary collection.

He has brought together his companions in these books—the great minds and hearts of the ages. They have been silently communing for a quarter of a century at the Center. From east to west and north to south a unique gathering of people and ideas has occurred—cross fertilizing and pollinating one another through the agency of human imagination.

The library is comparable to the remarkable collection of human fossils brought together at the American Museum of Natural History some years ago. These fossils represented some of the most significant links in the story of human evolution. Here were gathered the discoveries of the leading paleontologists of the twentieth century. Walking through this collection was like stepping into the strata of time—seeing our story unfold in front of us. There was a reverence in that exhibit hall, such as one rarely experiences in museums these days. We came to see these fossils in the late afternoon and stayed until closing time. As the lights began to dim in the hall and the door was locked behind us, I was suddenly overwhelmed with the notion of these ancient human presences communicating with one another through the night in that dark space. They were gathered for the first time—each one with a unique personal story, now made special by discovery and linkage to a larger universe story.

So it was with the books at the Center. Thomas' probing journey brought these volumes together. They have gathered and communed and have become moist soil for thought. Their seeds have spouted, grown, burst, decayed, and risen again. They have become rich compost for the mind and now they are being dispersed for a final time.

We walk slowly through the rooms, savoring their presence—the Church Fathers and the Chinese sages in the front conference room, the religious traditions and arts of Asia in the back room, western history, theology, and psychology in the hall, ecology books lining the workroom and Native American religions upstairs. The languages represented is staggering—Hindu Sanskrit volumes, Buddhist texts in Sanskrit, Pali, Chinese, and Tibetan, numerous editions of Dante, an Italian encyclopedia of art, and French and German books and dictionaries. How can one fathom such diversity?

As we begin to dismantle this collection, the spirits call out. The shaman's dismemberment is occurring. Pieces of him are broken off to begin again in new forms and circumstances. Hinduism to Los Angeles, Buddhism to New

Jersey, Confucianism and Daoism to Arizona, Asian arts to Pennsylvania, theology to Louisiana, psychology to San Francisco, Native American to Pennsylvania and Montana, ecology to New York and New Jersey, and Dante to North Carolina. The parts are being regrouped.

A woman comes into the Center in the midst of this dismemberment. Books and boxes are everywhere. She is caught unaware of the impending move. "But Tom won't you miss all this?" she asks plaintively. "Such a collection should be kept together," she observes. "It will be brought back together in time," she concludes. "Perhaps," says Thomas wryly, knowing it won't.

And yet, we sip tea in the kitchen and laugh at the world's follies swirling around us. We know somehow it will come together. What we have witnessed is the explosion of a vast seedpod of ideas. They are being carried across the winds of the continent to come to rest in colleges and universities, in programs and persons who will care for and nurture these companions as friends. "Aren't you sad to see this all go?" she asks me. "Of course, I'm devastated," I reply, "but the shaman's journey never ends." Indeed, at eighty, a new phase was only beginning.[2]

THE HERMITAGE AND WELL SPRING

In considering his return to Greensboro, Thomas was unsure of where he could live so as to continue his work and thinking. It was a significant move from New York, where he had been for many productive years and where he knew so many people. Indeed, including monastic life and teaching, he had lived in the New York area for nearly fifty years. Then Thomas's brother, Joe, and his wife, Jean, offered Thomas an apartment on top of a former stable on their property in northwestern Greensboro. Assured of independence in that setting, Thomas accepted their offer and renamed the stable, "The Hermitage." The name fit, as it was a quiet and hospitable place, nestled in a beautiful wooded area near a small pond. He moved there in the summer of 1995 and settled into a life of continued writing and public speaking. His schedule was conducive to reflection and a deepening of his vision for the Earth community. Thomas received visits from his family and from his religious order, from his former students and colleagues, and from friends across North America and abroad. With each visit he would share his latest musings.

8.1 The Hermitage, where Thomas lived after he retired to Greensboro, North Carolina.
Courtesy of Peggy Whalen-Levitt

Thomas lived comfortably in the Hermitage until 2003, when a shoulder injury required him to move into Greensboro's Well Spring Retirement Community, where his sister Margaret also lived. During his six years there, Thomas ingratiated himself with the nursing staff and was unfailingly courteous to the other residents. Indeed, on returning from lunch one day, he stopped to assist a woman in a wheelchair, pushing her back to her room. He kept his sense of humor lively, and his interest in current events, especially environmental issues, never diminished.

In these later years, Thomas had several small strokes, and a more serious one in 2008 occasioned his final move to Well Spring's skilled-care facility. After one of the early strokes, his thinking was slowed but not impaired. However, for about eight months afterwards he lost the ability to read. The stroke affected his capacity to name objects. He would laugh, saying, "I know what it is, I just can't say it." During that period, he labeled his room with post-it notes and retaught himself to remember and name things. With remarkable patience and persistence, and with the help of a reading tutor, he eventually regained his reading facility. This feat matched a lifelong drive to push ahead with his latest ideas and most recent insights. Nothing seemed to stop or discourage him, even with diminished energy in his later years.

RENEWING FAMILY RELATIONS

Thomas had a close association with his sister Margaret, who served as his personal assistant throughout this Greensboro period. She met with him twice daily to help with correspondence, presentations, appointments, visits, and travel plans. During these years, she assembled Thomas's papers and letters and sent them to his archives at Harvard. In addition, she served as family genealogist and historian, annually publishing the *Berry-Vize Patch Newsletter/Directory* and organizing reunions after their mother's death in 1980. Formerly a nun with the Daughters of Charity, Margaret had earned a PhD in English literature in 1956. Sharing her brother's global interests, she later earned a master's degree in South Asian Studies from the University of Pennsylvania in 1969. A longtime professor of English and Asian literatures at John Carroll University in Cleveland, she published three books and numerous articles, in addition to receiving Ford, Fulbright, and Danforth fellowships. Thus, for Thomas, she was an indispensable intellectual partner and assistant to the end.

Thomas also renewed connections with other siblings and their families. In particular, he had shared his ideas for many years with his brother, Jim. On retiring from the U.S. Air Force as a colonel in 1968, Jim settled with his wife, Mary, and their children in Raleigh, North Carolina. Initially an avid peace activist, Jim gradually turned to labor and environmental concerns. With Thomas's encouragement, he founded the Center for Reflection on the Second Law, an organization devoted to social and ecological issues. He collaborated closely with Thomas, and between 1982 and 1997 he wrote 180 provocative and insightful letters that were widely distributed. Jim also organized thirteen conferences at New Hope Camp and Conference Center in Chapel Hill, North Carolina. Thomas regularly participated in these—giving talks, meeting people, and encouraging his brother's work. He and Brian Thomas Swimme gave an all-day event there together on June 24, 1997.[3]

Thomas was also close to his brother, Joe, and his wife, Jean, who lived in the house on the property where the Hermitage was located. During Thomas's first year there Joe became ill, and Thomas was attentive to him and his family. Joe eventually succumbed to lung cancer in April of 1996. Joe and Jean's daughter, Ann Berry Somers, was especially close to Thomas in his final years. They frequently met for breakfast at the Oakcrest Café, where they had long and animated conversations. As a biology professor at the University of North Carolina in Greensboro, Ann explored Thomas's ecological concerns and brought these perspectives into her teaching and conservation work. The two shared a deep love of nature and its rich biodiversity. They commiserated on the struggle to maintain habitat for the community of local species, such as bog turtles, which are one of Ann's specialties.

THOMAS BERRY FOUNDATION

Both family and colleagues were keen to find ways to continue Thomas's work and spread his ideas. To that end, in October 1998, the Thomas Berry Foundation was created by John Grim, Mary Evelyn Tucker, and the lawyer Martin Kaplan, along with Thomas and his sister, Margaret. Thomas's nieces, Ann Berry Somers and Teresa Kelleher, both academics, later joined the board, along with Brian Brown and Amarylis Cortijo, Thomas's doctoral students at Fordham. The Foundation has promoted Thomas's ideas by establishing a website for Thomas, initiating his archives at Harvard, publishing his essays, overseeing translations, organizing the Thomas Berry Award and Lecture, founding the Forum on Religion and Ecology, and creating the *Journey of the Universe* project.

While John Grim and Mary Evelyn Tucker were working at Harvard in the 1990s, a new archive was being formed to honor significant environmental thinkers, called the Harvard Environmental Science and Public Policy Archives. It was originated by Professor William Clark, a specialist in sustainability science and policy at the Kennedy School at Harvard. When Tucker and Grim approached Clark about Thomas Berry's inclusion in this archive, he readily agreed. Clark appreciated the original contributions Thomas was making to rethinking human-Earth relations. He even offered to travel to Greensboro to speak with Thomas personally and invited him to send his papers and letters to Harvard. Over many years, these papers were indeed transferred there with the help of Margaret Berry.

The Thomas Berry Award was inaugurated in 1999 in Washington, D.C., when the Center for Respect of Life and Environment (CRLE) at the Humane Society of the United States (HSUS) created the award to honor Thomas's legacy.[4] Since then it has been presented to selected individuals who have modeled the "Great Work" in their teaching, writing, or public service.[5] The Forum on Religion and Ecology partnered with the Center for Respect of Life and Environment in presenting the award in its early stages and now sponsors the award.

PUBLISHING THOMAS'S ESSAYS

Spurred on by the formation of the Thomas Berry Foundation, the Greensboro years were marked by a steady effort to prepare Thomas's essays for publication. With the editorial help of Tucker and Grim, Thomas was able to publish *The Great Work: Our Way into the Future* (1999), *Evening Thoughts: Reflecting on Earth as a Sacred Community* (2006), *The Christian Future and the Fate of Earth* (2009), and *The Sacred Universe: Earth, Spirituality, and Religion in the Twenty-First Century* (2009). Mary Evelyn and John had begun this work during the Riverdale years and now made frequent trips to Greensboro to work closely with Thomas on each book. They helped select the essays, arrange them in a coherent order, and edit them. This was a detailed process, completed over two decades, as they collaborated with Thomas to adapt and update the essays from their earlier form in the Riverdale Papers. Those papers were often the results of talks and sometimes had to be changed from an oral to a written mode. There were frequently multiple versions of an essay on the computer, so they all had to keep a watchful eye for repetition. Then there was the challenge of finding the right publisher for each book and negotiating with a sympathetic editor at each press.

At several points Thomas expressed hesitations about publishing earlier papers because his thinking had developed considerably over the years. But eventually he was persuaded that these would show others the breadth of his thought. When these books were completed, they provided a larger public access to all of the major Riverdale Papers. Along with *The Dream of the Earth* (1988) and *The Universe Story*, written with Brian Thomas Swimme (1992), these books constitute Thomas's principal body of work on cosmology and ecology. A final book, *Thomas Berry: Selected Writings on the Earth Community*, was edited by Tucker and Grim in 2014 for the fifth anniversary of his death and the hundredth anniversary of his birth.

8.2 Thomas in his signature corduroy jacket.
Judith Emery

CIVIC, RELIGIOUS, AND EDUCATIONAL ACTIVITIES IN NORTH CAROLINA

During the last fourteen years of his life, Thomas was active in a variety of arenas in Greensboro and beyond. He lectured for local organizations and occasionally contributed a column or letter to the editor of the city newspaper. In his honor, the Greensboro Public Library established a biennial award for an individual or organization best embodying Thomas's work.[6] The Kathleen Clay Edwards Branch Library in Greensboro created a permanent tribute to him in the form of a mural in the rotunda ceiling featuring some of his key ideas.

Religious organizations that recognized the importance of Thomas's message included Episcopal parishes, the New Garden Friends Meeting, and the Unitarian-Universalist Church. Bishop Albert ("Chip") Maxwell of the North Carolina Episcopal Diocese met with Thomas in 2007 to discuss environmental stewardship. He reports being greeted by Thomas with a stack full of books and reading materials.

Various North Carolina colleges and universities invited Thomas to speak or sponsored seminars on his work. These included the University of North Carolina at Chapel Hill; Guilford College in Greensboro; the University of North Carolina, Greensboro; Elon University in Elon; and Warren Wilson College near

Asheville. In these academic settings, Thomas urged students not to ignore the ecological challenges of the twenty-first century.[7] He would often begin his talks diffidently and then continue eloquently without notes for an hour or more, mesmerizing his audiences. When he came north to Bucknell University in Pennsylvania to give a talk, a student said to Grim and Tucker the next day: "When I first saw him at the podium he looked like my grandfather and I wondered what he had to say to us. But with every ten minutes he lost ten years."

Warren Wilson College was committed to environmental issues early on and had established an Environmental Leadership Center in 1992.[8] Thomas and Brian Swimme served as advisers for the Center, and in time a Young Writers' Award was named there for Thomas. Near the college Marnie Muller, a freelance artist, created a large outdoor spiral forest walk illustrating the Universe Story. Even before Thomas's Greensboro residency, he had been a featured speaker, along with Brian, at the Western North Carolina Environmental Summit in Asheville on April 21–22, 1990. That meeting also occasioned Thomas's first encounter with Appalachian poet and environmentalist Thomas Rain Crowe, who was so taken with Thomas's writing that he later endorsed his book *The Great Work* and wrote a review of it.[9]

EDUCATION: THE CENTER FOR EDUCATION, IMAGINATION, AND THE NATURAL WORLD

Over his lifetime, Thomas made many contributions to education.[10] During his later years in Greensboro he was also able to assist in children's education. One of Thomas's close friendships during these years was with Carolyn Toben, who began an educational program for children. She recalls visiting him earlier in New York on a January morning with light snow falling. Thomas met Carolyn at La Guardia Airport without a hat or jacket. He had given his jacket away, she later learned, to someone "who needed it more than I did." Carolyn describes this first meeting as marked by extraordinary graciousness and hospitality.

After her husband's death in 1999, Carolyn inherited Timberlake Farm Earth Sanctuary in Whitsett, just outside Greensboro. For over three decades, the 165 acres of woods, meadows, ponds, and trails had been the family home. Carolyn now hoped to preserve the farm. After discussions with Thomas, she requested colleagues from the fields of history, geology, art, music, and creative writing to come to the farm to imagine how to proceed. For the next ten years, Thomas's inspiration guided the development of the Center for Education, Imagination, and the Natural World at the farm.[11] As Thomas reflected:

> The life of the child has always been *organized* around a real abiding world of beauty, wonder, and the intimacy of living processes. . . . the wind, frogs, but-terflies . . . not a manufactured electronic world of virtual reality. The child has a natural bond of intimacy with the natural world, a remarkable sense of identification with all living things.[12]

He continued:

> The long-term survival of our children will actually depend on a new relation-ship between the natural and the human worlds. Children need to develop within a whole cosmology of the sun, moon, stars; they need to awaken to a world to *relate* to as a communion of subjects, not to *use* as a collection of objects. Relationships are the primary context of existence, and children need to see us practice a *sympathetic presence* to the Earth, as a means for being in a mutually enhancing relationship to it.[13]

Center staff began to practice a *sympathetic presence* to the Earth with children on Timberlake trails and meadows. Programs like Awakening to Nature, Empathetic Listening, and the Poetry of Nature created a context in which children could experience a living relationship with the Earth. Visitors included Richard Louv, who wrote *Last Child in the Wilderness* and who was much inspired by Thomas.[14]

In 2006, the Center began a two-year program, "The Inner Life of the Child in Nature: Presence and Practice," where this learning could be shared with educa-tors and others with children in their care. The program culminated in a collec-tion of practices created by participants during their second year. In 2011, many of these essays were published in *Only the Sacred: Transforming Education in the Twenty-First Century*, edited by Peggy Whalen-Levitt.[15] The collection includes Thomas's essay "Our Children, Their Future." The Center also publishes a bian-nual journal, *Chrysalis*, and has published four books written by graduates of the Inner Life of the Child in Nature program.[16] "The Center," Thomas wrote in a

8.3 Thomas on his birthday, November 9, 1990, with the children of Amarilys Cortijo and Brian Brown (Alexis and Justin to left) and the children of Beatrice de Bary Heinrichs (Annalies in front, Johanna in back), with Fanny de Bary behind.
Gretchen McHugh, courtesy of Brian Brown, Amarilys Cortijo, and J. Murray McHugh

flier, "is a perfect context for the continuity of this work with children and the sacred. It has brought joy in the last years of my life, for the children have always been closest to my heart."

PHILOSOPHY AND PRACTICE: THE CENTER
FOR ECOZOIC STUDIES

Thomas was continually interested in how to bring philosophical ideas into relationship with social and environmental change. This challenge was taken up by a gifted attorney, Herman Greene, who was especially inspired by Thomas's book, *The Great Work*, as well as by the philosophy of Alfred North Whitehead. In 2000, Greene founded the Center for Ecozoic Studies (CES) in Chapel Hill.[17] He had met Thomas when he lived in New York City. After returning to North Carolina, he reconnected with Thomas at a conference Jim Berry organized in 1995. The Center is committed to developing the work of Thomas Berry, with particular attention to his historical analysis, cultural critique, philosophical ideas, and guidance for social reform.

The premise of the work of the Center is that humans are in the midst of two great transitions: a geo-biological change from the terminal Cenozoic era to the emerging Ecozoic era, and a historical change from industrial-economic societies to ecological-cultural (ecozoic) societies.[18] This premise creates a need to understand these transitions, advance ideas and actions for new modes of human presence on Earth, support people in their ecozoic journeys, and take action to foster ecozoic societies. In this spirit, the Center for Ecozoic Studies works in several areas: providing education concerning the "Ecozoic era" and the "Great Work," so that these terms and their meanings would become part of the global lexicon; supporting research, education, art, and action concerning ecozoic societies; assisting in the sharing of critical reflections, stories, and dream experiences of an Ecozoic era; and providing resources for individuals and groups engaged in the Great Work.

The Center has directed conferences and workshops on Thomas's ideas and publishes a quarterly journal, *The Ecozoic Reader*. In 2009, the year of Thomas's death, it compiled a large memorial volume of 152 tributes from people across the country and around the world.[19] In 2017, the Center published a series of twenty-six essays titled "Thomas Berry's Work," which resulted from a conference it organized in 2014.[20]

NATIONAL CONFERENCES AND TALKS

Thomas responded to numerous national requests for speaking engagements beyond North Carolina. He traveled north several times a year, including to New York City for the annual Teilhard meeting each spring. He participated in the conferences at Harvard entitled "World Religions and Ecology" between 1996 and 1998. At the culminating conference of the series at the American Museum of Natural History in New York on October 21, 1998, Thomas was the final speaker. The nearly one thousand audience members were so riveted that, even after a full day of talks, they begged the moderator to give him more time and rose to their feet at the end with resounding applause. Similarly, at the November 15, 1997

Epic of Evolution conference sponsored by the American Association for the Advancement of Science at Chicago's Field Museum of Natural History, Thomas received a standing ovation. He also spoke in August 2000 at the Millennium Peace Summit of Religious and Spiritual Leaders in New York. There his talk, titled "Evening Thoughts," was the keynote for the Thomas Berry Award Dinner honoring the Confucian scholar Tu Weiming at the Waldorf Astoria Hotel.[21] Its poetic qualities and stirring message moved many to tears.

During the Greensboro years, Thomas received numerous awards and honorary degrees in recognition of his contributions to human understanding of our place and role within the universe story.[22] Moreover, various conferences were held exploring his ideas on the unfolding of the Great Work. At Bellarmine College in Louisville, Kentucky, the Earth Spirit Rising conference took place on June 15-17, 2001, attended by a thousand people. Thomas was honored *in absentia* while his sister Margaret spoke on his behalf.[23] On November 3-4, 2002, the California Institute of Integral Studies (CIIS) held a conference in Berkeley called "The Cosmological Imagination" honoring Thomas's work. He attended and transfixed the audience with his remarks. Key thinkers and change agents from the Bay area also spoke at the conference.[24] Another major gathering took place in Toronto on May 13-16, 2004, titled "Spirit Matters: Wisdom Traditions and the Great Work."[25] Thomas did not attend, but the discussions reflected a dynamic engagement with his thinking.

INTERNATIONAL CONFERENCES

While Thomas traveled less than in his early years, he continued to go to Italy most summers for two programs in Assisi organized by Elisabeth Ferrero, professor of humanities at St. Thomas University in Florida. The first included the Study Abroad for the Earth programs (1991-1998), and the second included the Spirituality and Sustainability conferences sponsored by St. Thomas University and the Center for Respect of Life and Environment (1995-2000).[26] Rick Clugston, the director of the Center, was a co-organizer along with Elisabeth. Thomas was the keynote speaker in the conferences, which over the years drew other notable environmentalists, scientists, religious figures, and nongovernmental organization leaders.[27] The purpose of these conferences was to "identify and celebrate developments in religion, economics, science, education, politics, and the arts to promote eco-justice and sustainability."[28] Thomas's presence was appreciated by many:

> The presence of Fr. Berry in Assisi was not just the focal point of intellectual dialogue within the study abroad program and the conferences, for the entire city participated in the extraordinary events taking place during the summer months. The owners of the shops around the fountain in Assisi's main square would wait impatiently for *Padre Berry's* presence and open smile. The *Posta's* cook would always think of new treats to prepare for him. At sunset, as the colors of the sky take on muted and splendid shades in Assisi's *piazza*, at one of the coffee-shop-outside tables . . . observers would find Thomas Berry and a large circle of students, colleagues, friends from Assisi and abroad all around him. More than once someone had to go and fetch him, letting him know that dinner was getting cold.[29]

Joe Holland, a professor at St. Thomas University, recalls meeting Thomas at the Rome airport to bring him up to Assisi:

> Greeting Thomas as he exited from security area, I noticed he was wearing only a light jacket. When I asked if he had a warm coat, Tom said the jacket would be sufficient. Then I noticed he was carrying a small paper bag that looked like a lunch bag. So I asked him to what baggage area his luggage was being delivered. He looked at his little "lunch bag" and said quietly, "This is all I have." Tom thus personified the simplicity promoted by Saint Francis of Assisi, patron of the city where we had last met.[30]

THE PASSIONIST ORDER

In the fall of 2002, the Passionists celebrated their Sesquicentennial Jubilee in Philadelphia. In his keynote address, Thomas reviewed the history of the order in America while noting its recent decline in vocations. The Catholic Church itself, he observed, faces the most significant crisis in its modern history because, except for some of the nuns, neither the Church nor religious orders have adequately responded to the environmental crisis.

Thomas's continual call was for Christianity to move from an exclusive concentration on redemption toward a focus on creation. He felt that the attention to redemption had led to an otherworldly interest in personal salvation and an exclusive concern for human suffering that ignored the suffering of the Earth and the destruction occurring to the life systems of the planet. With this call toward creation and away from redemption, Thomas caused some tension within his own Passionist order as well as among other Christians. Indeed, it has taken several decades for churches to heed his call to care for creation.

The Ecozoic era, Thomas noted, requires a new religious spirit, a "third mediation," in which human-divine and human-human relations are supplemented by human-Earth relations. This implied cultivating a sense of Earth and the universe as the primary sacred community of which humans are a responsible part. For the Passionists, he concluded, this development means recognizing the ongoing devastation of Earth as planetary suffering analogous to that of the historical Christ and now perceived as the passion of the Cosmic Christ.[31] In this context, Thomas felt that the Passionists could renew their religious and spiritual identity.

Later in 2002, the Passionists celebrated the sixtieth anniversary of Thomas's ordination as a priest at a dinner at the Riverdale Center. Thomas expressed his gratitude for the order's ongoing support for his material well-being and recalled with affection his long association with it. Even so, Thomas also sharply questioned the Church's lack of environmental concern. In "The Christian Future and the Fate of Earth," Thomas warned that the future of the Catholic Church in America depends on its capacity to assume a religious responsibility for the fate of Earth.[32]

GREEN MOUNTAIN MONASTERY

In this vein, Thomas felt there was a need for a new expression of monasticism that incorporated an ecological and cosmological spirituality. To this end, he became a cofounder of the Green Mountain Monastery in Greensboro, Vermont, in 2007. This project took many years and was initiated by the Passionist nun, Gail Worcelo, who was later assisted by a lay associate, Bernadette Bostwick. Gail first heard Thomas speak at St. Gabriel's Passionist Monastery in Clarks Summit, Pennsylvania, in 1984. She eventually studied with Thomas, meeting him periodically at the Riverdale Center from 1988 to 1992. Thomas's 1994 paper "Women Religious: Voices of Earth" became a catalyst for both Gail and Bernadette.[33] Thomas suggested in that essay that women religious are called to meet the double crisis of our time: degradation of planetary life systems and human alienation from the Earth community.

Thomas's ideas were spreading among Catholic women religious seeking to accept this challenge in multiple ways. Many eco-learning centers and community-supported farms were being created by nuns.[34] Inspired by the New Story, sixty sisters from the United States and Canada met at St. Gabriel's Monastery on July 14-17, 1994. On that occasion the Sisters of Earth organization was born, which continues to hold biennial conferences inspired by Thomas's ideas.[35]

Four years later, in 1998, the Passionist sisters of St. Gabriel's Monastery began a discernment process to determine their future directions. Ideas submitted included Gail's proposal that she and Bernadette be given permission to found a new monastic community. They hoped to respond to the cosmological and ecological consciousness that Thomas Berry had aroused in them. The community eventually gave its approval, and, on June 1, 1999, Gail and Bernadette moved to Weston, Vermont, to begin their ministry, which later moved beyond affiliation with the Passionist sisters. Thomas visited Gail and Bernadette several times in their early years, working with them to articulate their mission.

In 2004, Gail and Bernadette purchased 160 acres of land with a farmhouse and barn in Greensboro, Vermont. Three years later, on October 13, 2007, the Green Mountain Monastery was dedicated on this land in a celebration presided over by Passionist priests Joseph Mitchell and Stephen Dunn.[36] The Thomas Berry Sanctuary was marked by a sculpture by the artist Frederick Franck (1909–2006), entitled *St. Francis and the Birds*. Franck's encomium at the base reads: "I dedicate this steel icon to the deathless spirit incarnate in one of the most precious of my contemporaries. Like Francis of Assisi, Thomas Berry's life testifies to the indestructible human spirit, the surviving triumph of human wisdom over all the follies and cruelties of our generation." It was on this land that Thomas was eventually laid to rest.

8.4 Frederick Franck sculpture at Green Mountain Monastery, Greensboro, Vermont.
Lou Niznik, courtesy of Jane Blewett

THOMAS BERRY'S FUNERAL AND MEMORIAL SERVICES

Visits to Thomas in North Carolina during those last years were filled with lively discussions punctuated by laughter over recollections of times past. Often, when a visitor arrived at his room asking, "How are you?" Thomas would look up saying with a laugh, "Not as good as I would like, but better than I deserve." On one occasion, when asked that question, Thomas paused and responded, "I recall that the Chinese understood that with aging comes wisdom. . . . I wonder what happened to me?" One visitor asked with some anxiety, "Thomas, where will you be after you pass on?" Without hesitation Thomas said, looking straight into her eyes, "I'll be where I've always been. Right here in the universe." This response reflected what he had written earlier: "we are as old as the universe and as big as the universe. This is our great self. We survive in our great self."[37]

Thomas's final days were calm, punctuated by the familiar routine of family visitors. He passed away peacefully in the early morning hours of June 1, 2009, at age ninety-four. His niece, Ann Berry Somers, was with him. According to his wishes, multiple memorial services were held. The first service, on June 3, 2009, was presided over by former Passionist provincial Father Terence Kristofak and held at St. Paul the Apostle Church in Greensboro. Besides Kristofak's homily, brother-in-law Gordon Forester remembered Thomas's life and career, with niece Ann Berry Somers adding reflections. Three days later, on June 6, a Mass was offered for Thomas at Immaculate Conception Monastery in Jamaica, New York, where he had lived before the Riverdale years. The Passionist provincial, Joseph Jones, presided, and Canadian Passionist Stephen Dunn delivered the homily. The third memorial was a Eucharistic celebration held on June 8 at Green Mountain Monastery in Vermont. Stephen Dunn officiated, and Ann Berry Somers delivered the homily. Thomas was then buried on the land next to a massive boulder, with Paul Winter's music bringing him to rest. Multiple obituaries in major national papers celebrated his life and legacy.[38]

That autumn, on September 26, a memorial service attended by over a thousand people was held at the Cathedral of St. John the Divine in New York. Before the memorial itself, the Thomas Berry Award was presented to Martin Kaplan, a longtime supporter of the work of Thomas, especially in the field of religion and ecology. Kaplan gave the accompanying lecture and spoke of the need to carry Thomas's vision forward.[39] In addition to Mr. Kaplan's speech, remarks were given by former senator Timothy Wirth, Ann Berry Somers of the University of North Carolina, Greensboro, Stephen Dunn of the University of Toronto, and Rick Clugston and Steven Rockefeller of the Earth Charter International Council.

Following the award ceremony was the memorial service for Thomas Berry—a celebration of his life and a gesture of gratitude from all present for his life work. It began with a momentous procession including members of the Omega Dance Company and the music of Paul Winter on his hauntingly beautiful soprano saxophone. Eugene Friesen offered an artistic tribute on his cello; Kathleen Deignan and Danny Martin sang stirring solos. The entire congregation came together in song.

The music, dance, and artistry in the memorial service combined to uplift the crowd and carry those gathered there out of those walls of stone into communion with the Earth community. Reflections were offered by the memorial organizers, Mary Evelyn Tucker and John Grim, as well as by Nobel Laureate Wangari Maathai and close colleagues of Thomas: Wm. Theodore de Bary of Columbia University, Brian Thomas Swimme of the California Institute of

8.5 Wangari Maathai at the memorial service for Thomas Berry at the Cathedral of St. John the Divine, September 26, 2009.
Nic Tuff

Integral Studies, and Sr. Miriam MacGillis of Genesis Farm. Brian Brown of Iona College read his poem on the "golden year" in Thomas's honor. These reflections gave a glimpse into the humanity and the brilliance of the man being remembered and honored there.

Paul Winter commented: "It was a summit meeting of wisdom-keepers . . . all Thomas' children."[40] Clare Hallward, who had come from Montreal, recalled:

> "I felt shaken as by a mighty wind, love as fire. We were all caught up in that beautifully orchestrated dance of joy unleashed. . . . Affording us a glimpse of what Thomas called the Grand Liturgy of the Universe. Words no longer suffice to convey the moment."[41]

Lauren deBoer, editor of *EarthLight*, reflected on why the participants were so moved:

> "Thomas represented an older, deeper, more primary source of wisdom, one we need so much today. He brought that out in people, gave expression to the

8.6 The Omega Dance Company performing at the memorial service for Thomas Berry at the Cathedral of St. John the Divine, September 26, 2009.
Craig Kochel

unexpressed in so many of us, made us feel less alone, less alienated, perhaps a little less sorrowful and more hopeful about what we can do about the desecration of the planet."[42]

Filled with that spirit of hope and healing, the graceful dancers, streaming banners, and redolent music gave a final farewell, along with the commitment, in the words of Martin Kaplan, to "choreograph our way into the future by listening intently to the music and dance of the Earth, and of all the species that share Earth with us."[43] In the following months, other memorials around the world honored the life and legacy of Thomas Berry. The arc of his life journey was complete; the resonances of his thought continue.

Interlude: The Arc of a Life

Thomas Berry.
Lou Niznik, courtesy of Jane Blewett

homas Berry's life journey started in Greensboro, North Carolina, in 1914 and ended there in 2009. He began surrounded by a large loving family and ended embraced by family and friends from all over the world. Those who met him felt enlivened by their encounter. Those who read him were often deeply changed. He influenced people in many disciplines, not only in religion and theology but also in law, economics, agriculture, education, and politics. Why was this the case?

Perhaps more than most academics, Thomas was widely read in his own field of history and religion, but also in other fields he chose to study. He was truly a renaissance person, continually seeking knowledge in new areas. The intense specialization fostered in higher education no longer lends itself to such breadth of exploration. In addition, Thomas was able to achieve a depth of understanding that was rare in his times and ours. Thus, he could converse with people of widely different backgrounds and expertise.

But how did he achieve such breadth and depth? This achievement may have been due to the time he set aside in the monastery for study without obligations to a family. His basic needs were provided. He did not have to earn a living, cover rent, support a family, cook meals, or pay for health care or education. Moreover, his monastic training gave him skills for study as it encouraged contemplation and discipline along with prayer and preaching. Thomas knew how to reflect and then synthesize what he was reading. And his insights were invariably original. Over many years he was able to study intensely in the monastery and collect a sizable library.

In addition, Thomas didn't begin university teaching until he was forty-three. He had time to prepare himself and gain exposure to other cultures—three years in Europe and travel in Asia. He was then ready to contribute in a university setting. For the next two decades, he worked intensely to train graduate students in the world's religions at Seton Hall, St. John's, and Fordham. During this period and beyond, he wrote numerous essays collected in the Riverdale Papers. He never stopped working, he never gave up writing, and he never indulged in despair. He was seeking not simply knowledge for its own sake or for publication of an article or book, but rather for an integral understanding of the arc of history.

Thomas pursued his work with grace and humor—a twinkle always in his eye and laughter ready to rise up. He was unfailingly kind, unstintingly generous. He had an irrepressible joy that spilled over into hospitality to whomever he met. People felt they were his close friends even after one meeting. He had an unusual charisma as well as a prophetic voice that could thunder at those disrupting Earth's ecosystems and roar at those institutions failing to respond. His criticisms of education, politics, business, and religion were usually scathing. But he was always identifying those who were change makers on the borders of the establishments.

What gave him his drive? It was a deep feeling for human suffering and a profound concern for the destruction of the life systems of the planet. He could not abide the withering of the Earth's beauty, the diminishment of its biodiversity, the marginalization of its struggling peoples. He brooded over the tragedies humans were inflicting or enduring.

A historical perspective was his way forward:

> I turned to history. Not to political or economic or social history, which were the dominant modes of interpreting history at the time, but to the newly emerging discipline of cultural history of the various peoples of the world. First there was need to appreciate the various classical traditions that had influenced the world so profoundly. This included the Hindu, Buddhist, Chinese, Japanese civilizations particularly. Then the biblical world with its Jewish, Muslim, Christian traditions. These were closer to my own language.
>
> But then I saw that there were two other traditions that were needed—one was the traditions of the indigenous peoples of the world, the other was the scientific tradition of the modern western world. How could all this be managed in any significant manner. Of course it could not be managed at the professional level of competence. But it could be managed at some level of understanding.
>
> (*Goldenrod*, 52)

He knew he would never be an expert in these traditions, but he felt that some general understanding was necessary at this point in world history. Humans needed to situate themselves in the larger diversity of cultures and religions.

But that was not enough. He realized that all cultures are embedded not only in human history, but also in Earth history. He therefore needed to expand his studies to geology and geography, ecology and the environment. And he never stopped. The epic of evolution embraced the cosmos as well, and he thus studied the formation of galaxies, stars, and planets.

The universe itself was calling him in a way that was unique and unrepeatable; the universe was asking him to tell its story. And so he did. The arc of history was urging him forward, not promising an easy path or even deliverance, but rather an ongoing struggle in the midst of tremendous odds. He knew there was no guarantee of success, but he rested his hopes on the possibility that the human spirit might indeed find a new path. He knew that the journey of the universe is woven with both chaos and creativity, with uncertain twists and turns. For Thomas, evolution moves into ever-deeper dimensions of complexity and consciousness.

Thus, he felt that the awakening of the human within evolutionary time was only just beginning. He drew on a steadfast hope beyond anything one can name or fully know. For him some of the sources for guidance were his historical studies and his understanding of Teilhard, along with his appreciation of Confucianism and indigenous traditions. This final section explores these influences as a tapestry he wove from within the arc of history. His sources of inspiration may contribute to our inspiration as well.

CHAPTER 9

Narratives of Time   ·

Although we have not been aware of it, we have in my lifetime been moving from human history to planetary history. From socio-political history to history of the biosystems of the planet. A new perspective has evolved which is still too difficult for most historians and most scientists to deal with.

Thomas Berry, *Goldenrod: Reflections on the Twentieth Century*

Momentous changes framed Thomas Berry's life—global economic depression, two world wars, and massive ecological devastation. He interpreted his journey in relation to these historical events, but not to them alone. Over a lifetime Thomas connected his historical studies with his expanding awareness of the evolutionary narrative of deep time. This vision was nurtured by his formation as a Christian and was further cultivated during his graduate studies, when Thomas associated the study of history with the Renaissance ideal of *homo universalis*, the capacity of humans to develop the broadest knowledge possible. His understanding of this perspective was inspired by the Western philosopher of history Giambattista Vico (1668-1744). Thomas eventually expanded this theory to include other human cultures as well as geological and cosmological time.

GIAMBATTISTA VICO AND THE AGES OF THE HUMAN

Vico was a seminal influence on Thomas's thought. Thomas wrote on Vico's major work, *The New Science of the Nature of the Nations*, for his doctoral dissertation at Catholic University.[1] As he stated: "Vico was the first person in the modern intellectual history of the West to understand that the human mind goes through different modes of understanding in the various periods of human cultural development" (*Goldenrod*, 72).

In his narrative of time, Vico posited three ages: the Age of the Gods (theocratic), the Age of the Heroes (aristocratic), and the Age of Humans (democratic). All societies passed through these repeating stages of cultural development. In the first age, powerful gods are revered among tribal peoples, who experience nature as living and who invoke nature with imaginative, ceremonial language. Aristocratic families dominate the second age of heroes with symbolic and heraldic languages. In the third age, reason predominates with languages that are discursive, analytical, and legal. Each age ends with a "barbarism of reflection," in which the distinct religion, language, politics, and jurisprudence of the age becomes an over-refinement that corrupts societies and eventually causes their collapse.[2] Thomas saw contemporary parallels to this periodic decline in the modern over-emphasis on reason and the diminishment of poetic intuition.

Vico observed that both non-Christian and later Christian communities transmitted the poetic wisdom of their founding achievements. Thus, the "ages" for Vico were not simply linear progressions that left earlier ages behind; each stage contained vestiges of prior periods, even as it was dominated by its own character in the course of history. This idea of cumulative cultural accretion provided Thomas with the insight that earlier intimacies with the natural world could be recovered by later ages.

In Vico's reflections on his "new science," reason was the dominant characteristic of the "Age of Humans," enabling its accomplishments. But an overemphasis on reason could also lead to what Vico called a "barbarism of reflection": endless analysis and objectification of the world. Thomas was deeply influenced by Vico's critique of reductive reason, especially a Cartesian approach that viewed reality as simply measurable and objective substance and thus available for unlimited use. Moreover, in Vico's thought humans create history, and, in that sense, they can know history in ways that they cannot know the natural world that is created by God.

Drawing on these perspectives from Vico, Thomas eventually concluded that a link between humans and the natural world was something to be discovered. The challenge of the present is for humans to recover intimacy with the natural world despite widespread ecological destruction. Thomas asked humans to imagine themselves into new roles inspired by ecological awareness. People must recover the mystique of subjectivity to avoid the trap of modern mechanism:

> Since the time of Descartes, Bacon, Galileo and Newton the effort of western intelligence had been to discover the mechanistic aspects of the universe as the exclusive explanation of the universe. The mystique of the universe as a community of ensouled realities disappeared in a definitive manner. The universe became a collection of objects. Only in this view could the plundering of the natural world take place with such disdain for the inherent grandeur and magnificence of the natural world.
>
> (*Goldenrod*, 71)

HISTORY AS THREE MEDIATIONS

Thomas later described history as involving three types of mediations: first, human-divine exchanges, as seen in religious traditions; second, the ways in which humans interacted with other humans; and, finally, human-Earth mediations, in which humans interact with Earth's ecosystems.[3] Thomas did not abandon his earlier studies in human-centric Western history, but he realized that humans were shaped by the long evolutionary history of the cosmos and the Earth:

> We need a more adequate understanding of the universe, of how it came into being, of its governing tendencies, and of the sequence of transformations whereby it has taken on its present forms of expressions. We need to know how the solar system and Earth came into being, how life developed on the planet, and finally, how we ourselves appeared and what our human role has been within this amazing process. All these things need to be understood as aspects of a spiritual as well as a physical process.

9.1 Statue of Giambattista Vico (1668-1744) in front of the Palazzo Di Giustizia in Rome, Italy.
iStock by Getty Images

Thus, the three mediations helped him to contemplate how humans were being shaped by cultural and cosmological values that, in turn, shape future evolutionary processes.[4]

In addition to Vico's philosophy of history, Thomas's historical thinking initially drew on complex patterns in the Hebrew Bible and on formative Christian thought that interpreted time in sacred, mythic ways. Especially significant for him were certain themes in Hebrew and Christian scriptures: the periodization in history; the Israelite covenant with the Divine; and apocalyptic language as a call to reinvention.

PERIODIZATION IN HISTORY

Thomas was aware that periodization—the division of something into historical periods—had been used as an organizational technique in ancient Near Eastern thought and texts. Records of the Egyptian rulers marked eras by associating them with a pharaoh's reign name. Thus, the ruling person, as a god-king, became an icon of the larger meaning of time. Periodization became more than simply a technique for organizing time; it was a way for the smaller self in society to participate in the larger figure of a cosmic ruler. Period names and terms became sacred icons of social and cosmological turnings in which spiritual worlds of meaning were mediated into human history.

The Israelite peoples adapted periodization as a way of thinking about, and participating in, past events filled with sacred revelation. Biblical names of Torah scripture such as *Exodus*, *Judges*, and *Kings* are specific references to seminal events in Hebraic history. Time, then, was not only increasingly segmented into period names, but most importantly was recognized as revealing a sacred purpose. In the Bible, the history of the chosen people is presented as a sacred history in which divine-human and human-human interactions are mutually amplified. Time is experienced as moving with purpose, as in a story.

Thomas was especially drawn to the second chapter of the Book of Daniel as an example of periodization in historical thinking. Here, the prophet Daniel interprets a dream of the Babylonian king, Nebuchadnezzar.[5] The king has a disturbing dream that he has not even told to his Chaldean diviners, yet he demands that they give their interpretation of that unknown dream. Upon their failure to do so, Daniel comes forward and not only tells the dream but also provides an interpretation with stunning historical implications:

> You saw, O king, and beheld, a great image. This image, mighty and of exceeding brightness, stood before you, and its appearance was frightening. The head of this image was of fine gold, its breast and arms of silver, its belly and thighs of bronze, its legs of iron, its feet partly of iron and partly of clay. . . . You, O king . . . you are the head of gold. After you shall arise another kingdom inferior to you, and yet a third kingdom of bronze, which shall rule over the Earth. And there shall be a fourth kingdom, strong as iron, because iron breaks to pieces and shatters all things; and like iron which crushes, it shall break and crush all these. And as you saw the feet and toes partly of potter's clay and partly of iron, it shall be a divided kingdom. . . . A great God has made known to the king what shall be hereafter. The dream is certain and its interpretation sure.[6]

In Daniel's interpretation, the decreasing value of the ore in the statue's body parts is analogous to the degeneration of Nebuchadnezzar's empire into divided kingdoms. Most importantly, Daniel draws from the dream an interpretation that acknowledges divine workings in time. Here, Thomas finds an insight that marks so much of his later thought, namely, that the dream drives the action. Historical periodization in Israel foreshadowed the participation of the larger human family in the wisdom of divine revelation in time through all three mediations. This led Thomas to search for a larger frame for the ages of human history, and eventually his search led to a cosmological sequence of transformations.

Influenced by biblical periodization and by Vico's formulations of the ages of history, Thomas observed: "The historical sequence of cultural periods can be identified as the tribal-shamanic period, the Neolithic village period, the classical civilizational, the scientific-technological period, and the emerging ecological period."[7] In making this periodization of history, he departed from a sense of history in which the emerging period shatters the preceding era. Rather, history involves nested stages in which dimensions of former periods endure and interact with the dominant age.

Yet, as Thomas had learned in his studies of Vico, each period distinctly shapes new cultural expressions and agendas. These historical dynamics, from the shamanic to the ecological era, emerged not from a wholly transcendent source, but from a sacred energy integrated into the three mediations. Each of these periods was a "macrophase" in which "a form is established that governs the basic modes of human activity of that period."[8] In these narrative periodizations of time, individuals and societies participated in larger visions of themselves and their role. Thus, humans could be inspired to do the "Great Work" of their time through the dynamic of the three mediations.

THE ISRAELITE COVENANT AND THE PROPHETIC CALL TO A "DAY OF THE LORD"

A second pattern from biblical history that influenced Thomas's thought was the idea of responsibility toward the covenant. In biblical history, the Israelite covenant reflects the three mediations: covenant obligations to the ever-present Divine are formulated, human ethical laws come forth, and settlement flourishes in a promised land. This ethical behavior of humans in relation to one another, predicated on responsibility to the divine-human covenant, gave rise to the promise of fertile land as the human-Earth mediation.

These three mediations are woven into the mythic expression of "a day of the Lord" in which people were promised for land, offspring, and a secure future. When they later neglected their responsibility to the covenant, the Israelite prophets warned of a different, more disastrous "day of the Lord." For Thomas, this reversal of the "day of the Lord" meant that a catastrophic cultural barbarism could emerge if a sacred dream became distorted or an end in itself. Thus, the prophets identified another type of sacred history that could reverse the promised dream.

Many of the prophets spoke of an imminent catastrophic "day of the Lord" because the Israelite people had lost their dream, their commitment to a divine covenant. For Thomas such biblical prophecy is manifest in the West's drive toward a promised future dream. However, sacred history in the Bible could lead to either beneficial consequences in that promised future or catastrophe resulting from disregard of the covenant. To Thomas, the modern wanton destruction of the natural world would also have apocalyptic consequences.[9]

Thomas realized that Israelite historical attitudes toward time and place—while cosmological in attributing creation to the Divine—eventually lost their mooring during the Babylonian Captivity and subsequent Second Temple period. That is, Israelite religiosity was increasingly removed from the natural world. The biblical world, then, collapsed the three mediations of their covenantal commitment. With the loss of human-Earth intimacies, only the first two mediations were recognized as revelatory. Nonetheless, the Israelite prophets alerted the people to the danger of losing the promise of fertile land and offspring, even as their eyes were fixed on a transcendent dream of restoring the Davidic kingdom.

THE APOCALYPTIC REINVENTION IN CHRISTIAN SCRIPTURES

The terror of the prophetic warning of a divine intrusion into human history is continued in the Christian New Testament.[10] The Hebrew scripture of Daniel *manifested* a new form of prophetic writing, namely, apocalyptic literature. The cataclysmic end of time, or "day of the Lord" in which judgment falls upon each individual, also carried over into the New Testament and appears in the Christian Book of Revelation (or the Apocalypse of John).

In the Book of Revelation, a thousand-year period, or millennium, is described as the time of an absolute promise and the presence of a righteous paradise for the faithful remnant before the final judgment. For Thomas, this millennial drive for paradise continues the older biblical dream of the covenant's promise. Indeed, for Thomas this became the key mythic idea underlying the modern drive toward economic and technological progress.[11] He also understood how such ethno-religious ideas as "chosen people," "promised land," and "righteous remnant" could mask the positive promise of religions and give rise instead to negative problems of religious ideology and intolerance. He often noted that apocalyptic thought has been used in the West to support ethno-nationalism, colonial dominance, economic injustice, and ecological devastation—in the age of globalization and imperialism from the time of Columbus to the present. Cosmological visions had multiple implications—for genuine inspiration as well as for exploitive manipulation.

LOSS OF COSMOLOGICAL STORIES AND APOCALYPSE

Cosmological stories, Thomas conjectured, are ways of orienting and grounding humans in the larger matrix of life.[12] They provide answers to questions such as: Where do we come from? Why are we here? What is our role? Such stories were narratives of time that aligned the day-to-day, or microphase, activities of a people with a vision of a macrophase cosmic story.[13]

When cosmological stories disintegrate, such as in the present diminishment of the Genesis story in relation to science, human communities experience dislocations, marked most acutely by a community's displacement from a larger universe of meaning. In such moments, the language of apocalypse may forestall catastrophe because although apocalyptic language communicates a feeling of loss and a sense of impending doom, it often calls for the transformations needed to recover cultural coherence. In the following passage, Thomas uses apocalyptic language to describe the modern environmental dilemma:

> If the supreme disaster in the comprehensive story of the Earth is our present closing down of the major life systems of the planet, then the supreme need of our times is to bring about a healing of the Earth through this mutually enhancing human presence to the Earth community. How to achieve this mode of presence is not always clear. That is why a new type of sensitivity is needed, a sensitivity that is something more than romantic attachment to

some of the more brilliant manifestations of the natural world. A sensitivity that understands the larger patterns of nature, its harsh and deadly aspects as well as its life-giving aspects, and is willing to see the human diminish such that other life forms might flourish.[14]

Thomas sees environmental degradation as a call for reorienting the human community away from overextended consumption and economic development. He calls for humans to limit their consuming desires in response to the massive extinctions in the natural world. He describes this sensitivity as an awakening to a "New Story" in which humans would willingly see their impact diminish so that the community of life might flourish.[15]

NARRATIVE TIME AND A NEW STORY

An emerging "New Story" functions in a macrophase capacity, as had the "Old Stories" found in religious scriptures. But this story initiates humans to a fundamentally different historical reality. Thomas began his 1978 essay on "The New Story" by acknowledging the following:

> We are in between stories. The Old Story—the account of how the world came to be and how we fit into it—is not functioning properly, and we have not learned the New Story. The Old Story sustained us for a long period of time. It shaped our emotional attitudes, provided us with a life purpose, and energized action. It consecrated suffering, integrated knowledge, guided education. We awoke in the morning and knew where we were. [16]

He believed that humans are now being called to reinvent themselves in all three mediations. They are being challenged to understand how the biological community of life relates to the cosmological emergence of the universe:

> The genetic coding that gives to the human its species identity is integral with this larger complex of codings whereby the universe exists, whereby the Earth system remains coherent within itself and capable of continuing the evolutionary process. To remain viable a species must establish a niche

for itself that is beneficial both for itself and for the surrounding community. The difficulty generally with this proposal is that our genetic endowment is considered to be a mere physical determination of our being, not also our richest psychic endowment, our guiding and inspiring force, especially when the human process has entered into a condition of pathological distortion.[17]

For Thomas, *self-realization* in the larger story calls for a reinvention of *ourselves* as participating in our genetic relatedness to Earth, as well as in the material elements of the universe. The challenge that Thomas himself underwent by integrating cultural and evolutionary history became his prophetic call. He called humans back from a hyper-individualism trapped in a use-relationship with an objectified, dead world. The three mediations evident in the cultural historical record inspired him to call for a communion experience with the Earth community as continuing the emergence of the universe.

THE HISTORICAL SELF AND THE CRISIS OF MEANING: AUGUSTINE OF HIPPO

Thomas was aware that such a struggle for deep transformation had also occurred earlier in Western history. Thus, it was Augustine of Hippo (354–430 CE) who influenced his idea of a self that participated in history, especially Augustine's reflections on the "City of Man" and the "City of God." Augustine sought to turn around the despair resulting from the sack of Rome by the Visigoths in 410 CE. He was responding to charges by non-Christians that Rome had fallen because Christians had halted the sacrifices to the ancestral gods. Augustine countered this charge by presenting an understanding of eternal versus temporal powers. He observed that Christianity offers eternal forces of redemption in the image of the "City of God" that turns one inward toward heavenly salvation and away from the material and worldly drives of the "City of Man." Augustine presents a Christian *apologia*, or defense, that imparts an innovative vision of a present and future time to the West.[18]

In the *City of God*, human imagination is the key to perceiving future directions and to achieving ultimate goals in the present. Augustine's city as a place that inspires human meaning-making also provided a dynamic setting for universal history because it is in this symbolic context of the city that the historical self emerges and consciously chooses a future.[19] Thomas sensed the overt and covert uses of the urban metaphor: Augustine connected overtly to the fall of Rome and covertly to his historical vision of time.

From Christ as Logos to the Jesus of History

In doing this, Augustine reimagined the Christ event in his historical narrative. Much earlier than Augustine, Christianity was understood as embodying a historical vision.[20] In this spirit, John's Gospel emphasizes that church communities are living, redeeming assemblies that believe in the Christ as Logos, or creative Word from which the cosmos continues to flow.[21] However, from Augustine's time onward the cosmological character of Christ as the Word incarnate in all reality was increasingly bracketed and often replaced by personal attention to the incarnate Jesus of history. While the idea of both the creative Father of the Trinity and the inspirational Spirit in scripture and in the visible world remained into the medieval period, individual salvation through personal identity with the sacrifice of Jesus became a goal of Christian life. In other words, Western Christian communities began to reorient themselves toward personal redemption and away from a cosmic theology of incarnation that embraced the world. Thomas felt that this turn toward redemption and escape from the world became widespread in Christian theology after the fourteenth-century Black Death, in which almost half the population of Europe died.

City of God as Reinvention

Earlier Roman pagan religions had had their own versions of a this-worldly revelation with Rome as sacred city. Citizens in this "City of Man," namely, Rome, maintained sacrificial relationships with ancestral lineages, ethnic identity, and geographical places. For Augustine these psychological and social dimensions of life related to a "City of Man" that was ending and in need of reinvention.

Augustine's sense of world history appears in his metaphor of a "City of God" that stands in contrast to the "City of Man."[22] This "reinvention" provides humans with a universal historical method that investigates each historical period so as to position it in one city or the other. These conceptions of the enduring good of the "City of God" and the facile, ephemeral, fallen character of the "City of Man" echo the classical Greek Platonic dualism of eternal ideas and corrupt matter. The entry of the incarnate Divine into the world, according to Augustine, reinvents sacred time and interrupts the seemingly eternal cycles of profane time in classical pagan Greek and Roman thought.

The metaphor of the city, for Thomas, also underscores Augustine's idea that civilization is an archetypal pattern transmitted by the classical gods and ancestors and implemented through human agency. In Greek classical thought, the city was an organization of humans who were bound by loyalties stretching across ties of language and kinship into sacred ancestral presences.[23] Augustine, however, introduces new criteria for self-actualization in the city; that is, he emphasizes activities for building the "City of God" that would endure after the end of time. Moreover, Augustine presents critical tools for identifying those discrete forces that bring about the development of each of the two cities.

Augustine and the Self in Historical Time

For Augustine, Christians yearning for redemption also grapple with momentous issues relating to the kingdom of God in future time. Augustine articulates his argument regarding the future in his *Confessions*.[24] Here, he develops a narrative of time in which human imagination is joined with intuition and rationality to glimpse and articulate future events. Augustine counters fatalistic views of history in which humans could not alter their fate, predominant in the classical period, by positing the presence of the "City of God" and describing creative human acts guided by the Spirit as choices in the historical process. In this way, Augustine reinvents the individual self as a locus of moral reasoning that counters the classical pagan idea that persons exist in a community of both living beings and their ancestors. Augustine's "self" is situated in a historical time that is linked to biblical salvation, as well as in a cosmos fashioned by One God manifest in three persons, the Christian mystery of the Trinity.

Thomas, Augustine, and the "New Story"

Thomas understood the power of Augustine's historical insights, and thus he used the term *New Story* as a metaphor for a comprehensive historical narrative. He strove to articulate an engaging story of human civilizations as part of a cosmological narrative that did not oppress others but that honored differences. This capacity to transform history resulted from the ability of humans to imagine their future.

Thomas does not simply transmit these influences from Augustine, but reinvents them. Thus, in his emphasis on the "New Story" and the "Great Work," he recognizes that humans emerge within the unfolding universe. In the "New Story," differentiation, subjectivity, and communion are the cosmological principles of an emerging universe. Each thing is different, has interiority, and is interconnected with other things. Later Thomas identified these cosmological principles with the symbolism of the Trinity.[25]

The "Great Work" of the human, now, is being "present to the planet as participating members of the comprehensive Earth community."[26] In this way, "the small self of the individual reaches its completion in the Great Self of the universe."[27] By realizing how life came to exist on Earth, people can embody their interdependent cultural and genetic inheritances.[28] Thus, Augustine's remarkable idea of individual self-awareness is given new directions in Thomas's thought.

DANTE AND CREATIVE TENSIONS

Augustine's influence on later medieval thinkers, such as Dante, was significant, and Thomas's historical analysis became even richer when he encountered the creative voice of Dante Alighieri (1265–1321). Thomas taught his masterpiece, the *Divine Comedy*, many times over the years. The literary force of Dante's writings is sufficient in itself to evoke admiration, but there was also a historical dimension to Thomas's appreciation of Dante. In 1964, he wrote a short article to explore this dimension: "Dante: The Age in Which He Lived."[29] There he observed that the turbulence of late medieval Europe evoked creativity from its greatest minds: Dante and others understood that holding the tension of opposing views opened the possibility of more creative resolutions.

Berry observed: "The major tensions of the period that produced such vitality were the tensions between faith and reason, religion and life, Church and state. These opposed forces evoked from each other a depth of expression of itself, which neither could have attained in isolation from the other."[30] This tension was also manifested in the shifting alliances in the Holy Roman Empire that eventually caused Dante's exile from Florence. These varying political alliances drew on the compelling historical vision of Joachim of Flora (1135–1202), who described spiritual ages of the Father, Son, and Holy Spirit. Joachim's sense of history is indebted to biblical periodization and to Christian views of time related to the Trinity. Dante was captivated by this perspective and saw Francis of Assisi (1181–1226) as ushering in the Age of the Spirit, thus resolving the tensions of history. Dante revered Joachim's vision and placed him in Paradise in the *Divine Comedy*.[31]

Thomas also recognized Joachim's historical periodization as an archetypal philosophy of history, and he maintained that Dante's efforts to live with tensions were a means of resolving them. Embracing a unifying view of history is a central core of Thomas's thinking. For him, history can be interpreted as a shared discourse that does not impose a dominant story on different historical voices. Thomas acknowledged this tension between dominant and particular in saying that a "New Story" would not necessarily be a single universal telling, but a narrative told by every aspect of the emerging universe process.

The political and spiritual tensions in the late medieval period were illustrated for Thomas in Dante's life. Thomas pointed out that Dante's literary examination of a person began with the question of where that person was from. For Dante, individual identity and value are necessarily connected to the meaning and purpose of time and place. Similarly, in Dante's final *Paradiso*, divine reality is a multiplicity bound in a dynamic unity. This idea is uniquely expressed by Thomas's understanding of the emergent whole. Each being tells its story—whether personal or social, whether human or other-than-human—in relation to the cosmos.

THE ARCHITECTONIC COSMOLOGY OF THOMAS AQUINAS

This perspective was also held by Thomas Aquinas (1225–1274), another major influence on Thomas Berry. Thomas's encounter with the work of Aquinas enabled him to see that historical diversity in creation results from cosmic processes.

Aquinas adapted the thought of Aristotle in his synthesis of medieval philosophy. In particular, he took Aristotle's idea of form embedded in matter as central. Like Aristotle, Aquinas saw form as the inner shaping dimension of reality that participates in Divine Being. This cosmological emphasis was a major influence on Thomas. He was particularly fond of quoting this passage from Aquinas: "The whole universe together participates in the divine goodness and represents it better than any single being whatsoever."[32]

In his interpretation, Thomas sees Aquinas as combining the first and third mediations: the human encounters the Divine by contemplating the universe in each existing being in the world. He often cited Aquinas's insight into the architectonic structure of the cosmos: "The order of the universe is the ultimate and noblest perfection in things."[33] For Thomas, the historical unfolding of evolution made possible the cosmological manifestation in every being.

Thus, Thomas moves beyond Aquinas's medieval worldview by drawing on modern evolutionary thought. For both Aquinas and Thomas, the universe is a revelatory source of ultimate mystery. Aquinas argued that eternal laws governed a seasonally renewing world, which was embedded in an unchanging universe that manifested divine principles. Thomas, however, moved into a scientific understanding of evolutionary time. Rather than a fixed universe fashioned as a hierarchical "chain of being,"[34] Thomas embraced the idea of a universe that was emerging in a process of constant change. Thus, he saw history as favoring neither "progress" nor anthropocentric needs and desires, but rather as a process of cosmogenesis.[35]

MODERN NARRATIVES OF TIME

Various modern historians and philosophers also influenced Thomas.[36] Three European historians stand out: the British historian of world civilizations, Arnold J. Toynbee (1889–1975); the German political scientist and historian, Eric Voegelin (1901–1985); and the British comparative historian, Christopher Dawson (1889–1970).

Arnold Toynbee taught at the London School of Economics and the University of London, where he emphasized the challenges that civilizations faced as they matured. His thinking was influential during the period that the United

9.2 Thomas Aquinas (1225-1274).
iStock by Getty Images

Nations was formed. Thomas was particularly attuned to Toynbee's sense of the diverse influences on multicultural civilizations, and he focused on the arts and literature as ways of understanding how a civilization is formed. He would cite Toynbee early in his teaching career as he contemplated world order and the cultural interactions that gave rise to shared patterns of social cultivation, economic trade, and political alliances. As Thomas in the 1970s began to see the significance of the environment in history, he moved away from speaking about large political units to an approach that explored cultural cosmologies in relation to local ecologies.

Eric Voegelin had escaped the Nazi takeover of Austria in 1938. His experience of the violence of a totalitarian regime enabled him to understand how Christianity could amplify totalitarian violence or lead to social order. Voegelin also drew on the historiographical dimensions of the Bible in Western thought to present his political philosophy.[37] Voegelin's influence on Thomas is especially clear in his concept of the "second Exodus": he posited that the prophets achieved a special insight into the sacred character of covenantal obligations and order. It was this insight that Voegelin called a "second Exodus." Thus the "second Exodus" was a form of transcendence that could only be obtained by moving beyond the limitations of social conditions. The prophets, according to Voegelin, called for this radical change beyond the scriptural covenant initiated by the first Exodus experience to a place where Israel could be a light to the nations.

Thomas appreciated Voegelin's insight about a "second Exodus" and expanded it with his own concern for "reinventing the human at the species level."[38] He saw this reinvention as a means of moving beyond the historical and economic fixations on unlimited growth, wealth accumulation, and endless consumption. Thomas would describe industrial extraction as dominated by an analytical "use" relationship that exploited the Earth. He interpreted this massive assault on Earth processes as manifesting the colonial age and its sense of humans as a "master species" subjecting all other species to its rational calculations. In a "second Exodus," humans should gain a cosmological understanding of their material needs and production as arising out of, and dependent on, the Earth community. Thomas saw the urgency of moving toward interactions that would enhance the mutual flourishing of humans and the Earth. This required a "Great Work" in which humans would reinvent their place in a cosmological order through new politics, economics, education, and religion.

Interest in deepening his understanding of European history also prompted Thomas to visit the British historian Christopher Dawson (1889–1970) in England in February 1954. Dawson was sixty-five and Thomas was nearly forty. This was at the end of Thomas's experiences in the tense Cold War years as an army chaplain in Germany. They spoke of the challenges of the postwar period and the recovery of Europe. It was three years later that the Common Market emerged out of the destruction of World War II, and eventually the European Community arose from out of the Cold War.

Dawson emphasized that religious traditions linked together historical epochs and held key insights for intercultural understandings. This was an insight that Thomas shared. To Dawson, Europe was becoming a meeting ground of indigenous and immigrant religions that were intertwining to create innovations.[39] Dawson's broad historical view of the flow of religious ideas and practices across the Eurasian continent influenced Thomas's search for the meaningful web of relations in human societies.

Thus, as Thomas returned to the United States in April 1954, he sought to enlarge the arc of his own journey by teaching the history of world religions and cultures. He received from Christopher Dawson the confidence—at a crucial moment of his life journey—to speak of the importance of religious and spiritual values in cultural history.[40] Dawson's insights underscored the meaningful web of relations that human societies establish through religion. Thomas realized that these relations could span historical periods, giving them a continuity often overlooked by historians with ethnic, sectarian, national, or ideological concerns.

In later reminiscences Thomas recognized Dawson's influence on his understanding of history:

> [His] insight into the dynamics of history of both Europe and Asia from the Neolithic until the present is, I think, quite extraordinary. His particular style of historical narrative I spontaneously adopted as the model for my own style. One of my basic differences from Dawson was my concern for the ecosystems of the planet as the larger context in which to understand history. For Dawson, the larger context of his thinking was the cultural development of peoples and nations.[41]

When Thomas called himself a "geologian" later in life, what moved him was a sense of this profound shift in his historical consciousness. He did not need to reject the cultural and historical influences that had shaped him. Rather, his insight into "New Story" perspectives acknowledged the abiding wisdom of the past while opening him to the creative present and the future of evolutionary unfolding. As he reflected: "My own thinking . . . might be described as bringing together Christopher Dawson and Teilhard de Chardin. These were the two dominant factors in my historical thinking" (*Goldenrod*, 70).

In summary, the key elements of Thomas Berry's historical vision may be seen in the following five points. First, historical reflection is a spiritual act that orients humans to their larger role in shaping and being shaped by history. Second, human history has traditionally been viewed only through the lens of social, political, or cultural history. Third, with evolutionary history humans are now seen as embedded in the dynamic unfolding of the Earth and cosmos. Fourth, history becomes an interpretive perspective for seeing that there are intimate connections between the thresholds of change in cosmic, Earth, and human evolution. Fifth, Earth, as the most immediate encounter of the human with the universe, is the primary setting in which history is disclosed to humans and humans understand and undertake their Great Work. It is this hope for the future that still radiates from Thomas's historical vision even as he contemplated the ecological and social crises of his times:

> The history of humanity cannot be set aside; the spiritual developments, the ancient symbols cannot be ignored. Humankind must simply become conscious of the deeper and more universal forces at work in its own development. . . . The need for a more mystical relationship with the Earth becomes more widespread, education becomes primarily initiation into a wisdom tradition rather than acquisition of factual data. A comprehensive program of spiritual reconciliation begins to emerge, since it is now clear that to save ourselves we must save the totality of the human community as well as the totality of the Earth upon which we live. We are beginning to understand the deeper dimensions of the present historical crisis.[42]

CHAPTER 10

Teilhard and the Zest for Life

Here we might step back a little to look at the work of Teilhard in some of its main concerns to understand more fully just where he fits into the history of this century. Indeed, he is the first person to outline, in some full detail and with some meaningful insight, the four phases of the evolutionary process: galactic evolution, Earth evolution, life evolution, human evolution. He sees all this in its encompassing unity, and with such descriptive detail of the outer process and the inner forces that sustained the unfolding sequence. Probably no one at the humanistic, spiritual, or moral level ever attended so powerfully to this evolutionary process as did Teilhard.

Thomas Berry, "Teilhard in the Ecological Age"

THOMAS BERRY AND PIERRE TEILHARD DE CHARDIN

Pierre Teilhard de Chardin was highly regarded by some of the leading thinkers of his time, including evolutionary biologist and first director of UNESCO, Julian Huxley, who wrote the introduction to *The Phenomenon of Man*.[1] Joseph Needham, the historian of science in China, called Teilhard "the greatest prophet of this age."[2] The world historian Arnold Toynbee spoke of him as "a great man of science and a great soul. His work gives our generation the comprehensive view it sorely needs."[3] Theologian Abraham Heschel described *The Phenomenon of Man* as "a most extraordinary book, of far-reaching significance for the understanding of man's place in the universe."[4] The neurologist Karl Stern wrote that "there is

10.1 Pierre Teilhard de Chardin (1881–1955).
Photo courtesy of Association des Amis de Pierre
Teilhard de Chardin

no doubt that later, when people will look back at our time as the dark ages of positivism, Teilhard's search will stand out like a flashing beam."[5]

In this same spirit, Thomas regarded the influence from Teilhard as integral to his thought.[6] He and Teilhard were both deeply concerned with the value and beauty of the universe in contrast to the otherworldly values and escapism often taught by religion. Teilhard argued for a "zeal for creation."[7] They both struggled to rethink the roles of traditional religious cosmologies in light of the scientific story of an evolving universe. They each wanted to reconsider the Christian commitment to a separate creation of the human by a transcendent Creator. They also felt that most natural scientists favored a materialist interpretation of evolution and thus positioned the human, by virtue of rational consciousness, as outside the mainstream of evolution. In this reductive view, subjectivity resides only in the human.

Both Teilhard and Thomas had a different view of subjectivity, or interiority, as a dimension of the entire evolutionary process. It was this affirmation of the human as part of the whole of cosmic emergence that gave Teilhard and Thomas a common sense of vision and purpose. For with this comprehensive vision came a zest for life and its future. They knew that zest and human energy had to be activated to build a viable future for both humans and the Earth. They called this the Great Work.[8] Ursula King has described this kind of zest as "a certain dynamic energy and movement, an aliveness that spurs us on, nourishes and sustains human attitudes, inspiring further action, growth and development, or it is simply understood as an alignment with the flow of life."[9] This alignment of human and Earth creativity is what Teilhard and Thomas sought to encourage for the benefit of the Earth community. Such alignment is indeed emerging, for example, in eco-cities, eco-design, biomimicry, and new sources of energy relying on wind, sun, and water.[10]

TEILHARD'S INTERIORITY AND THOMAS BERRY'S SUBJECTIVITY

Throughout his writings, Teilhard described evolution as both a physical and psychic process; matter has its physical without and its psychic within.[11] This is what Teilhard called interiority and Thomas called subjectivity—as in one of his most well-known phrases describing the universe as "a communion of subjects."[12] Their justification for such a view of inwardness in matter lies in inductive observation: if interiority exists at one point (as in human consciousness), it must exist throughout the evolutionary process.[13] This becomes evident in the increase in complexity and consciousness over the arc of evolutionary time. In this sense, human consciousness is not an aberration or addendum, but arises from out of the evolutionary process. Teilhard asserts:

> Deep within ourselves, through a rent or tear, an "interior" appears at the heart of beings. This is enough to establish the existence of this interior in some degree or other everywhere forever in nature. Since the stuff of the universe has an internal face at one point in itself, its structure is necessarily bifacial; that is, in every region of time and space, as well, for example, as being granular [material], coextensive with its outside, everything has an inside [spiritual].[14]

Teilhard saw the physical and psychic dimension of evolution as matter and spirit, differentiated yet intertwined aspects of reality.[15] For Teilhard, "spirit" was the "within" of all existence in the universe, inseparable from the visible, material "without" that humans could see, namely, matter.[16] In Teilhard's perspective, the elements of the universe are entangled in the process of evolution, pulled forward by the "within" of dynamic spirit. Teilhard describes this interior energy as drawing matter forward into patterns that result in greater complexity and consciousness. He observes that there are self-organizing principles or tendencies evident in matter that give rise to more intricate systems.[17]

From the first flaring forth of radiant particles to its present configuration, the universe has had a quantum of spirit—an interiority—that evolved inexorably toward a point that Teilhard named *omega*.[18] A phrase that Teilhard used for this universe process as it manifested on our planet was "the Spirit of the Earth."[19] Thomas affirmed and expanded this insight: "The spirituality of the Earth refers to a quality of the Earth itself, not a human spirituality with special reference to the planet Earth. . . . The human and the Earth are totally implicated, each in the other. If there is no spirituality in Earth, then there is no spirituality in us."[20]

In Teilhard's view, matter-spirit evolved and encircled the planet. On Earth successive evolutionary spheres became the lithosphere of rock, the hydrosphere of water, and, eventually, the biosphere of life surrounding the planet. This evolution over time of ever-increasing complexity and consciousness eventually emerged as life. Finally, there appeared self-reflexive consciousness in humans, giving rise to a mind-sphere around the globe, what Teilhard called the *noosphere*.[21]

Teilhard's perspective conveyed to Thomas a deepened sense of evolutionary history as diversified, having interiority, and wholly interconnected. This is what Thomas would later articulate in "The New Story" as differentiation, subjectivity, and communion.[22] The human connection to this evolutionary process changed forever the role of the human for Teilhard and for Thomas. The human could no longer be seen as something "created" apart from the whole of evolution. As Thomas would often say, echoing Teilhard and Julian Huxley, who supported Teilhard's thought, "The human is that being in whom the universe reflects back upon itself in conscious self-awareness."[23]

The deepening of interiority in the mind-and-heart of the human allows humans to participate in the all-embracing processes of the emerging universe.

For Thomas, the implications of such a planetary consciousness and a commitment to ecological awareness were clear. Teilhard realized that the collective
human consciousness, emerging in what he called the *noosphere*, had enormous
potential for creating a planetary community. Thus, he saw increasing centration
and unification within the universe. By "centration," he meant the intensification
of self-reflective consciousness.[24] By "unification," Teilhard expressed awareness
of a creativity and differentiation flowing from the unity of the universe. It is
this insight that Teilhard sought to communicate in one of his cherished phrases,
"union differentiates."[25] This feeling for the whole of the cosmos manifest in particular forms of existence informs Thomas's emphasis on differentiation in the
evolution of the universe.

In underscoring the unity of the universe, Teilhard affirmed the need to over-
come the divisive limits of political, economic, and cultural boundaries. In this
spirit, he was committed to the post–World War II efforts toward international
cooperation. Indeed, his ideas influenced those active in founding the United
Nations. Thomas, in turn, reflected on the evolution of human societies toward
greater awareness beyond the limits of the nation-state. This led to his appreciation of the World Charter for Nature ratified by the United Nations in 1982, and
later, the Earth Charter that was launched in 2000.

TEILHARD'S INFLUENCE ON THOMAS

Thomas first learned of Teilhard from John Cooper at Catholic University during
his graduate studies in the 1940s. However, he did not have a chance to really
absorb Teilhard's thought until Teilhard's writings became available in English in
the 1960s. Thomas writes:

> At the time, I was moving from theories of history such as those of Giam-
> battista Vico through the efforts at a universal history in the late nineteenth
> century to comparative history such as that of Arnold Toynbee and to that
> of the philosophy of history of Eric Voegelin. The acquaintance with Teilhard
> de Chardin made possible my moving into the realm of cosmology as history
> and human history as an extension of cosmology.
>
> (*Goldenrod*, 64)

He acknowledged that his study of history, while broad, was limited:

I already had extensive insight into the cultural history of the human community. What I did not have was an integral sense of the universe, as this was
available at the time through the new research that was being carried out
in both the microphase as well as the macrophase structure and functioning of the universe, also through paleontological research. I did not have any
adequate understanding even of the human evolutionary process. Nor did I
understand the relation of the human to the natural world.

(*Goldenrod*, 63)

Thomas had been more attentive to cultural history and religious cosmologies,
just as Teilhard had focused on geology and paleontology. As Thomas writes:

Teilhard was a person of immense significance for interpreting the vast
amount of data gathered by scientific research into the geological structure
and the sequence of living forms that occupied the planet over the millennia,
especially as these occurred in the Cenozoic period, the period leading up to
the appearance of the human. Of special importance was Teilhard's understanding of the earlier phases of human types that had existed during the past
three thousand years. He was extensively interested in the transition types, as
these had appeared throughout Asia and Africa.

(*Goldenrod*, 60)

Teilhard gave Thomas a new understanding regarding the significance of
cultural history. In his approach to history, Thomas had moved from simply
studying nation-states to examining the rich complexities of cultures. Through
Teilhard, he now realized that the universe is the ultimate context that shapes
human life and the dynamics of culture. Thomas describes Teilhard's central work,
The Human Phenomenon in this way:

This was the first great work that put together in a single narrative the story
of the universe from its primordial origins until the present. It established the
physical and the spiritual as two dimensions of the single reality of the universe
from the beginning. The story of the universe is the account of the movement

from the less complex to the more complex, from the lesser to the greater manifestation of consciousness, from lesser to greater freedom of expression. The long Cartesian separation of the physical and the psychic dimensions of the universe was ended. Mind was once again understood as a pervasive reality.

(*Goldenrod*, 62)

Thomas fully appreciated Teilhard's understanding of the psychic-physical character of the unfolding universe. For Teilhard and for Thomas, Cartesian mind-body dualism was an inadequate description of reality. For both of them, the universe is a singular reality differentiated by complex interiority. Thomas also obtained from Teilhard an appreciation for the law of complexity-consciousness, namely, that as organisms evolve from simpler to more complex, consciousness also increases. Forms of sentience exist in the world of nonhuman mammals, as well as in insects, birds, and fish. Ultimately, a unique form of self-consciousness, or reflexivity, emerges in the human order. From Teilhard, Thomas became aware of humans as a part of—not apart from—the evolutionary process. In other words, humans are integral to the whole cosmos:

This insight enabled Teilhard to identify the human story with the universe story. There was a single narrative, a continuity that had been lost over the centuries when in the western world the human was seen as such a distinctive being in the universe that every human individual had to be brought into existence by a unique disposition of the divine. With Teilhard the human, however distinctive, was a true Earthling.

(*Goldenrod*, 61)

From his encounter with Teilhard's thought, Thomas acknowledged that a new cosmological understanding began to emerge for him:

From this time onward, I had an assurance in my thinking that was not there previously. I had a basic understanding of the universe itself as the only self-referent mode of being in the phenomenal order. Every other being and every other activity was universe-referent. Only the universe was a text without a context. Every other form of being or knowledge or activity had the universe as its context.

(*Goldenrod*, 62)

This insight into the character of the universe also confirmed and expanded a position that Thomas acquired from Thomas Aquinas, who said: "The order of the universe is the ultimate and noblest perfection in things."[26] Teilhard provided a glimpse of the role of evolutionary science in explicating a modern understanding of this "order of the universe." He expresses it this way in *The Human Phenomenon*:

It was not until well into the nineteenth century, again under biology's influence, that the light finally began to dawn, revealing the *irreversible coherence* of everything that exists. Showing the interlinking of life—and soon after, of matter. Showing that the smallest molecule of carbon is a function of the total sidereal process, and that the smallest protozoan is structurally so interwoven with the web of life that its existence hypothetically cannot be extinguished without, from this very fact, the entire network of the biosphere unraveling. Showing that the *distribution, succession, and mutual interdependence of beings are born from their concrescence in a common genesis.* That time and space are organically joined together so as to weave together the stuff of the universe. This is the point we have reached—and as much as we perceive today.[27]

THE RADICAL SHIFT: COSMOGENESIS

Rather than a static universe, Teilhard's perspective points toward a sense of the universe as an ongoing *cosmogenesis*. Thomas saw that Teilhard radically challenged the views of cosmology articulated by both scientists and religious thinkers, namely, that the universe was fixed and determined in structure:

The real change in human consciousness . . . was the shift from cosmos to cosmogenesis. The sense of an abiding universe in which time moved in ever-renewing seasonal cycles was altered to a sense of the universe as a sequence of irreversible transformations. Cosmos gave way to cosmogenesis. This was perceived more clearly by Teilhard than by most scientists of his times.

(*Goldenrod*, 61)

In accepting Teilhard's view of a dynamic unfolding universe, or cosmogenesis, Thomas saw that the cosmos was not simply a determined thing in which everything exists; rather, cosmogenesis became the action of evolution at every moment, in every place, and in every being that exists.

As a stretcher-bearer during the trench warfare of World War I, Teilhard had intuited that there was meaning within a seemingly chaotic evolutionary process.[28] He wrote on the front lines, amid the suffering of war: "There is a communion with God, and a communion with the Earth, and a communion with God through the Earth."[29] Eventually, Teilhard came to realize that human participation in this communion brought one into the pressures of creativity and the depths of mystery. The process of communion was energized by the concentration and convergence of cosmic, planetary, and divine energies in the human. Humans are centered in the evolutionary whole, which, for Teilhard, is the "divine milieu" within which humans live, and breathe, and have their becoming. They are thus participating in cosmogenesis, the unfolding of deep time.[30]

These ideas were not well understood at the time, especially by the Catholic Church. Thus, Teilhard was exiled to China in the 1930s by his Jesuit order for his

10.2 Teilhard in World War I.
Photo courtesy of Association des Amis de Pierre Teilhard de Chardin

views on evolution. However, he continued his studies there, remaining throughout World War II. His research connected paleontological life with his geological understanding of transformations in the Earth's crust. His depth intuition was to connect these Earth-based observations with the emerging insights of physicists that the cosmos was expanding.[31] Cosmogenesis, for Teilhard, meant that the universe and Earth were in a state of continual emergence and development over time, as was discovered by astronomy, geology, biology, and paleontology.

This insight stood in stark contrast to major cosmological positions in Western religion and philosophy. In the Jewish and Christian traditions, the one-time creation of all existence is presented in the scriptural accounts in Genesis. Philosophy in the West, drawing on classical Neo-Platonic thought, held that a once-perfect cosmos had degenerated into its present forms. By the twentieth century, newer models of a dynamic universe challenged these older fixed cosmologies in religion and philosophy. At present, the contemporary "Standard Model" of physics describes all structures, from small-scale atomic structures to large-scale galactic structures, as organized processes in constant movement and change.[32]

This new evolutionary cosmology described the emergence of galaxies and solar systems, and eventually the rise of the first cells that evolved into multicellular organisms and complex life forms. It tried to respond to long-standing questions about how significant transitions had occurred: for example, how did galaxies emerge from a smoother, radiant universe? How did cells form and life begin? It was within this sea of questions that Thomas developed his first public presentation on Teilhard's thought.

THRESHOLDS: THOMAS BERRY'S PRESENTATION ON TEILHARD IN 1964

In 1964, when physicists in New Jersey were employing the Bell Labs radio telescope to detect the light from the birth of the universe, Thomas Berry, fifty miles to the east, was drawing on Teilhard's vision to offer his first reflections on the larger cultural implications of this new evolutionary cosmology. As Arno Penzias and Robert Wilson at Bell Labs were discovering that we live in an evolving universe, not a steady-state one, Thomas was trying to understand what the implications were for human culture and consciousness:

The account of how I became increasingly aware of the cosmological and bio-logical dimensions of existence is the story of my life. My quest for under-standing this larger context of things conditioned all the decisions I made about my life. I saw life within its larger context, eventually within the con-text of the universe itself (*Goldenrod*, 45).

Thomas was invited to speak at a conference on Teilhard at Fordham University in 1964, the first such gathering to focus on Teilhard's thought in the United States. He called his paper, "Threshold of the Modern World" and explored Teil-hard's sense of evolutionary pressures that bring about sudden transitions across evolutionary thresholds. This idea of sudden evolutionary change was consid-ered radical in scientific thought on evolution because it posited abrupt changes rather than the generally more accepted idea of a gradual process in which evo-lution left clear evidence of its forms of transition in the material, geological, or fossil record.[33] Thomas had assimilated Teilhard's view of evolution as a dynamic process in which matter evolved from simple particles into atomic structures and molecules, and eventually to galaxies and solar systems. The emergence of the human raised challenging questions about the appearance and source of self-reflexive consciousness.

In the midst of this, Thomas was trying to reconcile Teilhard's views of tech-nology, namely, as a positive expression of human evolution. Teilhard celebrated how technology was bringing humans to new thresholds. The challenge for Thomas was to reconcile this view with the environmental destruction arising from ever-expanding technologies. He felt these advancing technologies often became ends in themselves with unintended consequences.[34] Moreover, when used primarily for extraction of resources to feed an enlarged consumer appetite, technology became a tool for industrial exploitation.

It was in the midst of these pressing questions that Thomas presented his conference paper in 1964, which marked a watershed in his intellectual journey. Looking back at this moment, he wrote:

I was at the time trying almost desperately to reconcile my thoughts on the ecosystems of the Earth with the rising emphasis on technology. I had held this in abeyance during the years when I was simply studying the traditional history of peoples through their cultural phases. By this absorption in this direction I had avoided articulating any position of my own. I was dealing with scholarly data.

(Goldenrod, 64)

He reflects that at the Fordham conference something opened up:

> I took this opportunity to speak on Teilhard's idea of Threshold as an opportunity to examine the present threshold that we are now involved in since Teilhard himself was enabling our western historical vision to pass over a threshold. It was the threshold of the Technological Era. I made a great effort in this paper to accept Teilhard's ideas on the emerging period before us. I thought of the present age as a transition and adopted some of Teilhard's enthusiasm for the coming era with all its scientific and technological achievements as ultimately beneficial to the human.

(Goldenrod, 64)

However, Thomas later pulled back from this early acceptance of technology as largely beneficial for humans. While he had initially affirmed Teilhard's view of technology as manifesting an evolutionary unfolding of human consciousness, he now began to identify limitations in Teilhard's thought.[35] He observed that Teilhard inherited a modern faith in progress. This faith accounted for his confidence with regard to technology's role in what Teilhard called "building the Earth."[36] Such laudatory reflections on scientific research and technology did not always take into account technology's potential for disrupting Earth processes, as, for example, with nuclear power and genetic engineering.[37] This became a crucial point of difference for Thomas:

> I was so committed to the three positions of Teilhard on the psychic as well as the physical dimensions of the universe, of the identity of the human with the cosmological order, and the need to move from the redemptive emphasis to a creation emphasis in religious thought that I was for a time willing to accept some of Teilhard's optimism about the new age of scientific-technological controls over the course of Earth-human development.
>
> This did not last however. Almost immediately after this [1964] conference, I began to express a somewhat severe criticism of Teilhard for his sense

of human conquest over the forces of the natural world. The *Hymn to Matter* that he had written earlier in life seemed not to accord with the later effort to extend human technological controls over natural processes. These controls themselves were seen as natural processes in accord with Bergson's view that for humans to fly is strictly as natural as it is for birds to fly. In a sense, it is even more natural, since it is a further development of the natural processes.[38]

While Thomas felt that Teilhard was overly optimistic regarding technology, he resonated with the implications of the cosmology Teilhard articulated.[39] These implications took Thomas years to articulate, namely the profound connection of the human to the Earth as the outcome of cosmic evolution and the manifestation of the unity of the universe. Thus, while recognizing the continuity of his thought with Teilhard, he also was aware of his own distinctive turn toward ecology and the interdependence of life and nonlife. He called for a future in which humans acknowledge their deep relationships with the larger Earth community. Humans are dependent on the Earth not only for life and sustenance, but also for cultural meaning and creativity as cosmological beings.

Thus, Thomas embraced Teilhard's evolutionary vision of a dynamic unfolding universe bringing forth the human. At the same time, he struggled to articulate his own ideas about cultural history and ecology in an evolving universe, realizing that Teilhard and many of his contemporaries were not yet aware of the unintended consequences of industrialization. Thomas, nonetheless, acknowledged his significant debt to Teilhard: "This decision to become a critic of Teilhard as well as a follower in his monumental reorientations of western thought traditions established the basic identity of my own thinking. Without his work I would never have come to the synthesis of my own thinking" (*Goldenrod*, 65).

SEEING INTO EVOLUTION

Teilhard realized that understanding evolution would expand humanity's experience of the sacred. It is in this sense that he wrote: "For our age, to have become conscious of evolution means something very different from and much more than having discovered one further fact. . . . It means (as happens with a child when he acquires the sense of perspective) that we have become alive to a new dimension."[40] This awareness of evolution challenges us to *see*: "To try to see more and to see better is not, therefore, just a fantasy, curiosity, or a luxury. See or perish. This is the situation imposed on every element of the universe by the mysterious gift of existence. And thus, to a higher degree, this is the human condition."[41]

Teilhard understood that even empirical scientific research involved more than simply an analytical investigation of the world; it included the act of seeing the spiritual dimensions of matter in the evolutionary process. From this perspective of interiority, evolution is a movement in which the whole of the universe is active in each individuated material expression. Thus, Teilhard insisted that "union differentiates": namely, the whole of cosmic evolution is active in the creative emergence of each differentiated part of the universe.[42] Teilhard critiqued the dualistic split evident in religious worldviews in which God was seen as wholly transcendent and effecting change in the world from a realm separate from matter. He also objected to an atomistic worldview that reduced life, mind, and spirit to mere matter. Similarly, Thomas lamented a scientific viewpoint that presented matter as dead, inert, and simply functioning mechanically according to set physical laws.

10.3 Teilhard on an archaeological dig in China.

Photo courtesy of Association des Amis de Pierre Teilhard de Chardin

Drawing on his Christian orientation, Teilhard suggested that a deeper *seeing* into evolution could actually lead one toward an understanding of the Cosmic Christ as a numinous, ordering dimension of all reality (*Logos*). From this perspective, he viewed the universe as a "divine milieu."[43] This is the basis for Thomas's appreciation of Teilhard's turn from a redemption emphasis in Christianity toward a focus on creation. The turn was from an Augustinian sense of original sin and the fallen nature of the world toward the creativity of nature and the sacredness of the universe. For both Teilhard and Thomas, such a position still acknowledged disruptions in nature and degeneracy in humans. Indeed, Teilhard's vision arose from the massive suffering he witnessed in the trench warfare of World War I. However, from a broader viewpoint of developmental time, creativity and chaos were seen as an interwoven part of the evolutionary process. Teilhard's views on this and on original sin were a source of controversy within the Church.[44] This is one of the reasons why he was forbidden to publish his essays during his lifetime.

Thomas managed to avoid such theological scrutiny for a number of reasons. He never claimed to be a theologian, but rather a historian of religions. Moreover, his appreciation of diverse religious traditions and cosmological stories caused him to move away from the predominantly Christian terminology that Teilhard used. Thomas's intent was to appeal to a broader religious and cultural world than an only Christian one. He was also aware of the barriers that theological language often creates in a secular world, particularly among environmentalists. He hoped to reach a wider audience, one that was increasingly responsive to ecological and social concerns. He was also aware that Teilhard had not adequately understood other religious traditions and in this was very much a product of his colonial times.[45] Thomas's studies of religion, however, enabled him to affirm cultural differentiation and innovative views of humans in relationship to local ecologies and cosmologies.

In this spirit, Thomas moved forward by building on Teilhard's profound appreciation of the human within the whole of the universe. Thomas writes: "The human being emerges not only as an earthling, but also as a worldling. Human persons bear the universe in their being as the universe bears them in its being. The two have a total presence to each other."[46] This *presencing* of things to one another is a distinctive feature of Thomas's thought even as it reflects Teilhard's concept of interiority. Thomas spoke often of the universe as "a communion of subjects" to express his intuitions of intimacy with all life forms. Similarly, Teilhard wrote of this mutual attraction of things: "In the Divine Milieu all the elements of the universe touch each other by that which is most inward and ultimate in them."[47]

According to Thomas, the importance of this awareness of communion with the universe story should not be underestimated: "The reality and value of the interior, subjective, numinous aspect of the entire cosmic order are being appreciated as the basic condition in which the story makes any sense at all."[48] Thomas's emphasis on interiority in evolution is an important aspect of his turn as a historian toward his "New Story" approach. The inner patterning of all beings results from their long journey through evolutionary time. This interiority is what differentiates things as well as what brings them into communion with one another. Understanding the fullness of such relationships requires a bifocal approach, namely, through the lens of empirical study and through attunement to the evolutionary story. This approach enhances the human capacity to see existence as interdependent. Interestingly, Thomas saw this complementarity when he claimed that while Teilhard describes his central work, *The Human Phenomenon*, as science, he, Thomas, came to see this work as a narrative telling of the universe story.[49]

THE ORIGIN AND SIGNIFICANCE OF A "NEW STORY"

As Thomas immersed himself in Teilhard's thought, his ideas about a "New Story" began to emerge in the 1970s in relation to the ecological challenges the human community was facing. In a period of increasing assault on Earth's ecosystems, he proposed a "New Story" in his 1978 essay as a comprehensive basis for nurturing reciprocity between humans and fostering reverence between humans and the Earth.[50]

Thomas also became clearer about cosmological narratives as functional stories that arose not as simply abstract overviews, but as responses to questions of meaning for humans. In modernity, humans increasingly experienced themselves as alienated from one another, from God, and from nature. This alienation found particular expression in the post–World War II period with existentialist philosophy, as well as the death of God theology and the literature of the absurd.

This sense of estrangement spread to other parts of the world, transmitted with Western culture, globalization, and consumer materialism. Thomas presented a "New Story" as an important antidote to this disaffection, which was growing with increasing environmental degradation. He felt that a new context for human connection, purpose, and action was needed. In an attempt to untie the knots of the industrial mindset, he consistently challenged the folly of managerial control of the natural world, invoking beauty and wonder, intimacy and awe as antidotes to the ruthless economic pragmatism of extractive industrialization. Moreover, he spoke of "integral ecology" as a means for humans to participate in "a single integral Earth community."[51] Such participation involves ecological restoration, community building, agricultural renewal, environmental education, and social and political commitment toward justice, peace, and ecological flourishing. For Thomas, this was the role of a "New Story," namely, to continue what "functional cosmologies" had always accomplished: ways of activating the human energies needed for physical and psychic survival. With such energies he felt the Great Work could be invoked for the healing of the Earth. Thomas always stated that this New Story was not singular, but plural, and to be told by the Earth community. For example, humans around the world would tell it through their own cultural or religious perspectives.[52]

FROM OLD STORY TO NEW STORY

Thomas opens his "New Story" essay by observing: "We are in between stories." The old story was functional because "it shaped our emotional attitudes, provided us with life purpose, energized action. It consecrated suffering and integrated knowledge."[53] But while the meaning provided by traditional cosmological stories was no longer operative, adaptations of the old story were still evident. People turned to new age solipsism for existential assurance, to technological utopias for a constructed future, to scientific determinism for rational grounding, or to ethno-nationalism for a sense of belonging. However, for Thomas, none of these orientations were ultimately satisfying for present circumstances. He recognized the dysfunctionalism in religious, political, technological, and scientific communities and proposed a new story of how things came to be, where we are now, and how the human future can be aligned with the larger Earth community.

To communicate the values of this new universe story, it is necessary to identify the basic principles of the universe process: differentiation, subjectivity, and communion. *Differentiation* refers to the extraordinary variety and distinctiveness of everything in the universe. No two things are completely alike. *Subjectivity* is the interior, numinous component shaping all reality. *Communion* is the ability to relate to life and nonlife with awareness of distinctive subjectivities and differences. These three dimensions together create the grounds for the creativity of the universe. Thomas felt these three principles provided a comprehensive context that nested the cosmological, ecological, social, and personal dimensions of the human.

THE GREAT WORK AND THE ZEST FOR LIFE

For Teilhard and for Thomas, then, cosmic evolution provides the most comprehensive context for understanding the human phenomenon in relation to other life forms. This realization of cosmic interrelatedness for Teilhard is part of the *hominization* process whereby humans find their fuller identity and role.[54] *Hominization* implies for Thomas that humans as self-reflective beings need to understand how they belong to the cosmic whole and see their particular responsibility for the continuation of the evolutionary process in their day-to-day actions. This is what he called the Great Work. Humans have reached a juncture where they are realizing that they will determine which species will survive and which will become extinct amidst dramatic climate changes and loss of ecosystems and biodiversity. Humans are participants and partners in evolution as they become conscious of their place in this extraordinary, irreversible sequence of changes.

In all of this, both Teilhard and Thomas saw the vital importance of human energy, or action, as a way to participate more fully in the creative dynamics of evolution. Human creativity, for Teilhard, derives from a passionate dedication to meaningful action as an extension of cosmic creativity.[55] Both Teilhard and Thomas recognized this as the Great Work. A primary concern for Teilhard, and for Thomas, was the existentialist despair and ennui that pervaded Europe between and after the two world wars. They looked for a way forward. The spirit of the human needed to be brought together with the spirit of the Earth.

Here, a zest for life could nurture the flourishing of the Earth community. Teilhard recognized that an evolutionary worldview requires a shift in thinking and in moral commitment. A primary question for him was how to valorize human action and inspire the zest for life amid inevitable human suffering and natural disasters.[56]

CONTEMPLATION AND COMMUNION

A way to activate this exuberance for life and for the Great Work it evokes is through contemplation. Contemplation in the world's religions is often understood as an interior experience that demands a de-materialization and a transcendent leap into the Divine. Teilhard, however, radically reconceptualized contemplation in the age of science as a spiritual calling. He regarded scientific research as a means of participating in cosmic evolution.[57] As Teilhard observed, "For the first time in history humans have become capable not only of knowing and serving evolution but of loving it."[58] From this perspective, contemplation entails two powerful currents—evolution and love. To embrace the universe and the Earth is to be involved in a process in which one's particular love is universalized, rendered dynamic, and joined with a sense of evolution.[59]

For Thomas, this view embodies not simply an anthropocentric or human-centered love, but a love that reaches through the human to a larger world of other species. In other words, love has ecological and cosmological dimensions. Ecological contemplation, then, is one response to that call for renewal and restoration in which humans rediscover the relations between species. Moreover, Thomas recognized the cosmological dimension of love in many religions. Focusing on Asian religions, he reflected:

> What is remarkable throughout the Asian world is that terms designating supremely affectionate qualities carry ultimate cosmological significance. So in the Chinese world, *jen*, a term translated as love, benevolence, or affection, is not only an emotional-moral term, it is also a cosmic force. This can be said also of the virtue of *ch'eng*, translated as sincerity or integrity. In India the term *bhakti*, devotional love, was a cosmological as well as spiritual force. In Buddhist tradition the term *karuna*, compassion, is a supreme cosmic power.

Thus we find a pervasive intimacy and compassionate quality in the very structure of the universe and of the Earth itself.[60]

This insight into the cosmological dimension of love in the world's religions is resonant with Teilhard's sense of love pervading the universe.

Thomas understood that the human, caught in the technological trance of an industrial age, could lose this sensibility and be distracted indefinitely. His dream, in league with Teilhard, was for humans to undertake a contemplative and cosmological turn toward the living, interdependent Earth community. This turn away from an extractive worldview that sees everything as a "collection of objects" to be used was a frequent theme in his talks. Thomas would lean into the microphone and, lowering his voice, would ask how the audience felt when someone says, "You used me." Drawing out the implications of a use-relationship, he would say, "Earth gives freely to us every day; yet, we fail to see that giving. Instead we surrender ourselves to a consumer mentality requiring endless extraction. Soon, everything and everyone becomes a commodity that is subject to our use and exploitation."[61]

To break out of the grip of that mindset requires a contemplative renewal of love for the world. For Teilhard, such love is always synthesized in the personal. Here lies the point of contemplation of the world for Teilhard—the center in which all spiritual energy lies. By means of this personalizing force at the heart of the universe and of the individual, human activities become an expression of love. As Teilhard observed, "every activity is amorized."[62] Teilhard spoke of the renewal of love as a "second fire" akin to humans' first discovery of fire for warmth, security, and cooking. "The day will come when after harnessing space, the winds, the tides, and gravitation we shall harness for God the energies of love. And on that day, for the second time in the history of the world, we shall have discovered fire."[63]

This is a kind of boundless and renewable energy that both Teillhard and Thomas evoked—a love for the future that could indeed renew the face of the Earth. It requires an integrated story that could evoke for humans their role in the arc of Earth and universe time. For Thomas, this new story is told by everything that exists—the sun, the moon, the galaxies. Everything has a voice by virtue of its journey in time—mountains, rivers, trees, plants, and all species. As Thomas noted, it is a story awaiting multiple narrations with an ever-deeper confidence in the beauty and mystery of its unfolding.

CHAPTER 11

Confucian Integration of Cosmos, Earth, and Humans

No human mode of existence, of activity, or of value is possible except in a natural and social context. To awaken an individual to a consciousness of one's own being and to activate the full expansion of one's individual personality in this context are the primary obligations of society. The importance of this consciousness and this discipline can be seen when we consider how the entire order of the universe rests on the individual. Each individual becomes creator, sustainer, and fulfillment of the universe. . . . the Chinese discovered a more integral and more intimate presence of the universe and the individual to each other along with the discipline that would provide the functional efficacy needed by the individual.

Thomas Berry, "Individualism and Holism in Chinese Tradition"

Thomas Berry was profoundly influenced by the Confucian tradition and read widely in its texts and history. Even before he went to China in 1948, he had developed an interest in Confucianism, which deepened throughout his life. He began his studies of Chinese language in China and continued them on returning to New York. On the boat to China in 1948, he met Wm. Theodore de Bary from Columbia University, who was the first Fulbright scholar to China. They became lifelong friends, along with Ted's wife, Fanny.

The studies in Beijing were cut short by the movement of Mao's troops toward Beijing in December 1948 and the retreat of the Kuomintang (Chinese Nationalist Party). However, after Thomas and Ted returned to the United States, they worked collaboratively in the area of Asian studies and began the Asian Thought and Religion seminar at Columbia University. Ted de Bary became a leading

Confucian scholar and developed the field of Asian studies at Columbia, while Thomas founded the History of Religions program at Fordham University. Their abiding interest in the moral and spiritual dimensions of Confucianism was central to their friendship and their scholarly collaboration.

Thomas and Ted also recognized that the Chinese traditions of Confucianism, Daoism, and Buddhism were always interacting and mutually influencing one another. Indeed, they affirmed them as syncretic traditions that do not have mutually exclusive claims to truth, as do the Western religions. Thus, Confucianism and Daoism share the idea of following the Dao, the Way, and of various forms of cultivating *ch'i* (*qi*), or life force. Buddhism adapted into the Chinese context by using terms from Daoism, such as for emptiness. At the same time,

11.1 Statue of Confucius outside the Confucian Temple in Suzhou, China.
iStock by Getty Images

Buddhists taught filial piety using Confucian examples. For an individual to draw on practices or ideas from each of these traditions and to celebrate their different holidays was commonplace. To follow Confucian ethics in the family and society and to be buried in a Buddhist funeral was not considered contradictory. In the Ming dynasty the phrase "The three traditions are one" was widespread.

In addition, Ted and Thomas both developed a strong appreciation for the thought of Tu Weiming, one of the leading thinkers in the younger generation of contemporary Confucian scholars. These "New Confucian" scholars helped to keep Confucianism alive when they emigrated to Taiwan and Hong Kong after Mao came to power in 1949. This was particularly important with the destruction of Chinese traditions and institutions, such as Confucianism, in the Cultural Revolution. Tu emigrated from Kunming in western China to Taiwan, where he encountered the New Confucians during his university studies. He then came to the United States, where he did his doctoral work at Harvard.[1] He taught there for nearly thirty years and also directed the Harvard Yenching Institute.[2] He was invited back to China in 2010 to become the founding director of the Institute for Advanced Humanistic Studies at Beijing University.

Tu Weiming worked closely with Ted de Bary on issues of human rights, publishing books with him on the sources of such rights in the Confucian tradition.[3] He also wrote widely on the ethical and spiritual dimensions of Confucianism and the implications of the tradition for contemporary China.[4] His work was of great interest to Thomas, whose interaction with Weiming's thought was significant throughout the 1980s and 1990s. Similarly, Weiming had high regard for Thomas's understanding of Confucianism. In addition, he valued Thomas's deep concern for the future of the Earth community in light of the growing environmental crisis. Weiming continues to draw on Thomas's ideas on cosmology and ecology.

These three scholars, Ted de Bary, Thomas Berry, and Tu Weiming, along with others, have helped to reshape the understanding of Confucianism in the West. The conventional interpretation of this tradition in academia was as a political system that was at times repressive or a social system that could be hierarchical or feudalistic. While there are aspects of such control in the tradition, this is not the spirit or defining characteristic of Confucianism in theory or in practice. Moreover, it can be acknowledged that most premodern traditions have been used for power and control. The narrow interpretation of Confucianism in the West was also due in part to the lack of translations of Confucian texts and the

11.2 Tu Weiming.
Ai Bei

dearth of historical understanding of the complex historical development of this tradition in China and across East Asia.

As Ted de Bary assembled a team of translators and organized the Columbia University Press series Translations from the Asian Classics and the *Sources of Chinese Tradition* volumes,[5] this view of Confucianism would gradually change. In addition, he compiled key edited volumes on Confucianism as it developed in China, Korea, and Japan. Finally, he created courses at Columbia on the Asian classics, literature, and history that significantly expanded the understanding of Confucianism and the other traditions of Asia. All of this work took several decades and deeply influenced Thomas's ideas, as well as his teaching at Fordham. Thomas participated in many of the conferences and seminars that de Bary organized on Confucianism. Ted was immensely appreciative of Thomas's insights into the Chinese traditions, which Thomas expressed in the conference papers he wrote on topics such as "Individualism and Holism in Chinese Tradition" and "Affectivity in Classical Confucian Tradition."[6]

After returning from China, with the encouragement of Ted, Thomas continued to study the Chinese language and the classical texts of Confucianism, Daoism, and Buddhism. He supplemented this work with his wide reading of Chinese history, culture, art, and literature. He had a deep affection for Chinese poetry, especially the Tang dynasty poets Tu Fu and Li Po, who inspired his own writing of poetry. Thomas assembled an extensive library of books about China that included the classics in their original Chinese. Drawing on all of this material, he frequently taught Chinese religions at Fordham in the History of Religions program.[7]

What was key to Thomas's appreciation of Confucianism is seen in these lines:

> The main principle of Confucian thought is that the human is integral with the Earth and the entire universe. That this is compatible with modern cosmology is evident from the observations in contemporary physics that the universe is integral with itself throughout its vast extent in space and throughout its sequence of transformations in time. This is known as the cosmological principle.[8]

In addition to the cosmological dimensions of Confucianism, Thomas valued the comprehensive view of the human that this tradition offered, especially in its program of education and self-cultivation. This chapter will highlight Thomas's appreciation for the various dimensions of Confucianism: cosmological, political, educational, social, religious, and ecological. It will illustrate how a Confucian view of the interrelatedness of the universe permeates Thomas's thinking in many aspects and is relevant to his call for developing new human-Earth relations.

CONFUCIANISM AS AN ANTHROPOCOSMIC TRADITION

Confucianism has conventionally been described as a secular humanistic tradition focusing on the hierarchical roles of humans in the family, society, and politics. Thus, Confucianism is identified primarily as an ethical or political system of thought with an anthropocentric focus. However, upon further examination, and as more translations have become available in Western languages, this narrow perspective is being reexamined. This is one of the central contributions of the work of Ted de Bary, Thomas Berry, and Tu Weiming, each of whom elaborated on the religious, philosophical, and spiritual dimensions of this tradition. Thomas, for example, frequently described Confucianism as a "mystical humanism" to indicate that it is not simply a form of secular humanism. Similarly, Tu Weiming calls it "spiritual humanism," expressing a continuity between all orders of reality—Cosmos, Earth, and Human. He uses the term *anthropocosmic*, namely, the human is situated as a numinous, reflective being within the vastness of cosmos and Earth.[9]

Ted, Thomas, and Weiming have helped others view Confucianism as a profoundly religious and spiritual tradition in ways that are different from Western traditions. All three were key speakers at a Confucian Spirituality conference Tucker organized at Harvard in 1998.[10] The two volumes from this conference seek to expand the idea of "religion" itself to include more than criteria adopted from Western religious traditions, such as notions of God, salvation, and redemption. For example, they explore fresh notions of immanence and transcendence and the public impetus of religion to assist the common good. Moreover, Confucianism is being recognized for its ecological dimensions because of its affirmation of relationships not only among humans but also between humans and the natural world.[11] This was a central understanding of Thomas in his writing and teaching on Confucianism.

The Confucian worldview might be described as a series of concentric circles, where the human being is the center, not as an isolated individual but as embedded in rings of family, society, and government. Humans cultivate themselves and pursue learning in relation to these circles. In this way, they can positively influence order in the family and harmony in the state. This is especially clear in the classical text of the *Great Learning*, which Thomas would frequently cite:

> Those in antiquity who wished to illuminate luminous virtue throughout the world would first govern their states; wishing to govern their states, they would first bring order to their families; wishing to bring order to their families, they would first cultivate their own persons; wishing to cultivate their own persons, they would first rectify their minds; wishing to rectify their minds, they would first make their thoughts sincere, wishing to make their thoughts sincere, they would first extend their knowledge. The extension of knowledge lies in the investigation of things.[12]

All of these circles are contained within the vast cosmos itself. Thus, the ultimate context for the human is the "10,000 things," namely, nature in all its remarkable variety and abundance. Within this anthropocosmic worldview there is no radical separation between human and nature and the universe. Rather, a "continuity of being" exists between these realms.[13]

HISTORICAL DEVELOPMENT

Thomas would outline for his students the four major periods of Confucian thought and practice and then discuss texts from each period. The first stage is classical Confucianism, which ranges from approximately the sixth century BCE to the second century BCE. This is the era of the flourishing of the early Confucian thinkers, Confucius (Kong Fuzi), Mencius (Mengzi), and Xunzi. The second period is Han Confucianism, when the classical tradition was shaped into a political orthodoxy under the Han Empire (202 BCE–220 CE) and began to spread to other parts of East Asia. The Han period saw the development of the theory of correspondences between the microcosm of the human world and the macrocosm of the natural world. This idea was important to Thomas as he outlined the relationship of the human to nature. The third major period is the Neo-Confucian era from the eleventh to the early twentieth century. This includes the comprehensive synthesis of Zhu Xi (1130–1200) and the distinctive contributions of Wang Yangming (1472–1529). A fourth period emerges with the "New Confucians" after 1949 to the present.

While Ted de Bary was strongly influenced by Zhu Xi and his educational program, Thomas Berry and Tu Weiming were inspired by the thought of Wang Yangming, particularly his idea of innate knowing of the good. All of them were keenly interested in the further development of the Neo-Confucian idea of "forming one body with the 10,000 things." This refers to how persons identify with the myriad variety of the abundance of the world in both its natural and human forms. They also studied the influence of Confucianism as an educational and philosophical system that spread beyond China and shaped East Asian societies, especially Korea and Japan, along with Taiwan, Hong Kong, Vietnam, and Singapore. Each of them followed closely the revival of Confucianism in these regions as well as in China itself in the post-Mao era up to the present.

In the latter half of the twentieth century, as previously mentioned, a fourth epoch emerged called "New Confucianism."[14] This epoch represents a revival of the tradition under the influence of scholars who came to Hong Kong and Taiwan after Mao's ascendancy in 1949. They aspired to be in dialogue with Western philosophy and to address the contemporary need for a comprehensive philosophy of the way to be human. To this end, the New Confucians—Chi'en Mu and

Tang Junyi—founded New Asia College in Hong Kong in 1949. This later became the Chinese University of Hong Kong, and it is still a preeminent research center for Chinese studies, especially Confucianism.

In Taiwan, scholars reestablished a major Chinese research center, the Academia Sinica, which had been in Nanking since 1928. They developed a department for Chinese literature and philosophy, especially focusing on Confucian studies. Also in Taiwan the noted New Confucian scholars Mou Zongsan and Xu Fuguan taught at Tunghai University, where Tu Weiming studied. They, in turn, were students of Xiong Shili, a founder of New Confucianism who had remained on the mainland. In 1958, the key New Confucian leaders published "A Manifesto for a Re-appraisal of Sinology and Reconstruction of Chinese Culture."[15] This document emphasized that China could learn science and democracy from the West, but the West should learn something of a more integral wisdom from China, especially through Confucianism.

CONFUCIAN DESTRUCTION AND REVIVAL

The manifesto was necessary because Mao had changed the shape of modern China, and the revolution he created influenced both Chinese and Westerners in the 1950s and 1960s. Indeed, Thomas wrote a paper entitled "Mao's Great March" in which he described this march as a heroic journey in an attempt to free China of foreigners and gain power in China.[16] Thomas also recognized Mao's limits, especially his hostility to religions, his rejection of Confucianism, and his tyrannical rule. Mao felt that Confucianism was essentially a feudal tradition, anchored in ancient history. Thus, for his own ideas to flourish, he felt a radical break must be made with the past. The anti-Confucian campaigns during Mao's rule were virulent, especially during the Cultural Revolution from 1966 to 1976. However, after Mao's death in 1976, there was a gradual resurgence of interest in Confucian values in the People's Republic of China. In recent decades, this has even been encouraged by the government.

Indeed, the International Confucian Society held two major conferences in 1989 in Beijing and in Confucius's birthplace, Qufu, to explore the future of the Confucian Way. These conferences were held to commemorate the 2,540th anniversary of Confucius's birth and marked a renewed interest in Confucianism to balance the unsettling effects of the rapid industrialization and modernization of China. The conferences have continued to be held in Qufu, and, in September 2014, Xi Jinping became the first president to attend. He has been promoting Confucianism throughout his tenure in office, suggesting that China has its own cultural tradition to draw on that is different from Western religion and democracy. All of these uses of Confucianism clearly need to be interpreted through the dual lenses of political ideology and genuine efforts at cultural revival.

Since 2004, over five hundred Confucian institutes have been created around the world to promote understanding of Chinese culture. Numerous academic conferences have been held in China on Confucianism. For example, in September 2017, the eighth session of the World Confucian Conference was held in Qufu, with ninety papers by Chinese academics and sixty paper by foreign scholars. The theme was "Confucianism and a Community of a Shared Future for Mankind." In this spirit, Tu Weiming organized seven forums from 2011 to 2018 at the UNESCO heritage site of Songshan in Hunan Province. These have been attended by academics from China and abroad, as well as by government officials from this province of 94 million people. The title of the 2018 conference was "Multicultural Coexistence, Harmonious Symbiosis, Sharing Future." Similarly, Tu Weiming arranged for the World Congress of Philosophy to be held in Beijing in August 2018, the first time the conference was convened outside the West.

Clearly, there is a growing movement in China and across East Asia to reevaluate Confucianism for a sustainable future. This is part of a broader attempt to encourage the creation of "ecological civilization," drawing on the traditions of Confucianism, Daoism, and Buddhism, which has been promoted by a number of government leaders, including the former deputy vice minister for the environment, Pan Yue.[17] Ecological civilization is also now in the Chinese constitution and cited at the highest levels of government as a state policy. Whether it remains aspirational or realized is still a question, as China faces enormous environmental problems. These problems are being extended to other parts of the world with the ambitious development project called the Belt and Road Initiative.

On a popular level, Yu Dan, a media professor at Beijing Normal University, lectured on the *Analects* on China Central Television (CCTV) in 2006. These lectures were published as a book titled, *Confucius from the Heart: Ancient Wisdom for Today's World*, which has sold over 10 million copies. It is considered rather elementary by most scholars, but its popularity reflects something of the spiritual vacuum in contemporary China. Even accomplished China scholars, such as Michael Puett of Harvard, have helped to popularize Confucianism in their writings, classes, and talks.[18]

Moreover, since 2004, a "Chinese classics fever" has spread across the country, encouraged by the government and by newspapers. This has been promoted by the Ministry of Education through the teaching of Chinese language through the classics. In addition, in 2016, a massive National Chinese Classics Centre was established at the former Beijing Olympic Park. In the same year, the Ministry of Education launched a series of textbooks for teaching Chinese traditions, primarily through the Confucian classics.

MODELS OF CONFUCIAN FLOURISHING

It was Thomas's enduring concern to contribute to the contemporary search for a common future for the Earth community. Thomas rarely used the term *sustainability*, but instead preferred *flourishing*, as something that would point toward a vibrant future that humans could create. He recognized the need for new human-Earth relations and was deeply inspired by the Confucian tradition, which embodied a cosmological vision of such relations. Some of the primary Confucian philosophers who shaped Thomas's thinking in this regard are explored here. He drew on these philosophers throughout his teaching and writing life.

Confucius: Moral Rectification Extending Outward

The acknowledged founder of the Confucian tradition was known as the sage-teacher Kongzi (551–479 BCE). His name was Latinized by Jesuit missionaries in the sixteenth century as Confucius. Born into a time of rapid social change, Confucius was concerned with reestablishing political and social order through rectification of the individual and the state. The principal teachings of Confucius are contained in his conversations recorded in the *Analects*. Here, he emphasized the cultivation of moral virtues, especially humaneness (*ren*) and the practice of civility or ritual decorum (*li*), which includes filiality (*xiao*). Such virtues were exemplified by the noble person (*junzu*), particularly within the five relations, namely, between ruler and minister, parent and child, husband and wife, older and younger siblings, and friend and friend.

The essence of Confucian thinking was that to establish order in the society, one had to begin with harmony, filiality, and decorum in the family. Then, like concentric circles, the effects of virtue would reach outward to the society. Likewise, if the ruler was moral, it would have a ripple effect on the rest of the society and on nature itself, like a pebble dropped into a pond. This was true for the Confucian sage/teacher, whose influence could be seen in his students. This was a perspective that Thomas reflected on frequently and embodied in his life, especially in his teaching at Fordham. His students appreciated his sage-like wisdom and his search for moral depth and spiritual insight. Like a genuine noble person (*junzi*), he did not aspire to be a "guru" or to imprint his ideas on his students for their theses. He had an open mind-and-heart (*hsin*) and encouraged broad reading and reflection on genuine Confucian practice.

This Confucian practice was exemplified in humaneness and civility, which was at the heart of Thomas's interactions with students, visitors, scholars, and family members. These two virtues gave expression to human relatedness as a spiritual path. Through civility, beginning with filiality, one could repay the gifts of life both to one's parents and ancestors and to the whole natural world. Through humaneness, one could extend this sensibility of care to other humans and to all living things. In doing so, one became more fully human. The root of humaneness was considered to be filial relations. The extension of these relations from one's family and ancestors to the larger human family and to the Earthly family of the natural world was the means whereby these primary biological ties provided a person with the roots, trunk, and branches of an interconnected spiritual path.

For Thomas, as for all Confucians, humans, nature, and the cosmos were joined in the stream of filiality. From the lineages of ancestors to future progeny, intergenerational connections and ethical bonds were created. Reverence and reciprocity were considered a natural response to this gift of life from parents and ancestors. Analogously, through reverence for Heaven and Earth, as the great parents of all life, one realized one's full cosmological being and one's place in the natural order. Life flourishes from the individual radiating outward. This was a central aspect of Thomas's personal journey, as he was committed to the continuity of being of all life forms not only in a symbolic sense, but also in an evolutionary framework of interdependence. He would acknowledge that from the explosion of stars to the development of carbon-based life, there is a single unfolding reality.

Mencius: Botanical Cultivation of Self and Nature

Confucian thought was further developed in the writings of Mencius (c. 371–c. 289 BCE) and Xunzi (c. 300–c. 219 BCE), who debated whether human nature was intrinsically good or evil. These two thinkers had a strong influence on Thomas, although he placed himself firmly in the Mencian lineage. Mencius's argument for the inherent goodness of human nature gained dominance among Confucian thinkers and gave an optimistic flavor to Confucian educational philosophy and political theory. This perspective influenced the spiritual aspects of the tradition as well, because self-cultivation was seen as a means of uncovering this innate good nature. Mencius used the example of a child who was about to fall into a well. In such a situation humans would instinctively move to call out and rescue the child. This simple but penetrating example became an important part of the Confucian tradition, which affirmed that humans could develop this goodness further through education and self-cultivation. Thomas illustrated this perspective in his teaching, helping students to realize that they were not just reading ancient historical texts from the past, but were absorbing insight for the present. For him, as for all Confucians, the goodness of human nature could be fostered and tended, like a garden. This was both a spiritual and intellectual endeavor involving reflection and practice.

Mencius contributed an understanding of the process required for genuine self-cultivation. He identified the innate seeds of virtues in the human and suggested ways in which they could be encouraged to grow toward their full realization as virtues. Analogies taken from the natural world extended the idea of self-cultivation of the individual for the sake of family and society, to a wider frame of reference that also encompassed the natural environment. This can be described as a path of botanical cultivation, pulling up the weeds so as to cultivate the plants of virtues.

In addition to his teachings on personal cultivation, Mencius advocated humane government as a means to promote the flourishing of a larger common good. His political thought embraced appropriate agricultural practices and proper use of natural resources. In particular, he urged that the ruler attend to the basic needs of the people and follow the way of righteousness, not profit.

Xunzi: Ritual Relationship of Humans and Cosmos

Xunzi saw human nature as innately flawed, and thus he emphasized the need for education and ritual to shape human nature toward the good. He had a strong sense of the importance of ritual practice as a means of self-cultivation. Human desires need to be satisfied, and emotions such as joy and sorrow should be expressed in the appropriate degree. Thomas recognized Xunzi's contribution in this regard and affirmed the need for rituals to shape human emotions throughout a person's life. Rituals can provide the form for emotional expression in daily human exchange, as well as in rites of passage such as marriage and death. When Thomas performed a wedding or a funeral, he composed simple poetic comments that drew forth the joy of the couple or underscored the sorrow of loss.

Xunzi also had a highly developed sense of the interdependent triad of Heaven, Earth, and humanity that was emphasized also by many later Confucian thinkers. He wrote: "Heaven has its seasons; Earth has its resources; humans have their government."[19] Heaven here is understood as the guiding force of the Universe, and Earth as the natural world within which humans live and form communities. This was a central idea in Thomas's thought as well, especially as he began to explore cosmology. He frequently referred to the triad of Heaven, Earth, and humans as an interpenetrating cosmological worldview. He realized that modern Western philosophy and religion had left behind such an integrated worldview for a dualistic one that separated humans from nature and maintained a division between humans and the Divine as a transcendent being. This comprehensive cosmology was further developed in Neo-Confucian thought, which was a major influence on Thomas.

Zhu Xi: Forming One Body with All Things

Confucianism blossomed into a Neo-Confucian revival in the eleventh and twelfth centuries that resulted in a new synthesis of the earlier teachings. The major Neo-Confucian thinker, Zhu Xi (1130–1200), designated four texts from the canon of historical writings, as containing the central ideas of Confucian thought. The classical texts were the Four Books: the *Analects*, *Mencius*, the *Great Learning*, and the *Doctrine of the Mean*. The *Analects* are the sayings of Confucius, *Mencius* is the sayings of Mencius, and the *Great Learning* and *Doctrine of the Mean* are selections from the *Classic of Rites*. In 1315, these texts, and Zhu Xi's commentaries on them, became the basis of the Chinese civil service examination system, which endured for nearly six hundred years, until 1905. Every prospective government official had to take the civil service exams based on Zhu Xi's commentaries on the Four Books. The aim was to provide educated, moral officials for the large government bureaucracy that ruled China.[20] The influence, then, of Neo-Confucian thought on government, education, land, and social values was extensive and long lasting. Views regarding nature, agriculture, and management of resources were derived from Neo-Confucian understandings of the importance of humans working to cultivate and care for nature as a means of fulfilling their role in the triad of Cosmos and Earth. Thomas was keenly interested in this perspective.

Zhu Xi's synthesis of Neo-Confucianism was recorded in his classic anthology, *Reflections on Things at Hand* (*Jinsilu*).[21] In this work, Zhu formulated a this-worldly spirituality based on a balance of cosmological orientation, ethical and ritual practices, scholarly reflection, and political participation. The aim was to balance inner cultivation with outward investigation of things in concert with the dynamic changes of the natural world. Zhu Xi affirmed these changes as the source of transformation in both the cosmos and the person.

Thus, Neo-Confucian spiritual discipline involved cultivating one's moral nature so as to bring it into harmony with the larger pattern of change in the cosmos. Each moral virtue had its cosmological component. For example, the central virtue of humaneness was seen as the source of fecundity and growth in both the individual and the cosmos. By practicing humaneness, one could affect the transformation of things in oneself, in society, and in the cosmos. In so doing, one's deeper identity with reality was recognized as forming one body with all things. As the *Doctrine of the Mean* states: "being able to assist in the transforming and nourishing powers of Heaven and Earth, one can form a triad with Heaven and Earth."[22] This idea had a strong appeal for Thomas and constituted one of the primary aims of his life and work. He hoped to awaken in humans a cosmological understanding of their place in the dynamic processes of evolution. With this awakening comes the possibility of evoking human participation in the nourishing powers of the cosmos and Earth, thus releasing ecological energies for healing the Earth.

CONFUCIAN RELATIONALITY AND NATURE: EMBODIED FLOURISHING

From the classical texts to the later Neo-Confucian writings, there is a strong sense of nature as a whole in which human life and society flourish. Indeed, Confucian thought recognizes that the rhythms of nature sustain life in both biological forms and sociocultural expressions. This idea was central to Thomas's thinking as well. He saw that the immense reservoir of symbolic resources in Confucianism could reorient humans to become a life-giving presence on the planet, not a life-destroying presence. He felt that this holistic worldview is compatible with evolutionary biology.

For the Confucians, and for Thomas, the biological dimensions of life are dependent on nature as an organic continuum. Everything in nature is interdependent and interrelated. Most importantly, for the Confucians, nature is seen as dynamic and transformational. These ideas are evident in the *Book of Changes* and are expressed in the Four Books, especially in *Mencius*, the *Doctrine of the Mean*, and the *Great Learning*. They come to full flowering in the Neo-Confucian tradition of the Sung and Ming periods. Nature in this context has an inherent unity, namely, a primary ontological source (*Taiji*). It has patterned processes of transformation (*yin/yang*), and the five elements. Nature is dynamic and fluid, involving the flow of material force (*qi*). *Qi* can be cultivated by humans through graceful physical movements, such as *qigong* or *taiqi*, so as to be in greater harmony with the flow of *qi* in the natural world.

THE MORALITY OF NATURE: AFFIRMING CHANGE

For the Confucians, humans are "anthropocosmic" beings, not anthropocentric individuals.[23] The human is viewed as a microcosm in relation to the macrocosm of the universe. This is expressed most succinctly in the metaphor of humans as forming a triad with Heaven and Earth. In the classic Western Inscription of Zhang Zai the metaphor becomes a parental one:

Heaven is my father and Earth is my mother and even such a small creature as I find an intimate place in their midst. Therefore that which extends throughout the universe I regard as my body and that which directs the universe I consider as my nature. All people are my brothers and sisters, and all things are my companions.[24]

In this view, humans are one with the *qi*, the vital force that extends through the universe, uniting human and nature in a great family. Humans are responsible to the cosmos and Earth as they are born from these great cosmological powers. Therefore, they owe nature a kind of filial care and respect. This idea appears early on in the Classic of History.[25]

Such relationships were developed during the unification of China in the Han period (221 BCE–206 CE) with a complex synthesis of correspondences involving the elements, directions, colors, seasons, and virtues.[26] This need to consciously connect the patterns of nature with the rhythms of human society is very ancient in Confucian culture. It is at the basis of the anthropocosmic worldview wherein humans are seen as working together with Heaven and Earth to create harmonious societies. The resonances between self, society, and nature are constantly being described in Confucian texts and are evident in architecture as well in such structures as the Temple of Heaven and Temple of Earth, where offerings were made to ensure social and political harmony.

For Confucians, nature is not only inherently valuable; it is morally good. Nature, thus, embodies the normative standard for all things; it is not judged from an anthropocentric perspective. There is not a fact/value division in the Confucian worldview, for nature is seen as an intrinsic source of value. This idea was coherent with Thomas's view as well. He did not see the biological fact or reality of ecosystems as distinctive from their inherent value. In particular, for the Confucians and for Thomas, value lies in the ongoing transformation and productivity of nature. A term repeated frequently in Neo-Confucian sources is life-life (*sheng sheng*), reflecting the ever-renewing fecundity of life itself. In this sense, the dynamic transformation of life is seen in recurring cycles of growth, fruition, harvesting, and abundance, which reflect the natural processes of flourishing and decay in nature, human life, and human society. Change is thus seen as a dynamic force with which humans should harmonize and interact, rather than withdraw, in terms of personal cultivation as well as cultivation of the land.

In this context, Confucians do not view hierarchy as leading inevitably to domination. Rather, they see that value rests in each thing, but not in each thing equally. Everything in nature and society has its appropriate role and place, and thus should be treated accordingly. The use of nature for human ends must recognize the intrinsic value of each element of nature, but also its value in relation to the larger context of the environment. This idea was key to Thomas's thinking as well, especially in his ideas of law and Earth Jurisprudence. For Thomas, and for Confucians, each entity is considered not simply equal to every other; rather, each interrelated part of nature has a particular value according to its nature and function. Thus, there is a differentiated sense of appropriate roles for humans and for all other species. For Confucians, hierarchy is a necessary way for each being to fulfill its function. In this context, then, no individual being has exclusive privileged status in relation to nature. Rather, the processes of nature and its ongoing logic of transformation (*yin/yang*) are the norm that takes priority for the common good of the whole society.

HUMANE SOCIETY AND GOVERNMENT: GROUNDS FOR FLOURISHING

Confucians were mindful that nature was the basis of a stable society and that if nature was not tended carefully, imbalance would result. This was also Thomas's repeated warning. There are numerous passages in *Mencius* advocating humane government for the appropriate management of natural resources and for sustaining community life, Indeed, there are various passages in Confucian texts urging humans not to wantonly cut down trees or kill animals needlessly.

However, the establishment of humane society, government, and culture inevitably results in the use of nature for housing, for production, and for governance. In this sense, Confucians might be seen as pragmatic social ecologists (rather than deep ecologists) who recognize the necessity of forming human institutions—both educational and political—for a stable society. Establishing schools and training teachers have always been a key part of Confucian societies. Moreover, linking the educational system to the civil service exam system was intended to form a meritocracy of scholar-officials who could lead with moral governance. This is why Thomas appreciated Confucianism—for both its aspirational and its practical dimensions. He advocated the need for a functional cosmology that encouraged healthy agriculture, eco-cities, ecological economics, and environmental education.

Thus, it is clear that for Confucians, human cultural values and practices are grounded in nature and part of its structure, and thus humans are dependent on its beneficence. In addition, the agricultural base of Confucian societies has always been recognized as essential to the political and social well-being of the country. Humans prosper by living within nature's boundaries and are refreshed by its beauty, restored by its seasons, and fulfilled by its rhythms. For Confucians, and for Thomas, human flourishing is thus dependent on fostering nature in its variety and abundance; going against nature's processes is self-destructive. Human moral growth means cultivating one's desire not to interfere with nature but to be in accord with the great Dao of Nature. Thus, the "human mind" expands in relation to the "Mind of the Way."

In summary, for Confucians and for Thomas, harmony with nature is essential. Indeed, human self-realization is achieved in relation to and in harmony with nature. Humans can only attain their full humanity in relationship to both cosmos and Earth. For Thomas, this was a basis for a system of relations that included the concentric spheres of family, society, education, politics, and nature itself. He was inspired throughout his life by the Confucian tradition and its articulation of such a cosmological, ecological, and moral vision. He saw Confucianism not as a fossilized tradition, but as one that is vibrant and valuable for the needs of the Earth community today.

CHAPTER 12

Indigenous Traditions of the Giving Earth

The indigenous peoples of this continent tried to teach us the value of the land, but unfortunately we could not understand them, blinded as we were by our dream of manifest destiny. Instead we were scandalized, because they insisted on living simply rather than working industriously. We desired to teach them our ways, never thinking that they could teach us theirs. Although we constantly depended on the peoples living there to guide us in establishing our settlements, we never saw ourselves as entering into a sacred land, a sacred space. We never experienced this land as they did—as a living presence not primarily to be used but to be revered and communed with.

Thomas Berry, "The World of Wonder"

T homas saw Indigenous peoples' reverence for the natural and celestial worlds as an expression of "cosmovisions": visions that arise from stories of collective identity that express ongoing relations with plants, animals, places, and stars. He knew that diverse Native peoples on the North American continent grounded their livelihood in different relationships of kinship and reciprocity with the community of life in a bioregion. These cultural practices not only supported individuals in close interdependence with their surrounding world, but they also gave rise to communities that transmitted visionary paths into their futures.

Thomas's perception of Indigenous people's relationships with "place" was not predicated simply upon their being the first humans to occupy those lands.[1] Rather, as he wrote in *The Dream of the Earth*, "They have this position of honor not merely by their temporal priority, but also by their mystical understanding and communion with the continent."[2] These Native relationships influenced Thomas's broader thinking about Indigenous worldviews. In an era of global environmental crises, he saw Indigenous lifeways as indispensable for reestablishing a direct experience of Earth processes. The term *lifeway* is central for understanding Thomas's emphasis on Native traditions. It describes the close connections between territory and society, religion and politics, and cultural and economic life whereby Indigenous peoples have maintained their knowledge systems and formed basic subsistence patterns.[3]

MOVING BEYOND STEREOTYPES

Thomas clearly saw beyond the stereotypes of Indigenous peoples as "noble savages," "wild Indians," or "first ecologists." He also sensed that these stereotypes masked an ingrained American prejudice toward what Americans felt was "savagism." These realizations became central considerations as he developed his thinking about human-Earth relations. For Thomas, Native American thought arose from living communities that transmitted stories of a vital Earth embedded in a cosmos of interrelated beings. In contemporary American society, stereotypes blinded many to the diverse lifeways of American Indian peoples as well as to their shared ideals.

In the late twentieth century the American public gradually transitioned from seeing Native peoples as savages to viewing them as "first ecologists."[4] But this ecological stereotype also expressed the view that all Indigenous peoples were, and are, identical in their environmental practices. It romanticized all Native peoples as caring for and preserving a static natural world and reduced cultural differences to homogenized stereotypes. The diversity of Indigenous peoples was ignored in favor of a sanitized sameness.

Thomas's readings in Indigenous ethnographies and his meetings with Indigenous elders gave him a broader view of the contributions of Indigenous peoples to current ecological challenges. Much of his regard for Indigenous peoples arose from his awareness of the traditional spiritual resources they preserved, despite centuries of cultural subversion through conquest and colonialism. His graduate studies at Catholic University with John Cooper—a noted anthropologist among

Anishinabe/Cree Peoples—prepared him to reexamine Indigenous thought and practice years later.

Thomas read extensively in American Indian studies, biographies, and ethnographies before he initiated a course at Fordham in 1973 entitled "Religious Studies and the American Indian." He also taught a similar course at Barnard College during those years. His teaching and research led him to develop an extensive library of American Indian and Indigenous studies, including autobiographical writings and literature by Native authors. Indeed, an entire room on the second floor of the Riverdale Center, overlooking the Hudson River, was devoted to his Native American books.

ENCOUNTERS WITH NATIVE ELDERS

Thomas's understanding of Indigenous lifeways was also deepened through exchanges with Indigenous elders across North America. He valued the wisdom these contemporary First Nation leaders transmitted to their communities and beyond. He was respected in Native American circles because they saw his deep appreciation for the life of the Earth and its rich diversity. His teaching of Native American history and religions was also affirmed because Native peoples saw his authenticity and broad spiritual understanding of Native cosmovisions. Many appreciated his essay "The Historical Role of the American Indian," which was published in *The Dream of the Earth*.

Thomas hosted a number of Native American elders at the Riverdale Center in the 1970s and 1980s. Prominent among these were the Haudenosaunee/Seneca leaders Oren Lyons (b. 1930) and John Mohawk (1945-2006). Both taught at the State University of New York in Buffalo. Thomas wrote of Oren Lyons, "whose presence also has that remarkable quality of personal grandeur that I would associate with Shakespeare where he says of someone that all nature could stand up and say here is a man. As a model for what a human being might be, Oren Lyons would undoubtedly be one of the persons who would come into my mind immediately" (*Goldenrod*, 93).

In addition, Thomas welcomed the Muscogee/Creek traditional healer and activist Phillip Deere (1929-1985) and John Fire Lame Deer (1900/1903-1976), the Mineconju-Lakota spokesperson and author. He also participated on panels with

12.1 Oren Lyons, Faithkeeper of the Onondaga people of the Haudenosaunee Nation.

Mike Greenlar

Native American leaders who gathered at the Cathedral of St. John the Divine in New York for the Spiritual Summits in 1975 and 1984.

When he was nearly eighty years old, Thomas recalled several of his exchanges with Native elders across North America.[5] During the Earth and Spirit conference held in Seattle in 1990, he was given a special recognition in a ceremony by the Lummi Indians of the Seattle region of the state of Washington. At this time Ken Cooper *Chilasquaetum*, who was then cultural consultant for fish, timber, and wildlife of the Lummi Tribe in the Nooksak Basin of Washington State, gave Thomas his personal drum, with its leather-encased drumstick.

A year earlier Thomas had been invited to join an assembly of Ojibway and Six Nations Peoples and other Indian groups gathered at Cape Crocker in Georgian Bay. This was the "Four Winds Assembly" called by Anishinabe/ Ojibwa, Cree, and Haudenosaunee/Iroquois elders. They were meeting to discuss their future, and Thomas was requested to speak on this occasion. After he spoke, Chief Tom Porter, founding elder of the Mohawk Kanasio-hareke community in upstate New York, said in his speech that he had never heard a non-Indian speak so much like his grandfather and the older men of his memory. He turned and addressed Thomas as "Grandfather." Thomas referred to this as one of the most significant moments in his life: "It has ever since been a sense of assurance that what I have been saying makes sense. I know of no normative source that would give me more reassurance" (*Goldenrod*, 93).

At a gathering of Indian peoples from North America, Central America, and South America held in Toronto the following year, Thomas was the only white person invited to sit with the elders. This was a meeting in 1990 for the Indian Arts Restoration Project, at which Thomas reacquainted himself with Danny Beaton, who had been at the Cape Croker Reserve gathering. Danny Beaton, a Haudenosaunee/Mohawk artist, organized this event.

In May 1994, at a conference titled "Caring for Creation," Kiowa speaker Marilyn Bread presented Thomas with a plaque in recognition of his contributions to the understanding of Native American worldviews. This took place at Haskell Indian Nations University in response to an address he gave on the North American continent.[6]

COSMOLOGY AND NATIVE TRADITIONS

It was during the early 1970s that Thomas was developing his understanding of the relationship between cosmology and ecology in various cultural traditions. In using the term *cosmology*, Thomas emphasized symbolic ways of knowing the interrelationships between local bioregions and the sky-Earth-Sun horizon and the larger universe. In American Indian traditions, these ways of knowing often appeared in oral stories that observed and expressed affection for local places and life forms. This affection was creatively expressed in song, dance, food, language, and rituals, associated here with the term lifeway.

As Thomas developed his thinking about cosmology and ecology, he increasingly understood that Indigenous peoples had come to profound spiritual insights regarding the interdependent, or ecological, nature of reality. It became clear to him that Indigenous myths described ecological realities not only in their place-based homelands, but also in relation to living beings on the land. These relationships that were developed in oral traditions often extended out to spiritual beings in the stars and deep space, not as distant realities but as close kin.[7] His studies of cosmology acknowledged traditional environmental knowledge, or TEK. Thomas realized that Native American narratives described, as well as activated, these intimate relations and communications with numinous beings in the natural world. His awareness provided him with a perspective on comparative religious studies because he became aware that Indigenous lifeways could help clarify the human religious experience. For Thomas, Indigenous ways of knowing had not disappeared or been extinguished. Rather, they continued into the present to inform and provide guidance for their communities and to explain the ways humans should act responsibly in a living world.

INDIGENOUS RELIGIONS AND FLOURISHING LIFE

At a time when Indigenous studies were just entering universities, Thomas affirmed the intellectual and spiritual contributions by Native peoples to human history. He realized that Indigenous peoples could not be simply conceived as living archaic societies. They provided invaluable insights into the significance of symbolic consciousness in all human societies, and especially insights into Axial Age religions. Indigenous peoples were aware of their own particular historical transformations and transmitted narratives in complex renditions that explored continuity and change in relation to their ancestral roots.

For example, elders at Zuni and Hopi Pueblos, as well as similar settlements along the Rio Grande River, spoke of their clan relations with earlier Pueblo cultural expressions such as the magnificent ritual structures at Chaco Canyon. Similarly, Salish-speaking peoples in the Pacific Northwest reflected on how their ancestors related to their spiritually active volcanic region over centuries. Northern Plains Peoples transmitted detailed narratives about their journeys guided by spiritual beings from the stars and the deep blue of space, or by the spirit of tobacco or by an assembly of animal presences. These diverse cultural thought traditions also related to different subsistence practices for buffalo, salmon, or agricultural crops such as corn, beans, and squash. Many Native peoples reflected on their transitions as they had moved through different bioregions, while other Indigenous tribes knew they had lived for centuries, if not millennia, in one homeland. Through his studies, and in conversations with elders, Thomas understood that small-scale Indigenous societies had survived countless changes over time. They showed their spiritual resilience as a people by living respectfully within changing bioregions. Thomas wrote in his 1976 essay "The Future of the American Indian":

> The present discussion is directed to the Euroamerican in the hope that if he understands something of the human resources of the Indian he will become less an obstacle and more of a help. Our presentation is from the cultural-historical point of view. Studies of the tribal cultures of the world, of the more massive civilizations, of modern culture, and the prospects for the future can be a great aid in understanding any people. Within the larger complex of human cultural transformations each can be seen in itself and in its relations with the others. The history of each helps in understanding the history of the others. Against this background it can be seen that the culture of the American Indian is unique, one of the most admirable of all cultures, destined perhaps for a future historical role of wide significance.[8]

As Thomas studied and interacted with Native communities, he reflected on their troubled relations with dominant American society. As industrial societies distanced themselves from nature, he observed that they lost that pastoral sense of an ever-renewing cycle of seasons. Increasingly he saw how the historical forces of globalization favored societies that were intent upon extracting from the Earth as they sought industrial dominance. Native peoples could teach dominant societies how to shape a future in which the Earth was not regarded as simply a resource, but as the source of life itself.

Thomas recognized that certain forms of spiritual consciousness among Indigenous peoples guided their interactions with the surrounding world. Life was seen as a giving reality that called for a giving back on the part of the people. For example, the massive bison herds in the Great Plains provided the Native peoples of North America with their core subsistence, but also with a sense of life as sacred. This sensibility did not eliminate massive hunting at buffalo-jumps in which more animals often died than could be used. But even in driving the bison over the cliffs, Native peoples activated living relationships with the buffalo in the songs that celebrated their cycles of birth and death. Bison nourish Native communities with their bodies, just as they also nurture the symbolic thinking of the people because they are the life form from whom the people originated. In gratitude, Northern Plains peoples dance, dream, hunt, cook, and communicate with their buffalo ancestors.

PERSONHOOD: INTERIORITY OF LAND AND BIODIVERSITY AS KIN

In the narratives and ceremonies of Indigenous peoples, plants such as corn, beans, and squash, and animal species like deer, bison, and bear, are seen as "persons." Anthropologists who interacted with Indigenous peoples became aware of these personal relationships, which were often identified with kinship terms. They began to use the term *personhood* to describe Indigenous ways of experiencing an inner presence in the natural world. Thomas saw this as a knowledge of sacred immanence. Moreover, he conjectured that without that knowledge humans could lose their connection to the natural world.

Thomas also realized that Indigenous cultures had struggled to maintain their lifeways, even before the first encounters with Europeans. This struggle only intensified during the five centuries of settler colonialism, nation-state oppression, and forced assimilation into dominant societies.[9] His insights into these processes drew on an anthropology of personhood that had emerged in the 1960s.[10]

Thomas understood that the sense of personhood-in-nature is an awareness that is common to Indigenous cultures, though differently articulated by various Native societies. These forms of personhood reflected an interiority that was similar to, but different from, human personhood. Thomas described this interiority using the metaphor of *coding*. "Genetic coding" refers to shared, but differentiated, biological activities such as eating, breathing, reproducing, and dying. "Cultural coding" refers to the social patterns and broader practices that sustain a culture, expressed in rituals, celebrations, cuisine, and clothing. According to Thomas, cultural coding orients individual and social life and is dependent upon the genetic coding that humans share with the larger world.[11] The key connection is in the alignment of these related codings, namely, the close relations between cultural lives and genetic drives. Thomas would describe flourishing cultures as those in which rituals and patterns of cultural life were in alignment with genetic drives.

In his courses on American Indian religions, Thomas suggested that the ethnographies of Native peoples provided numerous examples of that close linkage of genetic and cultural coding. He would speak of the Omaha peoples of the Central Plains regions of North America and their ceremonial "Introduction of the Child to the Cosmos."[12] As a newborn child was held up to the sky by parents, other kin and clan would invoke the powers of the cosmos as a way of introducing the child to the world and the world to the child. Thomas saw this ceremony as an orienting ritual that culturally and genetically located a person's life trajectory in relation to spirit presences in the larger world. He understood the alignment of these codings not as an introduction of a child to a competitive world in which only the fittest survive. Rather, this was an introduction to a cooperative and collaborative universe in which life was received and lives were taken. Indigenous communities undertook ritual activities to affirm this reciprocal relationship.[13]

Thomas believed that contemporary American Indian elders promote the spiritual dimensions of life,[14] often encouraging and guiding individuals to receive revelations from spiritual beings in the natural world. Individuals and communities form a deep kinship with land and diverse life forms and express this kinship in ordinary ways. Thus animals, clouds, and natural patterns may appear on pottery, in face painting at ceremonials, and in the naming of newborns. Along with this deep coding, there are shared dream experiences, such as when other-than-human animals give permission for the hunt and when youngsters are given vision songs during a fast.[15] Thomas discussed the mystical character of these forms of kin-relatedness in his 1976 essay, "The Vision Quest of the American Indian."[16] He suggests that the spirits as numinous presences open individuals to their own inner world as it is connected to the interiority of the natural world.

THOMAS'S WORK WITH T'BOLI PEOPLES IN THE PHILIPPINES

In addition to his encounters with Native North American peoples, Thomas had significant interactions in the summers of 1982 and 1984 with T'boli peoples in the Tiruray highlands of South Cotobato on Mindanao Island in

12.2 T'boli children riding a water buffalo.
John Grim

the Philippines.[17] These visits were arranged by Rex Mannsman, a Passionist missionary to the T'boli near Santa Cruz Mission from 1963 to 1992. During the decades that he lived in Mindanao, Mannsman gradually turned from his initial work of evangelization and conversion among the T'boli to cultural preservation and economic empowerment. He was joined in this work by the Passionist priest Charles Adams from 1974 to 1980 and by the Irish Columban priest Sean McDonagh from 1981 to 1984. All three men were deeply influenced by Thomas's cosmological and ecological approaches.

Following Thomas's emphasis on the values in cosmologies, Mannsman organized an extensive multihour recording of the T'boli origin story, the *Tut Bulul*. In an effort to implement Thomas's sense of a functioning economy, Mannsman drew on T'boli traditional knowledge of agricultural wet rice farming and fish netting in nearby Lake Sebu. Santa Cruz Mission helped sponsor collective meetings of local village leaders, called *datu*, to discuss intervillage governance among the widespread T'boli groups in South Cotobato. The thrust of these meetings was to inform local T'boli about the various illegal land grabs and marketing schemes being foisted on the T'boli by local merchants and shopkeepers.

Santa Cruz Mission staff increasingly worked toward staving off T'boli land loss in the face of massive immigration by incoming Visayan Islanders leaving those heavily populated islands in the Philippines. Thomas's visits to this region deepened his understanding of the challenges facing T'boli peoples. When asked for advice from T'boli elders, he urged them "to touch lightly on the industrial-technological world and move into the Ecozoic Era."[18] He was concerned with the rapid economic and technological challenges facing the T'boli. Realizing that they had established cosmological relationships with their homelands, he felt that these cultural, natural, and ritual orientations would become increasingly central to their future as an ecological conscious-ness became more widespread in the Philippines. But first there needed to be a larger awakening in the Philippines to the level of environmental degradation that was taking place.

To that end, a pastoral letter from the Philippine bishops was released in January 1988 titled, "What Is Happening to Our Beautiful Land?"[19] Thomas's ideas were influential in shaping the letter. This document lays out a narrative of loss and calls for new practices drawing on tribal peoples' cosmological awareness:

> Our forefathers and our tribal brothers and sisters today still attempt to live in harmony with nature. They see the Divine Spirit in the living world and show their respect through prayers and offerings. Tribal Filipinos remind us that the exploitative approach to the natural world is foreign to our Filipino culture.[20]

COSMOLOGY AS PERFORMATIVE STORY

The cosmological consciousness of the living world is manifest among Indige-nous peoples in narrative performances, such as the T'boli recitation of their epic story of creation, the *Tut Bulul*.[21] With symbolic actions and chanting, the T'boli enter into relationships with local lands, animals, insects, and plants as cosmic persons. Through rituals and traditional stories, Native homelands and other-than-human persons become living archetypal, symbolic presences. In the Philippines and in North America, Thomas witnessed and affirmed these living expressions of interdependence. These rituals join with subsistence activities and symbolic understandings to form "religious ecologies,"[22] namely, traditional ways of understanding the interdependence of humans, other-than-human animals,

plants, and place. Moreover, these religious ecologies were integrated with cosmological narratives, forming interrelated webs of cultural wholeness, a sign of
flourishing lifeways.[23]

An exemplary expression of an Indigenous individual articulating such an
experience of his world was that of Nicholas Black Elk, a Lakota *wichasha wakan*
or shaman-healer.[24] Thomas often cited that striking moment in Black Elk's
youthful vision in which a black stallion sang a song:

> His voice was not loud, but it went all over the universe and filled it. There
> was nothing that did not hear, and it was more beautiful than anything can
> be. It was so beautiful that nothing anywhere could keep from dancing. The
> virgins danced, and all the circled horses. The leaves on the trees, the grasses
> on the hills and in the valleys, the waters in the creeks and in the rivers and
> the lakes, the four-legged and the two-legged and the wings of the wind—all
> danced together to the music of the stallion's song.[25]

This worldview of numinous presences dancing in relation to the song of the
black stallion reveals a religious ecology, namely, a Lakota symbolic vision of
an interdependent world. As an elder, healer, and leader, Black Elk presented a

12.3 Black Elk and family.
Courtesy of the Denver Library archives

powerful Lakota vision that occurred during his youthful illness. He later reenacted his larger vision in a ceremony called the "Horse Dance." Black Elk also developed shamanistic rituals manifesting the healing presences revealed in his visions. The visions found expression in Black Elk's spiritual life as a Lakota healer and Catholic catechist at Holy Rosary Mission.[26] In his talks and later writings, Thomas would describe Black Elk's religious visions as among the most significant of the twentieth century.

GRIEF AND TRAUMA AMONG INDIGENOUS PEOPLES

Thomas was aware of how the religious cosmologies and ecologies of Indigenous traditions were diminished in the traumatic history of colonial encounters. The loss of land, culture, spiritual direction, and a sense of belonging resulted in intense grieving. Thomas would cite one Omaha elder who painfully recalled the religious ecology of his people:

> When I was a youth, the country was very beautiful. Along the rivers were belts of timberland, where grew cottonwood, maple, elm, ash, hickory, and walnut trees, and many other shrubs. And under these grew many good herbs and beautiful flowering plants. In both the woodland and the prairies I could see the trails of many kinds of animals and could hear the cheerful songs of many kinds of birds. When I walked abroad I could see many forms of life, beautiful living creatures which *Wakanda* [the sacred power of creation] had placed here; and these were, after their manner, walking, flying, leaping, running, playing all about. But now the face of all the land is changed and sad. The living creatures are gone. I see the land desolate and I suffer an unspeakable sadness. Sometimes I wake in the night and I feel as though I should suffocate from the pressure of this awful feeling of loneliness.[27]

Thomas did not overlook this colonial history but rather considered its sobering historical challenges. He drew attention to the epidemic diseases that were brought by Europeans and that weakened many Indigenous societies. He lamented the five centuries of relentless military conquest, settler colonialism, and extractive mining.

Thomas also noted that any understanding of Indigenous peoples had to take into account the "civilizing" and "christianizing" of their communities. Such practices were legally justified by colonial nations, from the earliest encounters through papal bulls from the Vatican beginning in the late fourteenth century.[28] The papal bulls justified the European conquest and exploitation of Native peoples and their homelands as necessary for evangelization and conversion to Christianity. Moreover, these documents established a precedent that "discovery" legalized European, and eventually American, sovereignty over Indigenous ideas of community relationships held by the original inhabitants. These ideas of the Christian Doctrine of Discovery have been encoded in United States law, for example, in the Supreme Court case *Johnson v. McIntosh* (1823).[29]

Rather than concentrating on this victimization of Native peoples, Thomas chose to focus on how Indigenous peoples view humans, land, and biodiversity as intimately related and sustained by one another. He taught about diverse Indigenous perspectives on this view of Earth as a giving world in which humans respond in ritual gratitude to acknowledge the successful hunt or the plentiful harvest. He explored the ways in which Native peoples integrated their worldview into daily behavior, affirming the depth of symbolic thinking in their lives. He also realized that this view of a sacred universe was vulnerable as settler societies flooded into their lands, bringing values that affirmed private property, hyperindividualism, and Christian righteousness.

Thomas saw continuities between the devastating genocide of Indigenous peoples and the current "sixth extinction" of species. Associating Native peoples with a savage land, dominant social forces distanced the American ethos from nature and filled that vacuum with industrialization, unbridled population growth, and global patterns of consumption. Only by engaging in depth with both social and ecological justice, Thomas warned, could people transform the exploitative economies of industrial societies. Dominant societies needed to recover relationships with a flourishing Earth community. In part this entailed realizing that the children of dominant societies would not go forth into a future unless all the children, of all the species, went forth together. In Thomas's view, Native peoples transmitted these insights as some of them survived the trauma of assault by preserving this traditional knowledge of a sacred, interrelated universe.

INTERIOR RESOURCES OF NATIVE PEOPLES

Thomas presented his understanding of the importance of Native American lifeways in his 1988 essay titled, "The Historical Role of the American Indian."[30] Here, he described survival during the colonial period in relation to Native peoples' sense of profound relationships with the natural world. Thomas described these relationships as "interior resources" because they enabled Native Americans both to reflect on what had happened to them in the centuries of colonial oppression and to find ways forward guided by this interior resilience.

Thomas described first how Indigenous people were aware of having won a moral victory by enduring as distinct peoples after being displaced and subverted by Western colonial societies. This interior strength, he continued, flowed from the rich symbolic consciousness expressed in Native American myths, rituals, arts, and social life. Thomas also emphasized not only their heroic struggle with a significant enemy, but also the struggle of personal and tribal identity. It was this heroic endurance that led Thomas to speak of Indigenous "peoples of the Earth," because of their ongoing relations with spirits in the land, in plants, in animals, and in the cosmos. Thomas did not claim that these ideas and experiences are openly discussed by all Native individuals and communities, but they are shared patterns threaded within the historical lifeways of Native peoples both in the past and into the present.[31]

MORAL VICTORY AND ENDURANCE

In highlighting the moral victory of American Indian peoples, Thomas recognized the importance of self-determination, namely, the ability of a people to have their own voice in determining their future. Drawing on his own standpoint as a member of the dominant American society, he observed:

> We have won our battles with the Indian in the military-political order, in the possession of property, in the power to control the exterior destinies of the native peoples; but we have lost in the moral sphere to such a degree that we are ourselves amazed to discover the depth and violence of our destructive instincts, and this not just as a speculative truth, but as the lived reality of our own existence. That our deeds were sometimes done for "sacred" purposes and

with the highest cultural intentions is an irony that baffles any human effort of understanding.[32]

Two points converge here, namely, the historical denigration by dominant society of Native peoples as immoral "savages" and later the recognition of their moral leadership in environmental concerns. Thomas intuited that Indigenous and dominant communities are now mutually intertwined in all ways going forward.

Native American stories of community survival in the face of historical trauma provided a central insight for Thomas into the vitality and spontaneity at the heart of existence. Stories of endurance transmitted meaning for Indigenous communities in dark times when the stereotype of Native peoples as "savage" was still widespread in America. Most importantly, Thomas realized that Indigenous peoples taught respect and reverence for nonhuman voices within the community of living beings. This became a central theme in his emerging ecological insights:

> In reality, there is a single integral community of the Earth that includes all its component members whether human or other than human. In this community every being has its own role to fulfill, its own dignity, its inner spontaneity. Every being has its own voice. Every being declares itself to the entire universe. Every being enters into communion with other beings. This capacity for relatedness, for presence to other beings, for spontaneity in action, is a capacity possessed by every mode of being throughout the entire universe.[33]

Thomas saw in the diverse Indigenous worldviews and especially in the verbal character of their languages how all beings move in relatedness, response, and gratitude to one another. Preserving these insights is a moral victory and an inner resource for Native peoples that activates awareness of nature as a spiritual resource during times of need.

NATURE MYSTICISM FLOWING FROM CONSCIOUSNESS

When Thomas described Native peoples as embodying "nature wisdom," this phrase carried distinct meanings for him.[34] He described this mysticism as arising from "primordial experiences . . . [that] provide the foundations upon which the cultural systems of the various peoples are established. . . . [They] determine the distinctive psychic structure of individual personalities within the culture . . . [and] form the ultimate psychic support for the human venture itself."[35] Indigenous relationships with the natural world revealed a cosmological power that led to distinguished individual lives and unique cultural lifeways. Thomas described the cosmological character of Indigenous lifeways as singular among world cultures:

> I have indicated some of the efforts made by the Indian in order to situate himself within the numinous presence and to deepen his encounter with the sacred. This was the center and circumference of his existence. Nothing could be done of any significance apart from this presence. Outside this context nothing had meaning. Within this context all things had meaning, and the greatest suffering deepened rather than destroyed this meaning.[36]

Thomas also saw how Indigenous rituals made suffering a transformative power that created spiritual experiences in many forms, such as in sweat lodges, Sundances, potlatches, and Green Corn dances. These religious pathways deepen the integrity of individuals within, not apart from, the larger community of life. Ritual, art, literature, music, myth narrations, and lifeway activities are unique creative expressions of a universal dignity, beauty, and harmony that are especially manifest in local places. Thomas asserted: "Just as in the human order, creativity is neither a rational deductive process nor the irrational wandering of the undisciplined mind but the emergence of beauty as mysterious as the blossoming of a field of daisies out of the dark Earth."[37]

PEOPLES OF THE EARTH

It is within that "dark Earth" that Thomas found another resource of Indigenous peoples. Since the age of European expansion, Native peoples have struggled to survive colonial genocide and recover a voice in managing their own affairs. Moving beyond the description of Indigenous cultures around the planet as dispossessed peoples, Thomas chose to see Indigenous communities as "peoples of the Earth."[38] He felt that in significant cultural settings the current political and economic paradigms would be changed by "a process of transformation from below."[39] His study of history brought him to an understanding that deep change was not initiated or carried forward from the centers of human cultures and civilizations. Instead, the most profound historical transformations came from the margins and peripheries of dominant societies. At the symbolic and actual margins of existing urban civilizations were the peoples of the Earth.[40] Whether in the urban ghettos of Minneapolis and Los Angeles or in the rural areas of Pine Ridge Reservation in South Dakota, wisdom teachings among Native elders and youth continue to inspire resilience, often in forms of environmental concern and protection.

Peoples of the Earth were aware of the spiritual power of places as well as the pain that arises from the loss of those places. This sacrifice would lead to transformation. Thomas expressed this foundational concept in several ways throughout his life. In one such moment, he wrote: "All the great transition moments are sacrificial moments. Our present transition will not be accomplished without enormous sacrifice."[41] Again, he observed:

> How to sustain the pain of existence . . . how to give it meaning, then how to bring it under the influence of a transforming saving discipline: these are the basic challenges. Traditional religions consider all the forces in heaven and Earth must contribute to this transforming process, to this new birth. This is the meaning of initiation rituals found among Indigenous peoples.[42]

RELATIONS WITH THE LAND AS HEROIC IDEAL

Thomas noted and affirmed Indigenous peoples' "communion with the natural world" as an intimacy with the living Earth. He saw this as an intuitive grasp of a numinous mystery in nature that called forth reciprocity and gratitude for the traditional environmental knowledge that sustained the people. In describing Indigenous knowing of land, he realized that this personal-and-communal character of encounter with mystery was something unassimilated by the West. Thomas posited a power that came to Indigenous peoples as they struggled within the hardships imposed upon them by colonial societies. That struggle was a heroic call to recognize the history of the encounter and to reopen revelation in nature. It was with this realization that Thomas wrote:

> The Indians have never accepted human life as ordinary, as something that can be managed in a controlled or painless manner. They realize that life tests the deepest qualities within the human personality, qualities that emerge in heroic combat not merely with others, but also with oneself and with the powers of the universe. The sacred function of enemies was to assist one another to the heroic life by the challenge, even by the challenge of death. For this to be effective, however, it was necessary that there be a certain equality between the protagonists.[43]

There are a number of ideas expressed here that flow from insight into Indigenous heroic ideals. There is the sense of the heroic ethos as beyond rational control. There is the heroic test that identifies the deeper sensibilities and strengths of person and community. Furthermore, a point that obviously interested Thomas was the sacred function of enemies to activate nobility and heroism. His questions, of course, explored the inequities that settler colonialism and military engagements brought to Native communities. Yet this struggle clarified the peoples' positions and dreams.

Because the cosmic powers become a dimension of oneself and one's community, *nobility* defines the relation between humans and spirits in nature. The powers of the universe are not impersonal, alienated forces. Rather, their presence is experienced as a heroic interior call evoking one's deepest response. This effort is also a gift that is given to oneself and one's community as potential knowledge of oneself. Everything that challenges also potentially gives insight and presents obligations.

Thomas's consummate expression of interiority is his statement "The universe is a communion of subjects, not a collection of objects."[44] As an evocative phrase, it expressed not only his regard for the vibrancy of matter but also his abhorrence of deadening, objectifying worldviews. He was suspicious of a human cunning and calculation that objectified the other (land or people) for the benefit of the small, anthropocentric self.

Thomas's phrase "a communion of subjects," marks a seminal turn in his thinking. This idea of subjectivity within the natural world challenged dominant worldviews based on objectifying reality. Thomas spoke of a shared interiority between humans and other-than-human plants and animals. It was through an exploration of ecology that he came to a new mode of awareness of the community of living beings as being present to one another.

Thomas recalls an experience that illustrates the psychic distance between the worldviews of Western and Native peoples.

> Some years ago, in 1975, in this great Cathedral of St John the Divine I presided over a public discussion on Technology and the Natural World with Edgar Mitchell the Astronaut, Eido Roshi the Zen Master, and Lame Deer the Sioux Indian. When Lame Deer spoke he stood with the sacred pipe in his hands, bowed in turn to the four directions, west, north, east, and south. Then after lifting his eyes to survey this vast cathedral, he turned to the audience and remarked on how over-powering a setting this cathedral was for communication with the divine reality. But then he added that his own people had a different setting for communion with the Great Spirit, a setting out under the open sky, with the mountains in the distance and the winds blowing through the trees and the earth under their feet and surrounded by the living sounds of the birds and insects. It is a different setting, he said, a different experience, but so profound that he doubted that his people would ever feel entirely themselves or able to experience the divine presence adequately in any other setting.
>
> It made an overwhelming impression on me and lingers in my mind still and causes me often to reflect on what we have gained and what we have lost in the life style that we have adopted, on the encompassing technocratic, manipulative world that we have established, even on the sense of religion that we have developed.[45]

This passage provides insight into why Thomas called for a new cosmological story that would create the basis for mutually enhancing human-Earth relations going forward into our shared future.

Epilogue

The journey, the sacred journey of the universe, is the personal journey of each individual. . . . The universe is the larger self of each person, since the entire sequence of events that has transpired since the beginning of the universe was required to establish each of us in the precise structure of our own being and in the larger context in which we function.

Thomas Berry, "Cosmology of Religions"

Thomas Berry's life was one of constant movement forward, yet at every moment he was also communing with the deep presence in all reality. He never lost this sense of communion, and that is what allowed his vision to come alive. The foundations were laid in his youth with his experience of the meadow across the creek. Then, in the monastery, this experience deepened as the liturgy of the universe and the liturgy of humans were woven together.

It continued to grow in graduate school while he was studying the great ages of Western history and then the insights of the Asian religions. In his teaching years, he began to write essays that were bound into the blue books of the Riverdale Papers. With his immersion into Teilhard's evolutionary perspective, his own vision blossomed forth into the brilliance of "The New Story," *The Dream of the Earth*, and *The Universe Story*. The dream inspired others and this creativity flowed into poetry, music, and art. The Great Work emerged / flared forth in education, religion, ecology, and law.

Thomas wanted to align human imagination and ingenuity with the creativity of the universe and the Earth. This alignment, he felt, would result in eco-cities, green buildings, ecological economics, environmental education, organic farming, and nature-based arts. His hope for enhancing human-Earth relations gave new depths of meaning and direction to human life and work. This vision was grounded in the New Story of the universe unfolding. The voices of the other—especially the wisdom of women and Indigenous peoples—were also included in this story.

To evoke this vision of mutual *presencing*, Thomas had to transform his identity at every stage of his life. He moved gradually but steadily from his small self to his great self. He embraced *homo universalis*, the universal human of Western thought; the *Mahapurusha*, the Great Person of Indian thought; and the *junzi*, the sage of Chinese philosophy. He opened up his mind and heart beyond the limits of provincialism to enter into a communion of subjects.

Thomas left Greensboro to enter the monastery after witnessing a tension between nature and commerce in his youth.

Once in the monastery he enlarged the contemplative routine to include study and reflection.

After ordination he moved from reading theology to researching and teaching history, which was a stimulating change for him.

He broadened his focus from Western history to Asian and Indigenous history.

He knew he had to transcend American culture to find his deeper identity and calling. He did this with his studies in China and then when serving with the army in Europe.

When he returned to the United States, he wanted to go beyond teaching in the seminary to teach at a university. With some struggle, and on the verge of leaving his religious order, he was at last able to do this.

From the academic constraints of St. John's University, he moved to Fordham University, where he created a unique History of Religions program.

At Fordham, he integrated his scholarly pursuits with his cosmological vision in founding the Riverdale Center for Religious Research. Here he placed human and Earth history within a universe story.

And finally, after fifty years of work in New York City—studying, teaching, writing, and speaking—he returned home to North Carolina to continue the Great Work in the later years of his life.

Thomas Berry.
Lou Niznik, courtesy of Jane Blewett

At each stage he released his prior identity for something larger and more encompassing. That holism was visible in who he was—a Renaissance thinker always moving toward becoming a cosmic person. This was not something determined, but rather part of his destiny, emerging gradually over time and involving suffering and loss. But that struggle was composted into the Earth, where he grounded himself. There, in the Earth and cosmos he experienced the "divine milieu" that surrounded him. Thus, as he approached death, he could say, "I will be in the universe where I have always been."

Becoming a cosmic person, although a potential from birth, is an achievement of a lifetime. This is what Berry did over many years with humor, grace, and joy of spirit—not defeated by adversity or succumbing to cynicism or despair, but rather, again and again, expanding his personhood and vision to embrace the whole Earth community and the universe that holds it together.

The fire continues to burn brightly. This is the deep confidence he bequeathed:

Here we might observe that the basic mood of the future might well be one of confidence in the continuing revelation that takes place in and through the Earth. If the dynamics of the universe from the beginning shaped the course of the heavens, lighted the sun, and formed the Earth, if this same dynamism brought forth the continents and seas and atmosphere, if it awakened life in the primordial cell and then brought into being the unnumbered variety of living beings, and finally brought us into being and guided us safely through the turbulent centuries, there is reason to believe that this same guiding process is precisely what has awakened in us our present understanding of ourselves and our relation to this stupendous process. Sensitized to such guidance from the very structure and functioning of the universe, we can have confidence in the future that awaits the human venture.[1]

Appendix: Thomas Berry Timeline, 1914–2009

LIFE AT A GLANCE

November 9, 1914 Born in Greensboro, North Carolina

1933 1942 Seminary studies

May 30, 1942 Ordination at St. Patrick's Cathedral, Newark, New Jersey

1943–1948 Doctoral study, Catholic University of America, Washington, D.C.

1948 PhD from Catholic University of America, Washington, D.C.

1948 Study in Peking, China

1951–1954 Army chaplain in Ellwangen, Germany

1957–1979 University teaching

1957–1961 Seton Hall University

1961–1965 St. John's University

1966–1979 Fordham University

1970–1995 Director, Riverdale Center for Religious Research, Bronx, New York

1975–1987 President, American Teilhard Association

1995 Retires to Greensboro, North Carolina

June 1, 2009 Dies in Greensboro, North Carolina,

June 8, 2009 Buried in Greensboro, Vermont

EDUCATION/SEMINARY TRAINING

1928–1932 Mount St. Mary's Prep School, Emmitsburg, Maryland

1932–1933 Mount St. Mary's College, Emmitsburg, Maryland

1933–1934 Holy Cross Seminary, Dunkirk, New York

1934–1935 Novitiate, Our Mother of Sorrows Monastery, West Springfield, Massachusetts

August 15, 1935 First profession of vows, West Springfield, Massachusetts

1935–1936 St. Paul of the Cross Monastery, Pittsburgh, Pennsylvania

1936–1937 Immaculate Conception Monastery, Jamaica, New York

1937–1938 St. Michael the Archangel Studies Monastery, Union City, New Jersey

August 15, 1938 Final profession of vows, Immaculate Conception Monastery, Jamaica, New York

1938–1939 Immaculate Conception Monastery, Jamaica, New York

1939–1942 St. Michael the Archangel Monastery, Union City, New Jersey

May 30, 1942 Ordination, St. Patrick's Cathedral, Newark, New Jersey

1942–1943 Studying sacred eloquence (preaching), St. Gabriel's Monastery, Brighton, Massachusetts

1943–1948 Doctoral study, Catholic University of America, Washington, D.C.

1948 PhD, Catholic University of America

1948 Chinese language study in Peking, China

1959–1960 Sanskrit language study at Columbia University, New York City

TEACHING

1947–1948, 1949–1951 Holy Cross Seminary, Dunkirk, New York

1957–1961 Seton Hall University; assistant professor, Asian Religions

1961–1965 St. John's University; associate professor, Asian Religions

1963 Columbia University; seminar on the *Bhagavad Gita*

1966–1979 Fordham University; associate professor, History of Religions program

1972, 1973, 1974 University of San Diego; summer program on History of Religions

1973-1976 Barnard College; adjunct professor; courses on Contemporary
   Spirituality and Native American Religions
1973-1974 Drew University; adjunct professor

MAJOR PUBLICATIONS

1951 "The Historical Theory of Giambattista Vico" (PhD thesis)
1966 *Buddhism*
1971 *Religions of India*
1988 *The Dream of the Earth*
1991 *Befriending the Earth: A Theology of Reconciliation Between Humans and the
   Earth*, with Thomas Clark
1992 *The Universe Story: From the Primordial Flaring Forth to the Ecozoic Era—
   A Celebration of the Unfolding of the Cosmos*, with Brian Swimme
1999 *The Great Work: Our Way into the Future*
2006 *Evening Thoughts: Reflecting on Earth as a Sacred Community*
2009 *The Sacred Universe: Earth, Spirituality, and Religion in the Twenty-First
   Century*
2009 *The Christian Future and the Fate of Earth*
2014 *Thomas Berry: Selected Writings on the Earth Community*

CITATIONS/AWARDS/HONORARY DEGREES

1989 Annual Mission Award—U.S. Catholic Mission Association,
   Washington, D.C.
1992 Environmental Award—Prescott College, Prescott, Arizona
1992 James Herriot Award—Humane Society of the United States,
   Washington, D.C.
1992 Wheel of Life Award—Temple of Understanding, New York City
1992 Named Honorary Canon of the Cathedral of St. John the Divine,
   New York City
1993 Bishop Carroll T. Dozier Award for Peace and Justice—Christian
   Brothers University, Memphis, Tennessee

1993 Sacred Universe Award–Spiritearth Society, Campion Center, Weston, Massachusetts

1993 Alumni Association Award for Scholarship–Catholic University of America, Washington, D.C.

1993 Honorary Doctorate of Humane Letters–California Institute of Integral Studies, San Francisco

1994 Honorary Doctorate of Humane Letters–Loyola University, New Orleans

1994 Honorary Doctorate of Humane Letters–St. Thomas University, Miami

1995 Honorary Charter Member–Club of Budapest

1995 Literary Award for Nonfiction for *The Dream of the Earth*–Lannan Foundation, Santa Fe, New Mexico

1995 First "Green Dove" Award–Common Boundary, Bethesda, Maryland

1997 Keepers of the Lore Award for Ecological Service

1997 Honorary Doctorate of Humane Letters–St. Mary's University, Halifax, Nova Scotia

1997 Honorary Doctorate of Humane Letters–Loyola Marymount University, Los Angeles

1997 Award: "A Visionary Voice in the Merging of Ecology and Spirituality"–Open Center, New York City

1998 First Annual Jerry Mische Global Service Award–Global Education Associates, New York City

1998 Honorary Doctorate of Humane Letters–College of Mount St. Vincent, Riverdale, New York

1998 Thomas Berry Foundation founded, Washington D.C.

1998 Thomas Berry Lecture established–administered by the Humane Society of the United States until 2004, when the Forum on Religion and Ecology assumed leadership

1999 Thomas Berry Hall established–Whidbey Institute on Whidbey Island, Washington

2001 Francis of Assisi Award–Institute for Nature and Culture, De Paul University, Chicago

2002 Juliet Hollister Award–Temple of Understanding, New York City

2003 Frederick II Peace Prize–Pax Romana Earth Charter Project, Assisi, Italy

2003 Honorary Doctorate of Theology–Catholic Theological Union, Chicago

2008 Honorary Doctorate of Humane Letters–Elon University, Elon, North Carolina

Notes

INTRODUCTION: THOMAS BERRY AND THE ARC OF HISTORY

In his later years, Thomas Berry wrote some reflections on his early life in an unpublished manuscript, housed in the Thomas Berry Archives at Harvard University, which he titled *Goldenrod: Reflections on the Twentieth Century*. He chose the title to reflect the notion that the goldenrod plant can be an irritant for people. In this case Thomas hoped to irritate, so as to awaken people to the challenges facing the Earth community. Throughout the book, references to *Goldenrod* will appear in parentheses in the text.

1. As the process theologian John Cobb writes: "Thousands of people, perhaps tens or even hundreds of thousands, have been led to give real primacy to the task of living into the Ecozoic Age. No other writer in the ecological movement has had analogous effectiveness. . . . Berry's formulation has pride of place, and it may prove the most durable and effective of all." Quoted in Thomas Berry, *The Christian Future and the Fate of Earth*, ed. Mary Evelyn Tucker and John Grim (Maryknoll, N.Y.: Orbis Books, 2009), xi.

2. Carlton J. H. Hayes, *Nationalism: A Religion* (New York: Macmillan, 1960). Republished by Transaction Publishers, 2016. Thomas Berry was much influenced by Hayes's perspectives, especially from reading his widely used textbooks on European history.

3. President Eisenhower delivered his farewell speech on January 17, 1961, in which he warned of this growing alliance of industry and the military, especially with regard to a larger arms industry.

4. "Read the Charter," *Earth Charter Initiative*, www.earthcharter.org.

5. Such a new story was first told in book form in collaboration with Brian Swimme in *The Universe Story* (San Francisco: HarperSanFrancisco, 1992). It was first told in film form in the *Journey of the Universe*, written by Brian Thomas Swimme and Mary Evelyn Tucker and produced by Tucker and John Grim.

1. AN INDEPENDENT YOUTH

The description of Thomas's youth in the chapter was compiled from interviews with Thomas and family members by the authors, as well as from passages in his later unpublished writings and memoirs: *Goldenrod: Reflections on the Twentieth Century*; *An Appalachian View*; and *Lifetime Remembrances*.

1. *An Appalachian View*, 9–10.

2. Elizabeth Ernestine Vize Berry, 1890–1980, often called Bess, Bessie, or Betty.

3. *Berry-Vize Patch*, 17.

4. "Notes," *New York Times*, May 10, 1942, Magazine insert, 26.

5. They first moved to a home on 800 Douglas Street, where they lived until 1927, the year the construction of their brick home at 2106 Colonial Avenue was completed.

6. Thomas's oral account to authors Tucker and Grim.

7. Thomas's oral account to authors Tucker and Grim.

8. Interview with Andrew Angyal at Wellspring Retirement Community, Greensboro, N.C., September 11, 2003.

9. Thomas Berry, *Lifetime Remembrances* (unpublished manuscript, n.d.), 51.

10. At that time, North Carolina, the only state without a Roman Catholic diocese, was considered a vicariate, a mission territory. Not until 1924 would it officially become a diocese, when, with William J. Hafey as its first bishop, it became the Diocese of Raleigh. Until then, St. Benedict's was run as a mission by the Benedictine Community of Belmont Abbey, near Charlotte, North Carolina.

11. He did not identify ethnically as many other Catholics did, for example, as an Irish-Catholic or Italian-Catholic.

12. Mount St. Mary's is the second oldest Catholic educational institution in America after Georgetown University, which was founded in 1789.

13. *Rerum Novarum* (Of new things: rights and duties of capital and labor) was issued on May 15, 1891. The ideas on social justice described here also influenced Pope Francis in his encyclical, *Laudato Si*.

14. Indeed, Greensboro was where efforts were later made in 1960 to integrate the Woolworth lunch counter over significant opposition. Five months of sit-ins at the counter eventually resulted in service for African Americans.

15. At the Biltmore Estate in Asheville, North Carolina, Gifford Pinchot established the nation's first scientific forestry program. Pinchot and his Pennsylvania lumber family were aware of this degradation of forests across the country. Thus, they founded the School of Forestry at Yale in 1900 to counter these deleterious practices with the scientific management of forests, drawing on German techniques. Pinchot also founded the U.S. Forestry Service.

16. Thomas Berry, *The Great Work: Our Way into the Future* (New York: Harmony/Bell Tower, 1999), 12–20.

17. Berry, *The Great Work*, 12.

18. Berry, *The Great Work*, 13.

2. THE CALL TO CONTEMPLATION

1. The college and seminary were located in Maryland, as that state had been established as a safe haven for Catholics in the colonial period.

2. This is now known as the National Shrine Grotto of Mount St. Mary's University.

3. "Story of Mother Mary's Mountain," National Shrine Grotto, http://www.nsgrotto.org /history.html.

4. He also took classes in English, French, and German, as well as American history and mathematics and biology.

5. Cassian J. Yuhaus, C.P., *Compelled to Speak: The Passionists in America—Origin and Apostolate* (New York: Newman Press, 1967), 299–300.

6. The Passionists also had a public outreach through *Sign* magazine, which they published from 1921 to 1982. They now have a televised Sunday Mass and a website with news, spiritual programs, and reflections.

7. Thomas Berry, letter to Passionist Provincial Father Justin Carey, September 5, 1933. Original in Passionist Historical Archives.

8. Thomas Berry, letter to Passionist Provincial Father Justin Carey, September 13, 1933. Original in Passionist Historical Archives.

9. Thomas Keevy, "Thomas Berry CP: The Passionist Heritage in The Great Work," in "Thomas Berry's Work: Development, Difference, Importance, Applications," special issue, *The Ecozoic*, no. 4 (2017).

10. Thomas Berry, letter to his parents, December 18, 1933. Original in Harvard Archives.

11. The 1933–34 year at Holy Cross Prep included courses on religion, English literature, rhetoric and composition, Latin, Greek, analytical geometry, and calculus. "For many years Dunkirk was a center of Passionist education. In 1888 St. Mary's Monastery became home to the Passionist Preparatory Seminary, a seminary high school. Temporarily transferred to Baltimore from 1913 until 1920, the seminary returned to a new 75-acre campus on the shore of Lake Erie, a few miles west of Dunkirk. Holy Cross Seminary, or 'The Prep,' offered an atmosphere of study, prayer, and sports. A new wing was added in 1926, a seminary chapel in 1934, and some modernization in 1948. It eventually was accredited as a two-year college. From 1920 to 1932 the seminary hosted a men's retreat movement. After the seminary was closed in 1968, the Passionists attempted to run a variety of ministries there and rented the facility to the Association of Retarded Children from 1972 to 1976. By the mid-1980s, the last Passionist had left and the building was razed." Description on the Passionist Historical Archives site: http://www.cpprovince.org/archives /histsummary/dunkirk-sum.php.

12. "Father James Lambert C.P.," Passionist Historical Archives, http://www.cpprovince.org /archives/bios/12/12-1b.php.

13. He said the customary three Masses in his memory. Thomas Berry, personal letter to Father Ernest Welch, January 2, 1952. Original in Passionist Historical Archives.

14. *Christian Perfection and Contemplation* is a treatise on the operation of grace in the spiritual life based on Thomas Aquinas and other Catholic sources.

15. Thomas chose the full religious name of "Thomas a Mater Dei" (Thomas of the Mother of God). In this he followed the custom of Italian men in choosing a woman's name for a middle appellation, namely, Mary.

16. For Thomas, the historic Christ of the Gospels was identified with the cosmic Christ of St. Paul. Thus, all of creation was seen as a Divine Milieu, participating in the rhythms

of death and resurrection. St. John's Gospel opens with the statement that the Logos, the Word, is present from the beginning of time and thus humans are immersed in a sacred universe. From this perspective Thomas envisioned the Christian story as held within the larger Earth and universe story.

17.   Over the breast of their black religious habit a cloth emblem symbolizes their vocation: a heart emblazoned with a cross and the words *Iesu Xpi Passio* (The Passion of Jesus Christ). After Vatican II, as was the case in many religious orders, Thomas rarely wore the habit. He preferred simply a brown corduroy jacket and tie, reflecting his identity as a teacher and scholar.

18.   A Brother is a member of a men's religious order who is not ordained and has not taken Holy Orders.

19.   This custom of moving seminarians was to give familiarity with the different monasteries and cities, spread out the cost of seminary education, provide some help in the working of the monasteries, and give exposure to different teachers. The timeline for these stages in Thomas's path is as follows:

1934-1935: Our Lady of Sorrows Monastery, Springfield, Mass.—Novitiate
August 15, 1935: First profession of vows
1935-1936: St. Paul of the Cross Monastery, Pittsburgh, Pa.
1936-1937: Immaculate Conception Monastery, Jamaica, N.Y.
1937-1938: St. Michael's Monastery, Union City, N.J.
August 15, 1938: Final profession of vows, Immaculate Conception Monastery, Jamaica, N.Y.
1938-1939: Immaculate Conception Monastery, Jamaica, N.Y.
1939-1942: St. Michael's Monastery, Union City, N.J.
May 30, 1942: St. Patrick's Cathedral, Newark, N.J.—Ordination to the priesthood
1942-1943: St. Gabriel's Monastery, Brighton, Mass.—Studying sacred eloquence (preaching)

20.   Thomas Berry, *An Appalachian View* (unpublished manuscript, n.d.), 2. Unpublished reflections that Thomas compiled toward the end of his life.

21.   Berry, *An Appalachian View*, 2.

22.   Pierre Teilhard de Chardin, *The Divine Milieu* (New York: Harper and Row, 1960), 89.

23.   Teilhard de Chardin, *The Divine Milieu*, 89.

24.   Teilhard de Chardin, 66.

25.   Teilhard de Chardin, 67.

26.   The monastic daily schedule was as follows:

2:00   Awakened by wooden rattle. Matins and Lauds chanted in chapel.
3:00   Sleep.
6:00   Prime and Tierce chanted until 6:30.
6:30   Mass and Eucharist.
7:30   Breakfast: coffee and bread. The Great Silence ends.
8:00   Study or exercise.
9:00   Two morning classes, fifty minutes each.

11:00	Spiritual readings.
11:15	Solitary walk.
11:45	Sext and None chanted in chapel.
12:00	Noontime meal with devotional or educational reading.
12:30	Recreational period.
1:15	Rest for one hour.
2:15	Rosary and common spiritual reading in chapel.
3:00	Afternoon classes.
5:00	Bell for chapel assembly.
5:15	Vespers chanted in chapel, followed by one hour of prayer.
6:30	Supper or dinner.
7:15	Recreation period.
7:45	Announcements.
8:00	Compline chanted in chapel.
8:30	Return to rooms.
9:00	The Great Silence begins.

27.   In the steps toward ordination, Thomas took the four minor orders in November 1941, followed by the subdeaconate February 28, 1942, the deaconate March 19, 1942, and finally ordination May 30, 1942. Preparing for the priesthood in the Passionist community requires the following:

1. Seven years of study (three of philosophy and four of theology)
2. Several phases of religious commitment:

a. One year of Novitiate, focused on spirituality
b. Taking of vows

i) First profession (temporary vows) at end of Novitiate
ii) Final profession (final vows) at end of third year post Novitiate

c. Receiving a progression of ecclesiastical "orders," or rank:

i) Minor Orders
ii) Major Orders (culminating in ordination to the priesthood)
iii) Religious Orders

Historically, individual persons in the early church communities felt a calling or commitment to serve the community in various ways: publicly reading the scriptures at services (as lectors) or helping in the liturgies (as acolytes). Others served the physical needs of the community (as deacons), while the call to preside at the Eucharistic liturgy was specific to the bishop and priests. As time went on, the church community became more organized and a hierarchical structure evolved. Significantly, these various ministries of service within the community became ranked, ultimately identified as "orders." Eventually that ranking became directly related to the priesthood.

Many of these ministries are undertaken today (since Vatican Council II) by the laity (e.g., lectors), but at the time Thomas was preparing for the priesthood, all the orders were subsumed hierarchically in the priesthood, so that over the course of his years of study separate liturgical ceremonies bestowed these various ranks or orders on him. First were the minor orders (together), then subdeacon, followed by deacon, and finally priest.

28.   *Berry-Vize Patch*, June 8, 2000, 18.

29.   *New York Times*, May 8, 1942, 8.

30.   *New York Times*, April 7, 1942, 25.

3. STUDYING HISTORY AND LIVING HISTORY

1.   Thomas's earliest courses included a history seminar on the colonial period in Latin America, German grammar, a social statistics seminar, contemporary German and French philosophy, historical research and criticism, and American philosophy.

2.   John Tracy Ellis, "American Catholics and the Intellectual Life," *Thought* 10 (Autumn 1955): 545. Engel-Janosi served as president of the American Catholic Historical Association in 1947.

3.   Thomas Berry, *An Appalachian View* (unpublished manuscript, n.d.), 4.

4.   His first-year courses included Europe from 1815 to 1870 and Europe from 1870 to 1914; modern European historiography; a seminar on nineteenth-century political theory; the history of ancient philosophy; and a survey of nineteenth-century literature. In 1944–45 he took courses in anthropology, the prehistory of Near and Far Eastern culture, ancient history, God and society, and "primitive" morality. During 1945–46, Thomas added courses on revolutionary and Napoleonic era history; post-1865 United States history; the Catholic Church in the United States since 1884; the Middle Ages to 1150; Plato, patristic and medieval philosophy; and purpose and design in the universe. Thomas also completed courses in Middle and modern English literature, as well as on Islamic culture and its influence on the Christian West. In 1946–47 he worked on his dissertation while finishing classes. He submitted it in November 1947 while teaching again in Dunkirk at Holy Cross Prep.

5.   Thomas also studied with Father Vernon Moore, one of the first American Catholic clergymen to teach empirical psychology. At Catholic University of America he also encountered the distinguished church historian Monsignor John Tracy Ellis.

6.   Carlton J. H. Hayes, *History of Europe* (New York: MacMillan, 1949); and *Nationalism: A Religion* (New York: Macmillan, 1960; reprinted by Transaction Publishers, 2016).

7.   In his studies, he did not take up systematic analysis himself, but he appreciated philosophical perspectives. This was the case with his reading of the process philosopher Alfred North Whitehead (1861–1947), who had profound insights into the dynamic unfolding nature of all reality, and existentialist thinkers such as Karl Jaspers (1883–1969), who recognized enduring patterns of thought from ancient civilizations into contemporary societies. Each of these thinkers influenced Thomas, but their efforts to construct a systematic philosophy did not fit his historical approach. Similarly, he was sympathetic to

newer forms of contemplative mysticism, such as that of the Trappist monk Thomas Merton (1915–1968), and to the work of the Jesuit theologian Bernard Lonergan (1904–1984). While appreciative of their spiritual visions, however, he felt they lacked a larger historical context. Instead he was attracted to the cosmological and ecological positions articulated by, among others, the paleontologist Pierre Teilhard de Chardin, the anthropologist Loren Eiseley, and the ecologists Rachel Carson and Aldo Leopold.

8. Thomas wrote an extensive review of Voegelin's book for *Thought* (a Jesuit quarterly review) in spring 1958: Thomas Berry, "Order and History" *Thought* 33, no. 2 (1958): 273–278, https://doi.org/10.5840/thought195833219.

9. Berry, *An Appalachian View*, 4.

10. Rev. Gabriel Gorman, letter to Thomas Berry, March 30, 1948. Original in Harvard Archives.

11. Berry, *An Appalachian View*, 4.

12. Thomas Berry, "The Historical Theory of Giambattista Vico" (PhD diss., Catholic University of America, 1948), 90.

13. Berry, "The Historical Theory of Giambattista Vico," 117.

14. Andrew Angyal, interview with Thomas Berry at Wellspring Retirement Center, Greensboro, N.C., August 6, 2004.

15. Fr. Gabriel Gorman, letter to Thomas Berry, March 30, 1948. Original in Harvard Archives

16. Thomas Berry, letter to his parents, November 27, 1948. Original in Harvard Archives.

17. Ronald Beaton, C.P., letter to Thomas Berry from Hong Kong Maryknoll House, November 16, 1950. Original in Harvard Archives.

18. Thomas Berry, letter to Fr. Gabriel Gorman, June 30, 1949. Original in Harvard Archives.

19. This was not published but was included in his Riverdale Papers, vol. 3.

20. Thomas Berry, "Mao Tse-Tung: The Long March," Riverdale Papers, vol. 3 (New York: Riverdale Center for Religious Research), 94–95.

21. "John Dewey's Influence in China 1919–21" was included in his Riverdale Papers, vol. 3, 1–48. It was published as "John Dewey's Influence in China," in *John Dewey: His Thought and Influence*, ed. John Blewett (New York: Fordham University Press, 1960).

22. Blewett, *John Dewey*, 54.

23. Blewett, *John Dewey*, 56.

24. Berry, "John Dewey's Influence in China 1919–21," 46.

25. In this spirit, Ba Jin (1904–2005) later wrote his novel titled *The Family*, which criticized Confucianism and its rigidity.

26. A study that explores some of the educational ideals of transcendence embedded in Chinese civil society during this period is Prasenjit Duara, *The Crisis of Global Modernity: Asian Traditions and a Sustainable Future* (Cambridge: Cambridge University Press, 2014).

27. Berry, "John Dewey's Influence in China 1919–21," 43.

28. Berry, "John Dewey's Influence in China 1919–21," 48.

29. Blewett, *John Dewey*, 69.

30. Ted de Bary, letter to Thomas Berry, April 18, 1951. Original in Harvard Archives.

31. Thomas Berry, letter to Ted and Fanny de Bary, July 5, 1952. Original in Harvard Archives.

32. Thomas Berry, letter to Ted and Fanny de Bary, May 30, 1952. Original in Harvard Archives.

33. Thomas Berry, letter to his sister Ann, October 5, 1952. Original in Harvard Archives.

34. Thomas Berry, letter to Ted and Fanny de Bary, July 5, 1952. Original in Harvard Archives.

35. Berry, *An Appalachian View*, 3.

36. Thomas Berry, letter to Ted and Fanny de Bary, July 5, 1952. Original in Harvard Archives.

37. Thomas Berry, letter to Ted and Fanny de Bary, May 30, 1952. Original in Harvard Archives.

38. A dozen years later, in 1965, Thomas was one of five scholars invited by New York's Channel Five television to present a series of half-hour programs on Dante during the seven-hundredth anniversary of the poet's birth. Thomas's lecture focused on the background of Dante's life and work. In a later essay on the poet and his age, Thomas declares: "A Dante experience is one of the essential elements in any full cultural development of a western personality." See Thomas Berry, "Dante: The Age in Which He Lived," Riverdale Papers, vol. 4 (New York: Riverdale Center for Religious Research, 1974), 1.

39. Thomas Berry, letter to Father Ernest Welch, fall 1953. Original in Passionist Historical Archives.

40. Andrew Angyal, interview with Thomas Berry at Wellspring Retirement Community, Greensboro, N.C., January 3, 2004.

41. Thomas Berry, letter to Ted de Bary, April 1953. Original in Harvard Archives.

4. THE STRUGGLE TO TEACH

The chapter epigraph is from Thomas Berry, *Religions of India: Hinduism, Yoga, Buddhism* (New York: Columbia University Press, 1996; first published 1971 by Bruce-Macmillan), 194. Bruce-Macmillan also asked Thomas to write a book entitled *The Religions of China and Japan*, but he was never able to complete it because of so many other commitments at Fordham and Riverdale.

1. Throughout the 1950s, Thomas maintained a close correspondence with his family, especially with three of his sisters in religious orders: his older sister, Sr. Mary Elizabeth (Merse), a hospital administrator in Cochabamba, Bolivia, with the Daughters of Charity; Margaret (Sr. Margaret Ann), also a Daughter of Charity, a professor of English at St. Joseph's College, Emmitsburg, Maryland, and later a professor of English and Asian Studies at John Carroll University, Cleveland, Ohio; and Ann (Sr. Zoë Marie), a Maryknoll Sister serving in the Philippines as a biology teacher. In 1956, Thomas's sister Ann was diagnosed with breast cancer. During the year that she underwent treatment, Thomas often visited her at Maryknoll, New York. His letters to her reflect not only his feeling for her struggle, but also his admiration for her courage in confronting the disease that took her life on March 28, 1958.

2. Thomas Berry, letter to his sister Ann Berry (Sr. Zoë Marie), September 20, 1955. Original in Harvard Archives.

3. Thomas Berry, letter to his sister Ann Berry (Sr. Zoë Marie), September 14, 1956. Original in Harvard Archives.

4. Rev. Ernest Welch, letter to Thomas Berry, May 7, 1957. Original in Passionist Historical Archives.

5. Thomas Berry, letter to Rev. Malcolm Lavelle, May 20, 1957. Original in Passionist Historical Archives.

6. Thomas Berry, letter to Father Ernest Welch, May 16, 1957. Original in Passionist Historical Archives.

7. Rev. Malcolm Lavelle, letter to Thomas Berry, July 12, 1957. Original in Passionist Historical Archives.

8. Robert Wilken, CP, letter to Thomas Berry, September 20, 1957. Original in Harvard Archives.

9. Thomas Berry, letter to Mary Evelyn Tucker and John Grim, June 24, 1982.

10. They included Reverend Paul Yu Pin, Archbishop of Nanking, China, and Cardinal and president of the Republic of China's Fu Jen Catholic University; John Chang Myun, prime minister of the Republic of Korea; Kotaro Tanaka, chief justice of Japan, who later became president of Tokyo University; Ngo Dinh Diem, former prime minister of Vietnam and later president of the Republic of Vietnam; and John C. H. Wu, a distinguished Chinese jurist and minister of China to the Holy See who, months earlier, had been appointed professor of law at Seton Hall's newly founded School of Law.

11. Thomas Berry, "Missions, Missiology, and Oriental Culture," *Theology Digest*, Autumn 1958, 130.

12. It wasn't until the publication of Edward Said's book *Orientalism* in 1978 that these terms were seen as part of a colonialist bias with regard to cultures in Asia and the Middle East. Consequently, other terms came into use, such as the more accurate term *Asian*.

13. The "rites controversy" was ended by Pope Pius XII, who requested in 1939 that the Vatican Sacred Congregation for the Propagation of the Faith, which had prohibited honoring Chinese family ancestors in 1645, reverse the earlier prohibition against ancestor reverence.

14. This commitment also led him to found the Edith Stein Guild. During the 1950s Thomas had become acquainted with Leon Paul, a Jewish convert to Catholicism and founder of the Don Bosco House for youth in Brooklyn. Together they founded the Edith Stein Guild, an interreligious organization designed to foster mutual understanding between Jews and Catholics and to provide support for Jewish converts to Catholicism.

15. Later the name was changed to the Asian Thought and Religion Seminar.

16. These included the following papers: "Theological Synthesis in the Great Traditions: Shankara, Chu Hsi, St. Thomas," 1963; "Ritual in the Chinese Tradition" (1965); "Salvation Experience in Early Buddhism" with Abe Masao and Robert Olsen as discussants, 1966; "Nirvana Experience in Buddhism," 1967; and "Primary Causality in Asian Traditions," 1968.

17. Thomas Berry, "Oriental Philosophies and World Humanism," *International Philosophical Quarterly* 1, no. 1 (February 1961): 5–33. Later published as *Five Oriental Philosophies* (Albany, N.Y.: Magi Books, 1968).

18. Berry, *Five Oriental Philosophies*, 8–9.

19. Berry, *Five Oriental Philosophies*, 15.

20. Berry, *Five Oriental Philosophies*, 21.

21. Berry, *Five Oriental Philosophies*, 28.

22. Berry, *Five Oriental Philosophies*, 28.

23. This panel was chaired by Ted de Bary and consisted of the following presentations: Ellen Marie Chen, St. John's University, "Tao as the Great Mother"; Richard Mather, University of Minnesota, "Love in Chinese Buddhism"; Ronald Dimberg, University of Virginia, "Ho Hsin-yin's Concept of Friendship"; and L. K. Tong, Fairfield University, "Platonic Eros and Confucian *Jen*." Discussants were W. T. Chan, Chatham College, and Joseph Wu, Sacramento State. The Association of Asian Studies meeting that year was held in Chicago at the Palmer House from March 30 to April 1, 1973.

24. *Buddhism* was first published by Hawthorne Books in 1966 and in 1989 by Anima Press. When that press closed, it was brought to Columbia University Press and published as a new edition in 1996. It is still in print.

25. L. D. Barnett, trans., *Path of Light: Rendered for the First Time into English from the Bodhich-aryavatara of Santi-Deva. A Manual for Maha-yana Buddhism* (London: John Murray, 1947). Quoted by Thomas Berry in *Buddhism* (New York: Hawthorne Books, 1966), 105.

26. Barnett, *Path of Light*, 80; quoted by Berry, *Buddhism*, 105.

27. *Religions of India* was to be part of a two-volume work titled: *Oriental Religions: A Study of the Spiritual Formation of the Asian World*. The second volume was to be *Religions of China and Japan*, but this was never published because of Thomas's many other teaching and writing commitments.

28. Thomas Berry, "The Creative Present," in *Religions of India: Hinduism, Yoga, Buddhism* (New York: Bruce-Macmillan, 1971), 193.

29. Berry, "The Creative Present," 194.

30. Berry, "The Creative Present," 194.

31. Thomas Berry, "Asian Art," in *Encyclopedia Americana*, international ed., vol. 2 (New York: Americana Corporation, 1965).

32. Thomas said this in classes on Asian religions at Fordham attended by the authors.

33. Barbara Louise Morris, "To Define a Catholic University: The 1965 Crisis at St. John's" (master's thesis, Columbia University Teacher's College, 1977), 180.

34. Morris, "To Define a Catholic University," 40.

35. Morris, "To Define a Catholic University," 24.

36. Joseph Scimecca and Roland Damiano, *Crisis at St. John's: Strike and Revolution on the Catholic Campus* (New York: Random House, 1968), 22.

37. Scimecca and Damiano, *Crisis at St. John's*, 67–68.

38. Scimecca and Damiano, *Crisis at St. John's*, 85.

39. Thomas Berry, letter to Father General Theodore Foley, C.P., December 20, 1965. Original in Passionist Historical Archives.

40. This exchange focused on Thomas's paper entitled "Creative Revolution"; his letter to Vincentian Father Tinnelly (November 3, 1965); and his letter to the Passionist Superior General Theodore Foley in Rome (December 20, 1965). In particular, Rooney objected to Thomas's contract negotiations with Christopher Mooney, S.J., chair of Fordham's Theology Department, about a faculty appointment there and about his plans for a trip to Asia.

41. Thomas Berry, letter to Father Provincial Gerard Rooney, C.P., January 1, 1966. Original in Passionist Historical Archives.

42. Thomas Berry, letter to Father Provincial Gerard Rooney, C.P., January 18, 1966. Original in Passionist Historical Archives.

43. Berry, *Religions of India*, 194.

5. FROM HUMAN HISTORY TO EARTH HISTORY

The chapter epigraph can be found in at least two publications: Thomas Berry, "Religions in the Global Human Community," in *The Sacred Universe: Earth, Spirituality, and Religion in the Twenty-First Century*, ed. Mary Evelyn Tucker (New York: Columbia University Press, 2009), 34; and Thomas Berry, *Thomas Berry: Selected Writings on the Earth Community*, ed. Mary Evelyn Tucker and John Grim (Maryknoll, N.Y.: Orbis Books, 2014), 90.

1. Thomas Berry, "Patriarchy: A New Interpretation of History," in *The Dream of the Earth* (Berkeley: Counterpoint Press, 2015; originally Sierra Club Books, 1988).

2. Thomas Berry, letter to Christopher Mooney, March 17, 1966. Original in Harvard Archives.

3. Fordham had mandatory retirement at age sixty-five. Thomas taught a few more courses through fall 1981. He received tenure in June 1970 with rank of associate professor.

4. This work resulted in a series by Crossroad Publishing titled, *World Spirituality: An Encyclopedic History of the Religious Quest*, edited by Ewert Cousins and a distinguished board of scholars.

5. These included Jesuits Ladislas Orsy, Robert McNally, Robert Gleason, and Julius Hejja.

6. While there are now theology departments with comparative theology, such as Boston College and Loyola Marymount University, even today, there are no comparable MA or PhD History of Religions programs at a Catholic university in North America.

7. In Thomas's view, just as theology departments were incomplete without the history of religions, so too, without including Asian thought, Western philosophy could not claim to be a world philosophy. In this, he was in agreement with many other scholars of Asian philosophy and religion, such as Tu Weiming, formerly of Harvard and now of the Institute for Advanced Studies at Beijing University, and Roger Ames, emeritus professor from the University of Hawaii.

8. The Harvard Archives include Thomas's correspondence with Asian scholars such as Joseph Spae, at the Oriens Institute for Religious Research in Tokyo; John Blewett, S.J., Gino Piovesana, S.J., and William Johnston, S.J., at Sophia University in Tokyo; Raimon Pannikar at Benares Hindu University; Bede Griffiths and Richard DeSmet, S.J., in India; Tissa Balasuriya at Aquinas University College in Colombo, Sri Lanka; and Yves Raguin, S.J., in Taiwan. In the United States he corresponded with Ellen Marie Chen at St. John's University and Aelred Graham at Portsmouth Priory.

9. He had great admiration for both these thinkers and encouraged students to read widely in their works. He also helped organize a conference on Teilhard and Jung in November 1975.

10. These included PhDs in Hinduism (Stafford Betty, John Borelli, Gerald Carney, Richard Cefalu, Rev. William Cenkner, O.P., Christopher Key Chapple, James Francis Kenney, Rev. Frank Podgorski, Dennis Ryan, Daniel Sheridan), Buddhism (Brian Brown),

Japanese spirituality (Rev. John Brinkman, M.M.), Native American traditions (Rosalyn Amenta, Michael Delgado, Kathleen Duggan, John Grim, Donald St. John), Loren Eiseley (Suzanne McGuire), the journey symbol (Sister Marilyn Nichols, C.S.J.), eco-psychology (Rev. Valerio Ortolani, S.J.), Mircea Eliade (Robert Avens), the spiritual guide (Sister Donald Corcoran, O.S.B.), and spirituality for missions (Daniel Martin).

11. *L'Osservatore Romano* published the announcement the next day and also noted Pope John's ecumenical intention that the Council will be of service "not only for the spiritual good and joy of the Christian people but also an invitation to the separated communities to seek again that unity for which so many souls are longing in these days throughout the world." *L'Osservatore Romano*, January 26/27, 1959. See: *Acta Apostolicae Sedis* 51 (1959): 69; see also comments by Thomas F. Stransky, C.S.P., "The Foundation of the Secretariat for Promoting Christian Unity," in *Vatican II: By Those Who Were There*, ed. Alberic Stacpoole (Minneapolis: Winston Press, 1986), 64.

12. Pope Paul VI, *Gaudium et Spes* (Joys and Hopes), December 7, 1965, 1.

13. Key theologians included Gustavo Gutierrez of Peru, Leonardo Boff of Brazil, Juan Luis Segundo of Uruguay, and Jon Sobrino of Spain.

14. Thomas gave talks at Iona College, College of New Rochelle, Good Counsel College, Seton Hall University, St. Francis College, Boston College, John Carroll, St. Louis University, Rutgers University, Trinity College, Vermont, and Jewish Theological Seminary.

15. Machado continues as interreligious officer for the Federation of Asian Bishops' Conferences and for the Catholic Bishops' Conference of India.

16. In 1983 Ettore Di Filippo was appointed bishop of Isernia-Venafro in Italy, and in 1989 as archbishop of Campobasso-Boiano.

17. In 1977, in preparation for the Vienna Conference on Ecology, Thomas participated in a retreat for Catholic UN delegates and the next year worked with their Institute for the Theological Encounter of Science and Technology. His interest in creative aging in time led to Di Filippo's invitation for him to coordinate the 1980 International Forum on Active Aging at the Vatican's Castel Gondolfo and the 1986 Forum for Creative Aging in Italy. Thomas's article on aging became the preface for this book: Francis Tiso, ed., *Aging: Spiritual Perspectives* (Lake Worth, Fla.: Sunday Publications, 1982).

18. The UN World Charter for Nature was endorsed by all member states except the United States. It was followed some two decades later by the Earth Charter, which was issued in 2000. The Earth Charter expressed a vision of ecology, justice, and peace.

19. *Nostra Aetate* (In Our Time: Declaration on the Relation of the Church with Non-Christian Religions of the Second Vatican Council). Promulgated by Pope Paul VI on October 28, 1965.

20. *Nostra Aetate.*

21. Thomas also expressed this idea in a lecture delivered before the National Association of Diocesan Ecumenical Officers in San Antonio, Texas, on May 15, 1985, on the occasion of the twentieth anniversary of *Nostra Aetate*. The lecture was titled, "The Catholic Church, the Religions of the World and the New Story." Thomas observed that the world religions "contain not only a 'ray of the divine light' but even floods of light illuminating the entire religious life of the human community."

22. *Nostra Aetate.*
23. *Nostra Aetate.*
24. There was a similarly expansive proposal discussed the year after Thomas arrived at Fordham that was never realized. This was to create "A World University Under Jesuit Auspices," which would bring together the resources and create exchanges among many of the Jesuit institutions of higher education in Tokyo, Pune, Manila, Bagdad, Rome, and Namur. Thomas wrote to express strong support for this proposal. Thomas Berry, letter to Fr. Richardson, September 15, 1967. Original in Harvard Archives.
25. Thomas Berry, "Education in a Multicultural World," in *Approaches to the Oriental Classics: Asian Literature and Thought in General Education*, ed. Wm. Theodore de Bary (New York: Columbia University Press, 1959), 11–23; Thomas Berry, "The Spiritual Forms of the Oriental Civilizations," in *Approaches to Asian Civilizations*, ed. Wm. Theodore de Bary and Ainslie T. Embree (New York: Columbia University Press, 1964), 5–33.
26. Dr. Jose Pereira in the History of Religions program encouraged his students to do translations of Sanskrit texts and provide historical context and commentary.
27. While Thomas originated the term the "second axial age", his colleague Ewert Cousins wrote about it in his book *Christ of the 21st Century* (New York: Continuum, 1992). Since then, many others, such as Leonard Swidler and Karen Armstrong, have also drawn on the term.
28. "Confucius and Lao-Tse were living in China when all the schools of Chinese philosophy came into being, including those of Mo Ti, Chuang Tse, Lieh Tzu and a host of others; India produced the *Upanishads* and Buddha and, like China, ran the whole gamut of philosophical possibilities down to materialism, skepticism and nihilism; in Iran Zarathustra taught a challenging view of the world as a struggle between good and evil; in Palestine the prophets made their appearance from Elijah by way of Isaiah and Jeremiah to Deutero-Isaiah; Greece witnessed the appearance of Homer, of the philosophers—Parmenides, Heraclitus and Plato—of the tragedians, of Thucydides and Archimedes. Everything implied by these names developed during these few centuries almost simultaneously in China, India and the West." Karl Jaspers, *The Origin and Goal of History* (London: Routledge, 2011), 2. First published 1953.
29. Forum on Religion and Ecology at Yale: www.fore.yale.edu.
30. In a September 30, 1967, letter to his superiors, Thomas expressed frustration with the order's lack of innovation in spiritual formation for their new members. Such concerns for his order's spiritual vitality would remain unaddressed until the 1968 election of a more sympathetic provincial. Flavian Dougherty, C.P., and Robert Carbonneau, C.P., et al., *Celebrating 150 Years of Passionist Ministry in North America and Beyond: 1852–2002* (South River, N.J.: Congregation of the Passion, 2002), 48.
31. Thomas Berry, letter of September 30, 1967. Original in Harvard Archives.
32. Berry, letter of September 30, 1967, 2.
33. Berry, letter of September 30, 1967, 2.
34. Thomas links these topics to Carlos Castaneda's *Journey to Ixtlan: The Lessons of Don Juan* (New York: Simon and Schuster, 1972) and Joseph Campbell's *The Hero with a Thousand Faces* (New York: Pantheon-Knopf, 1949) in Thomas Berry, "Contemporary Spirituality,"

Riverdale Papers, vol. 4 (New York: Riverdale Center for Religious Research). Both of these works offer archetypal symbols of the soul's journey to selfhood.

35.   Berry, "Contemporary Spirituality," 2. Tucker and Grim took this course.

36.   Berry, "Contemporary Spirituality," 26.

37.   John Grim was a student in the class and reports on the visit to Leonard Bernstein's apartment.

38.   See Christopher Key Chapple, "Thomas Berry on Yoga, Buddhism, and Carl Jung," in *The Intellectual Journey of Thomas Berry: Imagining the Earth Community*, ed. Heather Eaton (Lanham, Md.: Lexington Books, 2014).

39.   Much of this correspondence is in the Harvard Archives, along with many letters of recommendations for students and others.

40.   Thomas Berry, "The Cosmology of Religions," in *The Sacred Universe*, 117; also in *Thomas Berry: Selected Writings*, 67.

41.   Berry, "The Cosmology of Religions," 117; Berry, *Thomas Berry: Selected Writings*, 67.

42.   Thomas Berry, "Religion in the Ecozoic Era," in *The Sacred Universe*, 99; Berry, *Thomas Berry: Selected Writings*, 67.

43.   Berry, "The Cosmology of Religions," 117; Berry, *Thomas Berry: Selected Writings*, 67. Heather Eaton develops these ideas in her essay "Metamorphosis: A Cosmology of Religions in an Ecological Age," in *The Intellectual Journey of Thomas Berry*.

44.   The following description of this discussion draws on the account of Christopher Chapple, "Thomas Berry on Yoga, Buddhism, and Carl Jung," in *The Intellectual Journey of Thomas Berry*, 59–60. The discussion occurred in June 1989 at the College Theology Society.

45.   From the research and writing of that year, Brian Brown published *The Buddha Nature: A Study of the Tathagatagarba and Alayavijnana* (New Delhi: Motilal Banarsidass, 1991), John Grim published *The Shaman: Patterns of Religious Healing Among the Ojibway Indians* (Norman: University of Oklahoma Press, 1983), and in Mexico Valerio Ortolani published *Personalidad ecologia* in Spanish in 1986 on eco-psychology.

6. FROM NEW STORY TO UNIVERSE STORY

1.   It was called Cardinal Spellman Retreat House and lasted from 1966 to 2011, when it was sold to the Hebrew Home for the Aged, along with the Riverdale Center for Religious Research. It was at 5801 Riverdale Avenue in the Bronx.

2.   Rene Dubos, a distinguished biologist, wrote books for a larger public, such as *So Human an Animal* and *The Dreams of Reason*. He advocated for an active stewardship of the land according to a Benedictine model. He popularized the phrase attributed to Jacques Ellul, "Think globally, act locally." Dubos interacted with Thomas over the years, especially at the Cathedral of St. John the Divine, where they both often lectured.

3.   Known as the Allien Estate, the residence was purchased by the order in 1924 and renamed the Vincent Strambi Residence. See Flavian Dougherty, C.P., and Robert Carbonneau, C.P., et al., *Celebrating 150 Years of Passionist Ministry in North America and Beyond: 1852–2002* (South River, N.J.: Congregation of the Passion, 2002), 46. Passionists lived there from 1927 to 1967, when it was renovated for the Riverdale Center.

4. Since 1960, he had proposed a religious research center at Riverdale for the study of the spiritual formation of humans. See Thomas Berry, letter to John Chrysostom Ryan, C.P., September 30, 1967. See also Dougherty and Carbonneau et al., *Celebrating 150 Years*, 48. Within two years after the election of Flavian Dougherty, C.P., as provincial in 1968, Thomas was authorized to found the Riverdale Center and to renovate the old Victorian mansion on the Riverdale property. Later, he also received strong support from a subsequent provincial, Brendan Keevey.

5. Other Passionists who were there for several years at the beginning were Fr. Sebastian Kolinovsky, keeper of the books; Fr. Ernest Hotz, supervisor of the 1970s house renovation; and Brother Leo DiFiore, business manager. Those who continued to live there were Fr. Neil Sharkey, theology professor at St. John's, Fr. Richard Scheiner, counselor and retreat master, and for several years, Brother Dan Sheridan. Brother Conrad Federspiel eventually moved in after 1979 and was a valuable assistant to Thomas in the later Riverdale years. Many visitors used the library, including Thomas's niece, Terry Kelleher, and Amarylis Cortijo, graduate students at Columbia and Fordham.

6. After Thomas left and returned to North Carolina, the ancient red oak was cut down by the Passionist priests who moved into the house. Having renovated the house at considerable expense, they feared the oak might fall on it in a storm. Concerned neighbors and students tried to prevent this occurrence, but to no avail. On a cold sunny winter day in 1995, there was a leave-taking ritual for the tree led by Sr. Miriam MacGillis, founder of Genesis Farm. This was attended by many in the area, as well as Fanny de Bary, former students of Thomas, including Tucker and Grim, and Thomas's sister, Margaret, who flew up from Greensboro, North Carolina, for the occasion.

7. Unpublished document on the Riverdale Center for Religious Research, 1972. Copy in Harvard Archives.

8. Unpublished document on the Riverdale Center.

9. Thomas Berry, "Bioregions: The Context for Reinhabiting the Earth," in *The Dream of the Earth* (Berkeley: Counterpoint Press, 2015), 166. Originally published by Sierra Club Books in 1988.

10. See his essay "The Hudson River Valley: A Bioregional Story," in *The Dream of the Earth*, 171–179 (1988 edition).

11. In 1997 Kennedy received the first annual Thomas Berry Environmental Award for Achievement in Restoring Ecological Health to the Hudson Valley from the College of Mount St. Vincent in Riverdale. John Cronin helped to establish a Great Work Award in honor of Thomas Berry that is given annually by the Environmental Consortium of Colleges and Universities along the Hudson River.

12. For Haenke's call for this conference, see https://www.context.org/iclib/ic03/haenke/.

    Continental congresses have since convened on the Great Lakes Bioregion (Michigan, 1986), Cascadia (British Columbia, 1988), the Gulf of Maine (Maine, 1990), Edwards Plateau (Texas, 1992), the Ohio River valley (Kentucky, 1994), Cuahunahuac—a hemispheric gathering (Mexico, 1996), the Flint Hills (Kansas, 2002), Katuah on the southern Appalachians (North Carolina, 2005), and the Cumberland Bioregion (Tennessee, 2009).

13.   Brian C. Campbell, "Growing an Oak: An Ethnography of Ozark Bioregionalism," in *Environmental Anthropology Engaging Ecotopia: Bioregionalism, Permaculture, and Ecovillages*, ed. Joshua Lockyer, James Veteto, and E. N. Anderson (New York: Berghahn Books, 2013).

14.   Berry, "Bioregions," 163–170 (1988 edition).

15.   See *Cross Currents*, Summer/Fall 1987, where four of Thomas's essays are published: "Creative Energy," "The New Story," "Dream of the Earth," and "Twelve Principles," along with essays by Brian Swimme ("Berry's Cosmology"), Arthur Fabel ("The Dynamic of the Self-Ordering Cosmos"), and John Grim ("Time, History, Historians in Thomas Berry's Vision").

16.   *The Dream of the Earth* was published while he was still at Riverdale. The rest of his books were published after he retired to Greensboro, North Carolina, although most of the essays were written during the Riverdale years.

17.   Brian Swimme and Thomas Berry, *The Universe Story: From the Primordial Flaring Forth to the Ecozoic Era—A Celebration of the Unfolding of the Cosmos* (San Francisco: HarperSan-Francisco, 1992). Brian Thomas Swimme and Mary Evelyn Tucker, *Journey of the Universe* (New Haven, Conn.: Yale University Press, 2011). Brian Thomas Swimme and Mary Evelyn Tucker, *Journey of the Universe*, directed by David Kennard and Patsy Northcutt (Livermore, Calif.: Northcutt Productions, 2011), DVD. Reissued by Shelter Island in 2013.

18.   Thomas Berry, *An Appalachian View* (unpublished manuscript, n.d.), 5–6.

19.   Berry, *An Appalachian View*, 6–7.

20.   Dennis Patrick O'Hara, "Thomas Berry's Understanding of the Psychic-Spiritual Dimension of Creation," in *The Intellectual Journey of Thomas Berry: Imagining the Earth Community*, ed. Heather Eaton (Lanham, Md.: Lexington Books, 2014).

21.   Thomas Berry, "The Earth Story," in *The Great Work: Our Way into the Future* (New York: Harmony/Bell Tower, 1999), 31.

22.   Berry, *An Appalachian View*, 6.

23.   Loren Eiseley, *The Immense Journey: An Imaginative Naturalist Explores the Mysteries of Man and Nature* (New York: Vintage Books, 1959).

24.   Five extinction periods have preceded the present one, in which the planet is losing dozens of species each day. All prior extinction periods have had natural causes, but this current one is caused by humans, especially by destruction of habitat. See Elizabeth Kolbert, *The Sixth Extinction: An Unnatural History* (New York: Henry Holt, 2014).

25.   Paul J. Crutzen and Eugene F. Stoermer, "The 'Anthropocene,' " *Global Change Newsletter* 41 (2000): 17–18.

26.   Berry, *An Appalachian View*, 8.

27.   The first telling in film form was the *Journey of the Universe* in 2011; see Swimme and Tucker, *Journey of the Universe*, DVD.

28.   Matt Fox founded the Institute in Chicago in 1978. It was there that Thomas and Brian first met in 1982, when Brian invited Thomas to Chicago to give a public talk. In 1983, Fox moved the Institute to California, where Brian came to teach after his year at Riverdale.

29.   In 1996, the Institute morphed into the Sophia Center in Earth, Art, and Spirit, which Jim directed until 2015.

30.   Brian Swimme, *The Universe Is a Green Dragon* (Santa Fe, N.M.: Bear and Company, 1984). This book sold over 90,000 copies.

31. Swimme, *The Universe Is a Green Dragon*, 119.

32. Santa Sabina was a place where Thomas spoke for several years. Then Brian continued to offer yearly seminars there and to develop various aspects of the New Story. Susannah Malarkey and Harriet Hope were dedicated to organizing these seminars, which lasted for ten years.

33. The participants included Mary Evelyn Tucker, who chaired the meeting; John Grim; David Griffin; Charlene Spretnak; Bruce Bochte; Michael Zimmerman; Matthew Fox; Marnie Muller; David Peat; Duane Elgin; Ralph Metzner; John Broomfield; Mary Leahy; Bill Free; Billy Holiday; Joe Meeker; Jean Lanier; Arne Naess; Ty Cashman; Ann Jacqua; Sidney Lanier; Betty Roszak; Bill Keepin; Jo Ann McAllister; Eleanor Anderson; Rex Weyler; Stuart Brown; Jurgen Kremer; Sandra Lewis; Lee Henderson; Ted Roszak; Sheila Gibson; and George Sessions.

34. Several people supported Thomas and Brian in writing this book, including Lavinia Currier and Laurance Rockefeller. Special mention should be made of Bruce Bochte, who was a stalwart friend and dedicated assistant in Brian's work over many years, especially in his books and video projects.

35. Thomas was president of the American Teilhard Association from 1975 to 1987, and Brian later became a vice president in 2005. Chapter 10 discusses the influence of Teilhard's thought on Thomas.

36. Berry, *An Appalachian View*, 5.

37. The 1986–87 series included Sally and Joe Cunneen, who offered reflections on thirty-five years of publishing *Cross Currents*; Roger Panetta of Marymount College, who spoke on the Hudson River valley; Chris Stearn, who spoke on agriculture and bioregionalism; and Roy Anderson of All State Insurance, who spoke on economics and the environment.

38. The authors are indebted to Steve Dunn for his help with this section on Port Burwell. The Centre there closed in 2000.

39. This event was professionally videotaped (produced by Dawn Macdonald of Villagers) and published by Twenty-Third Publications in both book form and as a thirteen-part video series. See Thomas Berry with Thomas Clark, *Befriending the Earth: A Theology of Reconciliation Between Humans and the Earth* (Mystic, Conn.: Twenty-Third Publications, 1991). Although it was not broadcast on CBC, it was featured on CityTV, a creative Canadian channel founded in 1972 by Moses Znaimer. By 1990, CityTV was a popular source of new ideas. *Befriending the Earth* was subsequently translated into several languages, including Korean and Spanish.

40. The Ecology Project in Guelph was led by Jim Profit, S.J., with the assistance of Christina Vanin, Tarcia Gerwig, Barbara Peloso, Marianne Karsh, and Yvonne Prowse. See Christina Vanin, "Understanding the Universe as Sacred," in Eaton, *The Intellectual Journey of Thomas Berry*. Reference to Guelph is on page 118.

   The Stations of the Cross is a Catholic devotional practice in which Christians walk by a series of images relating to the Passion of Christ. The images are placed on the side walls of many churches. Stations of the Cosmos opened up this practice to include the thresholds of transformation in the unfolding of the universe, Earth, and humans.

See a description and pictures of Stations of the Cosmos at http://thomasberry.org /publications-and-media/a-guide-for-praying-the-stations-of-the-cosmos.

See also the Cosmic Journey at the Maryknoll Ecological Park in Baguio City in the Philippines: https://ainterosculate.wordpress.com/2015/04/17/a-cosmic-journey -maryknoll-ecological-park/.

Nelson and Elaine Stover have created a Universe Story walk on their land at their home in Greensboro, North Carolina.

41. The church was completed in 2006. "Green Church," accessed May 11, 2018, http:// stgabrielsparish.ca/who-we-are/green-church/.

42. The theme of the conference was "Christian Voices and World Order." The papers were later published in 1979 by Global Education Associates as one in their series of publications called *The Whole Earth Papers*.

43. Personal communication to Mary Evelyn Tucker.

44. See www.genesisfarm.org.

45. Adapted from the Genesis Farm website.

46. These include Crystal Springs in Plainview, Mass. (Sr. Chris Loughlin, O.P.); Prairie Woods Franciscan Spirituality Center, Hiawatha, Iowa (Sr. Betty Daugherty, F.S.P.A.); Michaela Farm, Oldenburg, Ind. (Sr. Mary Ann Quinn, O.S.F.); White Violet Center for Eco-Justice, St. Mary-of-the-Woods, Ind. (Sr. Ann Sullivan, S.P.); Sisters Hill Farm, Standfordville, N.Y. (Sr. Mary Ann Garisto, S.C.); Homecoming Farm, Long Island (Sr. Jeanne Clark, O.P.); Waterspirit, Elberon, N.J. (Sr. Suzanne Golas, C.S.J.P.); Franciscan Earth Literacy Center, Tiffin, Ohio (Rita Wienken); EverGreen, (Sr. Barbara O'Donnell, H.M.); Loretto Earth Network, St. Louis, Mo. (Sr. Nancy Witter, S.L.); Heartland Farm, Pawnee Rock, Kans. (Sr. Betty Jean Goebel, O.P.); Crown Point Ecology Center, Bath, Ohio (Sr. Pat Sigler, O.P.); and Sisters of Earth (Sr. Mary Southard, Sr. Maureen Wild, S.C., Sr. Toni Nash). Others projects include Deep Time Journey Network, Princeton, N.J. (Jennifer Morgan); EarthRide Spirituality and Education Center, Scranton, Pa. (Jan Novotka); and EarthCommunity Center in Maryland (Jane Blewett).

47. This program is now housed with the Earth Ethics Institute at Miami Dade: see http:// www.earthethicsinstitute.org.

In 1988, McGregor Smith, Jr., was already an innovative and engaging educator at Miami-Dade College in South Florida. He had begun teaching there as a journalism instructor and after finishing his doctoral work on 'self-directed' interdisciplinary learning models he piloted an innovative program called Life Lab. Affectionately known as 'Mac' Smith, he would later use this model to build an Environmental Demonstration Center and offer a wide range of community education classes in all aspects of earth friendly and sustainable living. In that same year he attended the First North American Conference on Christianity and Ecology in Webster, Indiana, where Thomas Berry was a major presenter. This was his first exposure to a new functional cosmology as a basis for cultural transformation and it became a turning point that would shape the next decades of his personal and professional life. Shortly after, Mac invited a group of educators to meet in Florida and begin developing resources and curriculum materials for college courses based on the insights of Thomas Berry and Brian Swimme. The group called themselves the Earth Literacy Communion and their collaborative efforts created the substantive content of an Earth Literacy curriculum. In a unique partnership with St. Thomas University in Miami, these courses became a pilot for graduate and undergraduate accreditation at Genesis Farm and began to extend into several other colleges and universities. From these efforts, Mac also helped in the founding of Narrow Ridge, a bioregional Earth Literacy center in Washburn, Kentucky. To assure the longevity and financial and institutional support for these efforts, Mac also developed the Earth Ethics Institute at Miami-Dade College. It was founded with a mission of infusing Earth Literacy into all the academic disciplines and operations of its diverse campuses. He believed that every student and every faculty and staff member should be invited into the study of the evolutionary story of the Universe and Earth and be given the insights and tools for creating their lives in harmony with the mystery of Earth. (Adapted from the Genesis Farm e-newsletter, May 28, 2018.)

48. "Ridge and Valley Charter School," accessed July 13, 2018, www.ridgeandvalley.org.
49. Miriam MacGillis, email communication to authors, May 10, 2018.
50. See http://thomasberry.org/life-and-thought/berry-award-and-memorial-service/program-for-2009-thomas-berry-award-lecture.
51. Paul Winter, "Earth Mass," http://www.paulwinter.com/earth-mass/.
52. Thomas Berry, "Morningside Cathedral," in *Thomas Berry: Selected Writings on the Earth Community* (Maryknoll, N.Y.: Orbis Books, 2014), 195–196.

7. EVOKING THE GREAT WORK

1. John Grim and Mary Evelyn Tucker, "Teilhard de Chardin: A Short Biography," *Teilhard Studies*, no. 11 (Spring 1984). See the development of Teilhard's ideas in chapter 10.
2. In his considerations of human action, Teilhard was influenced by the thought of Maurice Blondel.
3. Pierre Teilhard de Chardin, *Writings in Time of War*, trans. René Hague (New York: Harper and Row, 1968), 32.
4. See his essay "The Great Work" in *The Great Work: Our Way into the Future* (New York: Harmony/Bell Tower, 1999).
5. This is now the Culinary Institute of America.
6. His other writings were also translated into English and kept in print by Harper and Row. *The Phenomenon of Man* was retranslated by Sarah Appleton-Weber as *The Human Phenomenon* (Eastbourne, UK: Sussex Academic Press, 1999).
7. Conservative Fordham University administrators initially insisted that Teilhard's name should not be used at a Catholic institution for the title of a research institute because his works were thought by some to contain certain theological "errors." The name was temporarily changed to the Human Energetics Institute. In 1967, permission was obtained to restore Teilhard's name.
8. The major files were sent to the Teilhard Archives at Georgetown University in 2006. From that time until the present, the Association has been based at Tucker and Grim's home, first in Pennsylvania and then in Connecticut.

9.   In 2017, on the fiftieth anniversary of the founding of the Teilhard Association, John Grim was given the Thomas Berry Award for his thirty years of service as president of the Association.

10. For a brief period, the Association met at General Theological Seminary on Twenty-First Street in lower Manhattan, when board member Bishop Mellick Belshaw was acting dean there.

11. Annual meeting speakers included Michael Murray, "Teilhard and the Nature of the Soul" (1968); George Maloney, S.J., "The Cosmic Christ from St. Paul to Teilhard" (1969); board member Theodosius Dobzhansky, "Evolution and Man's Conception of Himself" (1970); Jean Houston, "Teilhard and the Future of Consciousness" (1971); Sir John Eccles, Nobel biologist from Australia (1972); Edgar Mitchell (1973); Thomas Berry, "The Dynamics of the Future" (1974); Beatrice Bruteau, Gerald Feinberg, and Roger Wescott, "Creating the Future," at Trinity Wall Street (April 19, 1975); Margaret Mead, "An Anthropologist Looks at the Converging of the Peoples of the World Today," at International House (1976); and Robert Muller and Thomas Berry, "New Experiences of the Sacred," at International House (1977).

12. See teilharddechardin.org.

13. Arthur Fabel and Donald St. John, eds., *Teilhard in the 21st Century: The Emerging Spirit of Earth* (Maryknoll, N.Y.: Orbis Books, 2003).

14. On September 25, 1975, before the conference took place, Thomas wrote an appreciative note to Vilas: "Dear Skip, All best greetings and a sky full of thanks for your work on the Jung-Teilhard Symposium. It seemed almost impossible a year ago. But now mostly with your help, it seems about to become a reality and for some of us 'the event' of the season. It would be wonderful if we could produce a Symposium at least slightly equal to its subject, or at least catch sufficient of the light and power of these two men to make our great historical task a bit more bearable and creative for that vast number of people who presently populate this planet. All best wishes, Tom Berry."

15. The UN conference included an introduction by John Grim, president of the American Teilhard Association, followed by Brian Thomas Swimme with a speech entitled "The Universe Story: The Cosmic Context of Global Spirituality" and Mary Evelyn Tucker with a speech entitled "Global Connection." Bertrand Collomb, president of the World Business Council for Sustainable Development, addressed the topic of "Global Spirituality and Sustainable Development." Wangari Maathai, the Nobel Laureate who founded the Greenbelt Movement, delivered greetings from Kenya via a live telecast. This was followed by a talk entitled "Sustainability and Human Need" by Jeffrey Sachs, director of the Earth Institute at Columbia University. The program concluded with Steven Rockefeller, chair of the Earth Charter Drafting Committee, who gave a speech entitled "The Earth Charter."

16. Mary Evelyn Tucker and John Grim, eds., *Living Cosmology: Christian Responses to Journey of the Universe* (Maryknoll, N.Y.: Orbis Books, 2016). In 2017, it received a first-place award from the Catholic Press Association in the category of Science and Religion.

17. See his books, *The Sacred Universe* (New York: Columbia University Press, 2009) and *The Christian Future and the Fate of Earth* (New York: Orbis Books, 2009).

18. These were on Indigenous Traditions, Judaism, Christianity, Islam, Hinduism, Jainism, Buddhism, Confucianism, and Daoism, published by Harvard. *Shintoism and Ecology* was published in Japanese.

19. Thomas Berry, "Loneliness and Presence," in *A Communion of Subjects: Animals in Religion, Science, and Ethics*, ed. Paul Waldau and Kimberley Patton (New York: Columbia University Press, 2006).

20. This statement is used in many of Thomas's essays. See also Paul Waldau, "From the Daily and Local to the Communion of Subjects," in *The Intellectual Journey of Thomas Berry: Imagining the Earth Community*, ed. Heather Eaton (Lanham, Md.: Lexington Books, 2015).

21. See the Ecology and Justice series at Orbis Books. The advisory board members are Leonardo Boff, John Grim, Sean McDonagh, and Mary Evelyn Tucker. The series includes cosmology, with a book by Brian Swimme, *The Hidden Heart of the Cosmos*, and one by Thomas Berry, *The Christian Future and the Fate of Earth*.

22. Christina Vanin, "Understanding the Universe as Sacred," in *The Intellectual Journey of Thomas Berry*, 103–122.

23. See John Grim and Mary Evelyn Tucker, *Ecology and Religion* (Washington, D.C.: Island Press, 2014). For example, the Islamic concepts in the Qur'an regarding *tawhid* (unity of creation), *mizan* (balance), and *amana* (trust or stewardship) reflect values that have been interpreted in relation to the natural world. Furthermore, Islamic practices such as *hima* (protected sanctuaries) and *haram* (sacred precincts) represent ancient customs whose contemporary environmental implications are currently being explored.

24. See fore.yale.edu.

25. It offers a certificate of Specialization in Theology and Ecology through the Faculty of Theology at the University of St. Michael's College, part of the Toronto School of Theology in the University of Toronto. Founded by Passionist Stephen Dunn and later directed by Dennis O'Hara, the institute also sponsors lectures, conferences, and workshops. Deeply inspired by Thomas's thinking, its mission was described as follows: "In expressing our concern for the ecological crisis, the Institute seeks integrative methods for contributing to the healing of the Earth in all of its life systems. . . . Interdisciplinary by definition, the Institute facilitates serious contact between the theological disciplines and the scientific, cosmological, and cultural paradigm shifts that are shaping our times." Several leading theologians received their doctorates under Stephen Dunn's mentorship, including Heather Eaton, Laurent LeDuc, Jai-Don Lee, and Dennis O'Hara.

26. *Worldviews: Global Religions, Culture, Ecology*, and *Journey for the Study of Religion, Nature and Culture*.

27. This description of the Ecology and Justice series appears on the Orbis Books website: https://www.orbisbooks.com/category-202/.

28. See Mark Hathaway and Leonardo Boff, *The Tao of Liberation: Exploring the Ecology of Transformation* (Maryknoll, N.Y.: Orbis Books, 2009).

29. Thomas calls for an "integral ecologist" in his 1996 article "An Ecologically Sensitive Spirituality." This was later published in *The Sacred Universe* (New York: Columbia University Press, 2009), 135–136. For early uses of this term, see Sam Mickey, *On the Verge of a Planetary Civilization: A Philosophy of Integral Ecology* (New York: Rowman and Littlefield,

2014). Mickey lists 1995 as the first published usage by Thomas of "integral ecology." John and Mary Evelyn recall Thomas's oral usages of this phrase from the late 1980s. See also Sam Mickey, Sean Kelly, and Adam Robbert, eds., *The Variety of Integral Ecologies: Nature, Culture, and Knowledge in the Planetary Era* (Albany: State University of New York Press, 2017); and Sean Esbjorn-Hargens, "Ecological Interiority: Thomas Berry's Integral Ecology Legacy," in *Thomas Berry: Dreamer of the Earth*, ed. Ervin Laszlo and Alan Combs (Rochester, Vt.: Inner Traditions, 2011).

30.   This is confirmed by Mike Bell: "The need for a new jurisprudence was first identified by Thomas Berry who described destructive anthropocentrism on which existing legal and political structures are based as a major impediment to the necessary transition to an ecological age in which humans would seek a new intimacy with the integral functioning of the natural world." Mike Bell, "Thomas Berry and an Earth Jurisprudence: An Exploratory Essay," *The Trumpeter* 19, no. 1 (2003). Bell, a community adviser for Alaska's Inuit peoples, frequently visited Thomas in Greensboro to discuss ideas and share writings.

31.   See the history of the Earth Jurisprudence movement at Gaia Foundation: https:// www.gaiafoundation.org/what-we-do/earth-jurisprudence/story-of-origin-growing -an-earth-jurisprudence-movement/full-story-of-origin/.

It is stored at *Ecozoic Times*: https://ecozoictimes.com/reinventing-the-human/earth -jurisprudence/history-of-earth-jurisprudence/.

32.   "The outstanding thing about this work of Vico is that he was still dominated by his interest in jurisprudence even while he was attempting the difficult task of unifying philosophy and philology. At this time in his career he wished to show that the union of all divine and human knowledge was the work of jurisprudence, which used both philosophy and philology in the full understanding and exercise of its function." Thomas Berry, "The Historical Theory of Giambattista Vico" (PhD diss., Washington, D.C.: Catholic University of America Press, 1951), 51.

33.   Thomas Berry, *The Dream of the Earth* (Berkeley: Counterpoint Press, 2015), 160. Originally published by Sierra Club Books in 1988.

34.   Berry, *The Dream of the Earth*, 104.

35.   Berry, *The Great Work*, 161.

36.   Thomas Berry, *Evening Thoughts: Reflecting on Earth as a Sacred Community* (Berkeley, Calif.: Sierra Club Books and University of California Press, 2006).

37.   "Earth Jurisprudence for the Earth Community," in *Living Cosmology*, 223.

See Brian Brown's comprehensive statement of this perspective in "The Earth Jurisprudence of Thomas Berry and the Tradition of Revolutionary Law," in *The Intellectual Journey of Thomas Berry*.

38.   Christopher Stone, *Should Trees Have Standing? Towards Legal Rights for Natural Objects* (Los Altos, Calif.: William Kaufmann, 1974).

39.   Berry, *The Great Work*, 5.

40.   Berry, *Evening Thoughts*, 149.

41.   The UN Harmony with Nature website lists experts who are committed to Earth Jurisprudence: http://www.harmonywithnatureun.org/knowledgenetwork/all-members/.

42.   In 1992, at the Earth Summit in Rio, the United Nations issued the Convention on Biodiversity, which helped support this perspective.

43. Gaia Foundation: www.gaiafoundation.org.

44. Those attending included Liz Hosken, Ed Posey, Andy Kimbrell, Jules Cashford, Cormac Cullen, Brian Brown, Martin von Hilderbrand, and John Grim.

45. Cormac Cullinan, *Wild Law: A Manifesto for Earth Justice*, 2nd ed. (Claremont, South Africa: Siber Ink, 2002).

46. http://thomasberry.org/publications-and-media/every-being-has-rights.

47. africanbiodiversity.org.

48. "Earth Jurisprudence in a Cosmological Perspective," in *Living Cosmology*.

49. www.earthjurist.org.

50. Some ten years later, on October 27, 2017, a "Rights of Nature Symposium" was held at Tulane University Law School. It was subtitled "Driving Rights of Nature into Law—Opportunities, Risks, and Obstacles." It was organized by Thomas Linzey and sponsored by his Community Environmental Legal Defense Fund: www.celdf.org.

51. There is the distinction between rights and responsibilities; Indigenous peoples operate with responsibilities, whereas rights are a more "modern" concept. See Catherine Iorns Magallanes and Linda Sheehan, "Reframing Rights and Responsibilities to Prioritize Nature," in *Law and Policy for a New Economy: Sustainable, Just, and Democratic*, ed. Melissa Scanlon (Northampton, Mass.: Edward Elgar, 2017).

52. It is important to note that not all of the aspirations have been achieved in Ecuador. See Neema Pathak Broome and Ashish Kothari, "A Green Revolution Runs into Trouble," *Resurgence*, no. 307 (March/April 2018).

53. In subsequent years, Maria Mercedes Sanchez has been a leading force in the UN Harmony with Nature initiative, organizing annual Interactive Dialogues of the General Assembly; see http://www.harmonywithnatureun.org/chronology.html.

54. The Universal Declaration of the Rights of Mother Earth has also figured prominently in several International Rights of Nature Tribunals, the first of which was held in January 2014 in Quito, Ecuador. This was followed by International Tribunals in Lima, Paris, and Bonn, all held during the COP climate conferences, and Regional Tribunals held in Quito in Ecuador, in San Francisco and Antioch, California, in the United States, and in Brisbane in Australia.

55. www.therightsofnature.org.

56. Bolivian Plurinational Legislative Assembly, Law of the Rights of Mother Earth, accessed at World Future Fund: http://www.worldfuturefund.org/Projects/Indicators/motherearthbolivia.html.

57. New Zealand's Te Urewara National Park had been granted the same legal status in July 2016.

58. The Supreme Court of India later stayed the effect of the ruling pending the outcome of an appeal by the state government of Uttarakhand, which argued that its new responsibilities were unclear.

59. In Africa, a three-year training for Earth Jurisprudence practitioners was initiated by the Gaia Foundation, to explore both the philosophy and practice, and an endogenous approach to working with indigenous communities to revive their traditional knowledge, customary laws, and governance systems. The first African Earth Jurisprudence practitioners graduated in July 2017, and a second group has embarked on their training.

See https://theecologist.org/tag/earth-jurisprudence. This movement catalyzed the passage of a new resolution from the African Commission that recognizes sacred natural sites, ancestral lands, and customary governance systems as rooted in Earth Jurisprudence. The strategy is to open spaces in the dominant colonial human-centered legal system in Africa for the recognition of its plurilegal systems, which are derived from the laws of nature and promoted by the African Charter.

60.   Yessenia Funes, "The Colombian Amazon Is Now a 'Person,' and You Can Thank Actual People," Earther.com, accessed April 14, 2018, https://earther.com/the-colombian-amazon-is-now-a-person-and-you-can-thank-1825059357. See also Jens Benöhr and Patrick J. Lynch, "Should Rivers Have Rights? A Growing Movement Says It's About Time," https://e360.yale.edu/features/should-rivers-have-rights-a-growing-movement-says-its-about-time.

8. COMING HOME

This chapter's epigraph is from Thomas Berry, *Selected Writings on the Earth Community*, ed. Mary Evelyn Tucker and John Grim (Maryknoll, N.Y.: Orbis Books, 2014), 188.

1.   John Grim, "The Song of the Library" (unpublished poem, January 3, 1995).

2.   Mary Evelyn Tucker, "Reflections on Sending Out a Library" (unpublished manuscript, New Year's Eve, 1994).

3.   Jim passed away some months later, in September 1997, and his wife, Mary Elizabeth, passed away in January 1998.

4.   Thomas served for many years on the Center for Respect of Life and Environment (CRLE) board, and his ideas were much appreciated by John Hoyt, the president of HSUS. Rick Clugston, the executive director of HSUS, partnered with Elizabeth Ferraro, Dean Joseph Iannone, and Dr. Joe Holland from St. Thomas University to organize the Assisi conferences where Thomas spoke throughout the 1990s. Clugston was also a key leader in the drafting of the Earth Charter, to which Thomas made many contributions. In 1992 Thomas was given the James Herriot Award by the HSUS.

5.   The Thomas Berry Award recipients are John Grim, May 20, 2017; Brian Edward Brown, January 24, 2016; James Gustave Speth, November 8, 2014; James Conlon, July 18, 2013; Stephen Dunn, November 1, 2012; Martin S. Kaplan, September 26, 2009; Fritz and Vivienne Hull, October 15, 2007; Miriam Therese MacGillis, October 1, 2005; Reverend James Parks Morton, 2004; Steven C. Rockefeller, May 17, 2002; Tu Weiming, August 30, 2000; Brian Thomas Swimme, October 8, 1999; and Mary Evelyn Tucker, November 10, 1998.

6.   See http://thomasberry.org/life-and-thought/past-award-recipients.

7.   Joseph Cigna, "Speaker: Ignoring Ecology Is Dangerous," *Burlington Times-News* (Burlington, N.C.), January 14, 2000, C1–C2. In Elon University's Special Millennium Lecture series.

8.   This was led by John Huie and Margo Flood. The Center focuses on elementary school eco-training, a radio program (*Swannanoa Journal*), campus and city green walkabouts, and internships for promising subjects.

9.   Thomas Rain Crowe, "Attending to Our Future," review of *The Great Work*, by Thomas Berry, *The Bloomsbury Review*, January/February 2000, 3.

10.   His contributions included not only work at Warren Wilson College, but also inspiring work at Miami Dade University with McGregor Smith and Miriam MacGillis; at St. Thomas University in Miami with Elizabeth Ferraro, Joe Holland, and Joe Iannone; at Prescott College in Arizona through Drew Dellinger and Steve Snider; at Loyola University in New Orleans with Kathleen O'Gorman; at the University of Toronto with Steve Dunn, Dennis O'Hara, and Ed O'Sullivan; at Iona College in New Rochelle, New York, with Brian Brown, Kathleen Deignan, Kevin Cawley and Danny Martin; at Loyola Marymount University in Los Ángeles with Christopher Chapple; at Indiana University with David Haberman; at the University of Montana with Dan Spencer; and at the University of San Francisco with Sam Mickey. In addition, Jennifer Morgan has been active in the education of Montessori teachers. She has written a three-part series of books for children and adults: *Born with a Bang; The Universe Tells Our Cosmic Story* (Nevada City, Calif.: Dawn Publications, 2006); *From Lava to Life: The Universe Tells Our Earth Story* (Nevada City, Calif.: Dawn Publications, 2006); and *Mammals Who Morph: The Universe Tells Our Evolution Story* (Nevada City, Calif.: Dawn Publications, 2006). Moreover, she has created the Deep Time Journey Network to encourage the telling of the epic of evolution. See deeptimejourneynetwork.org. Betty-Ann Kisslove has also written a book for children, *Great Ball of Fire: A Poetic Telling of the Universe Story* (San Francisco, Calif.: Mearth Press, 2010).

11.   www.beholdnature.org.

12.   Quoted in Carolyn Toben, *Recovering a Sense of the Sacred: Conversations with Thomas Berry* (Whitsett, N.C.: Timberlake Earth Sanctuary Press, 2012), 96.

13.   Quoted in Toben, *Recovering a Sense of the Sacred*, 98.

14.   Richard Louv, *Last Child in the Wilderness: Saving Our Children from Nature-Deficit Disorder* (Chapel Hill, N.C.: Algonquin Books, 2005). Louv later wrote a piece for *Psychology Today* titled "The Giftedness of Thomas Berry": https://www.psychologytoday.com/us/blog/people-in-nature/200811/the-giftedness-thomas-berry.

15.   Peggy Whalen-Levitt, ed., *Only the Sacred: Transforming Education in the Twenty-First Century* (Greensboro, N.C.: Center for Education, Imagination and the Natural World, 2011).

16.   Andrew Levitt, *All the Scattered Leaves of the Universe: Journey and Vision in Dante's Divine Comedy and the Work of Thomas Berry* (Greensboro, N.C.: Center for Education, Imagination and the Natural World, 2015); Colette Segalla, *I Am You, You Are Me: The Interrelatedness of Self, Spirituality and the Natural World in Childhood* (Whitsett, N.C.: Center for Education, Imagination and the Natural World, 2015); Clay Lerner, *Opening Forgotten Sanctuaries: Recognizing Education as Sacred Encounter* (Greensboro, N.C.: Center for Education, Imagination and the Natural World, 2015); and Andrew Levitt, *Heron Mornings* (Greensboro, N.C.: Center for Education, Imagination and the Natural World, 2017), a collection of poetry. Peggy Whalen-Levitt's essay, "Thomas Berry's 'Communion of Subjects': Awakening 'The Heart of the Universe,' " was published in *The Ecozoic Journal*, a special issued entitled "Thomas Berry's Work: Development, Difference, Importance, Applications," no. 4 (2017).

17.   Herman Greene (b. 1945) holds degrees in Spirituality and Sustainability, DMin, United Theological Seminary 2004; Law, JD, University of North Carolina at Chapel Hill 1979;

Ministry, MTh and MDiv, University of Chicago Divinity School 1969 and 1970; Political Science, MA, Stanford University 1967; and Political Science, BA, University of Florida 1966. His professional life began at the Ecumenical Institute of Chicago, a division of the Church Federation of Chicago, where he lived and worked from 1967 to 1975. He practiced corporate, tax, and securities law with firms in New York City, Denver, Colorado, and Chapel Hill, North Carolina, from 1978 to 2017. He has served as board member and president of CES since its inception. He has spoken and published widely and has served on various boards.

18.   This paragraph was composed by Herman Greene to describe his work.

19.   Ecozoic Review, "A Tribute to Thomas Berry," special issue, *The Ecozoic*, no. 2 (2009).

20.   Ecozoic Review, "Thomas Berry's Work: Development, Difference, Importance, Applications," special issue, *The Ecozoic*, no. 4 (2017).

21.   This talk was published in *Evening Thoughts*, ed. Mary Evelyn Tucker (Berkeley, Calif.: Counterpoint Press, 2015). Originally published in 2006 by Sierra Club Books and University of California Press.

22.   Honorary degrees: California Institute of Integral Studies (1993); St. Thomas University, Miami, Fla., (1994); Loyola University, New Orleans (1994); Loyola Marymount University, Los Angeles (1997); St. Mary's University, Halifax, N.S. (1997); College of Mt. St. Vincent, Riverdale, N.Y. (1998); Catholic Theological Union, Chicago, Ill. (2003); and Elon University, Elon, N.C. (2008).

23.   This was sponsored by *EarthLight* magazine and Jim and Eileen Schenk's eco-village group, Imago. *EarthLight* magazine was edited by Lauren deBoer. The tenth anniversary issue in Spring 1999 was dedicated to Thomas Berry.

24.   The conference was organized by Robert McDermott and Sean Kelly; those who spoke included Maia Apprahamian, Lauren Artress, Chris Bache, Jim Conlon, Drew Dellinger, Christian de Quincy, Molly Dwyer, Larry and Jean Edwards, Jorge Ferrer, James Fournier, Matthew Fox, Linda Gibler, Gwen Gordon, Susan Griffin, Stanislav Grof, Kalli Rose Halvorson, Robert Hand, Sean Hargens, Nancy Conlee Hart, Mara Lynn Keller, Sean Kelly, Joanna Macy, Robert McDermott, Ralph Metzner, Wes Nisker, Rod O'Neal, Frank Poletti, Sheri Ritchlin, Betty Rosak, Ted Rosak, Jacob Sherman, Charlene Spretnak, Brian Thomas Swimme, Rick Tarnas, and Mary Evelyn Tucker.

25.   The conference was convened by Professor Edmund O'Sullivan of the Ontario Institute for Studies in Education at the University of Toronto, a longtime collaborator with Thomas in the field of ecology and education.

26.   Dr. Ferrero describes the process of developing these programs: "In the late 1980s, Dr. Iannone, Dean of Religious Studies at St. Thomas University, started a 'base community' concept. Thomas Berry's cosmology was at the center of our gatherings, with frequent visits by Dr. McGregor Smith, Director of the Environmental Center at Miami Dade College; Miriam MacGillis from Genesis Farm; and others. The resulting intellectual ferment changed many people's lives and work. Healing the Earth was conceived with important events open to the entire South Miami community. In October 1990, I knocked on Dean Iannone's office with a unique idea: a summer ecological study abroad program in Assisi, Italy, centered on Thomas Berry's cosmology. The following June,

Study Abroad for Earth was underway in Assisi with Fr. Berry as the Visiting Scholar for the next seven years." Elisabeth Ferrero, ed., *Thomas Berry in Italy: Reflections on Spirituality and Sustainability* (Washington, D.C.: Pacem in Terris Press, 2016), 20.

27. These included John Brinkman, Tony Cortese, Drew Dellinger, John Grim, Joe Holland, Hildur Jackson, Pamela Kraft, Miriam MacGillis, Gary McClosky, David Orr, Rodney Peterson, Lauren Ross, Karl-Ludwig Schibel, Rupert Sheldrake, Steve Snider, Brian Thomas Swimme, and Earth Charter drafters such as Steven Rockefeller, Mirian Vilela, and Mary Evelyn Tucker.

28. Ferrero, *Thomas Berry in Italy*, 21.

29. Ferrero, *Thomas Berry in Italy*, 22.

30. Ferrero, *Thomas Berry in Italy*, 180–181.

31. Robert Carbonneau, C.P., *The Passionists in the United States—St. Paul of the Cross Province: A Narrative History—The 1998 Provincial Chapter* (Chicago: Passionist Community Catholic Theological Union, 1998), 18–19.

32. In Thomas Berry, *The Christian Future and the Fate of Earth*, ed. Mary Evelyn Tucker and John Grim (Maryknoll, N.Y.: Orbis Books, 2009).

33. Published in *The Christian Future and the Fate of Earth*. ed. Mary Evelyn Tucker and John Grim (Maryknoll, N.Y.: Orbis Books, 2009).

34. For further information, see thomasberry.org.

35. Sisters of Earth is "an informal network of women who share a deep concern for the ecological and spiritual crises of our times and who wish to support one another in work toward healing the human spirit and restoring Earth's life support systems." See https://sistersofearth.wikispaces.com.

36. In 2012 Amie Hendani joined the community.

37. Berry, *Selected Writings*, 188.

38. Andrew Revkin, "Thomas Berry, Writer and Lecturer with a Mission for Mankind, Dies at 94," *New York Times*, June 3, 2009, http://www.nytimes.com/2009/06/04/us/04berry.html; Jon Thurber, "Thomas Berry Dies at 94; Cultural Historian Became a Leading Thinker on Religion and the Environment," *Los Angeles Times*, June 13, 2009, accessed March 13, 2018, http://www.latimes.com/local/obituaries/la-me-thomas-berry13-2009jun13-story.html (this same article also appeared in the *Washington Post*); Walter Schwarz, "Thomas Berry Obituary: Influential Christian Eco-philosopher—As He Put It, 'a Geologian,'" *The Guardian*, September 27, 2009, accessed March 20, 2018, https://www.theguardian.com/world/2009/sep/27/thomas-berry-obituary.

39. The talk focused on climate change and was a strong appeal to political and religious leaders to respond to the findings of the Intergovernmental Panel on Climate Change (IPCC) report for the common good of present and future generations.

40. Quoted in Tara C. Trapani, "Overview of Memorial Service," Thomas Berry and the Great Work, http://thomasberry.org/life-and-thought/berry-award-and-memorial-service/overview-of-the-thomas-berry-award-and-memorial-service.

41. Trapani, "Overview of Memorial Service."

42. Trapani, "Overview of Memorial Service."

43. Trapani, "Overview of Memorial Service."

9. NARRATIVES OF TIME

1.   Thomas's dissertation was entitled "The Historical Theory of Giambattista Vico." The translation of Vico used in this chapter is Giambattista Vico, *The New Science of Giambattista Vico*, revised and unabridged version translated by Thomas G. Bergin and Max H. Frisch (Ithaca, N.Y.: Cornell University Press, 1984).

2.   "Such people, like so many beasts, have fallen into the custom of each man thinking only of his own private interests and have reached the extreme of delicacy, or better of pride, in which like wild animals they bristle and lash out at the slightest displeasure. Thus no matter how great the throng and press of their bodies, they live like wild beasts in a deep solitude of spirit and will. . . . In this way, through long centuries of barbarism, rust will consume the misbegotten subtleties of malicious wits that have turned them into beasts made more inhuman by the barbarism of reflection than the first men had been made by the barbarism of sense." Vico, *The New Science*, 381, para. 1106.

3.   See Thomas Berry, *The Christian Future and the Fate of Earth*, ed. Mary Evelyn Tucker and John Grim (Maryknoll, N.Y.: Orbis Books, 2009), 8–13.

4.   In an attempt to give expression to his comprehensive vision, Thomas's early historical style of writing, evident in his books on Buddhism and the religions of India, tended toward an "engaged understanding." This is a style that German scholars described as *verstehen*, or participation in the actions and thought of another. See Wilhelm Dilthey, *Understanding the Human World*, ed. and with an introduction by Rudolf Makkreel and Frithjof Rodi (Princeton, N.J.: Princeton University Press, 2010); and Max Weber, "Objectivity in Social Science and Social Policy," in *The Methodology of the Social Sciences*, ed. and trans. E. A. Shils and H. A. Finch (New York: Free Press, 1949; originally published 1904). There is some continuation of this position in the "lifeworld" analyses from Edmund Husserl to Tim Ingold. In this line of thinking, *story* became Thomas's term for empathetic engagement with cultural narrations, and eventually with the unfolding narrative of the cosmos. As his essay writing developed, he integrated cultural history with scientific cosmology and ecological awareness. In doing this, Thomas realized that cosmological stories are not simply passively received by listeners. Rather, they draw listeners into an engaged, mutual interaction in which the story is present and alive in person and place. This implies a mutuality of give and take in which humans realize they are talking about the world that is also forming them.

5.   Thomas refers to this example in *The Dream of the Earth*, but he used this example repeatedly in his classroom teaching from the late 1960s forward. See Thomas Berry, *The Dream of the Earth* (Berkeley, Calif.: Counterpoint Press, 2015; originally published San Francisco: Sierra Club Books, 1988), 28.

6.   Daniel 2:31–45 in Herbert G. May and Bruce Metzger, eds., *The New Oxford Annotated Bible: Revised Standard Version* (New York: Oxford University Press, 1977), 1069–1070.

7.   Quoted in Anne Lonergan and Caroline Richard, eds., *Thomas Berry and the New Cosmology: In Dialogue with Gregory Baum, James Farris, Stephen Dunn, Margaret Brennan, Caroline Richards, Donald Senior, and Brian Swimme* (Mystic, Conn.: Twenty-Third Publications, 1987), 107–108.

8. This point also relates to the discussions of Vico below. For "macrophase" and an extended discussion of these periods, see Thomas's reflections in *Evening Thoughts: Reflecting on Earth as Sacred Community*, ed. Mary Evelyn Tucker (San Francisco: Sierra Club Books, 2006), 72-74.

9. See Berry, *The Christian Future*, 104.

10. See John Grim, "Apocalyptic Spirituality in the Old and New Worlds: The Revisioning of History and Matter," *Teihard Studies*, no. 27 (Fall 1992).

11. This idea has a lengthy development in Thomas's thought; one example is in the article "Dream of the Earth: Our Way into the Future," published one year before the book of the same title in *Cross Currents* 37, nos. 22/23 (1987), especially 207-208.

12. Thomas's conception of the reinvention of the human at the species level is particular to his later ecological phase of thought. His articulation of this conception is found throughout his writing, but one such discussion is in "The Cosmology of Religions," in *The Sacred Universe: Earth, Spirituality, and Religion in the Twenty-First Century*, ed. Mary Evelyn Tucker (New York: Columbia University Press, 2009), 126-128.

13. While Thomas's sense of reinvention owes more to Vico, there are also parallel conceptualizations in Benedict Anderson, *Imagined Communities: Reflections on the Origin and Spread of Nationalism* (London: Verso, 1983); and Eric Hobsbawm and Terrence Ranger, *The Invention of Tradition* (Cambridge: Cambridge University Press, 1983).

14. Berry, *The Dream of the Earth*, 212.

15. This articulation by Thomas of the impact of the human on the Earth is a precursor of the "Anthropocene era" idea now widely accepted. See the six conditions for the Ecozoic era in Thomas Berry with Thomas Clark, *Befriending the Earth: A Theology of Reconciliation Between Humans and the Earth* (Mystic, Conn.: Twenty-Third Publications, 1991), 96-103.

16. Thomas Berry, "The New Story: Comments on the Origin, Identification and Transmission of Values," *Teilhard Studies*, no. 1 (Winter 1978). Also published in Arthur Fabel and Donald St. John, eds., *Teilhard in the 21st Century: The Emerging Spirit of Earth* (Maryknoll, N.Y.: Orbis Books, 2003).

17. Berry, *The Dream of the Earth*, 208.

18. Thomas situates Augustine in the transmission of biblical historical consciousness into Christianity in various places throughout his writings. One such treatment is in Berry, *The Christian Future*, 104-106.

19. Thomas can be understood as holding to this position regarding the pervasive influence of the urban on Western intellectual life both in his readings of Dante and in his seminar at the Riverdale Center for Religious Research on "New York as Sacred City" in 1981.

20. See seminal studies of salvation history: Gerhard von Rad, *Old Testament Theology*, 2 vols. (New York: Harper and Row, 1962); and Hans Conzelmann, *An Outline of the Theology of the New Testament* (New York: Harper and Row, 1969).

21. Thomas often cited a particularly significant biblical text in this argument regarding the emphasis in Christianity on historical realism, namely, the First Epistle of John. "Something which has existed since the beginning, that we have heard, and have seen with our eyes; and we have watched and touched with our hands, the Word, who is life—this is our subject" (1 John, 1: 1-2).

22.   "In regard to mankind I have made a division. On the one side are those who live accord-ing to man; on the other those who live according to God. And I have said that, in a deeper sense, we may speak of two cities or two human societies, the destiny of the one being an eternal kingdom under God while the doom of the other is eternal punishment along with the Devil. . . . For the moment, therefore, I must deal with the course of the history of the two cities from the time when children were born to the first couple until the day when men shall beget no more. By the course of their history, as distinguished from their original cause and final consummation, I mean the whole time of their world history in which men are born and take the place of those who die and depart." Book 15, chap. 1. See, e.g., Augustine of Hippo, *City of God*, trans. Gerald Walsh, Demetrius Zema, Grace Monahan, and Daniel Honan (Garden City, N.Y.: Image, 1958), 323–324.

23.   Thomas was fond of citing Numa Denis Fustel du Coulanges, *The Ancient City*, published in Strasbourg in 1864, in which Fustel du Coulanges described the roles of religion in the political and social formation of Greece and Rome.

24.   "So in whatever way this mysterious pre-perception of future things goes on, it is not possible for a thing to be seen unless it is something existing. What exists now is not a future thing but present. Therefore, when future things are said to be seen, the things themselves which do not yet exist, that is, the future things are not seen, but rather their causes or signs perhaps which now exist. And so they are not future things, but things now present to those who are seeing, from which they foretell future things as conceived by their mind. Again, these conceptions exist now, and those who predict such things see them as present within themselves." Book 11, chap. 18. See, e.g., Augustine of Hippo, *Confessions*, trans. R. S. Pine-Coffin (New York: Viking Penguin, 1961), 268.

25.   Berry, *The Christian Future*, 56, 81.

26.   Thomas Berry, *The Great Work: Our Way into the Future* (New York: Harmony/Bell Tower, 1999), 8, 41, 190.

27.   Berry, *The Great Work*, 190.

28.   While Thomas did not draw extensively on Pierre Bourdieu's concept of *habitus*, he had read the phenomenologist philosophers, and Merleau-Ponty's reflection on embodied knowing interested him. See Maurice Merleau-Ponty, *The Visible and the Invisible*, ed. Claude Lefort, trans. Alphonso Lingis (Evanston, Ill.: Northwestern University Press, 1968); and Pierre Bourdieu, *The Logic of Practice*, trans. Richard Nice (Stanford, Calif.: Stanford University Press, 1990; originally published in French in 1980 by Les Editions de Minuit as *Le sens pratique*).

29.   This was originally written in 1964 but was later included in the unpublished Riverdale Papers. Thomas Berry, "Dante: The Age in Which He Lived," Riverdale Papers (New York: Riverdale Center for Religious Research, n.d.).

30.   "Certainly the greatest single decision made at this time was the decision to reject neither of these opposites, neither the natural nor the supernatural, neither faith nor reason, neither secular song nor religious asceticism, and neither logic nor mysticism. Condemnation was reserved for those who rejected one or the other of the opposed terms." See Berry, "Dante."

31.   See Marjorie Reeves, *Joachim of Flore and the Prophetic Future: A Medieval Study in Historical Thinking* (Stroud, UK: Sutton, 1999).

32. Thomas Aquinas, *Summa Theologica*, trans. English Dominicans (New York: Benzinger Brothers, 1948, Question. 47, Article. 1.

33. Thomas Aquinas, *Summa Contra Gentiles*, trans. Anton Pegis (Notre Dame, Ind.: University of Notre Dame Press, 1955), 2.45.10.

34. Arthur Lovejoy, *The Great Chain of Being: A Study of the History of an Idea* (Cambridge, Mass.: Harvard University Press, 1936).

35. See the essay by Caroline Richards, "The New Cosmology: What It Really Means," in *Thomas Berry and the New Cosmology*, 91–101.

36. For example, Thomas was influenced by such thinkers as Karl Marx (1818-1883). He drew on ideas Marx outlined in the *Communist Manifesto* regarding the limits of the human journey. Thomas was also influenced by the founder of academic history, Leopold von Ranke (1795-1886) who insisted that historical narratives should be based on empirical facts. The work of Ranke's student, Jacob Burckhardt (1818 1897), is especially noteworthy. Burckhardt's research into the Renaissance period established a method of investigating cultures through their creative arts. This appreciation of the arts was also developed by Wilhelm Dilthey (1833-1911) and Benedetto Croce (1866-1952), and is evident in Thomas's work.

37. In *Five Oriental Philosophies* (Albany, N.Y.: Magi Books, 1968), 38, Thomas wrote: "One of the few writers to understand this approach to the thought development of mankind is Eric Voegelin whose work on the cosmological, historical, and philosophical forms of symbolization in the first three volumes of his Order and History is of some importance in giving us an understanding of the conceptual modalities of thought that are most basic to the human mind." See also Thomas's review, "Order and History," *Thought* 33, no. 2 (1958): 273-278.

38. Thomas Berry, "Reinventing the Human," in *The Great Work*.

39. "The problem of Religion and Culture—the intricate and far-reaching network of relations . . . unites the social way of life with the spiritual beliefs and values, which are accepted by society as the ultimate laws of life and the ultimate standards of individual and social behavior; . . . these relations can only be studied in the concrete, in their true historical reality. The great world religions are, as it were, great rivers of sacred tradition, which flow down through the ages and through changing historical landscapes, which they irrigate and fertilize." Christopher Dawson, *Religion and the Rise of Western Culture* (New York: Doubleday, 1957), 12.

40. Thomas related in private conversations his meeting with Christopher Dawson during the period he was an army chaplain in Europe. Students at Fordham read many of Dawson's works: e.g., *The Making of Europe, Religion and Culture*, and *Religion and World History*. Thomas was especially interested in Dawson's ideas regarding religions as at the center of cultural life. He was also interested in Dawson's ideas about the cultural expansion now associated with "world history," namely, the encounters between the great civilizations of Eurasia, the Americas, and the Pacific Ocean.

41. Thomas Berry, *An Appalachian View* (unpublished manuscript, n.d.), 3.

42. Thomas Berry, "Contemporary Spirituality: The Journey of the Human Community," *Cross Currents* 24, nos. 2/3 (1974): 180 and 183.

10. TEILHARD AND THE ZEST FOR LIFE

The quotation in the chapter epigraph is from Thomas Berry, "Teilhard in the Ecological Age," *Teilhard Studies*, no. 7 (Fall 1982), 4. Also in Arthur Fabel and Donald St. John, eds., *Teilhard in the 21st Century: The Emerging Spirit of Earth* (Maryknoll, N.Y.: Orbis Books, 2003), 59. In this article Thomas presents his appreciation for Teilhard's ideas as well as areas in which his thought needs to be expanded. Teilhard has also been discussed in chapter 7.

1.   Julian Huxley, introduction to *The Phenomenon of Man*, by Pierre Teilhard de Chardin (New York: Harper and Brothers, 1959). In this book, Teilhard presents his fullest telling of the story of evolutionary processes. This was published posthumously in French in 1955 and in English in 1959. An updated English translation was published forty years later. See Pierre Teilhard de Chardin, *The Human Phenomenon*, trans. Sarah Appleton-Weber (Eastbourne, UK: Sussex Academic Press, 1999).

2.   Joseph Needham, foreword to *Teilhard de Chardin and Eastern Religions: Spirituality and Mysticism in an Evolutionary World*, by Ursula King (Mahwah, N.J.: Paulist Press, 2011), xi. Originally published 1980.

3.   Front cover of de Chardin, *The Phenomenon of Man*, 1959, hardback.

4.   Back cover of de Chardin, *The Phenomenon of Man*, 1959, paperback.

5.   Back cover of de Chardin, *The Phenomenon of Man*, 1959, paperback.

6.   Thomas Berry, "Teilhard in the Ecological Age," in *Teilhard in the 21st Century: The Emerging Spirit of Earth*, ed. Arthur Fabel and Donald St. John (Maryknoll, N.Y.: Orbis Books, 2003).

7.   Pierre Teilhard de Chardin, "The Sense of Man," in *Toward the Future* (New York: Harcourt Brace Jovanovich, 1975), 32.

8.   See introduction to chapter 7 for their use of the term *Great Work*.

9.   Ursula King, "The Zest for Life: A Contemporary Exploration of a Generative Theme in Teilhard's Work," in *From Teilhard to Omega: Co-creating an Unfinished Universe*, ed. Ilia Delio (Maryknoll, N.Y.: Orbis Books, 2014), 7.

10. For eco-cities, see ecocitybuilders.org, and for eco-design, see William McDonough and Michael Braungart, *Cradle to Cradle: Remaking the Way We Make Things* (New York: North Point Press, 2002). For biomimicry, see Janine Benyus, *Biomimicry: Innovation Inspired by Nature* (New York: Harper Perennial, 2002).

11. John Grim and Mary Evelyn Tucker, "Teilhard's Vision of Evolution," *Teilhard Studies*, no. 50 (Spring 2005).

12. Thomas Berry, "The Meadow Across the Creek," in *The Great Work: Our Way into the Future* (New York: Harmony/Bell Tower, 1999), 16.

13. The theme of interiority is central to John Haught's book, *The New Cosmic Story, Inside Our Awakening Universe* (New Haven, Conn.: Yale University Press, 2017).

14. De Chardin, *The Human Phenomenon*, 24.

15. Ursula King, *Spirit of Fire: The Life and Vision of Teilhard de Chardin* (Maryknoll, N.Y.: Orbis Books, 2015).

16. See reflections on this idea by Mary Evelyn Tucker, "The Ecological Spirituality of Teilhard," *Teilhard Studies*, no. 51 (Fall 2005). Also published in Kathleen Duffy, ed.,

Rediscovering Teilhard's Fire (Philadelphia: St. Joseph's University Press, 2010). See also Ursula King, "Ecology and Spirituality: A New Earth Consciousness and a New Earth Community," in *Christ in All Things: Exploring Spirituality with Teilhard de Chardin* (Maryknoll, N.Y.: Orbis Books, 2016), 165-194.

17. This is what Ilya Prigogene's research showed, namely, that "dissipative structures lead to self-organizing dynamics, which are manifest in evolutionary processes"; see Ilya Prigogene and Isabella Stengers, *Order Out of Chaos: Man's New Dialogue with Nature* (London: William Heinemann, 1984).

18. For Teilhard, *omega* has two distinct usages with broader implications: first, *omega* is definitely a central idea within the evolutionary process, analogous to "spirit," "Spirit of the Earth," and "christic." But it is not limited to that. *Omega* is also a transcendent term for the culminating convergence beyond evolution. See de Chardin, *The Human Phenomenon*, 192-193.

19. Pierre Teilhard de Chardin, "The Spirit of the Earth," in *Human Energy* (New York: Harcourt Brace Jovanovich, 1971, 19-47.

20. Thomas Berry, "The Spirituality of the Earth," in *The Sacred Universe: Earth, Spirituality, and Religion in the Twenty-First Century*, ed. Mary Evelyn Tucker (New York: Columbia University Press, 2009), 69.

21. Teilhard coined this term, *noosphere*, from the Greek word for mind (*nous*). His friend, Edouard Le Roy, S.J., also used the term, as did the Russian scientist, Vladimir Ivanovich Verdnasky.

22. See especially Thomas's appendix in *The Christian Future and the Fate of Earth*, ed. Mary Evelyn Tucker (Maryknoll, N.Y.: Orbis Books, 2009), 120-121.

23. Julian Huxley writes that "evolution was at last becoming conscious of itself." Introduction to *The Phenomenon of Man* (1959 version), 20. This introduction was not included in the later translation *The Human Phenomenon* in 1999. Teilhard includes this in his text: "The human discovers that, in the striking words of Julian Huxley, *we are nothing else other than evolution become conscious of itself.*" *The Human Phenomenon*, 154.

24. "In general, centration is the tendency of matter to organize itself around a center, a process that at the human level takes the form of the intensification of the central nervous system that gives rise to reflexive consciousness." Personal communication from the Teilhardian scholar John Haught, June 7, 2018.

25. See Teilhard's statement: "Whatever the domain—whether it be the cells of the body, the members of society, or the elements of a spiritual synthesis—*union differentiates.*" In every organized whole the parts perfect and fulfill themselves." *The Human Phenomenon*, 186.

26. Thomas Aquinas, *Summa Contra Gentiles*, trans. Anton Pegis (Notre Dame, Ind.: University of Notre Dame Press, 1955), 2.45.10. Thomas frequently quoted this line.

27. De Chardin, *The Human Phenomenon*, 151-152.

28. John Haught, *The Promise of Nature: Ecology and Cosmic Purpose* (Eugene, Oreg.: Wipf and Stock, 2004).

29. Pierre Teilhard de Chardin, *Writings in Time of War*, trans. René Hague (New York: Harper and Row, 1968), 14.

30. Pierre Teilhard de Chardin, *The Divine Milieu* (New York: Harper and Row, 1960).

31.   This is a crucial insight that Teilhard received from his fellow Jesuit, Georges Lemaître (1895–1966), a physicist at the Catholic University of Leuven and one of the earliest proponents of an expanding universe, of which, at the time, Einstein remained skeptical.

32.   The contemporary Standard Model, or Core theory, of reality states that quanta are fundamental to energy and matter. These quanta are designated as "force-field" or "matter-field" quanta. See Frank Wilczek, *The Lightness of Being: Mass, Ether, and the Unification of Forces* (New York: Basic Books, 2008), as well as Bruce Schumm, *Deep Down Things: The Breathtaking Beauty of Particle Physics* (Baltimore, Md.: Johns Hopkins University Press, 2004).

33.   Scientists Niles Eldredge and Steven Jay Gould later developed the theory of "punctuated equilibrium" in 1972 to explain such transitions in Earth history. See "Punctuated Equilibria: An Alternative to Phyletic Gradualism," in *Models in Paleobiology*, ed. T. J. M. Schopf (San Francisco: Freeman Cooper, 1972), 82–115. Reprinted in Niles Eldredge, *Time Frames: The Rethinking of Darwinian Evolution* (Princeton, N.J.: Princeton University Press, 1985), 193–223.

34.   Thomas was influenced by the thought of Jacques Ellul, *The Technological Society* (New York: Vintage Press, 1964).

35.   Berry, "Teilhard in the Ecological Age," in *Teilhard in the 21st Century*, 57–73. Teilhard's views of progress led him to speculate on eugenics, as did others of his generation. See the essays in the newsletter *Teilhard Perspective* (Spring/Summer 2018) for responses to these problematic statements, which did not represent the mainstream of his thought.

36.   Pierre Teilhard de Chardin, *Building the Earth* (Wilkes-Barre, Pa.: Dimension Books, 1965).

37.   See Pierre Teilhard de Chardin, *Science and Christ* (New York: Harper and Row, 1968).

38.   *Goldenrod*, 64–65. Both Teilhard and Thomas were deeply influenced by Henri Bergson's *Creative Evolution*, trans. Arthur Mitchell (New York: Henry Holt, 1911).

39.   Ilia Delio has worked on the relationship of Teilhard's thought to technology. In particular, she critiques transhumanism for its hyperindividualism: "Teilhard's vision of evolution is not based on personal enhancement (like the transhumanists) but on community and creativity." Instead, she observes that Teilhard "sees the convergence of human and machine intelligence as completing the material and cerebral sphere of collective thought." Ilia Delio, "Technology and Noogenesis," in *The Unbearable Wholeness of Being: God, Evolution, and the Power of Love* (Maryknoll, N.Y.: Orbis Books, 2013), 172.

40.   De Chardin, *Science and Christ*, 193.

41.   De Chardin, *The Human Phenomenon*, 3.

42.   De Chardin, *The Human Phenomenon*, 186.

43.   Pierre Teilhard de Chardin, "The Christic," in *The Heart of Matter* (New York: Harcourt Brace Jovanovich, 1979), 94. See Thomas's book of essays, *The Sacred Universe* (New York: Columbia University Press, 2009).

44.   See David Grumett, "Teilhard de Chardin, Original Sin, and the Six Propositions," *Zygon: Journal of Religion and Science* 53, no. 2 (May 2018): 303–330.

45.   Ursula King provides an important overview of Teilhard's interpretation of Asian religions in *Teilhard de Chardin and Eastern Religions*. As Joseph Needham wrote in the

foreword of this book: "The fact seems to be that Teilhard de Chardin never acquired a detailed knowledge of Asian religious beliefs and practices, although his general acquaintance with the peoples and cultures of Asia was much greater than is usually supposed," xiv.

46. Thomas Berry, "The New Story: Comments on the Origin, Identification, and Transmission of Values," *Teilhard Studies*, no. 1 (1978); also in Arthur Fabel and Donald St. John, eds., *Teilhard in the 21st Century: The Emerging Spirit of Earth* (Maryknoll, N.Y.: Orbis Books, 2003), 83–84; also in Thomas Berry, *The Dream of the Earth* (San Francisco: Sierra Club Books, 1988; reprint Berkeley: Counterpoint Press, 2015).

47. De Chardin, *The Divine Milieu*, 92.

48. Berry, "The New Story," in *Teilhard in the 21st Century*, 86.

49. Teilhard writes: "To be properly understood, the book I present here must not be read as a metaphysical work, still less as some kind of theological essay, but solely and exclusively as a scientific study. The very choice of title makes this clear. It is a study of nothing but the phenomenon; but also, the whole of the phenomenon." In *The Human Phenomenon*, trans. Sarah Appleton-Weber. Eastbourne, UK: Sussex Academic Press, 1999, ii. First published in English as *The Phenomenon of Man*, 1955.

50. Berry, "The New Story," in *Teilhard in the 21st Century*, 77–88.

51. See Sam Mickey, *On the Verge of a Planetary Civilization: A Philosophy of Integral Ecology* (New York: Rowman and Littlefield, 2014). Mickey lists 1995 as Thomas's first published use of "integral ecology"; John and Mary Evelyn recall that Thomas orally used this phrase from the late 1980s forward. See Sam Mickey, Sean Kelly, and Adam Robbert, eds., *The Variety of Integral Ecologies: Nature, Culture, and Knowledge in the Planetary Era* (Albany: State University of New York Press, 2017). See also Sean Esbjorn-Hargens, "Ecological Interiority: Thomas Berry's Integral Ecology," in *Thomas Berry, Dreamer of the Earth: The Spiritual Ecology of the Father of Environmentalism*, ed. Ervin Laszlo and Allan Combs (Rochester, Vt.: Inner Traditions, 2011).

52. See *Journey of the Universe and the World Religions* conference at Chautauqua, June 24, 28, 2018: http://www.journeyoftheuniverse.org/conference-at-chautauqua/.

53. Berry, "The New Story," in *Teilhard in the 21st Century*, 77.

54. For Teilhard's reflections on hominization and noosphere, see *The Human Phenomenon*, 110–129.

55. See Henri de Lubac, ed., Pierre Teilhard de Chardin/Maurice Blondel: Correspondence, trans. William Whitman (New York: Herder and Herder, 1967).

56. John Grim and Mary Evelyn Tucker, "An Overview of Teilhard's Commitment to 'Seeing' as Expressed in His Phenomenology, Metaphysics, and Mysticism," in *Pierre Teilhard de Chardin on People & Planet*, ed. Celia Deane-Drummond (London: Equinox, 2006).

57. Kathleen Duffy, *Teilhard's Mysticism: Seeing the Inner Face of Evolution* (Maryknoll, N.Y.: Orbis Books, 2014). Using a model of five concentric circles, Duffy explores Teilhard's mystical journey.

58. De Chardin, *Science and Christ*, 172.

59. Ursula King, "Love—A Higher Form of Human Energy in the Work of Teilhard de Chardin and Sorokin," *Zygon* 39, no. 1 (March 2004): 77–102.

60.   Berry, "Human Presence," in *The Dream of the Earth*, 20.

61.   This is a remembrance by the authors based on hearing Thomas's talks from the 1970s through the 1990s.

62.   De Chardin, *Science and Christ*, 171.

63.   Pierre Teilhard de Chardin, *Toward the Future* (New York: Harcourt Brace Jovanovich, 1975, 86–87.

11. CONFUCIAN INTEGRATION OF COSMOS, EARTH, AND HUMANS

The quotation in the chapter epigraph is from Thomas Berry, "Individualism and Holism in Chinese Tradition," in *Confucian Spirituality*, vol. 1, ed. Tu Weiming and Mary Evelyn Tucker (New York: Crossroad, 2003).

1.   Tu was on the faculty at Princeton (1968–1971) and Berkeley (1971–1981) before returning to Harvard in 1981 where he taught until 2010 when he returned to China to Beijing University. For an online intellectual biography, see http://www.iep.utm.edu/tu-weimi/.

2.   Among Tu Weiming's many influential books are *Commonality and Centrality: An Essay on Confucian Religiousness* (Albany: State University of New York Press, 1989) and *Confucian Thought: Selfhood as Creative Transformation* (Albany: State University of New York Press, 1985).

3.   Wm. Theodore de Bary and Tu Weiming, eds., *Confucianism and Human Rights* (New York: Columbia University Press, 1998); Wm. Theodore de Bary, *Asian Values and Human Rights: A Confucian Communitarian Perspective* (Cambridge, Mass.: Harvard University Press, 2000).

4.   Tu Weiming and Mary Evelyn Tucker, eds., *Confucian Spirituality*, 2 vols. (New York: Crossroad, 2003, 2004).

5.   The Translations from the Asian Classics series includes many volumes from different authors/translators. *Sources of Chinese Tradition* was published in two volumes, edited by Wm. Theodore de Bary and Irene Bloom: *Sources of Chinese Tradition*, vol. 1 (New York: Columbia University Press, 1964; revised 1999); and *Sources of Chinese Tradition*, vol. 2 (New York: Columbia University Press, 1965; revised 2000).

6.   Both of these papers were published in Weiming and Tucker, *Confucian Spirituality*, vol. 1.

7.   Thomas's studies included the other traditions of Asia, and he wrote a book on Buddhism and a book on the religions of India: *Buddhism*, (New York: Hawthorne Books, 1966; paperback edition by Crowell Publishers, 1975; since 1996 available from Columbia University Press); and *Religions of India: Hinduism, Yoga, Buddhism* (2nd ed., New York: Bruce-Macmillan, 1971; also Chambersburg, Pa.: Anima Books, 1992; since 1996 available from Columbia University Press).

8.   Thomas Berry, *Evening Thoughts: Reflecting on Earth as a Sacred Community*, ed. Mary Evelyn Tucker (Berkeley, Calif.: Counterpoint Press, 2015; first published San Francisco: Sierra Club Books and University of California Press, 2006), 85.

9.   See Weiming, *Commonality and Centrality*.

10.   The papers were published in two volumes; see Weiming and Tucker, *Confucian Spirituality*.

11.　Mary Evelyn Tucker and John Berthrong, eds., *Confucianism and Ecology: The Interrelation of Heaven, Earth, and Humans* (Cambridge, Mass.: Harvard Center for the Study of World Religions, 1998).

12.　See de Bary and Bloom, *Sources of Chinese Tradition*, 1999, 1:330–331.

13.　This term is used by Tu Weiming in his article "Continuity of Being," in *Confucianism and Ecology*.

14.　See John Makeham, *New Confucianism: A Critical Examination* (New York: Palgrave Macmillan, 2003).

15.　Mou Tsung-san, Carsun Chang, Tang Chun-i, and Hsu Fo-Kuan, "A Manifesto for a Re-Appraisal of Sinology and Reconstruction of Chinese Culture," in *The Development of Neo-Confucian Thought*, vol. 2, ed. Carson Chang (New York: Bookman Associates, 1962).

16.　Included in the unpublished Riverdale Papers. Thomas Berry, "Mao Tse-Tung: The Long March," Riverdale Papers, vol. 3 (New York: Riverdale Center for Religious Research), 94–95.

17.　See John Grim and Mary Evelyn Tucker, *Ecology and Religion* (Washington, D.C.: Island Press, 2014), 109–125.

18.　Michael Puett and Christine Gross-Loh, *The Path: What Chinese Philosophers Can Teach Us About the Good Life* (New York: Simon and Schuster, 2016).

19.　See de Bary and Bloom, *Sources of Chinese Tradition*, 1999, 1:171.

20.　This system had a direct influence on the civil service exam systems developed in the West. Indeed, the Enlightenment thinkers were attracted to Confucianism for its humanistic teachings and its emphasis on meritocracy in governance through the civil service exams.

21.　Chu Hsi and Lu Tsu Ch'ien, eds., *Reflections on Things at Hand: The Neo-Confucian Anthology*, trans. Wing-tsit Chan (New York: Columbia University Press, 1967).

22.　De Bary and Bloom, *Sources of Chinese Tradition*, 1999, 1:338.

23.　This term was described by Tu Weiming in *Commonality and Centrality*. He was drawing on the historian of religions Mircea Eliade.

24.　Zhang Zai, "Western Inscription," in de Bary and Bloom, *Sources of Chinese Tradition*, 1999, 1:683.

25.　This idea appears early in the Confucian tradition in one of the Five Classics, the Classic of History.

26.　See de Bary and Bloom, *Sources of Chinese Tradition*, 1999), 1:294–309.

12. INDIGENOUS TRADITIONS OF THE GIVING EARTH

The chapter epigraph is from Thomas Berry, "The World of Wonder," in *The Sacred Universe*, ed. Mary Evelyn Tucker (New York: Columbia University Press, 2009), 173.

1.　Particular names of Indigenous nations and peoples, such as Apsaalooke, are preferable to English translations, such as Crow, or more general references such as American Indian, Native American, First Peoples, First Nations, and Indigenous Peoples. As no one English term is preferable, these terms are used interchangeably here to refer broadly to the Indigenous peoples of the Americas.

2. Thomas Berry, *The Dream of the Earth* (Berkeley, Calif.: Counterpoint Press, 2015, 181.

3. Indigenous lifeways are ways of knowing the world that describe enduring modes of sustainable livelihood. See John Grim and Mary Evelyn Tucker, *Ecology and Religion* (Washington, D.C.: Island Press, 2014), 127–128. They are also prescriptive of what Peet and Watts call "ecological imaginaries." See R. Peet and M. Watts, *Liberation Ecologies: Environment, Development, Social Movements* (London: Routledge, 1996), 7. Ecological imaginaries refer to deep relationships between place and people that activate affective, cognitive, and creative forces at the heart of cultural life. When homelands of Indigenous peoples are literally cut down or mined away, the possibility of imaging oneself and one's community is torn asunder.

4. Often associated with Congressman and Secretary of Interior Stewart Udall's 1973 article, "Indians: First Americans, First Ecologists," in *Readings in American History 1973/1974* (Guilford, Conn,: Dushkin Publishing Group, 1973); also see Shepard Krech III, *The Ecological Indian: Myth and History* (New York: Norton, 1999).

5. This was in a letter to Anne Marie Dalton, a professor at St. Mary's University in Halifax, dated May 10, 1994.

6. Thomas Berry, *The Great Work: Our Way into the Future* (New York: Harmony/Bell Tower, 1999), 39. Among the comments in that essay is his reflection: "This presence of Native Peoples to the numinous powers of this continent expressed through its natural phenomena transmits an ancient spiritual identity."

7. For Thomas's understanding of the spiritual dynamics of philosophical thought, see his *Five Oriental Philosophies* (Albany, N.Y.: Magi Books, 1968), 5–6. Regarding his anchoring of cosmology in evolutionary processes, see Thomas Berry, "Contemporary Spirituality: The Journey of the Human Community," *Cross Currents* 24 (Summer 1974): 172–183. Berry wrote on page 173: "As part of this long cosmic process it can be said that the varied spiritual traditions scattered across the globe are not of yesterday, nor are they simply of the Earth. In some manner they were born when the galaxies appeared in the limitless swirl of space; the dynamic at work in this process has found unique expression in the formation of the green earth with its myriad forms of life and their completion in the human."

8. Thomas Berry, "The Future of the American Indian," *Cross Currents* 26 (Summer 1976): 133–142. A more extensive revised version is in *The Dream of the Earth* as "The Historical Role of the American Indian," 180–193.

9. See Roxanne Dunbar-Ortiz, *An Indigenous Peoples' History of the United States* (Boston: Beacon Press, 2014).

10. This terminology of personhood follows from the anthropological studies of A. I. Hallowell, which have influenced a generation of social scientists. For Thomas, Hallowell's perspective also provided a serious pathway for religious studies. See A. Irving Hallowell, "Ojibwa Ontology, Behavior and Worldview," in *Culture and History: Essays in Honor of Paul Radin*, ed. Stanley Diamond (New York: Columbia University Press, 1960), 207–244.

11. Thomas's concepts of genetic and cultural coding appear repeatedly throughout his work from the 1980s and can be found, for example, in the essay "Reinventing the Human," in *The Great Work*, 159–165. Interestingly, the Confucian scholar Tu Weiming found this analysis helpful in his own work.

12. Alice C. Fletcher and Francis La Flesche, *The Omaha Tribe*, 2 vols. (Lincoln: University of Nebraska Press, 1972). Originally published in 1911 by the Bureau of American Ethnology.

13. Fletcher's ethnography preserved and opened insight into Omaha Indian traditional wisdom. It is important to note also that her active support of allotment of Native land-holdings, especially through the Dawes Act, broke apart many Native communities.

14. See Michael McNally, *Honoring Elders: Aging, Authority, and Ojibwe Religion* (New York: Columbia University Press, 2009).

15. Hallowell developed the phrase "other-than-human" persons to convey this insight in "Ojibwa Ontology, Behavior and Worldview."

16. Author's mimeographed copy of "The Vision Quest of the American Indian" from course handouts, 1. These materials were initially developed for Thomas's course, "Religious Studies and the American Indian," taught in the fall of 1976.

17. Thomas's activities in the Philippines during the summer of 1984 included presentations at the Agala Museum on "Art in the Ecological Age"; at Immaculate Conception (Maryknoll) College on "Religious Responsibility for Earth"; at Illigin Institute of Technology on "Educating for the Ecological Age"; at Manila Asian Social Institute on "Ecology and Social Justice"; and at Santa Cruz Mission on "Primal Religion" (LAP).

18. Thomas developed his thinking about the "Ecozoic era" in tandem with these encounters with Indigenous peoples. He associated the appearance of that era with dream consciousness. Dreams as numinous, revelatory occasions continue to be a contemporary religious feature of Indigenous communities wherever Christian or Islamic evangelization has not campaigned against and eradicated that practice. Connections between the dream and the Ecozoic era are stated, for example, in the essay "Moments of Grace," in which Thomas writes: "What can be said is that the foundations of a new historical period, the Ecozoic Era, have been established in every realm of human affairs. The mythic vision has been set into place. The distorted dream of an industrial technological paradise is being replaced by the more viable dream of a mutually enhancing human presence within an ever-renewing organic-based Earth community. The dream drives the action. In the larger cultural context, the dream becomes the myth that both guides and drives the action." In Berry, *The Great Work*, 201. John Grim recalls that as Thomas's student studying the nature and thought of Indigenous peoples, he had extensive conversations with Thomas about the range of issues regarding the T'boli peoples, whom John visited in 1982. Thomas repeated this "touching lightly" phrase many times in talks and discussions from the 1970s until his death in 2009.

19. The Catholic Bishops' Conference of the Philippines, "What Is Happening to Our Beautiful Land? A Pastoral Letter on Ecology," accessed June 5, 2018, http://www.cbcponline.org/documents/1980s/1988-ecology.html.

20. Catholic Bishops' Conference.

21. Two studies of this interaction of narrative and ritual are Rukmini Bhaya Nair, *Narrative Gravity: Conversation, Cognition, Culture* (London: Routledge, 2002); and Eduardo Kohn, *How Forests Think: Toward an Anthropology Beyond the Human* (Berkeley, Calif.: University of California Press, 2013).

22. Though Thomas did not use this terminology, his thought was generative in the series of conferences at Harvard University in the late 1990s that gave expression to religion and ecology as a field of study. "Religious ecology" is developed in John Grim and Mary Evelyn Tucker, *Ecology and Religion* (Washington, D.C.: Island Press, 2014), 35–37.

23. An excellent example of this type of insight by an ethnographer is the work of a contemporary of Thomas Berry, namely, Gerardo Reichel-Dolmatoff, in *Rainforest Shamans: Essays on the Tukano Indians of the Northwest Amazon* (Devon, UK: Themis Books, 1997).

24. At first, Thomas drew extensively on the 1932 publication by John Neihardt, *Black Elk Speaks*. Gradually he included Neihardt's field notes edited by Raymond De Mallie. He was aware of the controversies that swirled about John Neihardt's original publication, which largely focused on attributions of statements in that text. More importantly for our considerations here, however, is the rich story that Black Elk provided of his life vision in the context of Lakota cultural life and place; see Raymond De Mallie, ed., *The Sixth Grandfather: Black Elk's Teachings Given to John Neihardt* (Lincoln: University of Nebraska Press, 1984), 19.

25. Nicholas Black Elk, as told through John G. Neihardt, *Black Elk Speaks* (Lincoln: University of Nebraska Press, 2000; originally published 1932), 35; and De Mallie, *The Sixth Grandfather*, 133.

26. This story of Nicholas Black Elk's religious life is evident in the works cited in note 24 as well as in Harry Oldmeadow, *Black Elk, Lakota Visionary: The Oglala Holy Man & Sioux Tradition* (Bloomington, Ind.: World Wisdom Press, 2018).

27. Melvin R. Gilmore, *Prairie Smoke* (New York: Columbia University Press, 1929), 36; cited in Joseph Epes Brown, *The Spiritual Legacy of the American Indian* (New York: Crossroad, 1991), 40.

28. See Steven Newcomb, *Pagans in the Promised Land: Decoding the Christian Doctrine of Discovery* (Golden, Colo.: Fulcrum, 2008).

29. N. Bruce Duthu, *American Indians and the Law* (New York: Penguin, 2008), 69–75. There are movements now to rescind the Doctrine of Discovery. See, for example, the Doctrine of Discovery list serv: DOD_STUDY_GROUP@LISTSERV.SYR.EDU.

30. This selection is included in *The Dream of the Earth*, 180–193. It is a more extensive version than an earlier work: Thomas Berry, "The Future of the American Indian," *Cross Currents* 26 (Summer 1976): 133–142.

31. This concept of lifeway, referenced earlier, is helpful because it picks up on the reflections of Indigenous individuals and communities on the interactive character of their thought and practice; see note 4.

32. Berry, "The Historical Role of the American Indian," 183.

33. Berry, *The Great Work*, 4.

34. Berry, "The Historical Role of the American Indian," 184.

35. Berry, "The Historical Role of the American Indian," 185.

36. Author's mimeographed copy of "The Vision Quest of the American Indian" from course handouts, fall 1973, 5.

37. Copy of "The Vision Quest of the American Indian," 31.

38. Berry, "The Historical Role of the American Indian," 185.

39.   Berry, "The Historical Role of the American Indian," 185-186.

40.   Berry, "The Historical Role of the American Indian," 185.

41.   Thomas Berry with Thomas Clarke, *Befriending the Earth: A Theology of Reconciliation Between Humans and the Earth* (Mystic, Conn.: Twenty-Third Publications, 1991), 132.

42.   Berry, "Traditional Religion in the Modern World," in *The Sacred Universe*, 9.

43.   Berry, "The Historical Role of the American Indian," 190.

44.   See Thomas Berry, "Our Way into the Future: A Communion of Subjects," in *Evening Thoughts: Reflecting on Earth as a Sacred Community*, ed. Mary Evelyn Tucker (Berkeley, Calif.: Counterpoint Press, 2015; first published San Francisco: Sierra Club Books and University of California Press, 2006), 17.

45.   Thomas Berry, "The Earth Community," in *The Dream of the Earth*, 8.

EPILOGUE

The chapter epigraph is from Thomas Berry, "Cosmology of Religions," in *The Sacred Universe: Earth, Spirituality, and Religion in the Twenty-First Century*, ed. Mary Evelyn Tucker (New York: Columbia University Press, 2009), 122-123.

1.   Thomas Berry, "The New Story," in *The Dream of the Earth* (Berkeley, Calif.: Counterpoint Press, 2015), 137. First published San Francisco: Sierra Club Books, (1988).

Bibliography

THE WORKS OF THOMAS BERRY (CHRONOLOGICAL)

BOOKS

Berry, Thomas. "The Historical Theory of Giambattista Vico." PhD diss., Catholic University of America Press, 1951.

——. *Buddhism*. New York: Hawthorne Books, 1966. Paperback edition by Crowell Publishers, 1975. Since 1996 available from Columbia University Press.

——. *Religions of India: Hinduism, Yoga, Buddhism*. New York: Bruce-Macmillan, 1971. Second edition: Chambersburg, Pa.: Anima Books, 1992. Since 1996 available from Columbia University Press.

——. *The Dream of the Earth*. Berkeley, Calif.: Counterpoint Press, 2015. First published San Francisco: Sierra Club Books, 1988.

Berry, Thomas, with Thomas Clark, *Befriending the Earth: A Theology of Reconciliation Between Humans and the Earth*. Mystic, Conn.: Twenty-Third Publications, 1991.

Berry, Thomas, with Brian Swimme. *The Universe Story: From the Primordial Flaring Forth to the Ecozoic Era—A Celebration of the Unfolding of the Cosmos*. San Francisco: HarperSanFrancisco, 1992.

Berry, Thomas. *Creative Energy: Bearing Witness for the Earth* (a selection of three essays from *Dream of the Earth*). San Francisco: Sierra Club Books, 1996.

——. *The Great Work: Our Way into the Future*. New York: Harmony/Bell Tower, 1999.

——. *Evening Thoughts: Reflecting on Earth as a Sacred Community*, ed. Mary Evelyn Tucker. Berkeley, Calif.: Counterpoint Press, 2015. First published San Francisco: Sierra Club Books and Berkeley, Calif.: University of California Press, 2006.

——. *The Sacred Universe: Earth, Spirituality, and Religion in the Twenty-First Century*, ed. Mary Evelyn Tucker. New York: Columbia University Press, 2009.

——. *The Christian Future and the Fate of Earth*, ed. Mary Evelyn Tucker and John Grim. Maryknoll, N.Y.: Orbis Books, 2009.

——. *Thomas Berry: Selected Writings on the Earth Community*. Selected and with an Introduction by Mary Evelyn Tucker and John Grim. Modern Spiritual Masters Series. Maryknoll, N.Y.: Orbis Books, 2014.

ESSAYS

——. "Our Need of Orientalists." *World Mission* 7 (Fall 1956): 301–314.

——. "Oriental Scholarship: A Challenge to Catholic Scholars." *World Mission* (1957).

——. "Missions, Missiology, and Oriental Culture." *Theology Digest*, Autumn 1958, 130.

——. "Order and History." *Thought* 33, no. 2 (1958): 273–278.

——. "Education in a Multicultural World." In *Approaches to the Oriental Classics: Asian Literature and Thought in General Education*, ed. Wm. Theodore de Bary, 11–23. New York: Columbia University Press, 1959.

——. "John Dewey's Influence in China." In *John Dewey: His Thought and Influence*, ed. John Blewett, 199–232. New York: Fordham University Press, 1960.

——. "Oriental Philosophies and World Humanism." *International Philosophical Quarterly* 1, no. 1 (February 1961): 5–33.

——. "Theological Synthesis in the Great Traditions: Shankara, Chu Hsi, St. Thomas." Unpublished manuscript, 1963.

——. "The Spiritual Forms of the Oriental Civilizations." In *Approaches to Asian Civilizations*, ed. Wm. Theodore de Bary and Ainslie T. Embree, 5–33. New York: Columbia University Press, 1964.

——. "Asian Art." In *Encyclopedia Americana*. International ed. Vol. 2. New York: Americana Corporation, 1965.

——. "Ritual in the Chinese Tradition." Unpublished manuscript, 1965.

——. "Salvation Experience in Early Buddhism." Unpublished manuscript, 1966.

——. "Nirvana Experience in Buddhism." Unpublished manuscript, 1967.

——. "Primary Causality in Asian Traditions." Unpublished manuscript, 1968.

——. "The Problem of Moral Evil and Guilt in Early Buddhism." In *Moral Evil Under Challenge*, ed. Johannes B. Metz, 126–133. New York: Herder and Herder, 1970.

——. "The Vision Quest of the American Indian." Unpublished manuscript, 1973.

——. "Contemporary Spirituality: The Journey of the Human Community." *Cross Currents* 24, nos. 2/3 (Summer/Fall 1974): 172–183. Reprinted in *The Sacred Universe*, ed. Mary Evelyn Tucker. New York: Columbia University Press, 2009.

——. "Mao Tse-Tung: The Long March." Riverdale Papers. Vol. 3. New York: Riverdale Center for Religious Research, 94–95.

——. "Cosmic Person and the Future of Man." Riverdale Papers. New York: Riverdale Center for Religious Research, 1975. Reprinted in *The Sacred Universe*, ed. Mary Evelyn Tucker. New York: Columbia University Press, 2009.

——. "The Future of the American Indian." *Cross Currents* 26 (Summer 1976): 133–142. A more extensive revised version is "The Historical Role of the American Indian," in *The Dream of the Earth*. Berkeley: Counterpoint Press, 2015. First published San Francisco: Sierra Club Books, 1988.

——. "The New Story: Comments on the Origin, Identification, and Transmission of Values." *Teilhard Studies*, no. 1 (1978). Reprinted in *Cross Currents* 37, nos. 22/23 (1987);

Teilhard in the 21st Century: The Emerging Spirit of Earth, ed. Arthur Fabel and Donald St. John. Maryknoll, N.Y.: Orbis Books, 2003. Also reprinted in *The Dream of the Earth*. Berkeley, Calif.: Counterpoint Press, 2015.

——. "Management: The Managerial Ethos and the Future of Planet Earth." *Teilhard Studies*, no. 3 (1980).

——. "Perspectives on Creativity: Openness to a Free Future." In *Whither Creativity, Freedom, Suffering*. Proceedings of the Theology Institute of Villanova University, 1–14. Villanova, Pa.: Villanova Theological Institute Publications, 1981.

——. "Classical Western Spirituality and the American Experience." *Cross Currents* 31, no. 4 (Winter 1981–1982): 388–399.

——. "Teilhard in the Ecological Age." *Teilhard Studies*, no. 7 (1982). Also in *Teilhard in the 21st Century: The Emerging Spirit of Earth*, ed. Arthur Fabel and Donald St. John. Maryknoll, N.Y.: Orbis Books, 2003.

——. "The Earth: A New Context for Religious Unity." In *Thomas Berry and the New Cosmology*, ed. Anne Lonergan and Caroline Richard, 27–40. Mystic Court, Conn.: Twenty-Third Publications, 1987.

——. "Economics: Its Effects on the Life Systems of the World." In *Thomas Berry and the New Cosmology*, ed. Anne Lonergan and Caroline Richard, 5–26. Mystic Court, Conn.: Twenty-Third Publications, 1987.

——. "Our Future on Earth: Where Do We Go from Here?" In *Thomas Berry and the New Cosmology*, ed. Anne Lonergan and Caroline Richard, 103–106. Mystic Court, Conn.: Twenty-Third Publications, 1987.

——. "Creative Energy." *Cross Currents* 37, nos. 22/23 (1987). Reprinted in *The Dream of the Earth*. Berkeley, Calif.: Counterpoint Press, 2015.

——. "Dream of the Earth: Our Way into the Future." *Cross Currents* 37, nos. 22/23 (1987). Reprinted in *The Dream of the Earth*. Berkeley, Calif.: Counterpoint Press, 2015.

——. "Twelve Principles." *Cross Currents* 37, nos. 22/23 (1987). A revised version published in *Evening Thoughts*, ed. Mary Evelyn Tucker. Berkeley, Calif.: Counterpoint Press, 2015

——. "The Spirit of the Earth." In *Liberating Life: Contemporary Approaches to Ecological Theology*, ed. William Birch, William Eakin, and Jay B. McDaniel, 151–158. Maryknoll, N.Y.: Orbis Books, 1990. Reprinted in *The Sacred Universe*, ed. Mary Evelyn Tucker. New York: Columbia University Press, 2009.

——. "Ecological Geography." In *Worldviews and Ecology: Religion, Philosophy, and the Environment*, ed. Mary Evelyn Tucker and John Grim, 228–237. Maryknoll, N.Y.: Orbis Books, 1994.

——. "Ecology and the Future of Catholicism." In *Embracing Earth: Catholic Approaches to Ecology*, ed. Albert L. LaChance and John E. Carroll. Maryknoll, N.Y.: Orbis Press, 1994.

——. "The Gaia Theory: Its Religious Implications," *ARC: The Journal of the Faculty of Religious Studies* 22 (1994): 7–19. Reprinted in *The Sacred Universe*, ed. Mary Evelyn Tucker. New York: Columbia University Press, 2009.

——. "The Cosmology of Religions." In *A Source Book for Earth's Community of Religions*, ed. Joel D. Beversluis, 93–98. Grand Rapids, Mich.: CoNexus Press, 1995. Also in *Pluralism and Oppression*, ed. Paul Knitter. Vol. 34. Published by the College Theology Society. Reprinted in *The Sacred Universe*, ed. Mary Evelyn Tucker. New York: Columbia University Press, 2009.

——. "Thomas Berry." In *Listening to the Land. Conversations About Nature, Culture, and Eros*, ed. Derrick Jensen, 35–43. San Francisco: Sierra Club Books, 1995.

——. "The Bush." In *Sculpting with the Environment*, ed. Baile Oakes, 8–12. New York: Van Nostrand Reinhold, 1995.

——. "The Viable Human." In *Deep Ecology for the Twenty-First Century*, ed. George Sessions, 8–18. Boston: Shambhala Publications, 1995. Reprinted in *The Great Work*. New York: Harmony/Bell Tower, 1999.

——. "The Meadow." In *Cathedrals of the Spirit*, ed. T. C. McLuhan, 220–221. San Francisco: HarperCollins, 1996.

——. "The Role of Religions in the Twenty-First Century." In *The Community of Religions: Voices and Images from the Parliament of the World's Religions*, ed. Wayne Teasdale and George Cairns, 182–188. New York: Continuum, 1996. Updated as "Religion in the 21st Century" in *The Sacred Universe*, ed. Mary Evelyn Tucker. New York: Columbia University Press, 2009

——. "The Universe Story; Its Religious Significance." In *The Greening of America: God, Environment and the Good Life*, ed. John E. Carroll and Paul Brockelman, 208–218. Hanover, N.H.: University Press of New England, 1997.

——. "The Universe, the University, and the Ecozoic Age." In *Doors of Understanding: Conversations in Global Spirituality in Honor of Ewert Cousins*, ed. Steven Chase, 79–96. Quincy, Ill.: Franciscan Press, 1997.

——. *What Does It Mean to Be Human? Reverence for Life Reaffirmed by Responses from Around the World*, ed. Frederick Franck, Janis Roze, and Richard Connolly, 50–56. Nyack, N.Y.: Circumstantial Productions, in cooperation with the UNESCO Institute for Education, 1998.

——. "The Hudson River Valley: A Bioregional Story." In *At Home on the Earth: Becoming Native to Our Place*, ed. David Landis Barnhill, 103–110. Berkeley, Calif.: University of California Press, 1999. Reprinted in *The Dream of the Earth*. Berkeley, Calif.: Counterpoint Press, 2015.

——. "Christianity in an Emerging Universe." In *Light Burdens, Heavy Blessings: Challenges of Church and Culture in the Post Vatican II Era*, essays in honor of Margaret R. Brennan, IHM, ed. Mary Heather MacKinnon SSND, Moni McIntyre, and Mary Ellen Sheehan IHM, 361–369. Quincey, Ill.: Franciscan Press, 2000.

——. "Christianity's Role in the Earth Project." In *Christianity and Ecology: Seeking the Well-Being of Earth and Humans*, ed, Dieter T. Hessel and Rosemary Radford Ruether, 127–134. Cambridge, Mass.: Harvard University Center for the Study of World Religions, 2000.

——. "On the Historical Mission of Our Times." In *Macroshift: Navigating the Transformation to a Sustainable World*, ed. Ervin Laszlo. Official Report of the Club of Budapest. San Francisco: Berrett-Koehler, 2001.

——. "Affectivity in Classical Confucian Tradition." In *Confucian Spirituality*, vol. 1, ed. Tu Weiming and Mary Evelyn Tucker, 96–112. New York: Crossroad, 2003.

——. "Individualism and Holism in Chinese Tradition: The Religious Cultural Context." In *Confucian Spirituality*, vol. 1, ed. Tu Weiming and Mary Evelyn Tucker, 39–55. New York: Crossroad, 2003.

——. "The Story and the Dream: The Next Stage in the Evolutionary Epic." In *The Epic of Evolution: Science and Religion in Dialogue*, ed. James B. Miller, 209–217. Upper Saddle River, N.J.: Prentice-Hall, 2004.

——. "Alienation in a Universe of Presence." *Teilhard Studies*, no. 48 (2004).

——. "Our Children, Their Future." In *Only the Sacred: Transforming Education in the Twenty-First Century*, ed. Peggy Whalen-Levitt. Greensboro, N.C.: Center for Education, Imagination and the Natural World, 2011.

——. "Dante: The Age in Which He Lived." Riverdale Papers. New York: Riverdale Center for Religious Research, n.d.

PAMPHLETS

——. *Five Oriental Philosophies*. Albany, N.Y.: Magi Books, 1968.

——. *The Lower Hudson River Valley: A Bioregional Story*. Brochure for the *Hudson River Bundle*. San Francisco: Planet Drum Foundation, 1985.

——. *The Ecozoic Era*. Eleventh Annual Schumacher Lecture. Great Barrington, Mass.: Schumacher Center for a New Economics, 1991. Also published as "The Ecozoic Era" in the following: *Guideposts to a Sustainable Future: The E. F. Schumacher Lectures, 1996*, ed. Mike Nickerson, Minneapolis: Voyageur, 1996; *The Other Half of the Soul: Bede Griffin and the Hindu-Christian Dialogue*, compiled by Beatrice Bruteau. Wheaton, Ill.: Quest Books, 1996; and *People, Land, and Community*, ed. Hildegarde Hannum, 191–203. New Haven, Conn.: Yale University Press, 1997.

——. *Human Presence on the North American Continent*. An Alfred P. Stiernotte Lecture in Philosophy. Hamden, Conn.: Quinnipiac University, 1994.

——. *Every Being Has Rights*. Twenty-Third Annual Schumacher Lecture. Great Barrington, Mass.: Schumacher Center for a New Economics, 2003.

INTERVIEWS AND CONVERSATIONS

——. "Earth Systems . . . Human Systems." In *Fugitive Faith: Interviews by Benjamin Webb*, ed. Benjamin Webb, 31–43. Maryknoll, N.Y.: Orbis Books, 1998.

——. Conversation in *The Forsaken Garden: Eco-psychology Restoring Earth, Healing the Self: Four Conversations on the Deep Meaning of Environmental Illness*, by Nancy Ryley. Wheaton, Ill.: Quest Books, 1998.

FOREWORDS, INTRODUCTIONS, AND PROLOGUES

——. Preface to *Aging: Spiritual Perspectives*, ed. Francis Tiso. Lake Worth, Fla.: Sunday Publications, 1982.

——. Foreword to *Meditations with Hildegard of Bingen*, by Gabriele Uhlein. Rochester, Vt.: Bear and Co., 1983.

——. Foreword to *Religious Life and Art: Hindu-Buddhist*, by Santosh N. Desai, 11–12. Vancouver, BC: Asian Research Service, 1986.

——. Foreword to *Meditations with Animals: A Native American Bestiary*, by Gerald Hausman. Santa Fe, N.M.: Bear and Co., 1986.

——. Foreword to *Earth, Sky, Gods, and Mortals*, by Jay McDaniel. Mystic, Conn.: Twenty-Third Publications, 1990.

——. Foreword to *To Honor the Earth: Reflections on Living in Harmony with Nature*, by Dorothy Maclean and Kathleen Thormod Carr, ii–ix. San Francisco: HarperSanFrancisco, 1991.

——. Foreword to *The Breathing Cathedral: Feeling Our Way into the Living Cosmos*, by Marthe Heyneman, xiii–xviii. San Francisco: Sierra Club Books, 1993.

——. Foreword to *Earth & Spirit: The Spiritual Dimensions of the Environmental Crisis*, ed. Fritz Hull. New York: Continuum, 1993.

——. Introduction to *Re-inhabiting the Earth: Biblical Perspectives and Eco-Spiritual Reflections*, by Mary Lou Van Rossum. Liguori, Mo.: Triumph Books, 1994.

——. Foreword to *Endangered Species: Saving the World's Vanishing Ecosystems*, by Anna Maria Caldera, 8–15. New York: Mallard Press, 1995.

——. Foreword to *Invested in the Common Good*, by Susan Meeker-Lowry. Philadelphia: New Society Publishers, 1996.

——. Introduction to *The Lost Gospel of the Earth: A Call for Renewing Nature, Spirit, and Politics*, by Tom Hayden, ix–xv. San Francisco: Sierra Club Books, 1996.

——. Foreword to *The Forsaken Garden: Eco-psychology Restoring Earth, Healing the Self: Four Conversations on the Deep Meaning of Environmental Illness*, by Nancy Ryley. Wheaton, Ill.: Quest Books, 1998.

——. Foreword to *Growing Up Green: Educating for Ecological Renewal*, by David Hutchison. New York: Teacher's College Press, 1998.

——. Introduction to *The Voice of the Infinite in the Small: Revisioning the Insect-Human Connection*, ed. Joanne Elizabeth Lauck and Brian Crissey, xix–xxii. Mill Spring, N.C.: Blue Water, 1998.

——. Foreword to *The Piracy of America: Profiteering in the Public Domain*, ed. Judith Scherff. Atlanta, Ga.: Clarity Press, 1999.

——. Foreword to *A Theology for the Earth: The Contributions of Thomas Berry and Bernard Lonergan*, by Anne Marie Dalton, v–viii. Ottawa, ON: University of Ottawa Press, 1999.

——. Foreword to *Transformative Learning: Educational Vision for the 21st Century*, by Edmund O'Sullivan, xi–xv. New York: University of Toronto Press, 1999.

——. Prologue to *Designing the Green Economy: For a Post-Industrial Transition*, by Brian Milani. Toronto, ON: Eco Materials Project, 2000.

——. Foreword to *Soulcraft: Crossing into Mysteries of Nature and Psyche*, by Bill Plotkin. San Francisco: New World Library, 2003.

——. Introduction to *Earth Age: A New Vision of God, the Human, and the Earth*, by Lorna Green. Lincoln, Nebr.: iUniverse, 2003.

——. Foreword to *Motivation for the Great Work: Forty Meaty Meditations for the Secular-Religious*, by John P. Cock. New York: Authors Choice Press, 2003.

——. Preface to *Earth Charter: A Study Book of Reflection for Action*, by Elisabeth Ferrero and Joe Holland. Morrisville, N.C.: Redwoods Press, 2005.

——. "Prologue: Loneliness and Presence." In *A Communion of Subjects: Animals in Religion, Science, and Ethics*, ed. Paul Waldau and Kimberley Patton. New York: Columbia University Press, 2006.

——. Foreword to *Wild Law: A Manifesto for Earth Justice*, by Cormac Cullinan. 2nd ed. White River Junction, Vt.: Chelsea Green, 2011.

UNPUBLISHED REFLECTIONS (HARVARD ARCHIVES)

——. *An Appalachian View*. Unpublished manuscript, n.d.

——. *Goldenrod: Reflections on the Twentieth Century*. Unpublished manuscript, n.d.

——. *Lifetime Remembrances*. Unpublished manuscript, n.d.

WORKS ABOUT THOMAS BERRY (ALPHABETICAL)

DOCTORAL THESES

Kwang Sun Choi. "The Sacred Journey of the Earth Community: Towards a Functional and Ecological Spirituality via the Cosmologies of Thomas Berry and Zhou Dunyi." PhD diss., University of Toronto, 2012.

Lee, Jai-Don. "Towards an Asian Ecotheology in the Context of Thomas Berry's Cosmology— A Critical Inquiry." PhD diss., University of Toronto, 2004.

O'Hara, Dennis. "The Implications of Thomas Berry's Cosmology for an Understanding of the Spiritual Dimensions of Human Health." PhD diss., University of Toronto, 1998.

Otu, Idara. "The Eco-theologies of Thomas Berry and John Zizioulas: Intimations for Ecojustice." PhD diss., University of Toronto, 2012.

GENERAL

Appolloni, Simon. *Convergent Knowing: Christianity and Science in Conversation with a Suffering Creation*. Montreal, QC: McGill-Queens University Press, 2018.

Barlow, Connie. *Green Space, Green Time: The Ways of Science*. New York: Springer-Verlag, 1997.

Bell, Mike. "Thomas Berry and an Earth Jurisprudence: An Exploratory Essay." *The Trumpeter* 19, no. 1 (2003).

Cigna, Joseph. "Speaker: Ignoring Ecology Is Dangerous." *Burlington Times-News* (Burlington, N.C.), January 14, 2000, C1-C2.

Dalton, Anne Marie. *A Theology of the Earth: The Contributions of Thomas Berry and Bernard Lonergan.* Ottawa, ON: University of Ottawa Press, 1999.

Dellinger, Drew. "Education for the Twenty-First Century on the North American Continent: An Address by Thomas Berry." In "Universe, Earth, Human: Reflections on the New Cosmology." Unpublished manuscript, 1997, 134-150.

——. "The Universe Is Celebration: An Interview with Thomas Berry." In "Universe, Earth, Human: Reflections on the New Cosmology." Unpublished manuscript, 1997, 16-33.

Eaton, Heather, ed. *The Intellectual Journey of Thomas Berry: Imagining the Earth Community.* Lanham, Md.: Lexington Books, 2014.

Ecozoic Review, "Thomas Berry's Work: Development, Difference, Importance, Applications." Special issue, *The Ecozoic*, no. 4 (2017).

Ecozoic Review, "A Tribute to Thomas Berry." Special issue, *The Ecozoic*, no. 2 (2009).

Ferrero, Elisabeth, ed. *Thomas Berry in Italy: Reflections on Spirituality and Sustainability.* Washington, D.C.: Pacem in Terris Press, 2016.

Grim, John. "The Shared Perspectives of Pierre Teilhard de Chardin and Thomas Berry." *Teilhard Studies*, no. 75 (Fall 2017).

——. "Time, History, Historians in Thomas Berry's Vision." *Cross Currents* 37, nos. 22/23 (1987).

Grim, John, and Mary Evelyn Tucker. "Thomas Berry: Reflections on His Life and Thought." *Teilhard Studies*, no. 61 (Fall 2010).

Laszlo, Ervin, and Allan Combs, eds. *Thomas Berry, Dreamer of the Earth: The Spiritual Ecology of the Father of Environmentalism.* Rochester, Vt.: Inner Traditions, 2011.

Lonergan, Anne, and Caroline Richard, eds. *Thomas Berry and the New Cosmology.* Mystic Court, Conn.: Twenty-Third Publications, 1987.

Louv, Richard. "The Giftedness of Thomas Berry." *Psychology Today*. Posted November 22, 2008. Accessed May 10, 2018. https://www.psychologytoday.com/us/blog/people-in-nature/200811/the-giftedness-thomas-berry.

Rain Crowe, Thomas. "Attending to Our Future." Review of *The Great Work*, by Thomas Berry. *The Bloomsbury Review*, January/February 2000, 3.

Revkin, Andrew. "Thomas Berry, Writer and Lecturer with a Mission for Mankind, Dies at 94." *New York Times*, June 3, 2009. http://www.nytimes.com/2009/06/04/ us/04berry.html.

Schwarz, Walter. "Thomas Berry Obituary." *The Guardian*, September 27, 2009. https://www.theguardian.com/world/2009/sep/27/thomas-berry-obituary.

Swimme, Brian. "Berry's Cosmology." *Cross Currents* 37, nos. 22/23 (1987).

Thurber, John. "Thomas Berry Dies at 94; Cultural Historian Became a Leading Thinker on Religion and the Environment." *Los Angeles Times*, June 13, 2009. http://www.latimes.com/local/obituaries/la-me-thomas-berry13-2009jun13-story.html.

Toben, Carolyn. *Recovering a Sense of the Sacred: Conversations with Thomas Berry.* Whitsett, N.C.: Timberlake Earth Sanctuary Press, 2012.

Trapani, Tara C. "Overview of Memorial Service." Thomas Berry and the Great Work. October 2009. Accessed June 29, 2018. http://thomasberry.org/life-and-thought/berry-award-and-memorial-service/overview-of-the-thomas-berry-award-and-memorial-service.

WEBSITES

Thomas Berry. http://thomasberry.org/.

FILMS

Thomas Berry Speaks. Produced by Marty Ostrow. Fine Cut Productions, 2006.

Thomas Berry: The Great Story. Produced by Nancy Stetson and Penny Morrell. 2002.

Journey of the Universe. Produced by Mary Evelyn Tucker and John Grim, Written by Brian Thomas Swimme and Mary Evelyn Tucker. Northcutt Productions, 2011. Dedicated to Thomas Berry.

ADDITIONAL WORKS CITED

Alighieri, Dante. *The Divine Comedy*, trans. John Ciardi. New York: New American Library-Penguin, 2003.

"American Mother Feted at Luncheon." *New York Times*, May 12, 1942, 22.

"'American Mother' Has 13 Children." *New York Times*, April 7, 1942, 25.

"'American Mother' Marks Day with 3 of Her 13 Children Here." *New York Times*, May 11, 1942, 10.

"'American Mother' Warns on Talking." *New York Times*, May 9, 1942, 8.

Anderson, Benedict. *Imagined Communities: Reflections on the Origin and Spread of Nationalism*. London: Verso, 1983.

Anthony, Carl. *The Earth, the City, and the Hidden Narrative of Race*. New York: New Village Press, 2017.

Aquinas, Thomas. *Posterior Analytics*, trans. Richard Berquist. South Bend, Ind.: Dumb Ox Books-St. Augustine's Press, 2008.

——. *Prior Analytics*, trans. Robin Smith. Indianapolis, Ind.: Hackett, 1989.

——. *Summa Contra Gentiles*, trans. Anton Pegis (Notre Dame, Ind.: University of Notre Dame Press, 1955).

——. *Summa Theologica*. Books 1–5. New York: Benziger Brothers, 1948.

Aristotle. *De Anima* (On the Soul), trans. Hugh Lawson-Tancred. New York: Penguin, 1987.

Auerbach, Eric. *Mimesis: The Representation of Reality in Western Literature*, trans. Willard Trask. Princeton, N.J.: Princeton University Press, 1953.

Augustine of Hippo. *City of God*, trans. Gerald Walsh, Demetrius Zema, Grace Monahan, and Daniel Honan. Garden City, N.Y.: Image, 1958.

——. *Confessions*, trans. R. S. Pine-Coffin. New York: Viking Penguin, 1961.

Barnett, L. D. *Path of Light: Rendered for the First Time into English From the Bodhicharyavatara of Santi-Deva. A Manual for Maha-yana Buddhism*. London: John Murray, 1947.

Benyus, Janine. *Biomimicry: Innovation Inspired by Nature*. New York, Harper Perennial, 2002.

Bergson, Henri. *Creative Evolution*. Mineola, N.Y.: Dover, 1998. First English translation 1911, trans. Arthur Mitchell. New York: Henry Holt. First published in French in 1907 as *L'Evolution creatrice*.

The Bhagavad Gita: Krishna's Counsel in Time of War, trans. Barbara Stoler Miller. New York: Columbia University Press, 1986.

Boff, Leonardo. *Cry of the Earth, Cry of the Poor*. Maryknoll, N.Y.: Orbis Books, 1997.

Bourdieu, Pierre. *The Logic of Practice*, trans. Richard Nice. Stanford, Calif.: Stanford University Press, 1990. First published in French in 1980 by Les Editions de Minuit as *Le sens pratique*.

Broome, Neema Pathak, and Ashish Kothari. "A Green Revolution Runs into Trouble." *Resurgence*, no. 307 (March/April 2018).

Brown, Brian Edward. *The Buddha Nature: A Study of the Tathagatagarba and Alayavijnana*. New Delhi: Motilal Banarsidass, 1991.

——. "Oh Watchman, What of the Night?" Unpublished poem, December 17, 1978.

Brown, Joseph Epes. *The Spiritual Legacy of the American Indian*. New York: Crossroad, 1991.

Campbell, Brian C. "Growing an Oak: An Ethnography of Ozark Bioregionalism." In *Environmental Anthropology Engaging Ecotopia: Bioregionalism, Permaculture, and Ecovillages*, ed. Joshua Lockyer, James Veteto, and E. N. Anderson. New York: Berghahn Books, 2013.

Campbell, Joseph. *The Hero with a Thousand Faces*. New York: Pantheon-Knopf, 1949.

Carbonneau, Robert, C.P. *The Passionists in the United States—St. Paul of the Cross Province: A Narrative History—The 1998 Provincial Chapter*. Chicago: Passionist Community Catholic Theological Union, 1998.

Carson, Rachel. *Silent Spring*. New York: Houghton Mifflin, 1962.

Castaneda, Carlos. *Journey to Ixtlan: The Lessons of Don Juan*. New York: Simon and Schuster, 1972.

Catholic Bishop's Conference of the Philippines. "What Is Happening to Our Beautiful Land?" 1988.

Conzelmann, Hans. *An Outline of the Theology of the New Testament*. New York: Harper and Row, 1969.

Cousins, Ewert. *Christ of the 21st Century*. New York: Continuum, 1992.

Crutzen, Paul J., and Eugene F. Stoermer. "The 'Anthropocene.' " *Global Change Newsletter* 41 (2000): 17–18.

Cullinan, Cormac. *Wild Law: A Manifesto for Earth Justice*. 2nd ed. Claremont, South Africa: Siber Ink, 2002. White River Junction, Vt.: Chelsea Green Publishing, 2011.

Dan, Yu. *Confucius from the Heart: Ancient Wisdom for Today's World*. London: Pan-Macmillan, 2010.

Dawson, Christopher. *The Age of the Gods: A Study in the Origins of Culture in Prehistoric Europe and the Ancient East*. Washington, D.C.: Catholic University of America Press, 2012. First published 1928.

——. *The Making of Europe: An Introduction to the History of European Unity*. London: Sheed and Ward, 1932.

——. *Religion and Culture* (Gifford Lecture, 1948). New York: Image Books-Doubleday, 1958.

——. *Religion and the Rise of Western Culture*. New York: Doubleday, 1957.

——. *Religion and World History: A Selection from the Works of Christopher Dawson*, ed. James Oliver and Christina Scott. New York: Image-Doubleday, 1975.

de Bary, Wm. Theodore. *Asian Values and Human Rights: A Confucian Communitarian Perspective*. Cambridge, Mass.: Harvard University Press, 2000.

de Bary, Wm. Theodore, and Irene Bloom, eds. *Sources of Chinese Tradition*. Vol. 1. New York: Columbia University Press, 1999.

——, eds. *Sources of Chinese Tradition*. Vol. 2. New York: Columbia University Press, 2000.

de Bary, Wm. Theodore, and Tu Weiming, eds. *Confucianism and Human Rights*. New York: Columbia University Press, 1998.

Delio, Ilia. *The Unbearable Wholeness of Being: God, Evolution, and the Power of Love*. Maryknoll, N.Y.: Orbis Books, 2013.

Dellinger, Drew. *A Love Letter to the Milky Way*. Mill Valley, Calif.: Planetize the Movement Press, 2002.

de Lubac, Henri. *The Faith of Teilhard de Chardin*. London: Burnes and Oates, 1965.

——, ed. *Pierre Teilhard de Chardin/Maurice Blondel: Correspondence*, trans. William Whitman. New York: Herder and Herder, 1967.

——. *The Religion of Teilhard de Chardin*. New York: Image Books, 1968.

——. *Teilhard de Chardin: The Man and His Meaning*. New York: New American Library, 1967.

——. *Teilhard Explained*. Boston: Paulist Press, 1968.

De Mallie, Raymond J., ed. *The Sixth Grandfather: Black Elk's Teachings Given to John Neihardt*. Lincoln: University of Nebraska Press, 1984.

Dilthey, Wilhelm. *Understanding the Human World*, ed. Rudolf Makkreel and Frithjof Rodi. Princeton, N.J.: Princeton University Press, 2010.

Dougherty, Flavian, C.P., and Robert Carbonneau, C.P., et al., *Celebrating 150 Years of Passionist Ministry in North America and Beyond: 1852–2002*. South River, N.J.: Congregation of the Passion, 2002.

Duara, Prasenjit. *The Crisis of Global Modernity: Asian Traditions and a Sustainable Future*. Cambridge: Cambridge University Press, 2014.

Dubos, René. *The Dreams of Reason: Science and Utopias*. George B. Pegram lectures. New York: Columbia University Press, 1961.

——. *So Human an Animal*. New York: Scribner's, 1968.

du Coulanges, Numa Denis Fustel. *The Ancient City*. Baltimore, Md.: Johns Hopkins University Press, 1980. First published in Strasbourg in 1864.

Duffy, Kathleen, ed. *Rediscovering Teilhard's Fire*. Philadelphia: St Joseph's University Press, 2010.

——. *Teilhard's Mysticism: Seeing the Inner Face of Evolution*. Maryknoll, N.Y.: Orbis Books, 2014.

Dunbar-Ortiz, Roxanne. *An Indigenous Peoples' History of the United States*. Boston: Beacon Press, 2014.

Duthu, N. Bruce. *American Indians and the Law*. New York: Penguin, 2008.

"The Earth Charter." Earth Charter Initiative website. 2000. http://earthcharter.org/discover/the-earth-charter/.

Eiseley, Loren. *The Immense Journey: An Imaginative Naturalist Explores the Mysteries of Man and Nature*. New York: Vintage Books, 1959.

Eldredge, Niles. *Time Frames: The Rethinking of Darwinian Evolution*. Princeton, N.J.: Princeton University Press, 1985.

Elgin, Duane. *The Living Universe*. Oakland, Calif.: Berett-Koehler, 2009.

Ellis, John Tracy. *American Catholicism*. Chicago: University of Chicago Press, 1956.

——. "American Catholics and the Intellectual Life." *Thought* 10 (Autumn 1955): 351–388.

Ellul, Jacques. *The Technological Society*. New York: Vintage Press, 1964.

Fabel, Arthur. "The Dynamic of the Self-Ordering Cosmos." *Cross Currents* 37, nos. 22/23 (1987).

Fabel, Arthur, and Donald St. John, eds. *Teilhard in the 21st Century*. Maryknoll, N.Y.: Orbis Books, 2003.

Fletcher, Alice C., and Francis La Flesche. *The Omaha Tribe*. 2 vols. Lincoln: University of Nebraska Press, 1972. First published 1911 by the Bureau of American Ethnology.

Funes, Yessenia. "The Colombian Amazon Is Now a 'Person,' and You Can Thank Actual People." Earther.com. Accessed April 14, 2018. https://earther.com/the-colombian-amazon-is-now-a-person-and-you-can-thank-1825059357.

Garrigou-Lagrange, Reginald. *Christian Perfection and Contemplation: According to St. Thomas Aquinas and St. John of the Cross*. Charlotte, N.C.: TAN Books, 2010. First published 1923.

Gilmore, Melvin R. *Prairie Smoke*. New York: Columbia University Press, 1929.

Global Education Associates. *The Whole Earth Papers*. New York: self-published, 1979.

Grim, John. "Apocalyptic Spirituality in the Old and New Worlds: The Revisioning of History and Matter." *Teihard Studies*, no. 27 (Fall 1992).

——. *The Shaman: Patterns of Religious Healing Among the Ojibway Indians*. Norman: University of Oklahoma Press, 1983.

——. "The Song of the Library." Unpublished poem. January 3, 1995.

Grim, John, and Mary Evelyn Tucker. *Ecology and Religion*. Washington, D.C.: Island Press, 2014.

——. "An Overview of Teilhard's Commitment to 'Seeing' as Expressed in His Phenomenology, Metaphysics, and Mysticism." In *Pierre Teilhard de Chardin on People & Planet*, ed. Celia Deane-Drummond. London: Equinox, 2006.

——. "Teilhard de Chardin: A Short Biography." *Teilhard Studies*, no. 11 (Spring 1984).

——. "Teilhard's Vision of Evolution." *Teilhard Studies*, no. 50 (Spring 2005).

Grousset, René. *The Civilizations of the East*, trans. Catherine Alison Phillips. London: Hamish Hamilton, 1931.

Grumett, David. "Teilhard de Chardin, Original Sin, and the Six Propositions." *Zygon: Journal of Religion and Science* 53, no. 2 (May 2018): 303-330.

Hallowell, A. Irving. "Ojibwa Ontology, Behavior and Worldview." In *Culture and History: Essays in Honor of Paul Radin*, ed. Stanley Diamond. New York: Columbia University Press, 1960.

Hathaway, Mark, and Leonardo Boff. *The Tao of Liberation: Exploring the Ecology of Transformation*. Maryknoll, N.Y.: Orbis Books, 2009.

Haught, John. *The New Cosmic Story, Inside Our Awakening Universe*. New Haven, Conn.: Yale University Press, 2017.

——. *The Promise of Nature: Ecology and Cosmic Purpose*. Eugene, Oreg.: Wipf and Stock, 2004.

Hayes, Carlton J. H. *History of Europe*. New York: MacMillan, 1949.

——. *Nationalism: A Religion*. New York: Macmillan, 1960. Reprinted 2016 by Transaction Publishers.

Hobsbawm, Eric, and Terrence Ranger. *The Invention of Tradition*. Cambridge: Cambridge University Press, 1983.

Hsi, Chu, and Lu Tsu Ch'ien, eds. *Reflections on Things at Hand: The Neo-Confucian Anthology*, trans. Wing-tsit Chan. New York: Columbia University Press, 1967.

I Ching or Book of Changes, trans. Richard Wilhelm and Cary Baynes. London: Routledge and Keegan Paul, 1968.

Jaspers, Karl. *The Origin and Goal of History*. London: Routledge, 2011. First published 1953.

Jin, Ba. *The Family*. Beijing: Foreign Languages Press, 2015. First published 1933.

Jung, Carl. *Memories, Dreams and Reflections*. New York: Pantheon Books, 1963.

King, Thomas, and James Salmon. *Teilhard and the Unity of Knowledge*. New York: Paulist Press, 1983.

——. *Teilhard's Mysticism of Knowing*. New York: Seabury Press, 1981.

King, Ursula. *Christ in All Things: Exploring Spirituality with Teilhard de Chardin*. Maryknoll, N.Y.: Orbis Books 2016.

——. "Love—A Higher Form of Human Energy in the Work of Teilhard de Chardin and Sorokin." *Zygon* 39, no. 1 (March 2004): 77–102.

——, ed. *Pierre Teilhard de Chardin: Writings*. Maryknoll, N.Y.: Orbis Books, 1999.

——. *Spirit of Fire: The Life and Vision of Teilhard de Chardin*. Maryknoll, N.Y.: Orbis Books, 2015.

——. *Teilhard de Chardin and Eastern Religions: Spirituality and Mysticism in an Evolutionary World*. Mahwah, N.J.: Paulist Press, 2011.

——. "The Zest for Life: A Contemporary Exploration of a Generative Theme in Teilhard's Work." In *From Teilhard to Omega: Co-creating an Unfinished Universe*, ed. Ilia Delio. Maryknoll, N.Y.: Orbis Books 2014.

Kissilove, Betty-Ann. *Great Ball of Fire: A Poetic Telling of the Universe*. San Francisco: Mearth Press, 2010.

Kohn, Eduardo. *How Forests Think: Toward an Anthropology Beyond the Human*. Berkeley: University of California Press, 2013.

Kolbert, Elizabeth. *The Sixth Extinction: An Unnatural History*. New York: Henry Holt, 2014.

Krech, Shepard III. *The Ecological Indian: Myth and History*. New York: W. W. Norton, 1999.

Leopold, Aldo. *Sand Creek Almanac*. Oxford: Oxford University Press, 1949.

Lerner, Clay. *Opening Forgotten Sanctuaries: Recognizing Education as Sacred Encounter*. Greensboro, N.C.: Center for Education, Imagination and the Natural World, 2015.

Levitt, Andrew. *All the Scattered Leaves of the Universe: Journey and Vision in Dante's Divine Comedy and the Work of Thomas Berry*. Greensboro, N.C.: Center for Education, Imagination and the Natural World, 2015.

——. *Heron Mornings*. Greensboro, N.C.: Center for Education, Imagination and the Natural World, 2017.

Liebes, Sidney, Elisabet Sahtouris, and Brian Swimme. *A Walk Through Time: From Stardust to Us*. New York: John Wiley, 1998.

L'Osservatore Romano (Vatican City, Italy), January 26/27, 1959.

Louv, Richard. *Last Child in the Wilderness: Saving Our Children from Nature-Deficit Disorder*. Chapel Hill, N.C.: Algonquin Books, 2005.

Lovejoy, Arthur. *The Great Chain of Being: A Study of the History of an Idea*. Cambridge, Mass.: Harvard University Press, 1936.

Magallanes, Catherine Iorns, and Linda Sheehan. "Reframing Rights and Responsibilities to Prioritize Nature." In *Law and Policy for a New Economy: Sustainable, Just, and Democratic*, ed. Melissa Scanlon. Northampton, Mass.: Edward Elgar, 2017.

Makeham, John. *New Confucianism: A Critical Examination*. New York: Palgrave Macmillan, 2003.

Marcel, Gabriel. *Refus a l'Invocation*. Paris: Gallimard, 1940. Translated in 1964 as *Creative Fidelity*.

Marx, Karl. *The Communist Manifesto*. New York: International Publishers, 2014. First published in German in 1848.

May, Herbert G., and Bruce Metzger, eds. *The New Oxford Annotated Bible: Revised Standard Version*. New York: Oxford University Press, 1977.

McDonough, William, and Michael Braungart. *Cradle to Cradle: Remaking the Way We Make Things*. New York: North Point Press, 2002.

McNally, Michael. *Honoring Elders: Aging, Authority, and Ojibwe Religion*. New York: Columbia University Press, 2009.

Meadows, Donella, Dennis Meadows, Jorgen Randers, and William Behrens III. *The Limits to Growth*. Falls Church, Va.: Potomac Associates-Universe Books, 1972.

Merleau-Ponty, Maurice. *The Visible and the Invisible*, ed. Claude Lefort, trans. Alphonso Lingis. Evanston, Ill.: Northwestern University Press, 1968.

Merton, Thomas. *The Way of Chuang Tzu*. New York: New Directions, 2010. Frist published 1965.

—. *Zen and the Birds of Appetite*. New York: New Directions, 1968.

Mickey, Sam. *On the Verge of a Planetary Civilization: A Philosophy of Integral Ecology*. New York: Rowan and Littlefield, 2014.

Mickey, Sam, Sean Kelly, and Adam Robbert, eds. *The Variety of Integral Ecologies: Nature, Culture, and Knowledge in the Planetary Era*. Albany: State University of New York Press, 2017.

Morgan, Jennifer. *Born with a Bang; The Universe Tells Our Cosmic Story*. Nevada City, Calif.: Dawn Publications, 2006.

—. *From Lava to Life: The Universe Tells Our Earth Story*. Nevada City, Calif.: Dawn Publications, 2006.

—. *Mammals Who Morph: The Universe Tells Our Evolution Story*. Nevada City, Calif.: Dawn Publications, 2006.

Morris, Barbara Louise. "To Define a Catholic University: The 1965 Crisis at St. John's." Master's thesis, Columbia University Teacher's College, 1977.

Nair, Rukmini Bhaya. *Narrative Gravity: Conversation, Cognition, Culture*. London: Routledge, 2002.

Nasr, Seyyed Hossein. *The Encounter of Man and Nature: The Spiritual Crisis of Modern Man*. London: George Allen and Unwin, 1968.

Newcomb, Steven. *Pagans in the Promised Land: Decoding the Christian Doctrine of Discovery*. Golden, Colo.: Fulcrum, 2008.

Nicholas Black Elk, as told through John G. Neihardt. *Black Elk Speaks*. Lincoln: University of Nebraska Press, 2000. First published New York: William Morrow, 1932.

"Notes." *New York Times*, May 10, 1942. Magazine insert, 26.

Noth, Martin. *The Deuteronomic History*. Sheffield, UK: JSOT Press, 1991.

Oldmeadow, Harry. *Black Elk, Lakota Visionary: The Oglala Holy Man & Sioux Tradition*. Bloomington, Ind.: World Wisdom Press, 2018.

Oliver, James, and Christina Scott, eds. *Religion and World History: A Selection from the Works of Christopher Dawson.* New York: Image-Doubleday, 1975.

Participants of the World People's Conference on Climate Change and the Rights of Mother Earth. *Universal Declaration of the Rights of Mother Earth.* April 22, 2010.

Peet, Richard, and Michael Watts. *Liberation Ecologies: Environment, Development, Social Movements.* London: Routledge, 1996.

Pope Francis. *Laudato Si* (Praise Be to You! On Care for Our Common Home). June 18, 2015.

Pope John XXIII. *Acta Apostolicae Sedis* 51. 1959.

——. *Pacem in Terris.* 1963.

Pope Leo XIII. *Rerum Novarum* (On New Things: Rights and Duties of Capital and Labor). May 15, 1891.

Pope Paul VI. *Gaudium et Spes* (Joys and Hopes). December 7, 1965.

——. *Nostrae Aetate* (In Our Time: Declaration on the Relation of the Church with Non-Christian Religions of the Second Vatican Council). October 28, 1965.

Plato. *Timaeus*, trans. Peter Kalkavage. Newburyport, Mass.: Focus Publishing, 2001.

Prigogene, Ilya, and Isabella Stengers. *Order Out of Chaos: Man's New Dialogue with Nature.* London: William Heinemann, 1984.

Puett, Michael, and Christine Gross-Loh. *The Path: What Chinese Philosophers Can Teach Us About the Good Life.* New York: Simon and Schuster, 2016.

Reeves, Marjorie. *Joachim of Flore and the Prophetic Future: A Medieval Study in Historical Thinking.* Stroud, UK: Sutton, 1999.

Reichel-Dolmatoff, Gerardo. *Rainforest Shamans: Essays on the Tukano Indians of the Northwest Amazon.* Devon, UK: Themis Books, 1997.

Richards, Caroline. "The New Cosmology: What It Really Means." In *Thomas Berry and the New Cosmology*, ed. Anne Lonergan. New London, Conn.: Twenty-Third Publications, 1987.

Said, Edward. *Orientalism.* New York: Pantheon Books, 1978.

Schopf, T. J. M., ed. *Models in Paleobiology.* San Francisco: Freeman Cooper, 1972.

Schumm, Bruce. *Deep Down Things: The Breathtaking Beauty of Particle Physics.* Baltimore, Md.: Johns Hopkins University Press, 2004.

Scimecca, Joseph, and Roland Damiano. *Crisis at St. John's: Strike and Revolution on the Catholic Campus.* New York: Random House, 1968.

Segalla, Colette. *I Am You, You Are Me: The Interrelatedness of Self, Spirituality and the Natural World in Childhood.* Greensboro, N.C.: Center for Education, Imagination and the Natural World, 2015.

Spretnak, Charlene. *The Resurgence of the Real: Body, Nature and Place in a Hypermodern World.* New York: Routledge, 1999.

Stone, Christopher. *Should Trees Have Standing? Toward Legal Rights for Natural Objects.* Los Altos, Calif.: William Kaufmann, 1974. Reprinted in 1996 and 2010 with different subtitles.

Stransky, Thomas, C.S.P. "The Foundation of the Secretariat for Promoting Christian Unity." In *Vatican II: By Those Who Were There*, ed. Alberic Stacpoole. Minneapolis: Winston Press, 1986.

Swimme, Brian Thomas. *Canticle to the Cosmos.* Berkeley, Calif.: Center for the Story of the Universe, 1990. DVD.

——. *Hidden Heart of the Cosmos.* Maryknoll, N.Y.: Orbis Books, 1999.

——. *The Universe Is a Green Dragon.* Santa Fe, N.M.: Bear and Company, 1984.

Swimme, Brian Thomas, and Thomas Berry. *The Universe Story: From the Primordial Flaring Forth to the Ecozoic Era*. San Francisco: HarperSanFrancisco, 1992.

Swimme, Brian Thomas, and Mary Evelyn Tucker. *Journey of the Universe*. New Haven, Conn.: Yale University Press, 2011.

——. *Journey of the Universe*. Directed by David Kennard and Patsy Northcutt. Livermore, Calif.: Northcutt Productions, 2011. DVD. Reissued by Shelter Island in 2013.

Teilhard de Chardin, Pierre. *Christianity and Evolution*. New York: Harcourt Brace Jovanovich, 1971.

——. *The Divine Milieu*. New York: Harper and Row, 1960.

——. *The Heart of Matter*. New York: Harcourt Brace Jovanovich, 1979.

——. *Human Energy*. New York: Harcourt Brace Jovanovich, 1971.

——. *The Human Phenomenon*, trans. Sarah Appleton-Weber. Eastbourne, UK: Sussex Academic Press, 1999. First published in English as *The Phenomenon of Man*, 1955.

——. *The Hymn of the Universe*. New York: Harper and Row, 1965.

——. *Science and Christ*. New York: Harper and Row, 1968.

——. *Toward the Future*. New York: Harcourt Brace Jovanovich, 1975.

——. *Writings in Time of War*, trans. René Hague. New York: Harper and Row, 1968.

Toynbee, Arnold. *A Study of History*. 12 vols. Oxford: Oxford University Press, 1934–1961.

Tsung-san, Mou, Carsun Chang, Tang Chun-i, and Hsu Fo-Kuan. "A Manifesto for a Re-Appraisal of Sinology and Reconstruction of Chinese Culture." In *The Development of Neo-Confucian Thought*, vol. 2, ed. Carsun Chang. New York: Bookman Associates, 1962.

Tucker, Mary Evelyn. "The Ecological Spirituality of Teilhard." *Teilhard Studies*, no. 51 (Fall 2005).

——. *Journey of the Universe: Conversations*. Directed by Patsy Northcutt and Adam Loften. New York: Shelter Island, 2013. Originally released by Northcutt Productions 2011 under the title *Journey of the Universe Educational DVD Series*. DVD.

——. *Moral and Spiritual Cultivation in Japanese Neo-Confucianism*. Albany: State University of New York Press, 1989.

——. *The Philosophy of Qi*. New York: Columbia University Press, 2006.

——. *Worldly Wonder: Religions Enter Their Ecological Phase*. Chicago: Open Court, 2003.

Tucker, Mary Evelyn, and John Berthrong, eds. *Confucianism and Ecology: The Interrelation of Heaven, Earth, and Humans*. Cambridge, Mass.: Harvard Center for the Study of World Religions, 1998.

Tucker, Mary Evelyn, and Christopher Chapple, eds. *Hinduism and Ecology*. Cambridge, Mass.: Harvard Center for the Study of World Religions, 1998.

Tucker, Mary Evelyn, and John Grim, eds. *Living Cosmology: Christian Responses to* Journey of the Universe. Maryknoll, N.Y.: Orbis Books, 2016.

——, eds. "Religion and Ecology: Can the Climate Change?" *Daedalus*, Fall 2001. https://www.amacad.org/content/publications/publication.aspx?d=845.

——, eds. *Worldviews and Ecology*. Maryknoll, N.Y.: Orbis Books, 1994. First published by Bucknell University Press, 1993.

Tucker, Mary Evelyn, and Duncan Williams, eds. *Buddhism and Ecology*. Cambridge, Mass.: Harvard Center for the Study of World Religions, 1997.

Tzu, Lao. *Tao Teh Ching*, trans. John C. H. Wu. New York: St. John's University Press, 1961.

Udall, Stewart. "Indians: First Americans, First Ecologists." In *Readings in American History 1973/1974*. Guilford, Conn.: Dushkin Publishing Group, 1973.

United Nations General Assembly. *World Charter for Nature*. Ratified at the Forty-Eighth Plenary Meeting, October 28, 1982.

Vico, Giambattista. *The New Science*, trans. Dave Marsh. New York: Penguin, 2000. First published 1725.

Voegelin, Eric. *Order and History*. 5 vols. Columbia: University of Missouri Press, 1999–2000. First published 1956–1987.

von Rad, Gerhard. *Old Testament Theology*. 2 vols. New York: Harper and Row, 1962.

Waldau, Paul, and Kimberley Patton, eds. *A Communion of Subjects: Animals in Religion, Science, and Ethics*. New York: Columbia University Press, 2006.

Weber, Max. "Objectivity in Social Science and Social Policy." In *The Methodology of the Social Sciences*, ed. and trans. E. A. Shils and H. A. Finch. New York: Free Press, 1949. First published 1904.

Weiming, Tu. *Commonality and Centrality: An Essay on Confucian Religiousness*. Albany: State University of New York Press, 1989.

—. *Confucian Thought: Selfhood as Creative Transformation*. Albany: State University of New York Press, 1985.

Weiming, Tu, and Mary Evelyn Tucker, eds. *Confucian Spirituality*. Vol. 1. New York: Crossroad, 2003.

—, eds. *Confucian Spirituality*. Vol. 2. New York: Crossroad, 2004.

Whalen-Levitt, Peggy, ed. *Only the Sacred: Transforming Education in the Twenty-First Century*. Greensboro, N.C.: Center for Education, Imagination and the Natural World, 2011.

White, Lynn, Jr. "The Historical Roots of Our Ecologic Crisis." *Science* 155, no. 3767 (March 1967).

Wilczek, Frank. *The Lightness of Being: Mass, Ether, and the Unification of Forces*. New York: Basic Books, 2008.

" 'Write to Your Boys in Service' American Mother of 1942 Says." *New York Times*, May 8, 1942, 12.

Wu, John C. H. *Beyond East and West*. London: Sheed and Ward, 1951.

Xi, Xhu. *The Chinese Classics: A Translation by James Legge*, trans. James Legge. 2 vols. Boston: Houghton Mifflin, 1882.

Yangming, Wang. *Instructions for Practical Living and Other Neo-Confucian Writings by Wang Yangming*, trans. Wing Tsit-Chan. New York: Columbia University Press, 1963.

Yuhaus, Cassian J., C.P. *Compelled to Speak: The Passionists in America—Origin and Apostolate*. New York: Newman Press, 1967.